W9-AFC-832

Salem Academy and College
Gramley Library
Winston-Salem, N.C. 27108

William Cowper

PR
3383
.K5
1986

WILLIAM COWPER

A Biography

James King

DUKE UNIVERSITY PRESS   DURHAM 1986

Salem Academy and College
Gramley Library
Winston-Salem, N.C. 27108

Frontispiece: William Cowper
From a crayon drawing by George Romney
By permission of the National Portrait Gallery

© 1986 Duke University Press
All rights reserved
Printed in the United States of America
on acid free paper ∞
Library of Congress Cataloging in Publication Data
appear on the last printed page of this book.
ISBN 0-8223-0513-5
The publication of this book was supported in part by funds
from the Duke Press Endowment for Humanities Publishing
made possible by the National Endowment for the Humanities
and contributions by friends of the Press.

To My Mother and
The Memory of My Father

Contents

Preface

THERE ARE over thirty biographies of William Cowper, so one would expect that most of the facts of his life have been accurately and carefully narrated. This is not the case, however. For a start, the nineteenth-century lives by William Hayley and Robert Southey are seriously flawed. Hayley, a close friend of the poet, deliberately concealed a great deal of material concerning Cowper's periods of depression; in addition, Lady Hesketh, the poet's executrix, prevented Hayley from seeing certain documents, and she forbade him to publish others. By our rigorous twentieth-century standards, Southey was an excellent editor and biographer, but he gained access only to a limited amount of information not known or used by Hayley. More recently, there have been major full-length biographies by Thomas Wright, Lord David Cecil, and Maurice Quinlan. Wright's biography is the most comprehensive of the three, but his work is based mainly on the thousand or so Cowper letters known to him, which he published in his edition of 1904. Wright, who was from Olney, had a very good knowledge of the town where Cowper spent so much of his life, but he did little research on other matters. Lord David Cecil's *The Stricken Deer* is a beautifully conceived and moving study, but he made no attempt to obtain new material on Cowper, his information coming mainly from Hayley, Southey, and Wright. Maurice Quinlan's study, subtitled "A Critical Life," is a competent book, but it does not go very far beyond Wright. The finest Cowper biography is Charles Ryskamp's *William Cowper of the Inner Temple, Esq.* This is a thoroughly researched and elegantly written book, but it stops at 1768, when Cowper was only thirty-seven.

There is a vast amount of manuscript material of great interest to the student of Cowper's life which has never been employed by any of his biographers. The King and Ryskamp edition of Cowper's correspondence for the Clarendon Press contains 1,306 letters, 200 of which have not been published before. As well, two-thirds of the 1,100 previously available letters include unpublished portions. N. C. Hannay's collection of Cowperiana, now at Princeton University Library, contains over 1,000 Cowper-associated manuscripts (as well as holographs [404] and copies [46] of Cowper letters); Dr. Hannay also transcribed virtually every reference to Cowper in all the likely archival locations in the United Kingdom and the United States. In addition, there is important documentation, not seen by Hannay, at Althorp, Norwich, Olney, The Bodleian Library, The Osborn Collection (Yale University Library), and Lambeth Palace Library. As a result of employing a wide range of sources not previously used by a biographer of Cowper, I am able to offer new information on virtually every aspect of Cowper's life, and, especially, on Theadora Cowper, Harriot Hesketh, Mary Unwin, the visit to Eartham, Hannah Wilson, and the last, grim years at Weston and in Norfolk.

Previous biographers have also been disinclined to treat Cowper's career as a writer—his work habits; the influence of other writers upon him; his negotiations with his publisher, Joseph Johnson; his critical reception in his own time; his fear of art; his rivalry with Pope; the autobiographical facts embedded in his poetical fictions. Cowper's writings grew out of his tormented life, and he is of interest largely because of his many splendid poems and letters. Indeed, at certain crucial times, Cowper's art *became* his life. In large part, then, this is a literary biography in which I have attempted to show the connections between Cowper's life and writings.

T. S. Eliot in *Tradition and the Individual Talent* said, "Poetry is not a turning loose of emotion, but an escape from emotion; it is not the expression of personality, but an escape from personality." Despite the affinities between Cowper's life and his art, he saw his writings as an "escape from personality" and—as he said—as "therapy." However, most biographical accounts of Cowper make no distinction between the man who suffered and the mind which created. As a result, little attention has been paid to Cowper's fine intellectual powers and rigorous, discriminating taste. In this book, I have endeavored to delineate both the man who experienced stark depressions and the writer who distilled those experiences into art.

In addition, I have devoted a great deal of attention to the translation of Homer, which Cowper felt was his great literary achievement and enduring monument. In his letters, Cowper left a detailed record of his progress on Homer, which he came to see as his vindication as a professional writer. Although our critical response is now rightly focused on the letters and original verse compositions, I have attempted to take Cowper at his own estimation and to demonstrate how crucial the Homer project was for him. Cowper was a man who became aware of ambition comparatively late in life, and in his dedication to Homer—and to his own claim to immortality—Cowper's passivity gave way to earnest, determined activity.

Cowper's "madness" is another major difficulty in assessing his life. In a letter to William Hayley, Cowper's first biographer, the poet's cousin and self-proclaimed custodian of his reputation, Lady Hesketh, firmly advised that the "biographer of Cowper, whoever he might be, shou'd not consider himself as the writer of a *novel*," and she went on to offer the opinion "that you should deal only in *Generals*, and by no means give a *particular* account of the Life of our friend." She was incensed by Samuel Greatheed's publication of his funeral sermon for Cowper in which he referred openly to the poet's mental sufferings, and she felt that a biographer could avoid what she must have seen as the distortion of fiction by eschewing embarrassing detail. Lady Hesketh wanted to avoid the truth. Nevertheless, her fears were well founded. The risk in offering a psychological interpretation of a subject's life is that his experiences may be reduced to simpleminded causes and effects, which do not fully reflect his existence. On the other hand, the biographer, in addition to his concern with the familial, social, historical, and cultural contexts in which his subject lived, must not neglect "psychological evaluation." Sir Isaiah Berlin has warned that "the invocation of historians to suppress even that minimal degree of moral or psychological evaluation which is essentially involved in viewing human beings as creatures with purposes and motives (not merely as causal factors in the procession of events), seems . . . to rest upon a confusion of the aims and methods of the humane studies with those of natural science. It is one of the greatest and most destructive fallacies of the last 100 years." Thus, if the biographer discovers a pattern which helps to remove the veil of obscurity from his subject's inner life, he has an obligation to offer his "reading" to his audience. In my opinion, Cowper's life was irrevocably altered by his mother's death when he was six. He was not unaware of the tremendous loss he endured and its effect on his subsequent existence. He wrote about this matter, and, in writing Cowper's life history, I have allowed him to guide me in my attempt to understand the workings of his mind.

Nevertheless, Cowper's own depictions of himself as the outcast have been taken too literally. As a result, he has usually been seen merely as a victim—of his own highly sensitive nature, of his morbid conviction of eternal damnation, and of religious enthusiasm. Although there is much truth in such a view of him, it does not provide a full (or *"particular"*) portrait. As well as being a victim, Cowper was also a skillful manipulator; he was frequently skeptical and damning of the talents of fellow writers; he was a person whom others often sought out for assistance and consolation. In this book, I have portrayed Cowper as a man who fought against the stark depressions which filled his existence. If this biography is revisionist, it is so in its emphasis on the tremendous strengths which resided in the heart of this reclusive man.

Indeed, from 1763, Cowper was in retreat from the world. However, his attitude toward retirement had changed markedly by 1779 and was to undergo further metamorphoses, his strong Evangelical convictions being largely dissipated by his religious crisis of 1773. As he approached fifty, he became more and more intrigued by the world he had abandoned, and in styling himself of "the Inner Temple, Esq." on the title page of his 1782 volume of verse, he signaled his return—if only in spirit—to the London world he had fled nineteen years before.

However, despite Cowper's desire to reenter the world, most of his life was spent in retirement, a situation which presents special problems for his biographer. The life histories of most individuals are best told in strict chronological order. However, Cowper's retired but intense life requires a different approach. The process of his life was often unduly slow, and a tenacious adherence to the temporal flux of his existence might make it seem what it was decidedly not: dull. In order to depict the intense inner vitality of Cowper, I have been mindful not only of his art—his poems and letters—but also of the artistry he displayed in friendship. I have given separate chapters to Cowper's major publications in order to document the genesis of an idea, the poet's often conflicting statements about his own abilities, his sense of accomplishment and failure, and his response to criticism. In a like manner, I have given special attention to Cowper's major friendships, lifting them out of the strictly chronological ebb and flow of his daily life. Although I place these portrait chapters at the appropriate places in the annals of the poet's existence, I have sometimes moved ahead within these chapters when I feel a particular incident or detail will allow me to evoke tellingly the essence of Cowper's involvement with a friend. I have tried to restrict myself in such matters so that the reader's indulgence is not trespassed. My aim has been to capture the quick, lively mind which led a sedentary existence. A quiet life can be dramatic, but its drama requires a special, distinctive sensitivity on the biographer's part.

Cowper claimed he was an outcast, and yet he had strong inner resources. Nevertheless, he ultimately saw himself as someone who was debarred from all that was good and satisfying from the time of his mother's death. Cowper often saw this exclusion in religious terms, and he perceived a hostile God as the force which plotted against him. His belief in such a power was so great that it destroyed his psychic well-being, forcing him to withdraw from the great Babylon of London and the life he led there. In later life, he attempted to return to the world he had abandoned many years before. Clearly, he had the ability to move against the hostile inner forces in a determined way. But the struggle was too great, and at the end of his life he saw himself as forsaken by man and God. He was—and remained—the castaway.

1
Berkhamsted and Westminster
(1731–1753)

1   WILLIAM COWPER is one of the great pasto-
ral poets of English literature. His hills, dales, brooks, spinneys,
and gardens are serenely beautiful. This is as it should be. Hertfordshire, the county of his birth, has no fenlands, no downs, no
sublime mountain ranges. There are no obvious edges, no sudden
contrasts—one landscape shades delicately into another. It seems an
unduly ordinary place. However, there are graceful, undulating
hills and patches of brightly colored golden barley and green grass,
of which Cobbett exclaimed: "Talk of pleasure-grounds indeed!
What that man ever invented, under the name of pleasure-grounds,
can equal these fields in Hertfordshire?"[1] E. M. Forster said this
county was "England at its quietest, with little emphasis of river
and hill; it is England meditative."[2]

Hertfordshire, then, was an appropriate place for a gentle, contemplative nature poet to come into being. William Cowper was
born there on November 15, 1731, in the prosperous market town
of Berkhamsted. This spot had witnessed, in 1066, the submission
of Edgar Atheling to William the Conqueror, and John II of France
had been imprisoned there in 1356. The Black Prince had been
especially fond of Berkhamsted, and Chaucer had been Clerk of the
Works there. However, it was a place of muted glory in the eighteenth century. All the principal buildings of its royal castle were
torn down by mid-century, although scanty remains were left behind. St. Peter's Church stood in the center of the town, and its
tower dominated the environs. It was at the now demolished Rectory of St. Peter's that William, John and Ann Cowper's fourth but
first surviving child, came into the world.

John Cowper was from one of the first families of Hertfordshire.
He was the son of Spencer Cowper the Judge, who at the end of his

career was puisne Justice of the Common Pleas, and his great-uncle was William, first Earl Cowper, twice Lord Chancellor. Although the Cowpers were not eager to admit it publicly, the mercantile origins of the dynasty were speculated upon and often laughed at by family members who had been told that the first Cowper had been "a *Scotch Pedlar,* who traveled out of Scotland with a Sack upon his back."[3] By 1642, the Cowpers had risen from such offices as Sheriff of London and Alderman to become baronets. They were a cultivated family. Sir William, the first holder of the family title, wrote verses on the death of Richard Hooker, and many of the eighteenth-century Cowpers, including John and his brother Ashley, were dedicated versifiers. Cowper claimed to have gained some of his inclinations and taste from his father, who was adept in the art of ballad making.

John's contributions to *The Poetical Miscellany* (1744) included *On Miss R[ope]r Having the Tooth-ach* and *The Client's Warning-Piece,* and, as his son said, John, who was born in 1694, had come to maturity when the best pieces in the same vein were produced by Pope, Swift, and Gay. John had been educated at Westminster School and at Merton College, Oxford, and was later a fellow of that foundation. In addition to his vocation as priest and Chaplain to the King, and avocation as poet, he was from 1731 joint patentee for making out commissions in bankruptcy. John was also a man of strong feelings, who inspired in his oldest son his own staunch brand of Whig patriotism. A person of extraordinary amiability, he could also be excessively morbid, especially in the company of the young and impressionable William: ". . . when I was about twenty years of age my father desired me to read a vindication of self-murder in the Persian letters . . . and to give him my sentiment upon the question. I did so and argued against it. My father heard my reasons and was silent, neither approving nor disapproving, from whence I inferred that he sided with the author against me."[4] As this incident shows, John, unlike his wife, was not an unduly demonstrative parent. Ultimately, however, Cowper saw his father as "excellent and Praiseworthy."[5] Despite nagging doubts, he was able in 1767, eleven years after his father's death, to "burst forth into Praise and Thanksgiving to God for having made me the Son of a Parent whose Remembrance was so sweet to me."[6] Having come to terms with God the Father, Cowper experienced more fully his love for his own father.

Cowper had even more tender recollections of his mother, Ann Donne, of Bedham Grange in Norfolk. The Donnes claimed to have

descended from Henry III by four different lines, including that of
Mary Boleyn, sister of Henry VIII's Anne, and from the noble families of Carey, Howard, and Mowbray. Ann's grandfather, William
Donne, was supposed to have been related to John Donne, the poet,
but such descent was probably collateral. Roger Donne, Ann's
father, a landowner and woolmerchant, died in 1722 when she
was nineteen. Her mother was Catherine Clench, the daughter of
Bruni [sic] Clench and Catherine Hippesley. Although Roger had
owned a great deal of land, he was not very prosperous; he was so
much in debt when he died that his legacies of £1000 to each of his
offspring could not be paid without selling property. Therefore,
Ann had to marry someone who could afford to take her without
a dowry. It is not known where the couple met, but John Cowper
did own a house in London in Red Lion Square, and Ann's maternal grandmother, Mrs. Clench, was living at nearby St. Martin-
in-the-Fields when the two became acquainted in 1727 (in 1726,
Ann had been engaged to Samuel Hudson of Great Yarmouth, who
died early in 1727).[7] In any event, John and Ann were married in
1728, and their first child, Spencer, was born the following year.

In his portrait of Ann when she was about twenty, Heins depicts
her as an exceptionally delicate, frail young woman, and this may
explain in part why, during the nine years that she was married,
only two children survived six pregnancies—this was a mortality
rate excessive even by the standards of the eighteenth century. Spencer died after five weeks. Nine months after his death, Ann and
John, twins, died within two days of birth. William came next.
After him was born, a year and a half later, Theodora Judith, who
died at the age of two. Thomas was born on October 9, 1734, and
died a fortnight later. Complications followed the birth of John,
her seventh child, on November 7, 1737, and Ann died six days later
at the age of thirty-four. Although Cowper's vivid recollections were
of his mother's passing, the infant deaths must have created a constant sense of gloom and foreboding in the Rectory. Cowper, as a
young child, might have felt especially blessed to be one of two
children to endure, but he may also have felt a totally irrational
sense of guilt in having survived when others had perished.

William must have been especially precious to a mother who had
lost so many children. As he recalled, Ann was a particularly sensitive parent, who gave her little boy a "biscuit, or confectionary
plum" before he left for school, who soothed his fevers with dabs
of lavender water, and who taught him to make patterns from the
violet, pink, and jessamine cuttings from the "tissued flow'rs" of her

garments.[8] Her son remembered her in a heightened, idealized way: "Every body loved her, and with an amiable character so impress'd on all her features, every body was sure to do so."[9] Her niece, Harriot Hesketh, had been told that Ann was "an angelick woman."[10] Cowper saw her as the embodiment of generosity and kindness, and he recalled with deep fondness her stealing into his room at the close of day: "Thy nightly visits to my chamber made, / That thou might'st know me safe and warmly laid."[11] Like many other children of well-to-do parents, Cowper may have attended his mother chiefly by appointment, many of the maternal responsibilities devolving to a nurse. Despite this, his memories of warmth and gentleness were associated with his mother. Indeed, Cowper may have had strong feelings of loss because he invested so much in the relatively few moments of each day which he spent in Ann Cowper's company. Although his grief seemed to diminish as his childhood progressed, her death was "ne'er forgot"; from the time of her passing, her son's life "pass'd . . . but roughly."[12]* The death of his mother was the strongest of Cowper's childhood remembrances. He recalled Ann's kindness and beauty, but the memory of her death was much sharper, penetrating to the very core of his being.

2   In his elegy of February 1790, *On the Receipt of My Mother's Picture Out of Norfolk,* Cowper recounted the sensations he experienced at the time of his mother's death:

> My mother! when I learn'd that thou wast dead,
> Say, wast thou conscious of the tears I shed?
> Hover'd thy spirit o'er thy sorrowing son,
> Wretch even then, life's journey just begun?
> Perhaps thou gav'st me, though unseen, a kiss;
> Perhaps a tear, if souls can weep in bliss—
> Ah that maternal smile! it answers—Yes.
> I heard the bell toll'd on thy burial day,
> I saw the hearse, that bore thee slow away,

---

* Ann was one of a new breed of parents in the eighteenth century who openly expressed their deeply felt feelings of affection to their children. In his important book, *The Family, Sex and Marriage in England, 1500–1800* (New York: Harper and Row, 1977), Lawrence Stone describes the growth of "affective individualism," and he argues that this phenomenon is reflected in the relations between some parents and their children (see, especially, 221–56, 405–78). The great irony of Cowper's early life is that the tenderness which Ann bestowed upon her child became, at the time of her death, the instrument of tremendous sorrow.

And, turning from my nurs'ry window, drew
A long, long sigh, and wept a last adieu![13]

Earlier, in a letter written in November 1784 to console Joseph Hill
on the death of his mother, Cowper said: "I while I live must regret
a comfort of which I was deprived so early, I can truely say that not
a week passes, (perhaps I might with equal veracity say a day) in
which I do not think of her."[14] His most extended prose description
of his remembrances is contained in his letter of February 27, 1790,
to Rose Bodham, the cousin who had sent him his mother's portrait:

> The world could not have furnish'd you with a present so ac-
> ceptable to me as the picture which you have so kindly sent me.
> I received it the night before last, and view'd it with a trepida-
> tion of nerves and spirits somewhat akin to what I should have
> felt had the dear Original presented herself to my embraces. I
> kissed it and hung it where it is the last object that I see at
> night, and, of course, the first on which I open my eyes in the
> morning. She died when I had completed my sixth year, yet I
> remember her well and am an ocular witness of the great fidel-
> ity of the Copy. I remember too a multitude of the maternal
> tendernesses which I received from her and which have endeared
> her memory to me beyond expression. . . . I was thought in
> the days of my childhood much to resemble my mother, and in
> my natural temper, of which at the age of 58 I must be sup-
> posed a competent judge, can trace . . . Her.[15]

These recollections of 1790 and 1784 are remarkably vivid, and in
recounting them Cowper provides a significant clue to his mental
state: he had not been able to come to terms with the death of his
mother. That event was the great sorrow of his life: Cowper's unhappiness arose from his sense of separation, isolation, and desertion.

Loss as a cause of depression was recognized in the seventeenth
and eighteenth centuries, and Burton in *The Anatomy of Melancholy* speculated on the role that fantasy can play in such situa-
tions.[16] After speaking of all kinds of loss, Burton poignantly enu-
merated the misfortunes to which the young are especially prone:
"If parting of friends, absence alone, can work such violent effects,
what shall death do, when they must eternally be separated, never
in the world to meet again?"[17] From childhood, Cowper's existence
was overshadowed by death, and his tragic life history, as we shall
see, provides an answer to Burton's question: Cowper's separation
from his mother worked "violent effects" upon his young heart. He

experienced not only great anguish but also tremendous guilt and anger. And yet, it must be admitted, the deep sorrow which invaded Cowper's childhood seems, at first glance, excessive. Of course, all children need a solid foundation of realized happiness upon which to build their lives, but many children experience great sadness and subsequently lead happy lives. And yet, as David Cecil has said, the key to Cowper's personality resides in his frail boyhood: "Cowper the child was like Cowper the man; a defeatist, hating decisions; frightened of the unknown, the creature, not the creator, of his own destiny."[18] Cowper's nature must have been inherently fragile, and, as he admitted, he "came from a house more than commonly subject to"[19] melancholia. It is perhaps impossible, therefore, to come to a full understanding of why William Cowper the motherless boy became Cowper the outcast. But it is true that if a young child is not able to accept the death of a parent (particularly, a mother), the subsequent life of that child can be filled with frequent and painful episodes of depression.

According to Freud, melancholia fills the soul when the process of grief has not—for some reason—been completed. Indeed, the child who cannot detach himself from the dead parent through the rite of mourning is often thrown into an existence of living death:

> Mourning is regularly the reaction to the loss of a loved person or to the loss of some abstraction which has taken the place of one. . . . In some people the same influences produce melancholia instead of mourning and we consequently suspect them of a pathological disposition. . . . The distinguishing mental features of melancholia are a profoundly painful dejection, cessation of interest in the outside world, loss of the capacity to love, inhibition of all activity, and a lowering of the self-regarding feelings to a degree that finds utterance in self-reproaches and self-revilings and culminates in a delusional expectation of punishment.[20]*

Later in his essay, Freud speaks further of the consequences which ensue when melancholia supplants mourning. "The melancholic displays something else besides which is lacking in mourning—an extraordinary diminution in his self-regard, an impoverishment of his ego on the grand scale. . . . This picture of a delusion of (mainly moral) inferiority is completed . . . by an overcoming of the instinct which compels every living thing to cling to life."[21] Recently,

* Cowper displayed Freud's "distinguishing mental features" of melancholia in the breakdowns of 1763, 1773, and, especially, 1794.

Evna Furman, John Bowlby, and others have argued more narrowly and precisely that the real or perceived loss of a parent, particularly the mother, can lead to serious repercussions in a child's development and in later life:

> An adult distributes his love among several meaningful relationships—his spouse, parents, children, friends, colleagues—as well as in his work and hobbies. The child, by contrast, invests almost all his feelings in his parents. Except in very unusual circumstances, this single relationship is therefore incomparably rich and intense, unlike any close adult relationship. Only in childhood can death deprive an individual of so much opportunity to love and be loved and face him with so difficult a task of adaptation.[22]

As well, the adult who has been given a warm and secure upbringing is usually able to invest his relationships with a similar benevolent sensibility. But what about the young child whose parent has been taken away?:

> Experiences of separation from attachment figures, whether of short or long duration, and experiences of loss or being threatened with separation or abandonment—all act . . . to divert development from a pathway that is within optimum limits to one that may lie outside them. In terms of [a] railway analogy, those experiences so act that the points at a junction are shifted and the train is diverted from a main line to a branch. Often, fortunately, the diversion is neither great nor lengthy so that return to the main line remains fairly easy. At other times, by contrast, a diversion is both greater and lasts longer or else is repeated; then a return to the main line becomes far more difficult, and it may prove impossible.[23]

A child is especially dependent upon his mother for love, and the youngster who grows to maturity without it sometimes assumes responsibility for such a deprivation—this is the route that the "diversion" often takes. If this affection has not been provided, the child deems himself accountable. Such a child is also often irrationally angry at the mother who has forsaken him.

Cowper did not complete the rite of mourning. In his imagination he clung relentlessly to his mother. Since he never fully detached himself from her, he spent his lifetime as the victim of melancholia. He turned the resulting guilt and anger against himself, creating within his being a God who hated him and would, like his mother, abandon him. Cowper's mother had bestowed love upon him, and he could in turn sometimes see himself as worthy of love. And yet guilt and self-loathing were much stronger emotions, and they frequently overwhelmed him: "But I live. That is my crime."[24] Cowper's heart was one torn between self-love and self-hatred. Although he saw himself at the mercy of a hostile God, his own divided heart was the source of his unhappiness. In 1733, George Cheyne claimed melancholia as the English malady—William Cowper is an extreme example of the truthfulness of that assertion.

Burdened by a depression which reached back to his mother's death in 1737, Cowper was an extremely passive person. He tended to allow events to overtake him. His overweening compliance with outside forces is in part explained by his preception of himself as powerless. If God took away his mother, he could spirit away anyone or anything beloved by Cowper. What could he do in the face of such an encroaching force? Why should he attempt to become the master of his own destiny? He told Margaret King that God beheld "with more complacency a suffering than an active courage."[25] The frightened little boy was locked up in the heart of the man.

3   Despite the sorrow which was not forgotten, Cowper looked back upon his childhood as a blissful time. "There was neither Tree nor Gate nor stile in all that country to which I did not feel a relation, and the House itself [at Berkhamsted] I preferred to a palace."[26] As a young boy, he even posed with a bow and arrow for a now-lost portrait, "waging war either with a *cock sparrow* or *bumble bee*."[27] These were seemingly idyllic days. Cowper was aware, however, that most people romanticize their earliest years, neglecting to take into account the acute sense of foreboding and isolation to which children are often prey:

> There are few perhaps in the world who have not cause to look back with regret on the days of Infancy. Yet, to say truth I suspect some deception in this. For Infancy itself has its cares, and though we cannot now conceive how trifles could affect us much, it is certain that they did. Trifles they appear now, but such they were not then.[28]

In his mother's home county of Norfolk, Cowper experienced some of the happiest times of his childhood. The coastline of that county and the peaceful beauties of its landscape beautifully depicted in the work of Gainsborough, Constable, and the Norwich school were not lost upon him. "No situation, at least when the weather is clear and bright, can be pleasanter," and the Norfolk coast remained for him the setting of pleasant days in "company with those whom I loved and by whom I was beloved."[29]

One person in the village of Catfield to whom Cowper was devoted was his cousin Harriot Donne: "an unaffected, plain-dressing, good-temper'd, cheerful" companion.[30] It was her mother who gave him his first books: *Pilgrim's Progress* and Gay's *Fables*. Cowper was soon "reckoned famous" for reciting *The Hare and Many Friends** in company.[31] His tastes were formed by his reading in Norfolk: "John Gilpin and John Calvin were part of him from the beginning."[32] It is also likely that he first witnessed the sea, the dominant image and symbol in his poetry, at Happisburgh, where his uncle was curate. There were frequent wrecks off that coast in the 1740s, and Cowper probably gained there for the first time a

* The little boy's interest in Gay's poem (no. 50 of *The Fables* [1727]) may have been derived to a large extent from his identification with the gentle hare who, although to "ev'ry creature" of the wood a "friend" (12), is abandoned by her companions at the advance of the cruel hunters:

> She starts, she stops, she pants for breath,
> She hears the near advance of death,
> She doubles, to mis-lead the hound,
> And measures back her mazy round;
> 'Till, fainting in the publick way,
> Half dead with fear she gasping lay. (15–22)

The hare's pitying calls for assistance are denied by the horse, bull, goat, sheep, and, finally, the calf:

> Shall I, says he, of tender age,
> In this important care engage?
> Older and abler past you by;
> How strong are those! how weak am I!
> Should I presume to bear you hence,
> Those friends of mine may take offence.
> Excuse me then. You know my heart.
> But dearest friends, alas, must part!
> How shall we all lament. Adieu.
> For see the hounds are just in view. (55–64)

The theme of the castaway is evident in this fable, and Cowper as a young child obviously found a strong personal resonance in the poem's poignant depiction of the fate of the loving, generous hare who is betrayed. As well, Cowper in his mature poetry often identified his destiny with that of animals (as in the "stricken deer" passage from book 3 of *The Task*), and he greatly admired Gay's fables and learned much from them. Indeed, one of Cowper's last efforts as a poet—in January 1800, three months before he died—was to translate three of Gay's fables, including *The Hare*, into Latin.

sense of the awesome and destructive majesty of the ocean. At "a time of life when I gave as little attention to religious subjects . . . I yet remember that the waves would preach to me . . . the Sight and Sound of the Ocean . . . often composed my thoughts into a Melancholy not unpleasing, nor without its use."[33] Cowper certainly associated his mother with the sea, identifying her in his poem to her memory as "a gallant bark from Albion's coast"[34] which had found a safe port, from which her son was cast adrift:

> Always from port withheld, always distress'd—
> Me howling winds drive devious, tempest toss'd,
> Sails ript, seams op'ning wide, and compass lost,
> And day by day some current's thwarting force
> Sets me more distant from a prosp'rous course.[35]

During childhood, however, Cowper coped with his mother's death. He had a great deal to forget, and the child, perhaps more than the adult, has to get on with the daily routine of life.

4   Before Ann's death, Cowper went to a dame school at Berkhamsted in his "bauble-coach" drawn by "Robin" Pope, the gardener. Later, in 1737, he went to Aldbury, a few miles from Berkhamsted, where he was under the care of the rector, the Reverend William Davis. Cowper went there because of the wretched conditions in the school at Berkhamsted, which from 1735 had been involved in a suit in chancery. He stayed at Aldbury only for a short time and was then sent about 1737 to 1739 to a "considerable school in Bedfordshire"[36] at Markyate Street on the Hertfordshire and Bedfordshire border. The headmaster, William Pittman, educated at King's College, Cambridge, and subsequently a Fellow there, had a considerable local reputation as a classical scholar. However, Cowper did not remember much about the school—except the torments of bullying:

> . . . my chief affliction consisted in being singled out from all the children in the school by a lad about fifteen years of age as a proper subject upon whom he might let loose the cruelty of his temper. I choose to conceal a particular recital of the many acts of barbarity with which he made it his business continually to persecute me. It will be sufficient to say that he had by his savage treatment of me imprinted such a dread of his very figure upon my mind that I well remember being afraid to lift my

eyes upon him higher than his knees, and that I knew him by
his shoe buckles better than by any other part of his dress.[37]

This is graphic recollection of thirty years later, and the horrors of
that event are heightened by Cowper's observation that his time on
trial at Markyate Street was made the more bitter because of the
"tenderness" he had experienced at home under a "most indulgent
mother."[38] Fortunately, the bully, who had obviously sensed his
little victim's vulnerability, was discovered and expelled from the
school, but that incident is the first piece of dramatic narrative in
Cowper's spiritual autobiography, where its position suggests that
what the child perceived and the man remembered was the deprivation of goodness and the onslaught of nameless evil.

At the age of eight, Cowper had "very weak eyes and [was] in
danger of losing one of them."[39] He was sent to the home of Mrs.
Disney, an oculist, where he remained for about two years. Later,
Cowper remembered the Disney household without affection, calling it a place "where Christianity was neither known nor prac-
tised."[40] Although he disliked Mrs. Disney, her regimen possibly
did his eyes some good (as an adult, he suffered only from inflam-
mations of the eyelids, with "specks" on his eyes). In those forlorn
years, Cowper had been separated not only from his father but also
from his brother.

Although the brothers had engaged in a now-lost correspondence
in rhyme, Cowper was reticent in his letters about youthful experiences shared with John. It could be that the six-year difference in
age prevented any close contact during childhood, and it is very
probable that John was the son favored by the father. John's career
at Felsted School and at Corpus Christi College, Cambridge, was
very distinguished. By the time he was thirty, he was well versed in
Latin, Greek, Hebrew, French, and Italian and was a fellow of his
college. Although an intuitive, sensitive person, John was obviously
not as highly strung as William, and it could well be that as a child
he had demonstrated a capacity for success more likely to gain his
father's approval than his older brother's retiring, timid demeanor.

As well, Cowper was isolated from Berkhamsted: "I believe no
man ever quitted his Native place with less Regrett than myself,
and were it not for the sake of a Friend or two that I have left behind me . . . , I should never wish to see either the place or any
thing that belongs to it again."[41] Cowper made this claim in 1757,
but, as he reminded John Duncombe two years later, all William
Cowpers were "Whimsical Fellows"[42] and in later life he looked

Salem Academy and College
Gramley Library
Winston-Salem, N.C. 27108

back fondly at his native town where, he reflected, he could pass through "unknowing and unknown" even though he had once been "a sort of principal figure."[43] As a young child, he probably perceived Berkhamsted not only as a place of intense sorrow but also as a refuge from Aldbury, Markyate Street, and Mrs. Disney.

5   In middle age, Cowper became the great spokesman against public schools in *Tirocinium*, where he echoed Fielding's Parson Adams: "Public Schools are the Nurseries of all Vice and Immorality. All the wicked Fellows whom I remember at the University, were bred at them."[44] On the basis of the poem of 1785, it is tempting to see Westminster as yet another entry in the list of unsatisfactory institutions Cowper attended. Although Cowper the Evangelical looked askance at Westminster, it was nevertheless the place where he acquired much of the classical lore and fluency in language which were abiding consolations throughout his life. It was also the proper place for a Cowper to deepen family ties and to learn his position in society. William Cowper would later scorn many of the tokens of worldly success, but he always retained an abiding trust in friendship and its benefits: influence, prestige, and assistance. Above all, he learned at Westminster to be a gentleman.

Westminster had long been the Cowper school when William matriculated there in April 1742. Part of John's ambition in sending his eldest son to his own school was, as Cowper facetiously put it, to assist his intention "to beget a Chancellor."[45] John also desired the strong Whig principles of Westminster (as opposed to its great Tory rival, Eton) to be instilled in his son from an early age; on that score, he need not have feared: Cowper remained his entire life an ardent and passionate Whig, even when Lady Hesketh, a fanatical Tory, attempted to convert him to her side.

Westminster had enjoyed a period of great renown under Richard Busby during the Restoration, and its second renaissance was under the leadership of John Nicoll from 1733 to 1753. During those twenty-one years, the boys included Rockingham, Portland, Howe, Keppel, Hastings, Impey, Churchill, Colman, Thornton, Cumberland, and Gibbon. When Cowper arrived, his school consisted of two buildings: the ancient monastic building next to the Abbey and the new dormitory for scholars which had been designed by Sir Christopher Wren, an old Westminster. The school was just above Thieving-Lane, but there was open ground in the Tothill Fields, between Westminster and Chelsea. There were 354 boys in

1742: 40 scholars in the college and the remaining town boys living
in boardinghouses in the neighborhood. Some of the students had
an opportunity to live with families, but no such consolation was
given to Cowper. He lived at Mrs. Playford's house on the north
side of Little Dean's Yard. The timid boy from Berkhamsted must
have felt deprived of the comforts of home, although Mrs. Playford
was probably more sympathetic than Mrs. Disney. Ann Playford,
seventy-one when Cowper stayed with her, was the widow of John
Playford, a distinguished music publisher who had been a friend of
Henry Purcell and Samuel Pepys, and she probably had a store of
amusing anecdotes to tell the boys who boarded with her. Nevertheless, the living quarters were cramped, and Cowper, during his first
year, was especially shy. Although there is no record of his having
been bullied as he was at Dr. Pittman's, his fear that he might be
remained with him, and the "tyranny of the older boys" was so
frightening to him that, "when in company with the Captain of
the School, he never durst look up at him, not lifting his eyes higher
than the boy's buckles."[46]

The school proper—one enormous room where, from Elizabethan
times until almost the end of the nineteenth century, all the boys
were taught—had eleventh-century walls and a hammer-beam roof.
There was only one division in the school: a curtain separated the
Upper and Under Schools from each other. There were two masters,
an Upper (Head) and an Under, and six ushers. The classics were
the basis for a Westminster education, as they were for every public
school of the time. A great deal of stress was placed on memorizing:
the rules of grammar, passages from the great authors, and the dates
of ancient history. Although Cowper would sometimes defend the
rigors of the system at Westminster, he felt that the boys were "generally made to draw in Latin and Greek Trammels too soon."[47] A
parent might be delighted with the learning in ancient languages of
his precocious son, but that child often "having exhausted his little
Stock of Attention & Diligence in making that notable Acquisition,
grows weary of his Task, conceives a Dislike of Study, & perhaps
makes but a very indifferent Progress afterward."[48] Cowper himself
did exceptionally well in this system, in contrast to his description
of a public school boy's regress. He was eventually head of his house
and third in the sixth form. When he left Westminster, he carried
with him the school's standards and, as he said, "valued a man according to his proficiency & Taste in classical Literature, & had the
meanest opinion of all other Accomplishments unaccompanied by
that."[49] Another legacy which the school bestowed upon him was

the capacity to work in a disciplined manner, independent of direct supervision. Such freedom can cripple some children, but it can liberate others. When he became a translator of Homer in middle age, Cowper looked back with a great deal of satisfaction to his study of Homer with Dick Sutton, a classmate. Cowper's ability to write his verse, his translations, and his letters in the rural isolation of Buckinghamshire must have been derived in part from the inner motivation John Nicoll felt to be the heart of a Westminster education and which he attempted to cultivate in his boys.

Richard Cumberland claimed that Nicoll cherished "every spark of genius which he could discover" in his students and was "determined so to exercise his authority, that our best motives for obeying him should spring from the affection, that we entertained for him."[50] For his part, Cowper cherished the religious sensibility which was instilled in him when Nicoll prepared him and the other boys for confirmation: "The old man acquitted himself of this duty like one who had a deep sense of its importance, and I believe most of us were struck by his manner, and affected by his exhortation. For my own part, I then for the first time attempted prayer in secret."[51] Cowper's other favorite was his usher in the fifth form, Vincent Bourne, a genial, lackadaisical person. Cowper obviously imbibed a great deal about Latin poetry and the art of prosody from Bourne, whose Latin verse he thought superior to Tibullus, Propertius, and Ausonius. He also liked his humor, drollery, pleasantry, good nature, and humanity. His slipshod manner of dress was objectionable, but his poetry made amends for this. "It is not common to meet with an Author who can make you smile, and yet at nobody's Expence, who is always entertaining, and yet always harmless, and who though elegant and classical to a degree not always found even in the Classics themselves, charms more by the Simplicity & playfulness of his Ideas, than by the neatness & purity of his Verse."[52] Cowper's enthusiastic description of Bourne's poetry can be applied to his own occasional verse, and he learned his lessons well from Bourne, between moments of comic drama: "I remember seeing the Duke of Richmond set fire to his greasy Locks, & box his Ears to put it out again."[53] Cowper also recalled affectionately his master in the fourth form, Pierson Lloyd, and in 1781 he translated William Vincent's Latin poem *To the Memory of Dr. Lloyd* into English.

During his time at Westminster, Cowper gained in self-confidence. He became a lively fellow who played games at the two Yards, and he later excelled at cricket and football. He cultivated his love of animals, keeping a tame mouse until she produced six youngsters and devoured them. A bout of smallpox "severely handled"[54] him, but he made a good recovery. There were visits to such curiosities as the lions kept at the Tower and the inmates of Bedlam. It was at Westminster that he realized for the first time that there were other men and boys who shared his own interests and quiet gentlemanliness. The boy from Berkhamsted who had entered the school as a docile, timid creature emerged six years later as a young man who could hold his own in conversation as well as in the classics.

Cowper's friends at Westminster included those who would become infamous or lead disreputable existences or be noted for the saintliness of their personal lives. Sir Elijah Impey was a friendly competitor with Cowper for school honors, and Cowper especially revered Warren Hastings, later the celebrated defendant in the East India debacle:

> Hastings! I knew thee young, and of a mind,
> While young, humane, conversable, and kind,
> Nor can I well believe thee, gentle THEN,
> Now grown a villain, and the WORST of men.
> But rather some suspect, who have oppress'd
> And worried thee, as not themselves the BEST.[55]

Cowper was quite friendly with Chase Price, the last boy—twentieth place—in the sixth form. Price was constantly involved in various schemes: land grants, Indian trade, and mining adventures. "Impetuous, resourceful, and passionately persevering, he was buzzing round, gathering information and retailing it, constantly scheming, and seeking great patrons under whom to act."[56] William Legge, later the second Earl of Dartmouth, sat beside Cowper in the sixth form; he became a deeply committed Evangelical, and Cowper characterized his former schoolmate as "one that wears a coronet and prays."[57] Another early friend—but not from Westminster—was Clotworthy Rowley, of a robust and unruly nature, who came from a distinguished naval family; he and Cowper were to be neighbors at the Inner Temple. Rowley eventually became Member of Parliament for Downpatrick for thirty years from 1771.

Cowper's closest alliances were with two men who shared his cultivated, quiet sensibility: Sir William Russell and Walter Bagot. Sir William, Cowper's "favourite friend"[58] at Westminster, drowned in 1757, and Cowper's poem to his memory, very much in the manner of Milton's *Lycidas* and clearly anticipatory of the sentiments expressed in the poem on his mother's portrait, is one of his finest evocations of the destructiveness of the sea:

Still, still, I mourn with each returning day,
Him snatch'd by Fate, in early youth away.

. . . .

See me—ere yet my destin'd course half done,
Cast forth a wand'rer on a wild unknown!
See me neglected on the world's rude coast,
Each dear companion of my voyage lost![59]

Walter Bagot had gone to Westminster with his older brothers, William and Charles, and two younger brothers, Richard and Lewis, later joined them there. Cowper was not personally acquainted with William (later Baron Bagot), but his brilliant reputation for English and Latin compositions had spread throughout the school; Charles was shy and retiring like Cowper and later became his neighbor at Chicheley, four miles from Olney; Cowper and Richard made nonsense verses together; Lewis (later Dean of Christ Church, Oxford, and Bishop, successively, of Bristol, Norwich, and St. Asaph) possessed, Cowper said, "the meekness of a Christian, and the good manners of a gentleman."[60] Despite the claims of his brothers, "Watty" was William's particular favorite.

Of all the friends Cowper made during the course of his life, Walter was the one most like him. He was the kind of person Cowper might have become had his inner torments been amenable to change. John Johnson said Walter was "the cheerfullest creature I almost ever met with, & I am laughing with him for ever."[61] A handsome boy but a distressingly slovenly dresser, only Walter's demeanor showed that he was an aristocrat. In youth, he had excelled at riding, hunting, and fishing, and he published his verse at an early age. Like Cowper, he was in youth and in later life devoted to the classics. "His divinity was of the old school, untouched with enthusiasm, unperverted by party."[62] Walter subsequently held the family livings of Blithfield and Leigh in Staffordshire. Cowper and Watty were "much intimate"[63] in their unaffected good natures, and it is fitting that Cowper's first extant letter (of March 12, 1749/50) is to him. That letter, jaunty and conspiratorial in tone and very much the letter of a young man full of swagger and the vigor of adolescent clowning, reveals the bonhomie shared by the two men: "Odd Enough! Two Friends corresponding by Letter at the Distance of a Mile & a half. An Indifferent person, would think we were afraid of seeing each other. No Rivers to interpose their Streams impassable; the Distance so Inconsiderable; the Weather fine, and both desirous of a meeting: Why then says that Indifferent person, what a Devil should hinder you?"[64]

After Westminster, the two drifted apart, and as Cowper told Lady Hesketh in 1785: "In the course, as I suppose, of more than twenty years after we left school, I saw him but twice;—once when I called on him at Oxford, and once when he called on me in the Temple."[65] When their friendship was renewed in 1782, Walter was a cultivated country parson, in whom Cowper saw a reflection of himself when he characterized him as a "good and amiable man": "I felt much affection for him, and the more because it was plain that after so long a time he still retained his for me."[66]

6   When Cowper was at Berkhamsted during the holidays, he looked up old friends and made new ones. John Duncombe, later to be the *Gentleman's Magazine*'s principal literary critic, and his father, William, who had quit the navy office in 1725 to pursue a life of literary leisure, were introduced to Cowper by either his father or brother. The Duncombes collaborated in the publication of some translations of Horace in 1757 and 1759, and Cowper was one of the friends who assisted them in that endeavor. Another friend was Richard Bard Harcourt, who attended Eton, Caius College, Cambridge, and Lincoln's Inn. In December 1757, Cowper told John Duncombe: ". . . tell me what is become of Dick Harcourt, I never hear from him or of him, & he is almost the only Man in your part of the World, that I want to hear of."[67]

Despite friends who lived nearby, Cowper was not anxious to visit Berkhamsted in the 1740s and 1750s. He was certainly not pleased by his father's marriage on January 8, 1740/41 (the year before Cowper enrolled at Westminster) to a widow, Rebecca Marryat. She was from Queen's Square, not far from Ashley's house, and John could easily have met her while staying at Red Lion Square and visiting his brother. Rebecca was approximately forty at the time of her second marriage (John was forty-seven) and was "long a cripple"[68] according to Cowper; her stepson's hostility is reflected in the comment he made at the time she died: ". . . my Mother:in: Law is dead and has left her fortune to be divided equally between my brother & myself—a division not very unlike Splitting a hair." Lady Hesketh declared that Rebecca Cowper was *"disagreeable enough in all Conscience,"*[69] and Cowper avoided Berkhamsted because of her presence. He was likely angry at his father for remarrying, and he must have compared his *"disagreeable"* stepmother to the angelic mother of his childhood memory. As well, he keenly felt the pressure of paternal expectations when at home, and he may have resorted to lying more than once:

> My father had given me a pair of silver shoe buckles which I kept till I wanted money and then sold them. The next time I waited on him at home the shoe buckles were missed and enquired after. I told him that being engaged at a match at football, and fearing that my buckles might be broken by kicks, I had put them into my waist-coat pocket, having hung my clothes upon a post; that while I was attentive to the sport, a blackguard boy, who had been lurking about us under pretence of looking on, had found an opportunity to steal them and carry them clear off.[70]

After Westminster, Cowper spent about nine months at home and was then sent to acquire the practice of law with an attorney. He was probably at home the following autumn, when his father suffered a serious "stroke of the dead Palsy" and "was judged to be in great danger."[71]

Affectionate remembrances of things past were second nature to Cowper. It was, however, in his temperament to feel most deeply only at moments of parting. Such was his final response to Berkhamsted: "I sighed a long adieu to fields and woods from which I once thought I should never be parted, and was at no time so sensible of their beauties as just when I left them all behind me to return no more."[72]

7   Cowper's career as a lawyer was determined from the time he was seventeen: on April 29, 1748, while still at Westminster, he was admitted to the Society of the Middle Temple, despite the fact that his name appeared on the school lists until 1749. As he himself said, he became a lawyer at his father's insistence: "I was bred to the Law. A Profession to which I was never much inclined, and in which I engaged rather because I was desirous to gratify a most indulgent Father, than because I had any hope of success in it myself."[73] Cowper's training in the law followed the common practice in the eighteenth century of having a would-be lawyer work at a firm before going on to the Inns of Court, which were usually places of amusement rather than serious study. He was apprenticed in 1750 to Mr. Chapman, an attorney and solicitor, who lived in

Greville Street, in the middle of the legal district, directly behind Furnival's Inn. He was a decent and kindly person, but Cowper found the "Tricks & illiberal Conduct of his fellow Clerks disgusting, and this association contributed to his dislike of the profession even after he moved to the Temple."[74] He received consolation in the summer of 1751 from an ally whom he should have intensely disliked: Edward Thurlow, the future Lord Chancellor. In that year, Thurlow was sent down from Caius College, Cambridge, because of insolent behavior and repeated absence from chapel. He was a coarse and brutal, but astute, devotee of law and literature. A contemporary said of him in 1754, when Thurlow was called to the Bar: "he was still idle and unfixed: he was a man of pleasure, and lost much of his time in social dissipation. If he read, nobody knew when he read; but in the midst of seeming inattention, and of utter neglect of the dull, technical studies of his profession, he sometimes betrayed a sleeping fire, and force of talent."[75] He could be kindly—he once spent £300 to establish a penniless daughter of a friend of his father's in a millinery shop.[76] It is a measure of the transformation of Cowper by 1751 that he, the boy who had previously been the victim of bullying, could become a close friend of a crass opportunist. However, Cowper looked upon Thurlow from the outset as someone who would protect him, and Thurlow may have seen in Cowper that refined part of himself he was forever at odds with and never able to accept fully.

Cowper had mastered a great deal of knowledge about worldly matters while at Westminster, where he had learned to present himself in a way by which his soft, genial nature would find acceptance. His closest literary friendships during the ensuing London years were with members of the Nonsense Club, which consisted of seven old Westminsters who dined together every Thursday. At his public school, Cowper had been trained to live according to the place in society of the Cowper and Donne families, and in his deportment, he always remained an aristocrat.

During his Westminster years, shadows from the past do not seem to have blighted this young patrician unduly. One of the great ironies of Cowper's early life is that he, who would later suffer severely from mental affliction and be confined in a private madhouse, could visit Bedlam with the smallest twinge of discomfort: "In those days when Bedlam was open to the cruel curiosity of Holiday ramblers, I have been a visitor there. Though a boy, I was not altogether insensible of the misery of the poor captives, nor destitute of feeling for them. But the Madness of some of them had such a humorous air, and displayed itself in so many whimsical freaks, that it was impossible not to be entertained at the same time that I was angry with myself for being so."[77] Only in 1763 did Cowper's past catch up with him; and from that time, he would be ensnared in the conflicts stemming from his mother's death.

In his early letters, however, especially those to Chase Price, Cowper portrayed himself as a libertine. He compared his sexual prowess to Price's ("And are you not a Coxcomb? Can you deny it? Is not your last Letter a Proof of it? Don't you there Brag of being better Qualified to entertain the Fair Sex than my Worship?"[78]), was proud of his dedication to licentious behavior, and evoked the life—his own at that time—of a rake from the beau monde: "Dancing all last Night; in bed one half of the Day & Shooting all the other half."[79] Cowper's advocacy of *liaisons dangereuses*, however, met a serious challenge when he began to court his cousin, Theadora, and his fragility in that instance manifests how much of his sophistication was merely masquerade.

2
Theadora

1   ALTHOUGH COWPER had visited his uncle Ashley and his family while at Westminster, he did not meet regularly with them until he was articled to Mr. Chapman. No. 30 Southampton Row became his unofficial residence: "I did actually live 3 years with Mr. Chapman . . . that is to say I slept three years in his house, but I lived, that is, spent my days in Southampton Row."[1] Ashley's house overlooked the gardens and fields of the Bedford Estates and the open land stretched away to Hampstead. "Chearful & happy I was wont to stray, / Through *Ducal Bedford's* fields to *Primrose-Hill,*"[2] Cowper said, echoing Thomas Gray's sentiments of 1759: "I am now settled in my new territories commanding Bedford gardens, and all the fields as far as Highgate and Hampstead, with such a concourse of moving pictures as would astonish you; so *rus-in-urbe-ish,* that I believe I shall stay here. . . . here is air, and sunshine, and quiet . . . to comfort you."[3] This Eden inspired exuberance in Cowper: "There was I, the future Lord Chancellor, constantly employed from Morning to Night in giggling and making giggle."[4]

Ashley Cowper, because of his small size, could one day, if his white hat was lined with pink instead of the customary yellow, his favorite nephew joked, be picked by mistake for a mushroom and "sent off in a basket."[5] Although Ashley published verse distinguished by crudity and blatant moralizing, Cowper thought, "No man has a better Taste than my Uncle, and my opinion of it is such that I should certainly renounce the pen for ever, were I to hear that he wish'd me to do so."[6] As a young man, Ashley "wrote some very pretty things, and had . . . a strong Turn for Poetry . . . ,"[7] and Cowper's propensity for verse drew uncle and nephew together. They also shared an obvious mixture of melancholic frailties: according to one of his daughters, Ashley "was subject *at times* to a degree of low Spirits, which would sometimes hang upon him for months together, and which were . . . affecting to see."[8] Ashley, who was a friend of Hogarth's, was more worldly, if not more intellectual, than his older brother John, Cowper's father, and in the 1750s it was sophistication and comfort which Cowper craved, and he came to enjoy "five Evenings in a week in the domestick Circle"[9] of Southampton Row.

By this time, Cowper "eyed the women, and made free / To comment on their shapes,"[10] and there were three attractive cousins at Southampton Row: Harriot (who eventually married Sir Thomas Hesketh), Theadora (who never married), and Elizabeth Charlotte (who married Sir Archer Croft). Cowper's fate would be inextricably linked with both Harriot and Theadora, but by the summer of 1752 he had become absolutely infatuated with Thea. An impartial account of 1754 reported her "grown tall and vastly improv'd."[11] She was learned in French, devout but not Evangelical, and an intelligent, lively letter writer. While others proclaimed Harriot the family beauty, Lady Hesketh called her sister a goddess: "her figure and her eyes would not have disgraced Madam Juno herself."[12] Harriot's description is matched in Cowper's evocation of his beloved in *A Song:*

> The sparkling eye, the mantling cheek,
> The polish'd front, the snowy neck,
>   How seldom we behold in one!
> Glossy locks, and brow serene,
> Venus' smiles, Diana's mien,
>   All meet in you, and you alone.[13]

Theadora is clearly the "Delia" of Cowper's amorous verse, and despite the traditionalism of these early poems, they would seem, like so much of Cowper's verse, to have a strong basis in autobiographical fact. During 1752 and 1753, Theadora said, "we saw each other *daily*."[14] Cowper pointed out Theadora to Walter Bagot one evening at the theater, and Bagot was convinced of the depth of his friend's attachment.[15] It was Thea who gave Cowper a red carnelian seal ring on which was depicted Omphale wearing the lion's skin of Hercules. Cowper was attracted by Thea's great beauty, but he also divined the deep well of unhappiness in her nature. From the start, theirs was a bittersweet love, a mixture of strong sexual attraction and similar melancholic inclinations.

2   Theadora was desolate when, after two years of seemingly idyllic courtship, the love affair began to go wrong. There were regrets, recriminations, partings, reconciliations, further partings. However, only in his "Delia" poems did Cowper ever allow himself to speak freely and directly of Theadora—and it is impossible in those poems to separate the man who suffered from the persona of wounded lover. In *Delia, Th'Unkindest Girl on Earth,* the speaker remonstrates against the lady who will not give him a lock of hair to protect it from the "spoiler," Time. The lover in this poem, unlike Pope's Baron, does not remove the lock by force, but, in language reminiscent of the conclusion to *The Rape of the Lock,* he warns Delia of the transience of earthly beauty:

> Yet when its sister locks shall fade,
>   As quickly fade they must,
> When all their beauties are decay'd,
>   Their gloss, their colour, lost,—
>
> Ah then! if haply to my share
>   Some slender pittance fall,
> If I but gain one single hair,
>   Nor age usurp them all—[16]

The speaker is perhaps describing the pain of William Cowper, but the reader is closed off from the biographical events. Cowper may be expressing his own anguish in these lines—:

> Rather, much rather would I be—
>   Be thus thy Scorn express'd—
> Detested and despis'd by thee,
>   Than by the World caress'd.[17]

—but the stance of the speaker is one taken in love poems by, among many others, Catullus, Wyatt, Donne, and Waller. Poems do not necessarily depict the reality of their creators' inner struggles, but they can often be used as corroboration. The young man who wrote these poems wanted to feel deeply, and he probably did. However, he was hesitant about genuine commitment. In *A Character,* which begins, "William was once a bashfull Youth," the speaker concludes that lovers "howe'er Sublime / Are fickle as the Weather."[18] When he revised the poem and shortened it considerably, Cowper came to a rather more sentimental conclusion about the transforming power of love: "Let the dear mind who wrought the change / E'en claim him for her own."[19]

Ultimately, Theadora was much more love's victim than Cowper, who had been entranced with the idea of being in love with its attendant exultations and depressions. Thea's heart was consecrated to her cousin. Finally, in about 1756, Ashley intervened and forbade marriage. It may have been for reasons of feared congenital melancholia present in both cousins and in Ashley himself, but William's father saw no objection to the match. It may have been due to the cousins' consanguinity, but this is unlikely since Major William Cowper had succeeded in marrying his first cousin, Maria Madan, in 1749 despite Judith Madan's dissent. According to Lady Hesketh, "There was no obsticle to [Theadora's] marriage with C. but his want of income for an establishment suited to their rank."[20] Harriot's claim may be the stated reason for the abandonment of marriage plans, but, as well, Ashley probably divined Cowper's lack of wholehearted devotion to Thea. In addition, the couple's constant quarreling likely indicated to him that the marriage would not work. At that time, Ashley's heart became "set, and his *Peace of Mind strongly interested* in their finding happiness independent of each other."[21]

However, the possibility of marriage was reopened by Ashley in August 1763 when he offered Cowper sinecure posts at the House of Lords and, by implication, his daughter's hand. Surprisingly, Cowper declined. In 1786, he told Harriot that when he and Thea

> met at Margate after having been for many years separated, that their Union wou'd have *then* been practicable, as he then, with the Place offer'd him, cou'd have maintained a family. He said he saw My dear Father, who always lov'd him *as a Son,* would have made no objections, and, that She herself was unchang'd—well, replied I, why did you *not* propose? To this question he replied what I can never forget. . . . "O yes I saw my Paradise before me—but I also saw the flaming Sword that must for ever keep me from it!"[22]

The "fiery sword" of Milton's Michael barred Adam and Eve from Eden; Cowper imagined that a similar divine injunction prevented him from entering wedlock.

Ashley's refusal seven years earlier was intended to put a public face on what might have been a multiplicity of private reasons. From the time of that break, Harriot encouraged "Conversation on this Subject as little as possible, certain that it cou'd answer no good end to either party."[23] There are no records of the immediate effects of the end of the affair on Thea. Her best friend, Georgiana

Poyntz, later the Countess Spencer, wrote her on June 6, 1756, accepting for ill-defined reasons the impossibility of the marriage, adding that "I think it would be only tormenting you for nothing & trying by an Ill tim'd advice to add to your Afflictions."[24] Earlier, on May 11, 1754, Georgiana told Thea that "Mamma said I think the best Thing Thea could do would be to marry Billy Cowper if she Can be Contented with a Little. He is a very good young man & I dare say will do very well in the world, besides he will have a pretty fortune when his father dies."[25] Mrs. Poyntz's advice would have been sound counsel had money been the only consideration. In any event, the cipher "repwoc" disappeared from the billets-doux of these two young ladies in 1756.

Without doubt, Theadora endured subsequent melancholy. In December 1762, after a painful operation for an abcess on her side, Thea's condition was said to be "a very critical one in many respects."[26] The disease was diagnosed the following month as St. Anthony's fire (erysipelas—a virulent and painful skin disease), and four doctors were in attendance. From the treatment, however, her aunt, Judith Madan, expected "nothing but an increase of her misery and uneasiness."[27] Mrs. Madan viewed her niece's illness as divine chastisement and, as a result, ultimately beneficial: "yet I dread the Life, the company She will again be involv'd in—how they will try to divert away Every Serious impression—thinking themselves most kind—when they can banish every thought, of what has past, during this Scene of awfull Events—from Her heart."[28] Georgiana, in her letters, was not blind to the possibility that "Dearest Thea's" illness might be psychosomatic: "it hurts me vastly . . . to find you so low spirited. I cannot help hoping it is partly owing to the effects of your illness, for so severe an attack as yours was last year must for a time weaken and ennervate all the faculties of the mind as well as the body. . . ."[29] Years later, Samuel Greatheed reported that she was "still living, single, but has many years been melancholy."[30] Although written fifty years after her first illness, Theadora's letters to Hayley are replete with sorrow: "I have long since been a Wanderer & a Vagabond upon the Face of the Earth."[31]

It is difficult to assess the nature of her various maladies and their seriousness. There is the strongest likelihood that the near relation that Cowper mentioned in August 1769 as filling a vacancy at Dr. Cotton's "Collegeium Insanorum" was Theadora.[32] Later that same month, Judith Madan told her daughter Maria that Thea had recovered but was in a weak state: "Sir Thomas talks of fetching her away to go to France with him, which She likes very well."[33] Throughout Thea's life, the stigma of rumored madness followed her. In 1804, Mrs. Maitland, a cousin, accosted Lady Hesketh with gossip that, "has lately come to my knowledge, but on which I will form *no* Judgment, till *you direct that judgement*. A Lady asserted that (to her knowledge) my dear Cousin Thea was a few years back *out of her mind:* that she went away from the house she was in, (somewhere near Cambridge I think) & was absent all night, having roamed about; & was found next day & brought back. . . ."[34] Lady Hesketh dismissed the allegation, but she did so in a hysterical manner: "I must next proceed to white wash my poor Sister, who I give my word of honor is perfectly free from any one part of the strange story you have heard ascribed to her!—that there is *nothing* people will not *say—assert—*and *Swear* to I have long been Convinc'd . . . my good Sister never was out of her mind in her whole life, I think I may venture to assert!"[35] The denial was certainly firm, but Harriot continued with the ludicrous suggestion: "that the *Story* may be true of *Some* Miss Cowper I pretend not to deny, but *assuredly not of my Sister.* So have the goodness to contradict it point blank I beseech you, for indeed you may with perfect Security."[36]

When he was dying, Cowper asked John Johnson to return to Thea "her father's watch which *she* had given him."[37] Only then did he name her as the person who bestowed it upon him. Thea outlived Cowper by almost a quarter of a century, but she spent her days in almost complete seclusion. Lady Hesketh told Cowper in 1785: "you know both my father and sister never were fond of Company, and I think this has increased greatly upon him lately even more I believe than even my Sister now finds pleasant, as he really does not wish to see even his nearest Relations."[38] Ashley had reacted bitterly to Cowper's refusal to marry Thea in 1763, and Thea, desolate when the engagement had been called off in 1756, never fully recovered from Cowper's betrayal of 1763. Harriot loved her sister but felt she was lazy and indolent. She was tolerant of Thea's failings, however, because of her misfortune in love: "we must look for the Cause of this I fancy in the early disappointment of her Heart."[39]

3   In *Adelphi*, there is no mention of Thea, but Cowper does relate the serious bout of depression he experienced at the time he moved to the Middle Temple in November 1753: "This being a

most critical season of my life and upon which much depended, it pleased my all-merciful Father in Christ Jesus to give a check to my rash and ruinous career in wickedness at the very outset. I was struck not long after my settlement in the Temple with such a dejection of spirits as none but they who have felt the same can have the least conception of. Day and night I was upon the rack, lying down in horrors and rising in despair."[40] One of his breaks with Thea surely came at this time. Does he refrain from mentioning her out of discretion or because he does not realize that his morbid feelings may have arisen in part because of the doomed relationship? The depression of 1753 obviously provided the first serious test of Cowper's young manhood, and the memory of his mother's seeming abandonment made it difficult for him to place his trust in a permanent alliance with Thea in marriage; his quarrels with her on that score likely provoked the "despair" at the Middle Temple.

Cowper tried to distract himself. He took refuge in reading George Herbert, whose verse turned his attention to religious matters: "I composed a set of prayers adapted to my necessity and made frequent use of them." Harriot whisked him away to Southampton. There, on a clear and beautiful morning while sitting on a ledge above the sea, his sorrow vanished: "Here it was that on a sudden, as if another sun had been kindled that instant in the heavens on purpose to dispel sorrow and vexation of spirit, I felt the weight of all my misery taken off. My heart became light and joyous in a moment."[41] He seemed to have escaped "dejection of spirits" in this romantic imbroglio.

Indeed, he confided to Chase Price the following year: "A certain Person who is not at all Dear to me to speak of, has given herself the Air of calling me a *Coxcomb* often before now; I am willing to allow *her* the Privilege of *calling* me so, because I know she cannot in reality think me one, and Love me as she does."[42] The "certain person" is probably Thea; their broken romance had been—temporarily—restored. In August 1758, approximately two years after his break with his cousin, Cowper was captivated by a sixteen-year-old beauty from the West Indies.[43] Later, in the early 1760s, he burned for the love of one of Edward Thurlow's mistresses.[44] These scanty, intriguing references are the only certain knowledge to survive of Cowper's amorous activities, but his letters from 1754 to 1762 display bravado in things sexual. He called John Duncombe "an honest old Whore"[45] and, in commenting on Martin Madan's newborn son, he told Duncombe that the baby "has a Foot much longer than yours already, so he is likely to be a Proper Man."[46] As a carefree youth, William Cowper actively pursued pleasure, but he had, as well, the uncanny ability to flee pain.*

This very same person, in the midst of composing his commonplace lover's complaints to Thea, could write verse which hints at the profoundest sorrow and anguish. In *Mortals, Around Your Destin'd Heads* written *c.* 1752–53 (there is a manuscript in Theadora's hand at the British Library, and the poem must have been written during their courtship), Cowper described the anguish of the human condition, employing language and imagery which anticipates *The Castaway:*

> Fondly we think all danger fled,
>   For Death is ever Nigh,
> Out-strips our Unavailing speed,
>   Or Meets us as we flie.

> Thus the Wreck'd Mariner may strive
>   Some Desart Shore to gain,
> Secure of Life, if he survive
>   The fury of the Main.

> But there, to Famine doom'd a prey,
>   Finds the mistaken Wretch,
> He but escaped the troubled Sea,
>   To perish on the Beach.[47]

Despite the share of sorrow that was his when he and Thea parted, Cowper in the mid-1750s was not, like Thea, destroyed by the affair. He could experience his first bout of intense depression and then have it miraculously lifted. He could plot amorous in-

---

* Cowper's sexuality has been much debated. A now missing letter from John Newton to John Thornton supposedly provided evidence that Cowper was a hermaphrodite. It is possible that Cowper in 1774 (the probable date of Newton's letter) believed that he was such, and Newton either mentioned Cowper's assertion to Thornton or, believing Cowper's claim, conveyed the information to Thornton as factually correct. Charles Ryskamp discusses this matter at length in *William Cowper of the Inner Temple, Esq.* (Cambridge: Cambridge University Press, 1959), 135–44, and comes to the sensible conclusion: "It is much more likely that Cowper's reputed hermaphroditism was a preoccupation resulting from his melancholia."

As well, the available evidence suggests that Cowper was an active heterosexual until 1763; after that, his diminution in self-esteem seems to have led to an eradication of sexual urges.

trigues after plans of marriage between himself and Theadora had been abandoned, just as he could compose conventional love poetry at the same time he hesitantly began to write verse whose grim melancholy anticipates his later work. In 1753, Cowper could separate and divide the sorrows and joys of his life from each other; in 1763, he would not be able to do so. He did not fully experience the anguish of the loss of Thea until that time.

3
London (1753–1763)

1   WHEN HE published his first independent volume of verse in 1782, Cowper asked to be announced as "William Cowper Esqr. of the Inner Temple."[1] In thus styling himself, he was affirming his status as gentleman, lawyer, and Londoner. Cowper was to find much comfort in his retreat from the world and, to a lesser extent, in fervent Evangelical Christianity. However, he always remained, if only in spirit, a citizen of London.

Later in life, Cowper described himself as "a batter'd actor upon this turbulent stage,"[2] but in the 1750s London was for him an exhilarating place, where he could be certain to have a central role in the worlds of letters—and amorous intrigue. In his early twenties, William Cowper was a charming and elegant beau, bound to society and fashion. He was a dilettante, although an especially learned one. He was of medium height, of sturdy rather than delicate build; he had light brown hair, dark hazel eyes, and a ruddy complexion. Romney, in his justly celebrated crayon drawing of 1792, captured the quick, darting, and virile aspects of Cowper's face. He caught a momentary glimpse of the handsome and sensuous young man of the 1750s and early 1760s.*

Throughout his life, Cowper possessed a "florid healthy Figure"[3]: he had "an interesting Countenance that expresses Intelligence & energy of Mind with Sweetness of Manners & a certain tender undescribable Mixture of Melancholy & Chearfulness, Gravity & Sportive Humour which give an admirable Variety of Attraction to his character."[4] Although not forward in conversation, "he could fall into their key, when started, as soon as any body."[5] From an early age, he adopted two distinct speaking voices: "The voice of Cow-

* Lemuel Abbott's portrait—also of 1792—depicts Cowper as country gentleman; Thomas Lawrence in 1793 emphasized the poet's gentility and timidity.

per in conversation was below the common pitch, and had that sort of obstructed tone in it which obtains in cases where the mouth is less open than is usually observed, and the lips in less active operation. But when raised for the purposes of reading or recitation, especially of poetry, it assumed another character, and without being over-loud was harmonious and distinct."[6] Although he had a slight tendency towards corpulence and suffered from indigestion, constipation, and other mild complaints, his physical health was always remarkably good. As late as 1798, John Johnson claimed Cowper "has *summer-looks* and *winter-looks,* more than any man I ever saw—but then in summer he is always *without doors,* and in winter always *within.*"[7]

As a robust young man, Cowper traveled to relieve the boredom of prolonged stays in London. He was "seldom seen there in summer"[8]: it was, after all, unfashionable to remain in London after the Season was over. Then, he would visit his cousin, Spencer Cowper, at Tewin-Water, or he might accept an invitation to Colne-Green, the seat of the Earls Cowper. In 1752 and 1753, he was in Norfolk at Catfield and Drayton, visiting his Donne cousins. He was especially fond of the sea, and he knew the fashionable summer resorts of Southampton, Taplow, Margate, Rottingdean, Weymouth, and Brighton as centers of "Idleness and Luxury, music, dancing, cards, walking, riding, bathing, eating, drinking, coffee, tea, scandal, dressing, yawning, sleeping."[9] He did, however, enjoy the more tranquil amusements of these watering places: "A walk to Nettley Abbey or to Freemantle or to Redbridge, or a book by the fire-side, had always more charms"[10] for him than any of the amusements he facetiously cataloged.

Cowper's lackadaisical life does not seem to have been unduly disrupted by his father's demise in 1756, when he was twenty-five. In middle age, however, a very different William Cowper regretted his earlier insensitivity:

> At a thoughtless age, allur'd
> By ev'ry gilded folly, we renounc'd
> His shelt'ring side, and wilfully forewent
> That converse which we now in vain regret.
> How gladly would the man recall to life
> The boy's neglected sire![11]

In 1763, seven years after his father's death, Cowper's London world collapsed, when he felt unable to defend himself in the essentially routine pursuit of a sinecure in his family's gift. Until that time, he chased "gilded folly." Cowper had suffered—perhaps he was unaware how deeply—from the break with Thea, and much of his London life was an attempt to escape from painful memories. It was in this existence of ease and graceful listlessness that, in his youth, he thought he found renewal. As an older man, he would have agreed with Horace Walpole: "We are absurd creatures; at twenty I loved nothing but London."[12]

2 "The happiness of London," Johnson once told Boswell, "is not to be conceived of but by those who have been in it. I will venture to say, there is more learning and science within the circumference of ten miles from where we now sit, than in all the rest of the kingdom."[13] Young William Cowper would have concurred in this judgment, but he would also have been well aware that his favorite city was dirty, smelly, and congested. Disgustedly, Horace Walpole exclaimed: "Prepare yourself for crowds, multitudes. In this reign all the world lives in one room. The capital is as vulgar as a county-town in the season of horse-races."[14] If one was prepared to brave the crowds, there was a variety of divertissements: the pleasure gardens of Vauxhall and Ranelagh, staged balls, masquerades, gambling dens, opera and theater, cock fighting, bull-and-bear-baiting, cricket, boxing, "disorderly houses." Undoubtedly, Cowper sampled all these delights.

At jovial gatherings, he was "able to drink 4 or 5 bottles of Claret without sensible effect."[15] Although naturally withdrawn, he could always muster a good story. His audience "knew something delightful was coming before it came. His eye would suddenly kindle and all his face become lighted up with the fun of the story, before he opened his lips to speak. At last he began to relate some ludicrous incident,—which, although you had yourself witnessed it, you had failed to recognize as mirthful. . . . So ready and so graceful in fact was the poet's fancy, that he knew how to make an amusing story out of nothing."[16] As well, Cowper could be mildly sarcastic and allow a vituperative remark to escape the usually carefree flow of his conversation. His habitual shyness was frequently conquered, and his enormous enthusiasms—for good verse, agreeable conversation, attractive women—would float to the surface. His ability at "mild and benevolent pleasantry" and "delicate humour"[17]—as well as his obvious literary talent—stood him in good stead with the other members of the Nonsense Club.

In 1787, John Newton told Hannah More that the "present Lord

Chancellor, Mr. Coleman of the Haymarket & the late Mr. Bonnel Thornton, were the three persons with whom Mr. Cowper was most intimate, when he resided in the Temple."[18] Edward Thurlow, since he was not at Westminster, did not qualify for membership in the Nonsense Club. In addition to Cowper, Colman, and Thornton, the other members were Robert Lloyd and James Bensley, and perhaps Chase Price and Charles Churchill. As in other literary clubs of the century, the members joined together for amusing chat, gossip, and the opportunity to receive sympathetic criticism and judicious encouragement.

In later life, Cowper was, at various times, Jeremy Sago, William Pindar, Andrew Fridze, Toot, and Giles Gingerbread, and this penchant for giving himself nicknames may have been part of his inheritance from the Club, where a premium was placed on literary disguises. The Club was, after all, a motley assemblage of young men, each in search of a literary identity. Like all young, would-be writers of their generation, they lived in the shadow of Samuel Johnson, against whose august—paternal—canons they rebelled. The group was also incredibly snobbish, and Cowper recalled that he did not as a dutiful member have much use for Thomas Gray or his poetry: "I was prejudiced; he did not belong to our Thursday Society & was an Eaton man, which lower'd him prodigiously in our Esteem."[19] Cowper was like Mr. Spectator, who "mixed" wherever he saw a "Cluster of People . . . tho' I never open my Lips but in my own Club."[20]

Cowper's confreres in the Club or "Thursday Society"* were as lively as he. George Colman the Elder, later a well-known dramatist, had been born in Florence in 1732 where his father was envoy to the court of Tuscany. His father died in 1733, and Colman was left as the charge of William Pulteney, later Earl of Bath. After Westminster, Colman entered Christ Church, Oxford, and, subsequently, in 1755, Lincoln's Inn. Although he was called to the Bar in 1757, he incurred the wrath of Pulteney for spending more time on the

---

* From the available evidence, it is difficult to determine how extensive Cowper's contacts were outside the Nonsense Club itself. He probably was not one of the "Geniuses" (Boswell's rather loose but memorable name for Wilkes, Churchill, and Lloyd, whom he encountered on May 24, 1763: "In a little, Mr. Wilkes came in, to whom I was introduced, as I also was to Mr. Churchill. Wilkes is a lively, facetious man, Churchill a rough, blunt fellow, very clever. Lloyd too was there, so that I was just got into the middle of the London Geniuses" (*Boswell's London Journal, 1762–1763*, ed. Frederick A. Pottle [1950], 266). Cowper was undoubtedly not as forward as his associates in the Club and probably did not pursue his literary interests much beyond his Westminster friends.

theater than the law. He did, however, establish himself in 1761 with the five-act comedy, *The Jealous Wife.* He and Cowper were similar in their genial, sometimes over-sensitive natures, and in 1785, after a considerable hiatus in their friendship, Colman assured him that he had "never lost the remembrance of the sweet counsel we took together. I have often thought of you with a most affectionate regret, and often mentioned you in terms that went not only from the mouth, but the heart . . . I am just what I was, just what you left me, the same feeling, fretful, fond, and I will say faithful, creature you once knew me."[21] Bonnell Thornton, a few years older than the other members of the Club, may have been its leader. His *Ode on Saint Cæcilia's Day, Adapted to the Ancient British Music,* written in 1749, was performed in 1763, with music by Dr. Arne, to considerable applause. Thornton's poem was a brilliant burlesque of the odes to the patroness of music by Dryden, Addison, Pope, and Smart. His most extensive literary activities, however, were in periodicals: the *Student* and the *Midwife* (with Smart), the *Connoisseur* (with Colman), the *Drury-Lane Journal,* the *St. James's Magazine,* the *Public Advertiser,* and the *Saint James's Chronicles.* Joseph Warton thought him delightful, and Boswell summed him up as a well-bred young man of independent means who was fond of writing: "So he employs himself in that way."[22]

Robert Lloyd and James Bensley were to die in their early thirties. Lloyd had been Westminster bred as well as educated: his father was "Tappy" Lloyd, for nearly fifty years a master at the school. Robert was an excellent scholar at school, but at Trinity College, Cambridge, and later in London, he led an undisciplined, carousing existence. As Boswell said, "Bachus leads him by the nose / And hence it is so wond'rous long / For Bachus' grips are mighty strong."[23] Lloyd, with Colman, wrote two burlesque odes to Gray and Mason in 1760, and in 1762 to 1763 he edited the *St. James's Magazine* with Thornton, with whom he quarreled. His old friend became his "inveterate enemy, in the quality of his most inexorable creditor."[24] In debt, Lloyd was thrown into the Fleet where he eventually died. James Bensley also went up to Trinity College, Cambridge. He was rusticated in 1754 for "grave irregularity and misbehavior by insulting the Vice-Master, the Dean, and other officers of the College."[25] He nevertheless went on to graduate in 1755; he was later at the Inner Temple and then Lincoln's Inn, where he was still a member in 1765 when he was killed by a fall from a horse. Cowper, who had been absent from London for almost two years when these two friends died, mourned their passings, but deplored the lives they had led: "Two of my friends have been cut off . . . in the midst of such a life, as it is frightful to reflect upon, and here am I, in better health and spirits than I can almost remember."[26] In this rare self-righteous mood, Cowper hoped that the tragic early deaths of these two men would be a useful memento mori to the surviving members of the Club.

Like Cowper and Bensley, Chase ("Toby") Price, whom William Combe called the *"Falstaff* of the present age,"[27] was of the Inner Temple as well as Westminster, where his disreputable career had begun. In his devotion to bawdy songs and prominent courtesans, his interests were very much those of Bensley and Lloyd. Cowper was intrigued with, and doubtlessly immeshed in, this manner of life in the mid-1750s. As he confessed to "Toby," their friendship was based on the cultivation of young men's vices. It was to Chase Price that he confided his early poems, some of which are now known only through Price's transcriptions.[28] Charles Churchill, who also died young, had attended Westminster, flown through Cambridge, served as curate in Somerset, Essex, and St. John's Westminster, but was completely devoted to spirits, mistresses, and the clap in the last three years of his tempestuous existence. He decribed himself to Garrick as "Half-Drunk—Half Mad—and quite stripp'd of all my Money."[29] Despite his devotion to a life that quickly became a rake's progress, Churchill was a satirist of uncompromising finesse, and it was this quality which Cowper recognized in the man he felt was the most accomplished writer of his London set: "It is a great thing to be indeed a Poet, & does not happen to more than One Man in a Century. Churchill, the great Churchill, deserved the Name of Poet. Such natural unforced Effusions of Genius, the World I beleive has never seen since the Days of Shakespear."[30] Churchill was a scapegrace—he never really learned to manage his existence. Cowper might well have identified with this aspect of Churchill; he obviously saw him as someone, like himself, who, despite precociousness and abundant talent, had ruined his life. His words about his death are especially poignant: "It is an affair of very little Consequence perhaps to the Wellbeing of Mankind, but I cannot help regretting that he died so soon."[31]

Unfortunately, there is little information concerning the actual meetings of the Club and the high jinks with which they were undoubtedly filled. Colman and Thornton did manage, however, one prank which suggests the sense of the ridiculous which inspired the Club's activities. Cowper had known them "many months and had dined and supped with them an hundred times" before he even suspected they were, like himself, aspiring writers—much less the editors of the *Connoisseur*. They encouraged him in March 1756 to try his hand at getting an acceptance from that illustrious publication, and then, a few days later, watched from a secluded corner in Dick's Coffee House as he called for a copy of the paper and beheld "the countenance no doubt of a man trembling lest his first attempt be rejected, and transported with joy to find himself actually in print."[32] Cowper's ribald portrait of Billy Suckling in *Connoisseur* 111 was probably his entrée to the Club, of which he was a member until 1762.

"Taste," the *Connoisseur* asserted, "is at present the darling idol of the polite world, and the world of letters; and . . . seems to be considered as the quintessence of almost all the arts and sciences." Indeed, it was the pursuit of this je ne sais quoi in literature and in a way of life that occupied Cowper's every waking hour. He knew and abided by all the rituals of the demimonde, and he was intimately acquainted with its canons. Cowper was especially hostile to those who did not observe society's whims of iron. His Billy Suckling did not have the requisite polish to survive in the refined—but often turbulent—world in which his creator lived: "I am intimately acquainted with one of these over-grown babies; who is indeed too big to be dandled in lap, or fed with a pap-spoon, though he is no more weaned from his mother, than if he had not yet quitted the nursery."[33] Cowper's demeanor had changed markedly from that of a timorous young boy from Berkhamsted deprived of his mother at an early age to that of a man-about-town who could, with some venom, attack the "lady-like gentlemen" who are too dependent upon their mothers.

Indeed, William Cowper the quintessential dandy is enshrined in his letter to John Duncombe of June 12, 1759:

> I have a great respect for your Virtues, notwithstanding that in your Letter to my Brother you talk Bawdy like an Old Midwife. You wonder I am not a more Punctual Correspondent; how the Devil should I be so, or what Subject can I possibly find to Entertain you upon? If I had a share in the Cabinet Councils of every Court in Europe, you would have no Pleasure in a Political Epistle; if I was a greater Philosopher than Sir Isaac Newton, you would think me a Fool if I should write to you upon the Subject of the Centripetal & Centrifugal Powers, the Solar System, and the Eccentrick Orbits of the

Comets; And as great a Lawyer as I am, I dare not Indulge myself in the Pedantry of my Profession, lest you should not understand me, or I should not understand myself.[34]

These high-flown words are well turned, and Cowper casts a sharply
ironical glance at Duncombe—and himself. As well, it is the letter
of a languid sophisticate who is competing with his friend to discover which of them is the more jaded. Cowper is also posing here—
he is searching for a tasteful blend of scorn and affection. Throughout the passage, he obviously speaks with assurance. Nevertheless,
his youthful shyness and sensitivity had not altered significantly.
He had merely applied a hard veneer to his tender spirit.

3   Joseph Hill, Cowper's closest friend during these years, was
not a member of the Nonsense Club, although he was very much on
its fringes. He had been born near Chancery Lane and was the son of
an attorney, Francis Hill. Joseph's father, who died when he was
eight, was the nephew and had served as the secretary of Sir Joseph
Jekyll, Master of the Rolls. Joe had "always lived in great intimacy"[35] with Ashley Cowper and his family, and "Sephus" (as he
was nicknamed) and Cowper became friends shortly after Cowper
left Westminster. Joe had probably first become acquainted with
Cowper's uncle in the office of Clerk of the Parliaments (Ashley was
the patentee of deputations in that place). In any event, Joe's life
was early devoted to the law: he served as a clerk in Chancery Lane,
qualified as both solicitor and attorney, and was later appointed
one of the Sixty, or Sworn Clerks in Chancery. Eventually, Hill became an eminently successful lawyer, who numbered the aristocratic
and wealthy among his clients.
     As a young man, Hill assumed a place in the legal world to
which the careers of Cowper's grandfather and uncle had earlier
been committed. He worked while Cowper played. These two men
were unlikely friends, but Joe was intrigued by Cowper's literary
aspirations, and Cowper was attracted by his friend's "warm heart"[36]
and steadfastness. Hill was later the financial mainstay of Cowper's
existence. However, in the early years of their friendship, it was
Cowper who had largess to bestow. He introduced Joe to Edward
Thurlow, who on assuming the Woolsack in 1778, gave Hill one
of the posts in his bequest: Secretary of Lunatics.
     Harriot Hesketh, who had known Hill at her father's home in
Southampton Row, told Hayley in 1801 about Joe's devotion to lit-

erature: "He is most perfectly a Man of honour & of honesty though bred in the above named Profession where it is not *always* to be found—beside that he is a man of letters—has an excellent & a strong understanding, is perfectly well inform'd, & has in my opinion a very Judicious & a very Critical Taste in Poetry, which he is very fond of, & in which I can always rely on."[37] Although Cowper truthfully recalled in 1769 the warmth of their friendship ("I remember you with all the friendship I ever professed, which is as much as I ever entertained for any man"[38]), the relationship in later years consisted of polite formality and duty letters. In their youths, however, Joe, a plain man, "close-button'd to the chin,"[39] indulged his flirtation with the muse in Cowper's company, and Cowper had a trusty companion who occasionally nudged him in the direction of the law.

The legal profession, into which Cowper had been reluctantly inducted, was not the happiest calling for a man of his capricious sensibility, and he attempted only halfheartedly to follow the choice of life which his father had made for him. He presumably left Mr. Chapman's sometime in 1753 and was living at the Middle Temple by November of that year. However, Cowper's knowledge of the law was acquired at Mr. Chapman's and certainly not at the Temples. The Inns of Court, which included the two Temples, only provided the requisite paper qualifications to practice law. To become a lawyer in the eighteenth century was often a matter of patience and luck. The aspiring barrister or solicitor cultivated connections at the Inns of Court, England's "University in a state of decay."[40] Such a young man might discuss law with his fellows, but the law was usually one topic among many. Sir William Holdsworth has put the matter well: "Legal education in the eighteenth century is a very melancholy topic. . . . The law student was obliged to get his knowledge of law by means of undirected reading and discussion, and by attendance in chambers, in a law office, or in courts."[41] At the Inns, there were many ceremonies which were leftovers from the past, but these events had become devoid of educational intent. Meaningless ritual had replaced legal training. The lack of a strict regimen at the Temples allowed Cowper to do what came naturally: drift. Addison's 1712 portrait of a Templar anticipates the "Inclinations" of Cowper the Templar:

> The Gentleman next in Esteem and Authority among us, is another Batchelour, who is a Member of the *Inner-Temple:* a Man of great Probity, Wit, and Understanding; but he has

chosen his Place of Residence rather to obey the Direction of an old humoursome Father than in Pursuit of his own Inclinations. He was plac'd there to study the Laws of the Land, and is the most learned of any of the House in those of the Stage . . . He is studying the Passions themselves, when he should be inquiring into the Debates among Men which arise from them. He knows the Argument of each of the Orations of *Demosthenes* and *Tully,* but not one Case in the Reports of our own Courts.[42]

Obviously, Cowper was one of many young men in the eighteenth century who, as Pope jested, studied "Shakespeare at the Inns of Court."[43]

Since he had been admitted to the Middle Temple in 1748, Cowper soon fulfilled the six years of membership which were required for a call to the degree of the Utter Bar. His proposal for acceptance was approved, and he was called in June. On June 11, 1754, he purchased chambers. In his spiritual autobiography, *Adelphi,* Cowper self-deprecatingly claimed that he had become "in a manner complete master"[44] of himself when he bought these rooms. From 1748 to 1753, he did not keep any of the published terms of the Middle Temple year, and he did not attend any of the formal ceremonies which were supposedly obligatory for members. He paid a fine at the time of his call to the Bar (£4. 10d. and another £14 for failing to appear at the six Vacation Exercises and the Candle Exercise[45]) to expiate his sins of omission. Like many others, he did not mend his ways—he did not have to. It was, moreover, a delightful home: "Looking into Pump-court in which there are Lime-trees, they are not unpleasant, and I can beside assure you on experience, that the sound of water continually pouring itself into pails and pitchers under the window, is a circumstance rather agreeable. In the country indeed, where we have purling brooks and such pretty things, a waterfall of the kind may be held rather cheap; but in the heart of London it has its value."[46] He had three further years of dining in hall and performing exercises. On the very day that these requirements were met, he resigned from the Middle Temple and transferred to the Inner Temple. On June 17, 1757, he purchased from William Henry Ashurst for £250 a chamber which was up one set of stairs, on the left, on the second staircase in Inner Temple Lane.[47] The Inner Temple was more fashionable than the Middle Temple. Its members were wealthier and presumably more sophisticated than those of the other Temple. These were Cowper's ideals in 1757, despite the fact that his grandfather and his uncle Ashley had belonged to the Middle Temple. Cowper was not rich, but he aspired at this time to the company of those who were. Years later, he looked back at what he considered wasted years, when he had had a chance to acquire a character of more importance in society. "But three years misspent in an attorney's office were almost of course followed by several more equally misspent in the Temple, and the consequence has been, as the Italian epitaph says, 'Sto qui.' "[48]

In later life, Cowper proclaimed his ignorance of the law, but many of his letters to Joe Hill are peppered with references and expressions which amply demonstrate that he had once been at least a semiserious student of it, and the light-hearted poem, *Nose Plaintiff, Eyes Defendant,* reveals an intimate knowledge of legal terminology. He formed a law library (later purchased by his cousin Spencer Cowper), and he acquired and worked through his cousin Martin Madan's case books.[49] There is at least some truth in Cowper's assertion from 1758: " 'Tis true enough that I am not fond of the law, but I am very fond of the Money that it produces, and have too great a Value for my own Interest to be Remiss in my Application to it."[50]

4   If the pleasures of London—and not the law—entranced the young Cowper, the delights of literature also fascinated him. Despite the later life of retreat, Cowper is a cosmopolitan writer, one whose turn of phrase shows an extensive knowledge of the finest writing produced in England during the eighteenth century. The Nonsense Club was his apprenticeship in the arduous task of learning to write in an off-hand, casual way. In his early as well as mature prose, there is conviviality and ease. Simple elegance is the hallmark of all his writing, and it was during his London years that Cowper learned the graceful use—and manipulation—of language.

Letter from an Owl to a Bird of Paradise (about 1760) is from the "first minister" of the Club to his cohorts, and that leader is not particularly concerned to hear that his role has been challenged: "Let them censure; what care I?" Although ostensibly defending his term in office, "Madge," the barn owl, is more interested in providing an account of a recent bout of diarrhea: "I have lately had a violent fit of the pip, which festered my rump to a prodigious degree. I have shed almost every feather in my tail, and must not hope for a new pair of breeches till next spring."[51] The outlandish spirits of this presidential address are matched in *A Dissertation on the Modern Ode* (*St. James's Magazine,* April 1763), which is a spirited attack in the manner of Lloyd and Colman on the ode-making excesses of the time. Such a poem can come forth "with equal propriety on the death of a king or a tom-tit, on a great minister, or a common whore, on the ruin of a nation, on the fall of a tobacco-box . . . Every object, in and out of nature, is matter enough for a modern to work upon, without fretting his imagination, or hazarding his judgment."[52] Cowper then goes on to give some recipes for this type of poetical enterprise. "Take MILTON, read his shorter poems, and particularly LYCIDAS, COMUS and SAMPSON; wherever you meet with an epithet, more especially, if it be a compound one, put it in your note-book; for as MILTON copied the antients, the more you steal from MILTON, of consequence the nearer you come to the antients."[53] If one wishes to conjure up emotion through sound, "W. C." advises reliance on Greek for "the soft manners of the female sex" ("ὲ ὲ ὲ ὲ ὲ ὲ ὲ ὲ ὲ ὲ ὲ ὲ ἐ") or "the hardy roughness of the male" ("Ωto toto toto toto toto toto toto to").[54]

The amusing facetiousness of these two epistles is also found in the more substantial, but earlier, *Connoisseur* essays (March–September 1756). In these papers, Cowper deals with a wide variety of subjects: mollycoddled Billy Suckling in no. 111, women-fleeing Christopher Ironside in no. 115, the not-keeping of secrets in no. 119, church manners and services in no. 134, styles of conversation in no. 138. In each of these essays, Cowper's captivating and gently ironical voice may be discerned.

Many of his observations in these essays simply echo sentiments expressed by other periodical writers early in the century. At times, it is impossible to hear a distinct literary personality.

> Critics in general are venomous serpents, that delight in hissing; and some of them, who have got by heart a few technical terms without knowing their meaning, are no other than Magpies. I myself, who have crowed to the whole town for near three years past, may perhaps put my readers in mind of a Dunghill Cock: but as I must acquaint them, that they will hear the last of me on this day fortnight, I hope they will then consider me as a Swan, who is supposed to sing sweetly at his dying moments.[55]

This passage in no. 138, if it lacks individuality, is at the very least a well-poised valediction to the readers of the *Connoisseur*. In no. 134, the speaker positions himself precisely between irony and justified anger when discussing the wretched state in which many country churches have been left to languish:

> The ruinous condition of some of these churches gave me great offence; and I could not help wishing, that the honest vicar, instead of indulging his genius for improvements, by inclosing his gooseberry bushes with a *Chinese* rail, and converting half an acre of his glebe-land into a bowling-green, would have applied part of his income to the more laudable purpose of sheltering his parishioners from the weather during their attendance on divine service.[56]

It is in finely tuned writing such as this that an anticipation of the mature writer can be seen. Cowper makes a serious point, but he couches the observation in mildly humorous language. The anonymous man-about-town who attacks Billy Suckling in no. 111 has a foil in Christopher Ironside, the writer of no. 115, who is weary of being chased by women:

> I am naturally a quiet inoffensive animal, and not easily ruffled, yet I shall never submit to these indignities with patience, 'till I am satisfied I deserve them. Even the old maids of my acquaintance, who one would think might have a fellow-feeling for a brother in distress, conspire with their nieces to harass and torment me. And it is not many nights since Miss *Diana Grizzle* utterly spoiled the only superfine suit I have in the world, by pinning the skirts of it together with a red-hot poker. I own my resentment of this injury was so strong, that I determined to punish it by kissing the offender, which in cool blood I should never have attempted. The satisfaction however which I obtained by this imprudent revenge, was much like what a man of honour feels on finding himself run through the body by the scoundrel who had offended him. My upper lip was transfixed with a large corkin pin, which in the scruffle she had conveyed into her mouth, and I doubt not that I shall carry the *memorem labris natam* from an old maid to the grave with me.[57]

Cowper is, of course, poking fun at Christopher, who views himself as a sufferer from the advances of women. In his depictions of both Billy and Christopher, he attacks male sensibilities which, for differing reasons, retreat from female company. There may be autobiographical hints in both these portraits; they certainly show that

Cowper was intimately aware of the fashionable—and unfashionable—in literary styles.

Indeed, in his early prose writings, Cowper displayed an obvious affinity with Addison and Steele. He looked at Gray and Mason with mild contempt for their attempts at a Miltonic manner. He himself had read deeply in Milton, whose poetry he had first encountered at the age of fourteen, and he saw *Lycidas* as the finest pastoral in English. Cowper especially admired the "Liveliness of the Description, the Sweetness of the Numbers, the Classical Spirit of Antiquity that prevails in it."[58] In *The Task* and in his translations of Homer, he would attempt to rekindle the magic of Milton's blank verse: "Was there ever any thing so delightfull as the Music of the Paradise Lost? It is like that of a fine Organ; has the fullest & the deepest Tones of Majesty, with all the Softness & Elegance of the Dorian Flute."[59]

Matthew Prior was another poet Cowper valued for his experiments in language: ". . . with admirable success, [he] has embellished all his poems with the most charming ease."[60] However, Cowper's early verse betrays a good ear but no striking interest in metrical innovation. He was to be concerned with that issue later. It was then that he was able to draw upon his early reading. Cowley and Butler among the established poets and Churchill, Colman, and Lloyd from his own generation were other writers from whom he took inspiration. As a young man, he even admired Pope, and he told John Johnson that "he once passed Pope's Lodgings, when a boy, and looked for him but he was not to be seen—"[61] Later, Cowper would see his own poetry as a retreat back to a Miltonic wilderness in direct opposition to Pope, whose "oily smoothness" and avoidance of "a manly rough line"[62] then disgusted him.

5   A young man in search of amusement and literary fame cannot, unless he has an independent income, live by these alone. This was the painful lesson that Cowper learned when he realized that to stay in London he would have to find employment. Ironically, it was his pursuit of funds which led to expulsion from that paradise.

The only work which Cowper had undertaken in a consistent fashion in the 1750s and 1760s was as a Commissioner of Bankrupts, a position which brought him £60 a year. His father had been a patentee for making out such transactions, and Cowper may have begun such work shortly after John's death in 1756. It is doubtful whether he ever exercised any of the powers such an office bestows, and he became extremely upset when he was forced by his uncle, Ashley, to become involved in the preparations to qualify as Clerk of the Journals in the House of Lords.

Ashley, the patentee of this position and others by virtue of the office of Clerk of the Parliaments, held his appointments under a grant sealed in the first year of the reign of George I. His father had at that time purchased the office for £18,000 so that his sons William and Ashley could obtain comfortable livings from its considerable profits. Ashley never attended at the House of Lords, although he was responsible for the transactions of all its business. The minor clerks and the head clerk frequently bickered, and there was a great deal of agitation caused by the fear that positions could be lost by whim of the Cowper family. In April 1763, the Clerk of the Journals, Francis Macklay, died, and William de Grey, who was married to Cowper's cousin, Mary, resigned the offices of Reading Clerk and Clerk of the Committees. Ashley, probably in an attempt to provide his nephew with sufficient financial resources to marry the heartbroken Thea, offered the two most lucrative posts, those held by de Grey, to Cowper, and the Clerkship of the Journals to Mathew Robert Arnott, a family friend.

The offices that de Grey held were public; the clerks in those departments took minutes and read acts and papers before the peers. The Clerk of the Journals enjoyed a much more private occupation: he transcribed the minutes of the House into journals and made copies of these; he had also "always been considered as a private Clerk to the Clerk of the Parliaments."[63] Cowper, who had, at first, eagerly accepted his uncle's wishes, changed his mind and asked simply for the Clerkship of the Journals, which he "flattered" himself "would fall fairly and easily within the scope" of his abilities. "Like a man in fever, I thought a change of posture would relieve my pain, and, as the event will show, was equally disappointed. . . . But behold the storm was gathering."[64] Ashley agreed to this alteration in plan and notified the House of his intended appointments. The storm broke when William Macklay, who had been brought into the office of Clerk of the Journals by his father, objected vociferously to Ashley's arbitrary use of power. Cowper described Macklay as his "enemy" and "opponent"[65] but he may well have realized that he was the man in the right.

Cowper was summoned to the Bar of the House to defend his claim to the appointment, and, with even a rudimentary knowledge of law, he should have been able to master the technical details he would be asked. He was unable, however, to do this; in fact, the prospect of a public performance terrified him, becoming the focus of incredible anxiety. A different William Cowper from the young man who had previously led a pleasant, easeful life sprang into being. This new man was unutterably tormented, convinced of his essential wretchedness. Cowper's letters and other prose until 1763 are elegant but austere—it is difficult to see a vulnerable human being with whom to empathize. Cowper's early poetry, however, anticipates the person who will now tell, perhaps in too full and unguarded a fashion, of the miseries of his despairing heart. To outward appearances, Cowper did not appear to be suffering. His surface seemed unruffled. He was always a passionate man, but the passions ran deeply into his divided being.

In *Adelphi,* Cowper described the nightmarish world into which he was plunged. "My continual misery at length brought on a nervous fever. . . . A finger raised against me was now more than I could stand against. In this posture of mind I attended regularly at the office."[66] He could not concentrate: "The feelings of a man when he arrives at the place of execution are probably much like what I experienced every time I set my foot in the office."[67] As in 1753, he escaped in August to "cheerful company, a new scene" at Margate, where he encountered Ashley and Theadora. Ashley, who may well have offered the Clerkships to Cowper in order to assist the separated lovers, now told him that he could marry Thea if he obtained the sinecure, but, as we have seen, the "Flaming sword" barred him from "Paradise." The traumas of thwarted love were added to his already "continual misery."

But the "continual misery" is difficult to decipher. In 1753, there had been a break with Thea; ten years later, she could have been restored to him. He then irrevocably rejected her. The earlier crisis had likely centered on commitment, on changing from carefree bachelor to dedicated husband. The events of 1763 involved a similar psychic process. His lightsome existence would have been modified by the ogre of work, even if it was of the most desultory kind. Lingering on the edges of childhood, he did not want to move into the world of experience. His angelic mother belonged to the realm of innocence.

Cowper "recover[ed] his spirits" during the next two months, but upon his return to London in late October he was once more faced with his forthcoming audience at the House of Lords. "I looked forward to the approaching winter and regretted the flight of every moment that brought it nearer, like a man borne away by a rapid torrent into a stormy sea from which he sees no possibility of return-

ing, and where he knows he cannot subsist . . . But the stress if
the tempest was yet to come. . . ."⁶⁸ London, which had been for
so long a safe harbor, became his prison. Cowper hoped "madness"
would overtake him and prevent his appearance at the House. He
constantly thought of suicide and remembered the discussion of
that topic he had had with his father years before. He became convinced that others were talking about him and that notices in the
newspapers referred to himself. However, his overwhelming fantasy
was of self-murder. He took a coach to Temple Wharf.

> Now came the great temptation, the point to which Satan had
> all the while been drawing me. . . . My mind was as much
> shaken as my body, distracted betwixt the desire of death and
> the dread of it. Twenty times I had the phial at my mouth and
> as often received an irresistible check, and even at the time it
> seemed to me that an invisible hand swayed the bottle down-
> wards as often as I set it against my lips. I well remember that
> I took notice of this circumstance with some surprise, though
> it affected no change in my purpose. Panting for breath and in
> a terrible agony, I flung myself back into the corner of the
> coach. A few drops of the laudanum which had touched my
> lips, besides the fumes of it, began to have a stupefying effect
> upon me. Regretting the loss of so fair an opportunity, yet
> utterly unable to avail myself of it; determined not to live, and
> already half dead with anguish of spirit, I once more returned
> to the Temple.⁶⁹

Cowper began to consider other ways in which he could do away
with his body. However, he was a hapless, would-be suicide whose
intentions were continually being frustrated by a mysterious force.
He attempted to puncture himself through the heart, but the blade
of his knife broke away. Then, he tried to hang himself.

> I pushed away the chair with my foot and hung at my whole
> length. While I hung I heard a voice say distinctly three times,
> "'Tis over, 'tis over, 'tis over." Though I am sure of the fact,
> and was so at the time, yet it did not at all alarm me or affect
> my resolution. I hung to long that I lost all sense, all conscious-
> ness of existence. When I came to myself again I thought my-
> self in Hell. The sound of my own dreadful groans was all that
> I heard, and a feeling like that of flashes, just beginning to
> seize upon me, passed upon my whole body. In a few seconds
> I found myself fallen with my face to the floor.⁷⁰

A serving woman in the dining room heard the noise of Cowper's drop to the ground and entered his room. Embarrassed and finally devastated by the enormity of the despair welling up inside himself, he asked her to send for a friend. This friend summoned Ashley, who realized the Clerkship had to be abandoned. His audience at the House having been canceled, Cowper experienced an incredible sense of guilt at having attempted suicide. The floodgates of extreme depression had been opened and would never again be closed completely. Frequent black waves of self-revulsion would remain with him.

Cowper had previously seen his appearance at the Bar as the great obstacle. When that impediment was removed, the depression refused to vanish. Indeed, his sufferings intensified: "Life appeared now more eligible than death only because it was a barrier between me and everlasting burnings. My thoughts in the day became still more gloomy and the visions of the night more dreadful. One morning as I lay between sleeping and awake, I seemed to myself to be walking in Westminster Abbey, walking till prayers should begin; presently I thought I heard the minister's voice and hastened towards the Choir; just as I was upon the point of entering, the iron gate under the organ was flung in my face with a jar that made the Abbey ring."[71] Cowper would always have an awesome sense (even during the height of his Evangelicalism) of exclusion from God's love and mercy. He attributed this to his commission in 1763 of the unforgivable sin of despair.* This conviction terrified him, justifying to him the self-loathing he constantly experienced. He became restless and withdrawn.

"Desertion is the only evil that a Christian cannot bear,"[72] Cowper claimed. He felt alone, helplessly alone. Emptiness and listlessness enveloped him, making him afraid of some loss, the danger of

---

* Strictly speaking, the unforgivable sin in Christian doctrine is against the Holy Spirit and occurs when a person, who having attained belief, subsequently apostatizes. One of the central biblical references for this is Hebrews 6:4–6: "For it is impossible for those who were once enlightened, and have tasted of the heavenly gift, and were made partakers of the Holy Spirit, and have tasted the good word of God, and the powers of the world to come, if they should fall away, to renew them again to repentance." For Cowper, even in 1763, having attempted suicide in a state of despair was tantamount to rejection of the "heavenly gift" and the committal of the unforgivable sin. His conviction of having done exactly this was increased in 1773, well after his conversion of 1765, when he again attempted suicide. Cowper's knowledge of theological doctrine in this matter likely derives from Archbishop Tillotson's sermon, "Of the Unpardonable Sin against the Holy Ghost" (see *Letters* 1, 26 and n.).

which he was not fully aware.[73] He had lost that "instinct which compels every living thing to cling to life."[74] His "decent outside," Cowper asserted, concealed inner "rottenness of heart."[75] He was, he also believed, a criminal—however, he was not certain whether he had committed a crime or been unjustly condemned.

It was at this time that strong religious feelings first entered Cowper's existence. Before, he had looked askance at any of the manifestations of Pietism which had become fashionable. Pietism itself, which stressed the religion of the heart and felt experience, was alien to him. As well, he certainly was not interested in the dissenting tradition, which also placed a strong emphasis on the individual's careful sifting of the presence of God in the recesses of the self. Furthermore, he had shown no concern with the developments in the Anglican church which were attempts at assimilating the dissenting tradition. His Christianity had been one which was centered on "reason, common-sense, and attainable morality which are the hall-marks of the rational and respectable pragmatism of the Augustan Age."[76] He would have agreed with Samuel Richardson's tremendous ire against the Methodists' condemnation of John Tillotson, the Latitudinarian divine, with whose sermons Cowper was well acquainted.[77] The novelist asserted in 1742 that "a new Sect, lately sprung up, called *Methodists,* with great Pretences to *Meekness,* and intolerable *Conceit* and *Vanity,* at present seek publicly to depreciate the Memory and Works of that truly great Man."[78] In 1763, whatever religious views Cowper held were minimal, having "relapsed into a total forgetfulness of God with the usual disadvantage of being the more hardened for having been softened to no purpose."[79]

From 1763, Cowper was drawn more and more to a strong conviction of God's presence in human life. This young man who had previously scoffed at strong religious feelings became engulfed in deeply felt religious experience. However, Cowper's conversion to a doctrine which emphasizes the stirrings of the heart was a slow one, which reached its height only in 1765. Even then, he would be an Evangelical by default. Nevertheless, in 1763, Cowper's beliefs underwent a profound change, as he became convinced of God's providential love. His existence was transformed into one in which the consolations of religion made up for the desolations of life.

The agent of this remarkable transformation in Cowper's life was not his brother, although he was an ordained priest in the Church of England. This was because John's religious convictions at this time were probably close to William's. Rather, the apostle of change was Cowper's cousin, Martin Madan, a convert to Evangelicalism. Martin, a forceful, dedicated and extremely persuasive person, attempted to comfort his cousin with his newly found religious zeal. Educated at Westminster, Christ Church, Oxford, and the Inner Temple, Martin had been called to the Bar in 1748. Up to 1750, Martin's life had been very much like his cousin's until one fateful evening "being in a coffee-house, [he] was requested by [some friends] to go and hear [John Wesley], who they were told, was to preach in the neighbourhood; and then to return and exhibit his *manner* and *discourse* for their entertainment."

> He went with that intention, and just as he entered the place, Mr. Wesley named as his text *"Prepare to meet thy God"* with a solemnity of accent which struck him, and which inspired a seriousness that increased as the good man proceeded in exhorting his hearers to repentance. He returned to the coffee-room, and was asked by his acquaintance "if he had taken off the old Methodist?" To which he answered, *"No,* gentlemen, but he has taken me off." From that time he withdrew from their company altogether, and in future associated with persons of a different stamp.[80]

Wesley himself provided an account of Madan's conversion: "This Mr Madan, [Wesley] said, was a famous mimic, and came to hear him in order to take him off, but was himself taken off his Deism . . ."[81] Martin's mother in 1754 recorded her impression of the incredible transformation in her son's sensibility: "Never was so th[o]rough a Change, sure, ever wrought in a Human Heart. . . . Martin constantly reads Prayers morning and evening in his Family."[82] For the remainder of his turbulent life, Martin's religious vision buoyed him up; in this regard, he is unlike his cousin William Cowper, whose overwhelming sense of exclusion would ultimately topple his religious convictions. After his encounter with Wesley, Madan obtained his license to become an itinerant preacher; he was eventually ordained deacon and priest in the Church of England. He had been Chaplain at the Lock Hospital for a year when he was summoned by Cowper, who had previously scorned his cousin's fervor. He now saw Martin "as a burning and shining Light, and as one of those who having turned many to Righteousness, shall shine hereafter as the Stars for ever and ever." Martin insisted that his cousin proclaim a lively faith in Jesus, "not merely an acquiescence in the Gospel as a truth, but an actual laying hold upon and embracing it as a salvation wrought out for and offered to me personally and particularly." Cowper could not assent to such a creed, but his soul was pierced with a sense of "[his] bitter ingratitude to Christ" and "those tears which I had thought it so impossible for me to shed burst forth abundantly." Martin's soothing ministrations seemed to work: "The wounded spirit within me was less in pain but by no means healed."[83]

Then the waves of depression returned. "At every stroke my thoughts and expressions became more wild and incoherent. When they ceased, they left nothing but disorder and a confused imagination behind them; all that remained clear was the sense of sin and the expectation of punishment. These kept undisturbed possession all the way through my illness without interruption or abatement."[84] Cowper saw himself as a damaged archangel who had been punished for rebellious behavior. Lucifer's words in *Paradise Lost* ("Evil be thou my good")[85] haunted him. He was, he thought, a malignant being who had called down upon himself his own painful destruction. At other times, he imagined himself an unwary Job whom God allowed Satan to ply with endless tortures.

Cowper thought a "Spirit" guarded the tree of life from his touch.[86] He would attempt to recite the Creed but when he came to the "second period of it, which professes a belief in Christ, all traces of the form were struck out" of his memory.[87] Absolute despair burned in his heart "like . . . [a] real fire, and [he] concluded it an earnest of those eternal flames which should soon receive" him.[88] When John arrived from Cambridge to tend his older brother, he "was pierced to the heart at the sight"[89] of William's misery. "I laid myself down in bed, howling with horror, while my knees smote against each other. In this condition my brother found me; the first word I spoke to him (and I remember the very expression) was, 'Oh brother, I am damned—damned. Think of eternity, and then think what it is to be damned.' "[90] John, deeply worried about his brother's constantly fluctuating sensibility, decided that William required the services of Dr. Nathaniel Cotton, who kept a madhouse at St. Albans. When Cowper left London for St. Albans in December 1763, it was almost a final parting. Only for a few fleeting moments twenty-nine years later in 1792, en route back to Buckinghamshire from Sussex, would he again visit his beloved city. But Cowper did become the wonder of those he left behind.

On February 26, 1791, the impressionable James Boswell was at a dinner where one of the guests was a Mr. Sharpe. Cowper's name came up during conversation, and Boswell was jarred by Sharpe's frightful account:

. . . for with a great deal of genius and even pleasantry, he has at bottom a deep religious melancholy. . . . He has been woefully deranged—in a strait waistcoat—and now is sometimes so ill that they take away his shoebuckles, that he may have nothing within his reach with which he can hurt himself. It seems he apprehends himself to be in a state of *reprobation*, being impressed with the most dismal doctrines of Calvinism. I was quite shocked to hear of such a state of mind. My own was good by comparison.[91]

Johnson's biographer felt relieved by Sharpe's gossip. It was a particularly black melancholia that could compete with Boswell's.

4
The Life of Retreat (1764–1767), Mary Unwin, and John Newton

1   In *Adelphi,* Cowper depicted himself as a godless young man, one who was ignorant of and even hostile to divine love. In that spiritual autobiography—in accordance with the conventions of the genre—he portrayed himself as a person who had with great perverseness ignored a multitude of warnings and strange happenings ("prefiguring types"[1] he called them) in which God had amply shown providential love. Although a member of the Church of England, he was undoubtedly not a deeply religious person during the 1750s and early 1760s. During the dark hours he experienced in 1763, however, this amiable man saw himself as Satan and the prey of Satan—in any event, an outcast of God.

Before he arrived at the Collegium Insanorum on December 7, 1763, Cowper had known Nathaniel Cotton slightly.[2] Cotton, who had been trained under Boerhaave at Leyden, had acquired a considerable reputation at Dunstable, Bedfordshire, and St. Albans for his serene and pious manner: his "company was much courted and highly relished by all his acquaintance, being most amiable and engaging . . . and bearing the character of a skilful and experienced Physician."[3] A devout man, Cotton had been a friend of Phillip Doddridge, whose *Practical Discourses on Regeneration* and *Rise and Progress of Religion in the Soul* Cowper came to admire, and also of Edward Young, whose *Night Thoughts* served as one of Cowper's models for writing confessional verse. Cotton's tenderness extended to his patients. He never took in more than ten at a time, and the usual number was three or four.

Cowper became violent when he first arrived at Cotton's: "I . . . made such resistance that three or four persons were employed to compel me, and as many to take me out again [of the coach], when I arrived at the place of my destination." During his first five months at the Collegium, he continued in a highly delusional state, with attempts at suicide.

> The chief difficulty now lay in finding opportunity for the purpose. I was narrowly watched, and the more narrowly as my design became continually more and more apparent. At length, however, I flattered myself that I had carried my point. As I sat by the fireside, I saw something glister in the cinders, and picking it up unobserved by the servant, I found it to be a large stocking-needle. The better to conceal it, I thrust it into the paper hangings by the bedside where the curtains covered it and where I could easily reach it in the night. I went to bed and slept some hours. Waking, I recollected my purpose, felt for the needle and found it. With my finger, as I lay on my left side, I explored the pulse of my heart, thrust in the needle, nearly to the head. Failing in the first attempt, I repeated it, and did so ten or a dozen times, till at length having broke the point of it in a rib, I was obliged to give over.

While in this "state of insanity," two "remarkable occurrences" happened, "the one in the beginning, the other towards the latter end of [his] malady." Cowper was later inclined not to relate these events, but he realized that it was his "duty to conceal none of God's dealings . . . however uncommon they may have been, and with whatever suspicious colours they may appear to others." In the first, he saw himself "suddenly enclosed in a temple as large as a cathedral."

> One of [the] cupolas was vertically over my head and formed the most radiant appearance. The whole edifice was built with beams of the purest light, mild and soft indeed, but bright as those of an unclouded sun. . . . At first I was willing to draw some favourable inferences to myself from so extraordinary an exhibition. But Satan quickly persuaded me that it had been made with no other view than to increase my regret for the loss of that glory which I had just seen a glimpse of, but which was now irrecoverably lost and gone.

According to Cowper, the second event was "still more remarkable." During a violent storm, he was struck by the "uncommon blackness" of a cloud:

> there appeared suddenly in the midst of it the form of a fiery hand clenching a bolt or arrow of lightning. I kept my eye

steadily fixed upon it, having been so long acquainted with despair that I was afraid of nothing, and watched it with a most undisturbed attention. Instantly the hand was lifted up towards the meridian and let fall again towards the earth till it seemed to reach the top of the opposite wood—as if in the very act of transfixing an enemy.

These were the two most startling incidents to overtake Cowper's "confused imagination." These "uncommon" and "suspicious" events were hallucinatory, and they show how disordered his mind had become. Neurosis had given way to psychosis.

Indeed, Cowper became "so familiar with despair as to have contracted a kind of hardiness and indifference" to it. By May 1764, he was amenable to conversation. Cotton captured his attention with amusing stories. "By this means I became capable of entering with some small degree of cheerfulness into conversation with the doctor. . . . He observed this seeming alteration with pleasure. Believing as he well might that my smiles were sincere, he thought my recovery well nigh completed, though they were in reality like the green surface of a morass—pleasant indeed to the eye but a cover for nothing but rottenness and filth." Gradually, he became more responsive to Cotton's support and generosity. On July 25, when his brother visited him, he was at first reserved. Later that day, he was deeply touched when John assured him that his despair was merely a delusion. The depression then started to fall away, but only bit by bit. Cowper suffered further periods of intense anxiety, which penetrated him completely.

One day, however, he opened the Bible at the verse in Romans concerning "propitiation through faith in [Christ's] blood."

> Immediately I received strength to believe it. Immediately the full beams of the sun of righteousness shone upon me. I saw the sufficiency of the atonement He had made, my pardon sealed in His blood, and all the fulness and completeness of my justification. In a moment I believed and received the Gospel. . . . My eyes filled with tears and my voice was choked with transport.

Shortly before, Cowper had a vision of ineffable tenderness. He had a dream in which "the sweetest boy I ever saw" came dancing up to his bedside. "He seemed just out of leading strings, yet I took particular notice of the firmness and steadiness of his tread." This apparition, a vivid evocation of happy innocence, filled Cowper with deep pleasure and served "to harmonize" his troubled spirit.[4] Here, he caught a glimpse of the strong, self-reliant child he might have become had his mother lived. The world of dreams always held him in thrall, and he was deeply sensitive to the clues they could provide to his inner world: "They have either tinged my mind with melancholy or filled it with terrour, and the effect has been unavoidable. If we swallow arsenic, we must be poison'd, and he who dreams as I have done, must be troubled."[5] Cowper would experience nightmares of incredible horror as an older man, but as his melancholia began to wane in 1764 he awoke this particular morning to a gratifying "sense of delight."[6] The cloud of horror had passed away.

As the depression lifted, Cowper became aware of a God who cherished him and desired his redemption. He also became convinced of the truths of Evangelicalism. Cowper's interest in such devotion was nurtured by Cotton, although the doctor himself was not markedly Evangelical. Cowper's gradual conversion would reach a heightened pitch and then subside. He was Evangelical in his espousal of the truths of the inner heart and in his insistence on experiencing and describing the emotional effects of God's goodness. For a decade, this devotion became a bulwark against the depressions he had experienced in London.

Cowper now became obsessed with his past obliviousness to providential warnings. He recalled two early incidents when God had delivered him from death: once when his gun cocked itself as he was forcing his way through a hedge, and once when a piece of brick falling from a high building narrowly missed him.[7] Cowper saw himself as having disregarded the significance of these events. As he recovered his equilibrium, he realized the extent to which he had been negligent of divine love. Previously, he felt, he had endured experience but missed its meaning.

This new religion of the heart, in which a powerful and majestic God allowed him to feel the full ardor of divine love, brought great comfort. Cowper, deprived of his mother in childhood and divested now of worldly expectations, longed for the warm embrace of an all-caring and all-protecting God. "It is impossible to say," he claimed, "with how delightful a sense of His protection and fatherly care of me it pleased the Almighty to favour me."[8] Cowper never completely abandoned this vision of God's startling intervention in his life, but he later came to believe that the God who could transform all men had decided irrevocably against himself. His mother had been torn away from him, and, later, the God who had seemed to restore the lost tenderness of which he had been dispossessed would become a malevolent trickster, intimating that He might—or, more likely, might not—redeem him.

In 1764, Cowper's faith removed him from the society in which he had once existed. He no longer had to be concerned with establishing himself in a profession. In fact, Evangelicalism—with its fervent denial of the temporal—was attractive to him because at a stroke it removed him from a world in which one had to strive for success (in his withdrawal he had originally sought "tranquil death"[9]). Cowper simply had to allow the calm indwelling of providental love to fill him. He thought he had found the ideal synthesis between natural and spiritual man. For ten years, this creed provided him with a great deal of comfort.

However, Cowper's "despair" and newfound religion alienated him from family and friends. His military cousin, Spencer Cowper, "the mover of [a] storm"[10] against him, disowned him. Ashley resisted such impulses, but Cowper would have been aware of his uncle's views on suicide: "What must we think of *Those* who not only break thro' all Laws of *Moral Obligation,* but even dare to act in defiance of a *Divine Command?* To imbrue our *Hands* in our *Blood,* is in *us* the most daring *Impiety*—a *Sin,* of all others the most *dreadful,* as 'tis the only one that cannot be *repented of* . . . In a Word—He that meanly quits his *Station,* or quarrels with his *Command,* in time of *Danger* and *Distress,* by putting an End to his *Being,* is no better than a rank *Coward*—a *Traitor* to Himself—and a *Rebel* against his *Maker.*"[11] Ashley's own "low Spirits"[12] may have led him to contemplate the ultimate rebellious act. In 1763, however, Cowper felt a deep sense of guilt in having attempted suicide, and his uncle's contemptuous abuse of those who "break thro' all Laws of *Moral Obligation*" weighed heavily upon this sensitive young man. In turn, Cowper saw his London compatriots in the Nonsense Club as "professed infidels" and the life he had led in London as one of "fancied happiness" and "empty dreams." His former friends were "wand'rers, gone astray / Each in his own delusions."[13]

Cotton was at first concerned "lest the sudden transition from despair to joy should terminate in a fatal frenzy,"[14] but in a short time he became convinced that Cowper had recovered. Nevertheless, Cowper remained with him for another full year. In June 1765, so that he and William could conveniently visit each other, John Cowper obtained rooms for his brother at Huntingdon, sixteen miles from Cambridge. On June 17, after having been "partly in bondage and partly in the liberty wherewith Christ had made me free,"[15] Cowper left St. Albans.

2   *Adelphi* tells of Cowper's misspent youth. It is a narrative which graphically portrays the demonic world into which its protagonist was thrown in 1763. Although a stark tale, it only intermittently hints at the chilling horrors to come. There were five intense depressive episodes in Cowper's life, those of 1753, 1763, 1773, 1787, and 1794. Apart from those of 1763 and 1794, information on these collapses is scanty. If his conduct during all of these was similar, the breakdowns included delusions of hearing voices, acute paranoia, and a total sense of worthlessness; suicide attempts (except in 1753 and 1794) then followed. Cowper, especially from 1774, saw his existence predetermined by the sin of despair of which suicide is the symbolic act, and despair he felt was the unforgivable offence[16]: "Can any sin committed in so terrible and tempestuous a moment deserve what I must suffer? For that first sin involved in it all that follow'd as absolutely unavoidable."[17]

The first threads in the web were the difficulties Cowper encountered in his courtship of Theadora. The second occurrence, as we have just seen, was in 1763, when Cowper was scheduled to appear before the House of Lords and his right to become Clerk of the Journals was under dispute. In 1773, he was engaged to marry Mrs. Unwin, and he lapsed into depression when his relationship with her was about to be converted from that of adopted son to husband. William Unwin's death in November 1786 and the departure of Lady Hesketh from Olney in December 1786 seem to have been the causes of the breakdown which lasted for the first six months of 1787, and Mary Unwin's failing health—the approaching death of his substitute mother—in 1794 prompted the final episode. The common strand in all these incidents was Cowper's inability to cope with loss or change. In 1753, he was fearful of losing Theadora; in 1763, his claim to a sinecure was disputed; in 1773, he faced the possibility of being deprived of Mary Unwin as a mother and having to take up the role of husband; in 1786, he lost William Unwin and Harriot Hesketh; in 1794, he was afraid Mary Unwin was about to die. Cowper's five major depressions were, in various degrees, psychic reenactments of his great loss of 1737, although Cowper often saw these breakdowns as divine chastisement.

Indeed, God's extreme and incomprehensible animosity toward him became a part of Cowper's everyday life from 1763. In 1792, he confessed to Hayley: "I cannot indeed say that I have ever been actually deprived of understanding, but near thirty years ago I had a disorder of mind that unfitted me for all society."[18] However, religious despair and the fear of having committed the "unforgivable sin" were manifestations—not the causes—of his "disorder of mind." Cowper's mother had abandoned him; although he did not realize it, he relived that loss when he imagined that God hated him and would cast him aside. He perceived himself as having become, unawares, worthy of God's hatred. Against every inclination in his being, he was Cain—the malicious outsider who had brought perdition down upon himself. Unable "to accept melancholia as a psychic state with only internal meaning, [Cowper explained] his emotional state as evidence of his relation to God."[19]

3   When he left St. Albans, Cowper was accompanied by a servant, Sam Roberts, who had watched over him there, and by a boy, Dick Coleman, whom he rescued from what he felt would have been a life of degeneracy.* Cowper would later lament his involvement with the good-for-nothing Coleman, but Sam Roberts gave years of devoted service and was with Cowper until 1795.

Huntingdon was a singularly beautiful spot. William Cobbett described it as "one of those pretty, clean, unstenched, unconfined places that tend to lengthen life and make it happy."[20] It was a

---

* Coleman was seven or eight years old in 1765. On November 12, 1766 (*Letters* 1, 155–56), Cowper provided Joseph Hill with this description of his little charge: "He is the Son of a drunken Cobler at St. Albans, who would have poisoned him with Gin, if Providence had not thrown it in my way to rescue him. I was glad of an Opportunity to shew some Mercy in a place where I had received so much, and hope God will give a Blessing to my Endeavours to preserve him. He is a fine Boy, of a good Temper and Understanding, and if the Notice that is taken of him by the Neighbours . . . don't spoil him, he will probably turn out well." In the same letter, Cowper discounted his generosity by saying that he intended in a year or two to deal with him as he did his servant. Then, he would be "old enough to do all the Business for which I shall want him, and of a right Age to be taught the Trade and Mystery of a Breeches' Maker. This though not so cheap a way as keeping no Servant, will yet be a considerable Saving to me. . . ." Cowper here provides a reasonable explanation of his motivations in taking Coleman under his wing. However, Cowper likely had a strong sense of identification with as well as empathy for this young waif. From 1763 to 1765 he had relived the acute sense of loss he had experienced as a boy of six. Having gotten back in touch with this aspect of his past, he attempted in a truly selfless, but perhaps unconscious, way to show kindness to a deprived, vulnerable child.

pleasant retreat, which had a card assembly, dance assembly, race-course, and bowling green, but Cowper had nothing to do with these. He lived alone, and he was careful in the cultivation of friends. Huntingdon was for him an expensive place, and at this time he became—as he would for much of the remainder of his life—financially dependent upon Joseph Hill.* Dependency was the least attractive of Cowper's traits, particularly when it concerned debts or gifts which he knew he simply could not repay. Having suffered acute deprivation as a child, he acted childishly in such matters. He thought he had an inalienable right to the largess of others. Cowper always lived as a gentleman, and he expected others to assist him in maintaining the style to which he had become accustomed. He was never overly concerned to deprive himself of unnecessary expenses, but he did pay back the material benefits given to him by others with generous thanks and steadfast devotion. At Huntingdon, he came to a crisis in his living arrangements when

---

* Cowper's financial position is difficult to decipher from the extant documents. The following financial history has been abstracted from the figures provided by Lady Hesketh in letters (British Library and Princeton) to various correspondents. The poet's estate at his death amounted to £976.10.2, after a debit of £600.2.9. was discharged. A portion of the estate was accrued from the remainder (£630.18.0) of the £1,000 payment by Joseph Johnson in 1792 for the translation of Homer—the only other remuneration Cowper received for his writings was the "profits" from the 1793 editions of his two volumes of original verse; there was also a substantial sum (£615.15.6) from the pension granted in 1794.

William and his brother were considering in 1763 an offer of £800 for their father's London house in Red Lion Square, but the proceeds of the actual sale are not known. When William's brother died in 1770, he left a balance of £700, and William probably received £200. He instructed Hill to sell stock for £100 (1766), £100 (1767), £400 (1772; £300 was due on John's behalf to Corpus Christi College, Cambridge), and £200 (1790). There was £100 in stocks in John's name when William died.

Until he sold his own stock in 1790, Cowper had presumably retained £300 in stocks from 1772. During the Olney years, his only other income would have been £20 per year for the rental of his Inner Temple chambers (which his tenant gave Hill a great deal of trouble in collecting) and an annual grant of £20 from the Earl Cowper (it cannot be deduced with any certainty when this gift was bestowed). From 1768 to 1786 (when he received additional yearly gifts totaling £100 from the Earl Cowper, William Cowper his cousin, Harriot Hesketh, and Theadora Cowper), his stocks would have generated comparatively little interest (3 or 5 percent), and Hill obviously subsidized (he was assisted by the Cowper family in this matter) the average yearly request of the poet for £100. At Cowper's death, Hill claimed £237 as the "Balance of his Account of Moneys advanced to Mr. Cowper."

Susanna Powley, Mrs. Unwin's daughter, claimed his mother "sunk 1800£ of her property in consequence of taking [Cowper] into her care."

he imprudently spent in three months what should have lasted a year.

As a partial solution to this difficulty, Cowper became a boarder on November 11, 1765, at the home of the Reverend Morley Unwin, who from 1746 to 1762 had been master of the Huntingdon school. Cowper, who met Morley's son, William, at a church service, moved to the Unwin residence to save money, but he discovered in the family "the most comfortable social folks" and was delighted with all four members of the family: Morley; his wife, Mary; and their children, Susanna and William. "The Old Gentleman carries me to Cambridge in his Chaise. He is a Man of Learning and good Sense, and as simple as Parson Adams. His Wife . . . is Young compared with her Husband . . . I find a House full of Peace and Cordiality in all its parts, and am sure to hear no Scandal." Although there is the appearance of serenity in this description of the Unwin family, Cowper was—immediately after meeting Mrs. Unwin—obsessed with "possibly find[ing] a place" in that household. "From the moment this thought struck me such a tumult of anxious thoughts seized me that for two or three days I could not divert my mind to any other subject. I blamed and condemned myself. . . . But still the language of my mutinous and disobedient heart was, give me this blessing or I die." Calm was restored only when he received "some degree of assurance of success" in this endeavor from God.[21]

However, Cowper's portrayal in his memoir of his initial encounters with Mary Unwin in the autumn of 1765 is exceedingly discreet. In fact, Cowper never depicts Mary Unwin in *Adelphi*—he simply assures the reader of the extraordinary bond that soon arose between them: "Let it suffice to say I found we had one Faith, one Lord, and had been baptized with one baptism of the Spirit."[22] Indeed, Cowper's autobiography concludes, abruptly, as soon as he is installed in the Unwin house: "I have lately received a blessing from His hand which shines as bright as most of the foregoing favours, having the evident stamp of His love upon it, and well deserving to be remembered by me with all gratitude and thanksgiving."[23] For the remainder of their long sojourn together (until Mary Unwin's death in 1796), Cowper perceived her friendship as the "blessing" of God, and it was thus natural that he concluded his account of God's intervention in his life by introducing the person who for many years would be the temporal embodiment of divine protection. Mary, a laconic but vigorous person, was the first of three strong-willed women who found Cowper an intriguing challenge.

In 1767, Cowper placed his mother and Mary Unwin at the beginning and end, respectively, of his autobiography. Although he does not vividly evoke either woman, the absence of commentary speaks eloquently of the central theme of the narrative: loss and reunion. Cowper's memoir ostensibly celebrates the renewal of God's love in Cowper's heart, but it is also the story of a man who loses his mother early in life and, after a great emotional crisis, discovers a substitute. In 1790, Cowper confessed to Mrs. King that Mary Unwin had "supplied to me the place of my own mother, my own invaluable mother, these six and twenty years. Some sons may be said to have had many fathers, but a plurality of mothers is not common." In the same letter, he said that the two poems he had written to Ann and Mary had given him "more pleasure in writing than any that I ever wrote."[24]

There can be no doubt that Mrs. Unwin possessed an extraordinary charm as far as Cowper was concerned. She, who was "more polite than a Dutchess,"[25] was a draper's daughter from Ely. At the age of eighteen in 1742, she married Morley and went to live in Grimston, Norfolk. In Arthur Devis's now-lost portrait of 1750, she is "sitting under a Tree upon a circular bench. She is habited in a White Satin Gown, blue quilted petticoat, with a hoop, hanging sleeves, holding a flat Hat in her right hand covered with light blue silk, her left pointing towards a Town in the distance with two churches—a Spire and a Tower. She is painted with a fresh coloured countenance, auburn hair, a mob cap tied under her Chin and wearing a stiff stomacher."[26] Mary "found the farmers' Wives and daughters so much beneath her own mental Standard, that to gratify her Mr. U. repaired to Huntingdon."[27] Mrs. Unwin's cultivation is emphasized in a letter from Elizabeth Pennington, the daughter of the Rector of All Saints', Huntingdon, to Samuel Richardson, the novelist, on April 4, 1756:

> . . . I yesterday drank tea with a lady whom I believe you have heard me mention in the number of my particular friends; her name is Unwin, a clergyman's wife who lives in the Town, a woman [of clear] Piety, extensive reading, fine taste and sound judgement, whose conversation is relish'd by scholars, liked by the witty and approved by the good; *You*, my dear Sir, was our theme, and when I have said she has a fine taste,

etc., I need not attempt to say how much she admired you; she
beg'd of me as a particular favor, that I would present her
compliments to you, that tho' unknown to you, she might have
the secret pleasure of having given that [   ] testimony of her
[   ] esteem for so great a Man.[28]

Richardson, quite rightly, was pleased by this tribute, and when
Miss Pennington wrote again, on December 2, 1756, she told Richardson that Mrs. Unwin longed to meet him "some future day & is
impatient for a call to town, that she may embrace the first opportunity of paying a visit she has so long been desirous of."[29] In
addition to her literary pursuits, Mrs. Unwin "retained much gaiety,
and fondness of Dress and Company. They visited all the principal
families of the town. . . . She was thought at that time a sensible
and accomplished though far from handsome Woman."[30] Up to the
age of forty-one, Mrs. Unwin was a person of some claim to taste
and polite company who had found Norfolk distasteful and had
insisted on leaving; she seems to have enjoyed Huntingdon well
enough, but her "extensive reading" and "fine taste" may have set
her apart from the other inhabitants of the town.

Cowper, immediately after meeting Mary, was overcome with
"anxious thoughts"; she underwent a similar change.

> Mrs. U. became a stranger every where but at home; and with
> her company dismissed her amusements. Prayers, as personified
> by Homer, had never paid a visit to the Old Clergyman's House,
> but now they made it their constant abode. . . . Mrs. U. be-
> came a Franche Religieuse, and the attachment natural between
> the Convert and the Converter, together with the Aversion dis-
> covered by Mr. U rendered the former two almost inseparable.
> They walked much, and avoided meeting, as well as visiting,
> any of their neighbours.[31]

The transformation of Mary Unwin is startlingly like that Cowper
had experienced two years before. They were persons who had once
lived very much in the world and, in both lives, an outside force
struck with such intensity that their destinies were irrevocably altered. Harriot Hesketh frequently (from 1792) referred to Mrs.
Unwin as the "Enchantress,"[32] but it was Cowper who entered
Mary Unwin's life and refashioned it.

This friendship flowered quickly. At Mary's insistence, Morley
allowed Cowper's rent to be halved when Ashley warned his nephew

that his allowance from the family might be withdrawn.[33] However, Morley, sixty-two at this time, did not approve of the strong religious alliance formed between Cowper and his wife. The devotions which the young stranger led "appeared to occupy the hearts of all the family except the Master, who as he could not shelter others from their enchantments determined to keep himself out of their way."[34] Despite this, Cowper's description of a day at Huntingdon suggests amiable tranquility:

> We Breakfast commonly between 8 and 9, 'till 11, we read either the Scripture, or the Sermons of some faithfull Preacher of those holy Mysteries: at 11 we attend divine Service which is performed here twice every day, and from 12 to 3 we separate and amuse ourselves as we please. During that Interval I either Read in my own Apartment, or Walk or Ride, or work in the Garden. We seldom sit an hour after Dinner, but if the Weather permits adjourn to the Garden, where with Mrs. Unwin and her Son I have generally the Pleasure of Religious Conversation 'till Tea time. . . . After Tea we sally forth to walk in good earnest. Mrs. Unwin is a good Walker, and we have generally travel'd about 4 Miles before we see Home again. When the Days are short we make this Excursion in the former part of the Day, between Church time and Dinner. At Night we read and Converse as before 'till Supper, and commonly finish the Evening either with Hymns or a Sermon, and last of all the Family are called in to Prayers.[35]

As we have seen, Morley Unwin obviously perceived malignity lurking beneath this calm, seemingly unruffled surface. His resentment may have been only a religious one. Nevertheless, the force of his antipathy was probably much deeper and more personal: "When Mr. C. came to board in the family, a sudden and obvious revolution took place, apparently as much against the inclination of the old Gentleman, as that of France against Lewis 16th's."[36] This "revolution" was probably sexual as well as religious. Cowper certainly saw Mrs. Unwin as a mother—apparently, he was not physically attracted to her. However, there might have been an erotic component in her affection for him. There was certainly talk in Huntingdon of "unguarded conduct" and "Improprietys"; Cowper mentioned to his aunt, Mrs. Madan, "the black and shocking Aspersions which our Neighbours here amuse themselves with casting upon our Names & Conduct."[37] This gossip apparently arose in response to the afternoon walks, but the townspeople might have sensed the intensity of Mrs. Unwin's devotion to the young aristocrat. If her interest in Cowper had sensual undertones, she transmuted such feelings into religious ardor. Despite this, Susanna claimed her mother "could never love more than one person at a time,"[38] and Morley obviously felt excluded by his wife's devotion to the "Converter." Father and daughter saw Cowper as an intruder who invaded their uneventful, sequestered lives.

Cowper, probably unaware of the ripples in the pond, continued to act in his habitually shy manner: "When any one visited them . . . [he] spoke little, often reclined in his Chair, with his eyes nearly closed; but if an Idea was started that excited his attention, he delivered a few sentences, which were certain to be received as an Oracular decision of any question that had been agitated."[39] He did speak freely and without reserve to Mary Unwin—although his speech was still filled at that time with the conventional phraseology of the Evangelicals. When she became extremely ill in 1767, he confessed to Mrs. Madan: "She is the chief Blessing I have met with in my Journey since the Lord was pleased to call me. . . . Her Illness has been a sharp Trial to me."[40] The relationship, then, was not only of mutual edification but also of real intimacy. As much as they understood the forces controlling their destinies, they shared those secrets with each other. For Cowper, Mary had "a very uncommon Understanding, [had] read much to excellent purpose."[41]

The friendship between Cowper and Mrs. Unwin was accidentally strengthened by the sudden death of Morley Unwin, who fell from his horse on June 29, 1767, as he was riding to his Cure: "he was flung to the Ground with such Violence, that his Scull was fractured in the most desperate manner."[42] Cowper was pleased that Morley's previous insensitivity to Evangelical doctrine disappeared as his life ended on July 2: "He was one of those many poor deluded Persons [who] denied the Divinity of our Lord and infinite Merit of his Sufferings."[43] Indeed, Morley's death deepened a resolve that Cowper and Mrs. Unwin had made to leave Huntingdon in order to further their Evangelical beliefs in "an Abode under the Sound of the Gospel."[44] Cowper had become angry at what he considered to be the dissolute ministry at Huntingdon: "It is a Matter of the utmost Indifference to us where we settle, provided it be within the Sound of the Glad Tidings of Salvation."[45] The persistence of gossip also made it essential that Cowper and Mrs. Unwin leave Huntingdon.

4   William Unwin's friend, Dr. Conyers, told John Newton, the Evangelical curate of Olney, of Mrs. Unwin's bereavement and of her desire to leave a community whose religious beliefs no longer matched her own. When Newton introduced himself to her and Cowper on July 6, 1767, he offered to find them a suitable place to live "within the Sound" of his ministry. On August 10, 1767, Cowper recounted that "on Monday last we went to see our friend Newton at Olney, and to take a View of the Place where we trust the Lord has fix'd the Bounds of our Habitation."[46] Only two weeks after he and Mrs. Unwin had settled into their own home in Olney in February 1768, Cowper complained dejectedly to Mrs. Madan that "We had no sooner taken Possession of our own House, than I found myself called to lead the Pray'rs; . . . A formidable Undertaking you may imagine to a Temper & Spirit like mine. I trembled at the apprehension of it, and was so dreadfully harass'd in the Conflict I sustain'd upon this occasion . . . that my Health was not a little affected by it."[47] This "Undertaking" must have been particularly dire for a young man whose London world had collapsed only five years before when he had been unable to appear in public. Newton's diary shows that Cowper was required to lead prayer meetings at the "Great House," an unoccupied mansion on the outskirts of Olney that Newton had procured for religious meetings.

If Mary Unwin was for Cowper the serene mother, John Newton was a harsh, domineering father. He was a small, slight man with a huge nose. The contrasts in his nature were also extreme. In adolescence, he had been a blaspheming atheist; in early manhood, he was a renegade gone native on the west coast of Africa; in middle age—when Cowper met him—he had become a vigorous Calvinist. This man of action, who threw himself earnestly, sometimes violently, into a multiplicity of projects during the course of his long life, had been born in London on July 24, 1725, the son of a commander in the Mediterranean merchant navy. He attended school in Essex and, after having been impressed on to HMS *Harwich* in 1743, he spent several years at sea. Eventually, he became involved in slave trading. Newton's journals record the horrors and cruelties of that profession, and he freely admitted in later writings the dissipation with liquor and slave girls in which he had partaken. These worldly ways, along with the sins of "Free-thinking" and "blasphemy," came to an end on March 10, 1748, when, during a violent storm which nearly capsized his ship, Newton was suddenly converted. Though he was tormented during subsequent days about

his past sins and profanities, he wrote in his diary that he knew
when, after four anxious weeks, his ship arrived safely at port, "that
there [was] a God who hears and answers prayers. I was no longer
an infidel."[48]

This conversion is vividly related in *Authentic Narrative* (1764),
together with Newton's unassailable conviction that his plight had
been "on the whole, unique in the annals of the church."[49] Unlike
Cowper, he saw himself as a survivor: "I was preserved from every
harm, and having seen many fall on my right hand and on my
left . . . the Lord was pleased to lead me in a secret way."[50] Previously, "whether I looked inward or outward, I could perceive nothing but darkness and misery. I think no case could be more dreadful
than mine."[51]

After his conversion, Newton returned to England where he married his beloved of many years, Mary Catlett. After taking ill on the
eve of another voyage, he decided in 1754 to retire from the sea and
to become a preacher "to show what the Lord could do."[52] He became an enthusiastic disciple of George Whitefield and applied for
orders; though unsuccessful at his first attempt, he was ordained
deacon on April 29, 1764, and priest on June 17. Thereafter, he was
a staunch defender of Evangelicalism.

Evangelicalism, which, as we have seen, became a dominant mode
of religious expression in eighteenth-century England, is a direct
descendant of the Pietist movement in continental Europe. The
particular manifestation of that creed which strongly influenced
the English theological tradition in the eighteenth century was the
Moravian, by way of John Wesley:

> Wesley, who visited the European headquarters of the Unitas
> Fratrum [the Moravians], was deeply impressed by the sincerity
> of their simple faith and the joy of their Christian life. Equally
> was he delighted by their communal type of Christian living
> and the care which they took of orphans and the very old. He
> could not but contrast the "top of the mind" religion of so
> many Englishmen with this "bottom of the heart" religion of
> the followers of Count Nicholas Von Zinzendorf. . . . Among
> [these people] he discovered the meaning of experimental reli-
> gion.[53]

Wesley was also moved by the extemporary preaching and prayers
of the dissenting tradition, but he held firm to his devotion to the
Church of England. Methodism, as practiced by Wesley, attempted
to appropriate Dissent and Pietism to the Anglican communion.

Anglican Evangelicalism, the tributary of Methodism to which
Newton as well as Cowper can be assigned,[54] goes back to November 1729 in Oxford when John Wesley and four friends formed the
"Holy Club," which met to discuss the New Testament. In this
year, William Law's *Serious Call to a Devout and Holy Life* appeared, and Wesley's group espoused Law's view that "either reason and religion prescribe rules and ends to all the ordinary actions
of life, or they do not; if they do, then it is necessary to govern all
our actions by these rules, as it is necessary to worship God."[55] To
Wesley, faith was "a firm assent to all the propositions contained in
the Old and New Testaments."[56] Wesley held this doctrine until
May 24, 1738, when he was attending a prayer meeting on Aldersgate Street in London. Suddenly, he felt himself overcome by an
overwhelming sense of God's providential love. This was the moment of conversion: "I felt my heart strongly warmed. I felt I did
trust in Christ, Christ alone, for salvation, and an assurance was
given me that He had taken away my sins, even mine, and saved
me from the law of sin and death."[57] Using the Sermon on the
Mount as a precedent, John Wesley and the other Methodists began
open-air preaching in April 1739. Lay preachers were appointed
and societies which met during the week for prayer, praise, and fel-
lowship sprang up in many places. Although all Methodists agreed
on stressing the Gospel of Salvation, they were from the outset divided on the Calvinist conception of Election, which states that
God elects some for salvation and damns the remainder.

From the beginning, the Methodists also encountered fierce clerical opposition. In *The Imposture of Methodism Displayed* (1740),
William Bowman called them "furious disciples of Anti-Christ,
reverend scavengers, filthy pests and plagues of mankind."[58] As
well, various splinters soon developed within Methodism: the Wesleyan, the Whitefieldian, and the loyal Anglican. Newton and Cowper are, of course, members of the latter group: ". . . while Wesley
had a profound regard for the traditions of the primitive Church
of the first five centuries, the Evangelicals turned for precedents to
the age of the Reformation and to the writings and examples of the
Puritans for the theological if not the liturgical attitudes of the latter. On the whole, however, the distinguishing mark of the Evangelical Anglicans was their stricter Churchmanship, as shown by
the fidelity to the Book of Common Prayer and their submission to
episcopal authority."[59] Ultimately, then, Newton was deeply suspicious of both Wesley's Arminianism and Whitefield's rigorous
Calvinism, as Cowper's remark to him of December 21, 1781, makes

clear: "Mr. Wesley has also been very troublesome . . . , and assented in perfect harmony of sentiment with his brother Fletcher, that Mr. Whitfield disseminated more false doctrine in the nation, than he should ever be able to eradicate. Methinks they do not see through a glass darkly but for want of a glass, they see not at all."[60]

Wealthy converts to Evangelicalism such as Cowper's classmate at Westminster, the Earl of Dartmouth, and the Russia merchant, John Thornton, bought livings, sent preachers of the new persuasion to these parishes, and provided further financial assistance. John Newton, who arrived at Olney in May 1767, saw pastoral work as far more important than the peripatetic vocation: "I wish well to irregulars and itinerants. I am content that they should labour that way who have not talents to support the character of a parochial minister."[61] Another preference Newton held was for vigorous preaching. William Grimshaw, the curate of Haworth, Yorkshire, who was called the "Black Bull," was frequently criticized for his coarse ranting in the pulpit, but Newton did not support this judgment; he admired Grimshaw's methods of intimidating a congregation.

Newton's own convictions are stridently presented in *Cardiphonia* (1781), a two-volume collection of letters written during the 1760s and 1770s. Among these is his insistence on the pride of learning: "Death will soon sweep away all that the philosophers, the virtuosi, the mathematicians, the antiquarians and other learned triflers are now weaving with so much self applauded address."[62] Like most Evangelicals, Newton held fast to the opinion that virtually every action in one's life should have as its end the glorification of God: "Alas, what are parts and talents, or any distinctions which give pre-eminence in life, unless they are sanctified by the grace of God, and directed to the accomplishment of his will and glory."[63] As well as emphasizing the futility of learning, Newton dubbed imagination a tool of Satan and stressed the hopeless depravity of man: "Surely man in his best state is altogether vanity."[64]

In the second volume, Newton warned a young churchman to use more propriety; to an evidently intelligent correspondent he gave the warning: "Be careful to avoid losing your thoughts, whether in books or otherwise, upon any subjects which are not of a direct subserviency to your grand design."[65] One of Newton's harshest scoldings was given to a woman who had been seen at a theater: "if there is any practice in this land sinful, attendance on the playhouse is properly and eminently so. The theatres are fountains and means of vice . . . and I can hardly think there is a Christian upon earth who would dare to be seen there."[66] This correspondent evidently ceased writing after receiving this letter, and Newton was bewildered by her silence.

The review of *Cardiphonia* in the *Monthly Review* of September 1781 was harsh but prescient: "We are disgusted with vanity in any form; but when it assumes the dress of religion, we are more than disgusted:—we are really shocked. . . . We are not at all surprized to hear men of such principles, as this Writer espouses, exclaim so bitterly against reason. They are conscious of an irreconcilable hatred between the common sense of mankind, and a faith that sets all reason and nature at defiance!"[67] Though he knew his certitudes frequently irritated others, Newton felt compelled to advance them. He lived in a world of black and white. He did not recognize gray, the color of Cowper's fraught existence.

In 1767, at the beginning of their curious friendship, Newton attempted to emulate Cowper; later, he tried to persuade Cowper to become as strong and as self-reliant as he was: "The first six [years] I passed in daily admiring and trying to imitate him; during the second six, I walked pensively with him in the valley of the shadow of death."[68] Newton remained intensely competitive, refusing to believe that Cowper's alienation from God could in any way rival his own past depravity.

Newton's passions were visible to all who knew him; Cowper's were locked up in his soul. Newton hit out against a world of vanities, whereas Cowper felt that sin had taken up residence within his own heart. During the years when Cowper's "Heart burned within . . . and melted in Tears of Gratitude and Love," he cherished the well-intentioned care and guidance Newton bestowed upon him. Nevertheless, the poet and the dogmatist were destined to part. Eventually, Cowper had to "stand against" Newton when he told him that even though his vision of spiritual reality was not consistent with Newton's, it was nevertheless true: "That a Calvinist in principle, should know himself to have been Elected, and yet believe that he is lost, is indeed a Riddle, and so obscure that it Sounds like a Solecism in terms, and may well bring the assertor of it under the suspicion of Insanity. But it is not so, and it will not be found so." Cowper's often vaunted Calvinism was a theological doctrine he used solely against himself. As R. D. Stock has wisely said, "it was not doubt of God's existence . . . that drove Cowper into the gulf"[69]—it was Cowper's conviction that God hated him. This punitive God was a creation of Cowper's haunted imagination, and Newton was never able to dislodge this belief. Since this vision of God seemed irrational and unscriptural to Newton, he thought it an idle chimera. Cowper desperately asserted that salvation was not as simple as Newton proclaimed. Newton's "secret way" was not his.

After Newton left Olney in 1780 to take up the Rectorship of St. Mary Woolnoth in London, Cowper said "[t]he Vicarage became a Melancholy Object."[70] Newton, however, had been at odds with his congregation. Even Mary Unwin had not been exempt from his wrath, as an undated fragment[71] (about 1774–75) to her "Dear Friend & honoured Pastor" reveals. In her letter, Mary promised to attend church services regularly in the future—she had lapsed because of his ministrations to Cowper.

Much later, in September 1786, Newton again passed censure on Mrs. Unwin. He had been told by some people from Olney that Cowper, Mrs. Unwin, and their guest, Lady Hesketh, had been acting in an unseemly, worldly way. Cowper, usually guarded in letters to Newton, dropped the mask of compliance:

> Your letter to Mrs. Unwin concerning our conduct and the offence taken at it in our neighbourhood, gave us both a great deal of concern, and She is still deeply affected by it. Of this you may assure yourself, that if our friends in London have been grieved, they have been misinformed; which is the more probable because the bearers of Intelligence hence to London are not always very scrupulous concerning the truth of their reports; And that if any of our serious neighbours have been astonish'd, they have been so without the smallest real occasion. Poor people are never well employed even when they judge one another, but when they undertake to scan the motives and estimate the behaviour of those whom Providence has exalted a little above them, they are utterly out of their province and their depth.[72]

This is the strongest reprimand that Cowper ever bestowed upon Newton. For him, this is sharp language, and he is insisting that Newton is out of his "province" and "depth." The break between Cowper and Newton evolved slowly, but his "Friend" became—in Cowper's last extant letter—"Sir."[73]

Even before he left for London, Newton sensed his estrangement from Cowper. He told Mary Unwin in April 1779 that he hoped his friendship with him would continue "as in times past." In the same letter, he wistfully delineated the contradictory impulses within himself: "Ah what a difference between what I really am, what I may perhaps sometimes appear, in the kind but partial judgment of my friends. The difference ought to humble me, I wish I could say it does."[74] Cowper was able to accept the discrepancies in Newton's character when he was completely withdrawn in the world of Olney, but as he began to look beyond rural Buckinghamshire, he found himself in fundamental—often severe—disagreement with him. He would then refuse to act a part and practice dissimulation. The ties that bound them became brittle and then decayed.

5
Olney (1767–1786)

1   COWPER AND MRS. UNWIN finally moved into
Orchard Side, their home at Olney, on February 15, 1768.[1] Earlier,
from September until October 23, 1767, they stayed with the Newtons while the Vicarage was being refurbished, and they were then
at the Vicarage while Orchard Side was readied for them.[2] Cowper
and Mrs. Unwin went to Olney at Newton's invitation, and John
and Mary were their only friends there. In addition to the Newtons, Cowper and Mrs. Unwin were the sole residents of the town
to keep servants. They obviously did not maintain a household of
the grandeur of nearby Gayhurst, the estate of the Wright family,
but they did not live like most citizens of Olney, many of whom
existed in direst poverty. It was a straitened existence. Cowper came
to know the gossip of the town, and his acts of charity to the impoverished were frequent and generous. Yet, he was, inevitably, isolated. He was "Sir Cowper" or the "Esquire," his dress, language,
and demeanor betraying his past.* Thus, Cowper's rank as gentleman as well as transplanted Londoner made him a remarkable outsider in rural Buckinghamshire, and to a large extent, his power to
evoke this pastoral landscape in his poems and letters was derived
from his "foreign" sensibility.

    Cowper's home in Olney was at the center of the village, not, as
he mentions in his verse epistle to Lady Austen, "Deep in the abyss
of Silver-End."[3] Olney is a pleasant if unremarkable place with a
long broad street widening into the three-cornered market where

---

* Cowper was particularly concerned about his appearance. In the morning, he
wore a cambric cap with a turned up border, bunched at the back, and fastened
with a ribbon. He breakfasted, read, and wrote in this manner. He would wear
a dark brown wig for walking, and he would exchange this for a powdered
peruque for dinner and the remainder of the day.

Orchard Side is situated. The Ouse coils around the town, and Cowper enjoyed walking on the outskirts of the meadows which bordered the river. Orchard Side, with imitation embattlements hiding the roof, was elegant if somewhat austere; Mrs. Unwin and Cowper occupied the western—supposedly less desirable—half of the house. From their front windows, they could easily see the Shiel Hall (used as the Town Hall), the small hexagonal Round House or town prison, and the three large elms which overshadowed the Round House. Three inns (The Swan, The Bull, and The Royal Oak) fronted the other two sides of the triangle, and two drapers, the carrier, and Wilson the barber were there also. Cowper's house may have been at the center of Olney, but at the back of his garden there was a greenhouse to which he could retreat. When "our severest Winter, commonly called the Spring"[4] was over, this "cabinet of perfumes"[5] was transformed into a "summer parlour," where "the sound of the wind in the trees, and the singing of birds, are much more agreeable to our Ears, than the incessant barking of dogs and screaming of children."[6] Cowper delighted in this secluded recess, but he was frequently seduced by the beauties of the garden itself. Between the summer house garden and the Vicarage garden was the orchard from which Cowper's house obtained its name; eventually, Cowper and Newton had a doorway made in the wall of the Vicarage garden, which allowed the two couples to visit each other without going through the town.

Nevertheless, it was not always possible to escape Olney. Cowper's alliance with Newton meant that the townspeople felt that they could call upon him as well as the curate for spiritual and temporal advice. Cowper even provided legal counsel. "They cannot be persuaded," he said ruefully, "that a head once covered by a legal periwig can be deficient in those natural endowments that it is supposed to cover."[7] He interceded, upon request, with prominent friends, such as the Earl of Dartmouth, who had power and influence. He fed the poor and clothed the naked through monies supplied by John Thornton and Robert Smith, the rich Nottingham banker. The destitute of Olney consisted for the most part of the lacemakers, who had a large but not very prosperous industry there, and it was to their aid that Cowper often applied himself. Mrs. Unwin was generous to the distressed as well, as Newton recorded in his diary for February 2, 1779: "A poor young Woman, who had nearly perished in the street last week, has been relieved & supported by Mrs. U—— for a few days, till an answer can be obtained from her friends."[8]

In *The Task,* Cowper delineated the joys and shortcomings of the country, but the ambivalent nature of his response is also found in the letters which relate the births, marriages, illnesses, and deaths that were a part of its existence: "few that court Retirement, are aware / Of half the toils they must encounter there."[9] In his own life, Cowper viewed the life of rural retreat as the best alternative available in a fallen world. But he was keenly aware of the rigors it presented. He told of the many deaths in childbirth, of the countless victims of smallpox epidemics, of having to abandon his house for a week when the corpse of a servant girl putrefied.

The frequent acts of small-mindedness and cruelty which were carried out at Olney in the name of religion deeply bothered him. In August 1780, Benjamin Page, the curate who replaced Newton, and Maurice Smith, his warden, had given orders for the pew in the Olney Church assigned to Warrington, a hamlet in the parish, to be altered without calling a vestry meeting, and the parish subsequently refused to pay Thomas Raban, the church carpenter. Raban, caught in the middle, used this incident to pour abuse on Page, whom he intensely disliked. Page retaliated by dispensing with Raban's services at a time when sixteen victims of smallpox were waiting to be buried in coffins which Raban should have made. Newton, from the confines of St. Mary Woolnoth, sided with the carpenter, and Cowper wrote a poem supporting "poor Tom Raban." Cowper also took a keen interest in the sexual mores of the town. He was not shocked when old Nat Gee "disgraced his grey hairs by very unseasonable alliance with a girl of ten years of age,"[10] but he was disturbed by, and was reluctant to talk about, William Pearce's homosexuality until the report which had been "in the way of whisper" for eighteen months became "noise and clamour": "Two boys, One called Butcher, and the other Beryl, are his accusers. They have repeatedly professed themselves ready to authenticate the charge under Oath, and one of them alledged it in presence of his wife and to his face. His reply was a clenched fist, and a thrust into the street."[11] From his bedroom window, Cowper was disappointed to observe Geary Ball, once a devoted Evangelical, center his life "in filling his glass and emptying it."

He is now languishing in a dropsy, and in the prime of life labouring under all the infirmities of age. He solaces himself, I am told, with the recollection of somewhat that passed in his experience many years ago, which although it has been followed by no better fruits than will grow at an Alehouse, he dignifies with the name of Conversion. Sows are so converted when they are washed, and give the same evidence of an unchanged nature by returning to the Mire. . . . So long as he was able to crawl into the street, his journey was to the Royal Oak and home again. And so punctual were we both, I in cleaning my teeth at my window and he in drinking his dram at the same time, that I seldom failed to observe him. But both his legs are now blistered, and refuse to assist him in poisoning himself any longer.[12]

Cowper's compassion gives way to severity in his account of Geary Ball; ultimately, his quick, vivacious fancy was more intrigued by the drollery of village life than by its tragedies.

Sensitive to idiosyncracy in behavior and speech, Cowper's letters are repositories of amusing, colorful anecdotes about Olney and its inhabitants. He was wryly amused at a public flogging in November 1783 when Francis Boswell, a young man accused of stealing from Griggs the butcher, displayed a remarkably stoic demeanor as the lashes hit his back.

The Beedle who perform'd it had filled his left hand with red Ocre, through which after every stroke he drew the lash of his whip, leaving the appearance of a wound upon the skin, but in reality not hurting him at all. This being perceived by Mr. Constable Henshcomb who followed the beedle, he applied his cane without any such management or precaution to the shoulders of the too merciful Executioner. The scene immediately became more interesting, the Beedle could by no means be prevailed upon to strike hard, which provoked the Constable to strike harder, and this double flogging continued, 'till a Lass of Silver End, pitying the pitiful Beedle thus suffering under the hands of the pitiless Constable, joined the procession, and placing herself immediately behind the latter, seized him by his capillary Club and pulling him backward by the same, slapt his face with a most Amazonian fury.[13]

Three years earlier in August 1780, Cowper had been alarmed when his favorite pet hare, Puss, gnawed through "the Strings of a Lattice Work" and escaped Orchard Side. He sent Richard Coleman to retrieve the wily hare, but Puss eluded capture.

She ran right through the Town, and down the Lane that leads to Dropshort. A little before she came to the House, [Richard] got the Start and turned her. She pushed for the Town again,

and soon after she Enter'd it, sought Shelter in Mr. Wagstaff's
Tan Yard, adjoining to old Mr. Drake's. Sturges's Harvest Men
were at Supper, and saw her from the opposite Side of the way.
There she encountered the Tan Pits full of Water, & while she
was struggling out of One Pit & Plunging into another, and almost drowned, one of the Men drew her out by the ears, and
secured her. She was then well washed in a Bucket, to get the
Lime out of her coat, and brought home in a Sack at 10 o'clock.
The Frolic cost us four Shillings, but you may suppose we did
not grudge a Farthing of it. The poor Creature received only a
little Hurt in one of her claws, and in one of her Ears, & is now
almost as well as ever.[14]

Four years later, Cowper's fear that Puss might make another bid
for freedom had amusing consequences. After dinner on March 29,
1784, the hare had been released from her pen into the parlor for
her evening playtime. Just then, the maid announced that Mr. Grenville, who was standing for parliament, wished to pay a visit. Flus-
tered, Cowper told the girl that Mr. Grenville would have to be
"refused admittance at the grand Entry, and referred to the Back
door as the only possible way of approach."

Candidates are creatures not very susceptible of affronts, and
would rather I suppose climb in at a window than be absolutely excluded. In a minute, the yard, the Kitchen and the
parlour were filled. Mr. Grenville advancing toward me, shook
me by the hand with a degree of cordiality that was extremely
seducing. As soon as He and as many others as could find chairs
were seated, he began to open the intent of his visit. I told him
I had no vote. . . . Thus ended the conference. Mr. Grenville
squeezed me by the hand again, kissed the Ladies, and withdrew. He kissed likewise the Maid in the kitchen, and seemed
upon the whole a most loving, kissing, kind-hearted gentleman.[15]

Olney offered Cowper many opportunities to employ his sharp eyes
and whimsical pen. Nevertheless, as we shall see, he came to see it
as a place whose inhabitants had narrow, suspicious sensibilities.

2   Cowper's time when he first arrived at Olney was largely
taken up with assisting Newton and collaborating with him. This
may have been a hazardous enterprise, but he had little else to do.

In her most unguarded statement about Cowper, Mary Unwin described the difficulties which confronted him: "Had he followed either of the three professions in his earlier days, he might have been not only laying a foundation but also raising the fabric of a distinguished character, and have spent the remaining portion of his life in endeavoring to maintain it. But the life of a mere gentleman, very few or any, are equal to support with Credit to themselves; or Comfort to their friends."[16] And it was the life of a "mere gentleman" that Cowper pursued. He dressed "with exactest order & neatness, *and look[ed] like an old Nobleman.*"[17]

There were congenial walks, which Newton rather elegiacally recalled in 1781: "with what pleasure should I steal away to visit the Spinney, the great tree, the Colonnade wall, the Temple, & all the pretty thickets & copses in that neighbourhood."[18] Cowper also conferred innumerable acts of spontaneous kindness. One who had been born at Olney recalled as an old woman: "I was born *the next house to them,* at Olney—and my father's Cottage fronted 'Squire Cowper's garden—and he has often put fruit in at our window, for my mother and me, as we sat at work, when he was going past out of his Garden."[19] This uneventful life of retreat was shattered in September 1769 when Cowper was summoned to tend his brother at Cambridge.

During the crisis in the Temple, Cowper had called upon John for assistance, and his brother had journeyed from Cambridge to be with him. However, Martin Madan had provided Cowper with the comfort that he sought. At Huntingdon, the brothers had seen each other once a week and conversed on spiritual topics. Because John did not share his older brother's earnest religious convictions, a coldness soon developed between them. After Cowper took up residence at Olney, he and John exchanged visits only once a year. John was reserved but polite to William, conforming to his brother's—and Newton's—devotions. "This through the goodness of his natural temper he was enabled to carry so far that though some things unavoidably happened which we feared would give him offence, he never took any: for it was not possible to offer him the pulpit. Nor when Mr. Newton was with us once at the time of family prayer could we ask my brother to officiate, though being himself a minister and one of our family, the office seemed naturally to fall into his hands."[20] This unspoken division between the brothers disappeared only when John was dying.

John Cowper's Cambridge was vastly different from William's London and Olney. Whereas Cowper had enjoyed a dilettantish existence in London, succeeded by a reclusive life at Olney, John had always been studious, and he served as Praelector (1765) and Bursar (1767) of his college, Corpus Christi. He was a poet himself— the brothers had exchanged rhyming letters—and had composed panegyrics on the death of George II and the accession of George III, on George III's marriage, on the birth of the Prince of Wales; he contributed verse to the *Gentleman's Magazine,* and, in 1761, the brothers shared the work of translating the first eight cantos of Voltaire's nine-canto *Henriade* (John translated 1–4, William 5– 8). As young men, the brothers were outwardly fond of each other. Cowper said, "his behaviour to me had always manifested an uncommon affection."[21]

John was known at Cambridge for his dedication to scholarship and his college, and John's obvious sense of purpose did not sit well with his older brother in the 1750s and 1760s. When Cowper attempted to find meaning in a rigorous devotion to Evangelicalism, this was a commitment repugnant to the Cambridge don, who, according to his brother, lived with a "view to the praise of men" and whose couch "was strewn with volumes of plays to which he had frequent recourse for amusement."[22]

To a contemporary at Cambridge, John, "a short, thick, well-set man," seemed "to be of a robust constitution."[23] In the last twelve months of his life, however, his health failed rapidly. His final sickness manifested itself as a dropsy which was said to be "the effect of an imposthume in his liver." Cowper's description of the horrific last illness of his brother is confirmed by Richard Gough, a close Cambridge friend: John was "nervously affected to such a degree that he would latterly break out into the most violent Screams, like hysterics, without any external effect: but to the last appeared in high health & went off rather suddenly in the night."[24] In *Adelphi,* Cowper recorded his brother's physical discomforts, but in the main he provided a testimonial to his brother's conversion to Evangelical beliefs.

Cowper went to Cambridge for about ten days in September 1769, and during that time John seemed to recover his strength. Cowper left him "so far restored that he could ride many miles without fatigue."[25] Six months later, on February 16, 1770, Cowper was again called to Cambridge. When he arrived there, John was extremely cheerful, assuring William that he would soon be well. Cowper's "situation at this time was truly distressful." He "learned from the physician that, in this instance, as in the last, [John] was in much greater danger than he suspected."[26] However, John did

not seem to have one "serious thought," constantly refusing to be
drawn into the "spiritual turns" William sought to introduce into
their conversations. Finally, he agreed to pray with William.

> He seemed as careless and unconcerned as ever, yet I could not
> but consider his willingness in this instance as a token for good
> and observed with pleasure that though at other times he dis-
> covered no mark of seriousness, yet, when I spoke to him of the
> Lord's dealings with myself, he received what I said with affec-
> tion, would, pressing my hand, look kindly on me and seemed
> to love me the better for it.[27]

Three days later, John had a "violent fit"[28] of asthma, and for the
next month—until he died on the 20th of March—he was in constant pain. During this final illness, John's reserve broke down and
he confessed how moved he had been by Cowper's earlier agony in
the Temple and "conversion."[29] As his death approached, John became convinced of the utter goodness of his older brother and
longed for the close relationship with him that he had never had:
"O brother, I am full of what—I could say to you."[30]

Like his older brother before him, John became obsessed with
his previous indifference to divine love, and he realized how obliv-
ous he had been to his older brother's struggles.

> What comfort have I in this bed, miserable as I seem to be?
> Brother, I love to look at you. I see now who was right and who
> was mistaken, but it seems wonderful that such a dispensation
> should be necessary to enforce what seems so very plain. I wish
> myself at Olney. You have a good river there, better than all
> [the] rivers of Damascus. What a scene is passing before me!
> Ideas upon these subjects crowd upon me faster than I can give
> them utterance.[31]

A day or two later, he told William how unsympathetic he had
been to his sufferings:

> When I came to visit you in London and found you in that
> deep distress—I would have given the universe to have adminis-
> tered some comfort to you. You may remember that I tried
> every method of doing it. When I found that all my attempts
> were vain, I was shocked to the greatest degree. I began to con-
> sider your sufferings as a judgment upon you, and my inability
> to alleviate them as a judgment upon myself. When Mr. Madan
> came, he succeeded in a moment. This surprised me, but it does

not surprise me now. He had the key to your heart which I had not.[32]

With a sense of having turned away from worldly things, John prepared to meet death under the tutelage of his brother. "There is that in the nature of salvation by grace when it is truly and experimentally known which prompts every person to think himself the most extraordinary instance of its power. Accordingly, my brother insisted upon the precedence in this respect, and upon comparing his case with mine would by no means allow my deliverance to have been so wonderful as his own."[33] The sibling rivalry which had existed between the brothers received its final ironic twist when John insisted that the life William had led had been the more worthy and thus proclaimed his own conversion the more remarkable.

John looked askance at his previous devotion to language when he evoked the new language of the heart which his older brother had taught him. John spoke of his birth and then checked himself: "Brother, I was born in such a year, but I correct myself. I would rather say, 'In such a year I came into the world.' You know when I was born."[34] The next morning, Cowper was called to be a witness of his brother's final moments. When he entered his brother's room for the last time, he found him in a deep sleep, lying perfectly still, seemingly free from pain. "I stayed with him till they pressed me to quit the room and in about five minutes after I had left him, he died."[35] Although Cowper claimed that he "felt a Joy of Heart upon the Subject of my Brother's Death, such as I never felt but in my own Conversion,"[36] he was so much affected by the loss that the Master and Fellows of Corpus Christi advised him to leave Cambridge before the funeral.

William was overcome with grief for the brother with whom he had only then become intimate. Death had forged a powerful bond between them, as John's deathbed expression of appreciation of his brother makes clear:

> Brother, if I live, you and I shall be more like one another than we have been, but whether I live or live not, all is well and will be so. I know it will. I have felt that which I never felt before and am sure that God has visited me with this sickness to teach me what I was too proud to learn in health. I never had satisfaction till now. The doctrines I had been used to referred me to myself for the foundation of my hopes and then I could find nothing to rest upon: the sheet anchor of the

soul was wanting. I thought you wrong yet wished to believe as you did. . . . You suffered more than I have done before you believed these truths, but our sufferings, though different in their kind and measure, were directed to the same end.[37]

John's words to William are haunting in their simple beauty and heartfelt love. Selflessly, he told his older brother the truth: William was a kind, generous, devoted person. In turn, William clearly acted the role of the responsible older brother when John died in the winter of 1770. He did not suffer a major period of depression at that time: he mourned his brother at the time he died and through the act of writing the second part of *Adelphi* (*The Brothers*).

3   In the first section (1767) of *Adelphi*, Cowper described his sinfulness from childhood onwards, which culminated in the depression over the Clerkship in the House of Lords; he then told of suicide attempts and incarceration at Dr. Cotton's; he concluded the narrative with the moment of spiritual illumination, which transformed his life and gave assurance of salvation. Three years later, Cowper wrote an account of John's final days which he then joined to the earliest segment concerned with his own spiritual destiny. The timid William Cowper of the earlier narrative is remarkably different from the confident William Cowper in the second portion, and it is in *Adelphi* that the first hints of Cowper's mature artistry can be discerned.

Throughout *Adelphi*, Cowper demonstrated a remarkable power to appropriate symbolic meaning to what might seem coincidental, improbable, or fantastic events. This spiritual autobiography is an extended "emblematical representation" of the William Cowper who in his poems and letters was to write elegantly and movingly of nature and ordinary events as a reflection of God's intervention in a postlapsarian landscape. As well, *Adelphi*, in its precise and controlled use of language, shows itself as the work of the William Cowper who earlier composed the facetious, but nevertheless disciplined, prose of the five *Connoisseur* essays.

This element of simple elegance is lacking in the letters from 1764 to 1778. These missives are replete with biblical quotation and paraphrase. There is a great deal of religious fervor in these letters but very little of Cowper's personality. His letters to his cousin Maria Cowper and her mother, Judith Madan, reflect these preoccupations. Maria, the wife of Major William Cowper and Martin Madan's sister, was an unusually accomplished woman. She was sufficiently skilled in French to act in Racine's *Athalie,* and she was so successful in this endeavor that she desired to become an actress. She poured her intense religious feelings into her letters, as did her mother, Judith Madan, the only daughter of Judge Spencer Cowper, Cowper's grandfather. A correspondent of Pope's, she was forced to curtail her literary interests when she married Captain Martin Madan, of the King's Own Regiment of Horse, and she found a great deal of solace in religion after she came to know Lady Huntingdon and John Wesley about 1749.

Since Joe Hill and Lady Hesketh were hostile to his newfound religious convictions, it was natural that Cowper write instead to Mrs. Cowper and Mrs. Madan, and in a letter of July 18, 1767, to Mrs. Madan, he described his alienation from Harriot in language which his aunt would understand and appreciate.

> I have a great Regard for Lady Hesketh, a sincere Affection; and am therefore glad of Opportunities to lead her thoughts, as far as the Lord shall enable me, to the Things that belong to her Peace, so that I never write to her without attempting it. But there are wide Gaps in our Correspondence, which nevertheless proceeds after a Fashion. . . . Though she is every thing that's Aimiable among men, yet I fear the Vail is upon her Heart, for I have heard her speak Shibboleth plainly, nor does the Abundance of her poor Heart seem to be what it should be. Yet the Lord may have purposes of Grace toward her, which I beseech him to manifest in his own time.[38]

Cowper would later be drawn back in the 1780s towards what is "Aimiable among men," and it was then that he wrote his most beautiful letters to Harriot.

4   After his brother's death, Cowper returned to his daily routine at Olney. Newton urged him to lead prayers, to visit the sick, and to accompany him on several preaching tours outside Olney. Newton also gave him copying chores—in one of the volumes of Newton's diary there is a commentary on the first chapter of St. John's Gospel entirely in Cowper's hand. However, early in 1771, Newton engaged Cowper in a different kind of venture: they were to write hymns for the Sunday schools and weekly meetings of the Olney congregation. William Hayley later spoke of the "intense

zeal with which [Cowper] engaged in this fascinating pursuit"[39] but saw it as injurious to his fragile mental condition. William Bull perceived it as beneficial because it was "altogether in conformity with [Cowper's] religious sympathies" and "adapted to his peculiar tastes."[40]

The *Olney Hymns,* which Newton referred to as "my hymn-book,"[41] were a momentous contribution to the Evangelical cause. After their publication in 1779, the hymns appeared in thirty-seven editions before 1836, many of the individual hymns finding their ways into other collections. Before Methodism and Evangelicalism gained momentum, the singing of metrical psalms had been customary in the Church of England. Thomas Sternhold and John Hopkins had translated and metrically versified the psalms in their edition of 1562; a new version of this collection by Tate and Brady had appeared in 1696 and was widely used. Cowper in 1756 had playfully commented on these "improvements":

> The good old practice of psalm-singing is, indeed, wonderfully improved in many country churches since the days of *Sternhold* and *Hopkins;* and there is scarce a parish-clerk, who has so little taste as not to pick his staves out of the New Version. This has occasioned great complaints in some places, where the clerk has been forced to bawl by himself, because the rest of the congregation cannot find the psalm at the end of their prayer-books; while others are highly disgusted at the innovation, and stick as obstinately to the Old Version as to the Old Stile. The tunes themselves have also been new-set to jiggish measures; and the sober drawl, which used to accompany the first two staves of the hundreth psalm with *gloria patri,* is now split into as many quavers as an *Italian* air.[42]

Evangelicals, such as Newton, rebelled against the psalms, new and old style, which were the staple of Church of England services; John Wesley, in a harsher vein than Cowper, castigated "the miserable, scandalous doggerel of Hopkins and Sternhold."[43] Gradually, Watts, Charles Wesley, and others replaced psalms with hymns which stressed in plain language the joyous news of Christ's love for each individual soul. Simplicity and clarity were certainly Newton's aims in his 282 hymns:

> There is a style and manner suited to the composition of Hymns, which may be more successfully, or at least more easily attained by a versifier than by a poet. They should be Hymns,

not Odes, if designed for public worship, and for the use of plain people. Perspicuity, simplicity, and ease, should be chiefly attended to; and the imagery and colouring of poetry, if admitted at all, should be indulged very sparingly, and with great judgment.[44]

As one would expect, John Newton's hymns "are fired by a vision of Christian experience that begins with [his] conviction of God's providential intervention in his own life and proceeds to sweep across history."[45] Newton was a versifier—Cowper a poet. His sixty-seven hymns, the majority of which were composed 1771–72, are at their best when they are lyrical utterances. As Donald Davie has pointed out, Cowper is a vastly different kind of hymn writer from Watts, Wesley, and Newton who utter "their hymns as it were from the pulpit, [whereas] Cowper is one of those who sit at their feet, reporting faithfully how it seems to him, there, in the pew."[46] In fact, many of Cowper's poems in this collection have a disturbing open-endedness, a lack of the resolution that is expected in hymns. The speaker in *The Contrite Heart* (no. 9) is despondent:

> The saints are comforted I know
>   And love thy house of pray'r;
> I therefore go where others go,
>   But find no comfort there.[47]

Cowper claimed that this hymn was based on Isaiah 57:15, yet his verse is markedly different from the scripture passage where God says:

> I dwell on a high and holy place,
> And also with the contrite and lowly spirit
> In order to revive the spirit of the lowly
> And to revive the hearts of the contrite.

God provides His comfort to the "lowly" but Cowper is excluded— his heart is not revived.

Cowper's extraordinary passivity—his willingness to accept the role of outcast—is evident elsewhere in the *Olney Hymns*. In *Contentment* (no. 19), the "Fierce passions" that discompose the mind are like "tempests," while "calm content and peace"[48] are found only in faith. Cowper becomes "still" in order to be "taught" to be content in *Peace after a Storm* (no. 41); previously, he had wandered but this led only to doubts and fears. God, however, "Subdues the disobedient will; / [And] Drives doubt and discontent away."[49]

Cowper dramatized his helplessness in these poems. Like his puta-
tive ancestor, John Donne,[50] he pleaded with God, "Repair me now,
for now mine end doth haste."[51] From 1765 to 1773, he felt, intermittently, that such a restoration was possible. In no. 52, which George
Eliot said was "as lovely and rich as the pomegranate and the
vine,"[52] the speaker describes himself as once a "groveling creature"
who "wanted spirit to renounce / The clod that gave me birth."
Suicidal intentions have been done away with, however, by a loving God who has sent him "from above, / Wings such as clothe an
angel's form, / The wings of joy and love."[53]

In passages in the *Olney Hymns* where he evokes the sea, Cowper portrays this God as a mighty force who can subdue the tempests
of the ocean and the wayward soul:

> O LORD, the pilot's part perform,
> And guide and guard me thro' the storm
>
> . . . .
>
> Dangers of ev'ry shape and name
> Attend the follow'rs of the Lamb,
> Who leave the world's deceitful shore,
> And leave it to return no more.
>
> Tho' tempest-toss'd and half a wreck,
> My Saviour thro' the floods I seek;
> Let neither winds nor stormy main,
> Force back my shatter'd bark again.[54]

The irony here is that God is also the author of these storms. Indeed, Cowper's God in the *Olney Hymns* is Janus-like. He is both
the tender Lamb and the cruel Avenger. In *Welcome Cross* (no.
36), Cowper suggested that he would become a castaway if as a
"true-born child of God" he was not subjected to "chastisement":

> Did I meet no trials here,
> No chastisement by the way;
> Might I not, with reason, fear
> I should prove a cast-away:
> Bastards may escape the rod,
> Sunk in earthly, vain delight;
> But the true-born child of GOD,
> Must not, would not, if he might.[55]

If God loved him, he would punish him severely, brutally if necessary, in order to make him worthy of salvation. Thus, during pe-

riods of religious enthusiasm and relatively good mental health, the "trials" were an obvious way to monitor the process of personal salvation. Ultimately, however, Cowper came to see himself as a Sisyphus, whose chastisement consisted of difficult, ever frustrating toil. In *Adelphi,* Cowper told of God's beneficent intrusion in his life; in the ostensibly more public and impersonal forum of congregational hymns, he wrote another spiritual autobiography—this one dramatizes in vivid detail his relationship with a loving but sadistic God.

5   During these years, when Cowper was immersed in Evangelical practices and beliefs, his correspondence with old friends dwindled; he attempted to sever himself from Joe Hill with this finical reply: "Believe me my dear Friend truly sensible of your kind Invitation, tho' I do not accept it. My Peace of Mind is of so delicate a Constitution, that the Air of London will not agree with it."[56] Harriot Hesketh told Hayley that the "idea [of working on the hymns] never quitted him night or day, but kept him in a *constant fever,* add to this, that when he left the Church, it was to attend their prayer meetings."[57]

However, Newton felt that Cowper's "delicacy of sentiment"[58] in religion declined after three or four years at Olney; in his first days there, Cowper had declared his fervent obedience to divine will "so that the sweat ran down his face, in the open air & in a very severe frost."[59] Newton believed, rightly, that Cowper's decreasing ardor contributed to the severe depression which began in 1773. Cowper's intense, almost fierce, Evangelicalism had largely arisen as a defense against the feelings of self-loathing which had invaded him at the Temple. He simply could not sustain this emotional commitment, and he became more susceptible to inner hostile forces as his zealous devotion to his newfound religion abated.

However, the potential transformation of Mary Unwin from the role of mother to that of spouse was the single most important element in the breakdown. Morley Unwin had evidently intimated that, should he die, "Mr. Cowper might still dwell with Mary"[60]: the "intimate and growing friendship" between Cowper and Mrs. Unwin "led them [Newton claimed] in the course of four or five years to an engagement for Marriage, which was well known to me, and to most of their and my friends, and was to have taken place in a few months, but was prevented by the terrible Malady which seized him about that time."[61] This betrothal was undoubtedly prompted by Olney gossip about two unmarried people living together. According to Hayley, "some good over righteous People *told them both,* that out of *respect to the Forms of the World;* they *ought to be married*—& my own private opinion is, that, at one particular Time, an ill judg'd & unreasonable Fuss on this Subject overwhelm'd the fine faculties of our dear feeling friend."[62] The approaching departure from Olney of Susanna, who married Matthew Powley in 1774, contributed to the decision. In Huntingdon six years earlier, talk of "Improprietys" had influenced the move to Olney.

Whatever the forces were which contributed to the engagement, it would have been an emotionally impossible alliance for Cowper. The possibility that through marriage he would lose his new mother was simply too much for him. A "terrible Malady" did not seize him in 1773 and prevent the marriage; he became acutely ill in 1773 because marriage was for him a frightful prospect. Lady Hesketh is sometimes an unreliable interpreter of her cousin's life; she disliked Mary Unwin and wanted Cowper's blighted romance with Thea to be seen as his great love; however, her comments on the broken engagement of 1773, made in 1801, seem just: "of one thing I am *absolutely certain,* that however strong his friendly attachment to Mrs. Unwin was and however gratefully he return'd her Care and Kindness to him, I am convinc'd he never had a thought of Her that interfered with the Remembrance of his early attachment—He himself told me that he had always consider'd Mrs. U: as a Mother—he was then in perfect health, and I am sure spoke the *truth* as he felt it!"[63]

The depression which overtook Cowper in January 1773 was similar to his debilitating time in the Temple ten years earlier. He became convinced of his essential wretchedness and heard voices which confirmed this fear. He made further attempts at suicide, which were frustrated by the close vigils maintained by Mary Unwin and the Newtons: "What opportunities of Suicide had I, while there was any Hope, except a miserable, a most miserable moment, in 73? that moment lost, all that follow'd was as sure as necessity itself could make it. How are opportunities to be found where the intention is known, watch'd and guarded against? Oh monstrous dispensation!"[64] Finally, in late January or early February 1773, Cowper experienced a nightmare, "before the recollection of which, all consolation vanishes."[65] In this dream, he heard the dreadful words: "Actum est de te, periisti" ("It is all over with thee, thou hast perished"). The engagement to Mrs. Unwin was immediately broken, and he moved to the Vicarage, under the care of the Newtons, in April. He did not return to Orchard Side until May 23, 1774. John Newton provided this account:

> As the House which we used to call Orchard side, fronted the Market-place, he was afraid of the noise & hurry of the Fair-day; & desired to pass that day & night at the Vicarage. But he staid with us for fourteen months, & as he could not then be safely left by himself, he was seldom a minute at a time, out of the sight of one or other of us, by night or day, while he staid under our roof.[66]

The move to the Vicarage was really motivated by Mrs. Unwin's supposed "aversion" to Cowper: "I believed that every body hated me, and that Mrs. Unwin hated me most of all; was convinced that all my food was poisoned."[67] So intense was Cowper's sense of deprivation in 1773 that he felt that Mary Unwin, his second mother, despised him.

Before 1773, Cowper considered, at times, that he might possibly be forgiven the sin of despair. In a letter to Mrs. Newton of October 7, 1773, Mary Unwin told of the damage this breakdown had inflicted upon him: "The Lord is very gracious to us; for though the cloud of affliction still hangs heavy on Mr. Cowper yet he is quite calm & persuadable in every respect. . . . It is amazing how subtilly the cruel adversary has worked upon him. & wonderful to see how the Lord has frustrated his wicked machinations. . . . A most Marvellous story will this Dear Child of God have to relate when by His Almighty power he is set at liberty."[68] Unfortunately, he was never able to utter such a song of liberty. He thought his task was to placate a vengeful God. He did not realize that the savage God resided in the heart of William Cowper.

Newton and Mrs. Unwin delayed getting in touch with Nathaniel Cotton, but at last Newton journeyed to St. Albans to obtain his advice. Cotton recommended bleeding and prescribed medicine; his directions were followed, but Cowper's recovery was slow. The severity of the depression began to lessen in mid-1774, and he inched toward recovery. Newton told Thomas Bowman on June 21, 1774:

> Mr. Cowper's burden is something lighter, he spends almost his whole time in gardening, which was always his favourite amusement, but within this 13 months he was incapable of attending to it. Once or twice of late, some little incidents have drawn a smile from him, which was a new Phanomenon for nothing like

a Smile had been seen upon his face for about 16 months. He will occasionaly converse a little about the garden or such indifferent things. He is certainly better for air & exercise. But the stress . . . of his disorder remains the same.[69]

When Cowper returned to Orchard Side in 1774, his nightmares were so frightening that Mrs. Unwin remained in his room throughout the night in order to comfort him. This arrangement continued at least until 1786 when he told Harriot Hesketh about it: "It is a long time for a Lady to have slept in her cloaths, and the patient at first sight seems chargeable with much inhumanity who suffers it."[70] For the remainder of his life, Cowper had the conviction of having committed the unforgivable sin of despair, and January and February remained times of great anguish. From January 2, 1773 until his death, certain of being the castaway, he never again attended public worship. After 1774, he did not even wish to enter the Vicarage: "When asked, he has often pointed at the Church, & said, 'While I am banished from the House of God, where I have known so much of his presence, I cannot bear to sit down in the house of a friend.' "[71] Cowper terrifyingly evoked this banishment in this poem:

Hatred and vengeance, my eternal portion,
Scarce can endure delay of execution:—
Wait, with impatient readiness, to seize my
    Soul in a moment.

Damn'd below Judas; more abhorr'd than he was,
Who, for a few pence, sold his holy master.
Twice betray'd, Jesus me, the last delinquent,
    Deems the profanest.

Man disavows, and Deity disowns me,
Hell might afford my miseries a shelter;
Therefore hell keeps her everhungry mouths all
    Bolted against me.[72]

In the "fleshly tomb" that had become his life, Cowper was "buried above ground." Before the crisis of 1773, he had been deeply afraid that he was one of the outcasts of God; after 1773, his case was unique—he was "the last delinquent," who could not find refuge even in hell.

6   Before 1781, there was to be only one other new friend in the neighborhood of Olney: the Reverend William Bull, the dissenting

minister of Newport Pagnell Independent Church. Bull, who was born at Irthlingborough, Northamptonshire, in 1738, was admitted in 1759 to Daventry Dissenting Academy and five years later accepted the pastorship at Newport Pagnell, where he also took in students for instruction. Eighteen years later, in 1782, Bull founded his own academy for dissenting ministers, which admitted two students the following year. John Thornton, the wealthy patron of Newton, provided a great part of the funds for the support of this institution, and Bull's activities with the school brought him into close contact with members of the Clapham Sect, including Zachary Macaulay and Thomas Babington. Despite his commitment to the religious values of John Wesley, Bull's divinity was much like that of a charming, idiosyncratic Thomas Browne. Bull's religion may have been of the eighteenth century, but he had the courtly manners and gentility of a retired, seventeenth-century parson. He prided himself on his eccentricity: he once cut a small niche in his garden wall through which he could contemplate the neighboring landscape; he was not at all bothered by the brickwork a few inches from his nose.

John Newton had not been amused by such whimsy when he met Bull in 1768; he had thought "lightly" of him. However, he was much moved when he heard this large, clumsy man preach a funeral sermon of considerable grace and elegance in August 1775: "I can remember when I look'd upon him with much indifference," John told his wife, "and could but just keep up a common civility with him. But what a changed man. Now I seem to shrink into nothing before him, to be a poor empty superficial creature. I could be silent half a day to listen to him, and am almost unwilling to speak a word for fear of preventing him."[73] Amused—and probably amazed—at the prospect of anyone who could reduce her husband to silence, Mary rejoined: "I think Mr. Bull is Your *pope*."[74]

By October 1775, Newton had taken steps to renew his friendship with Bull. However, despite Bull's insistence, he did nothing to promote a meeting between Bull and Cowper. Bull was deeply agitated by this, as his heartfelt lament to Newton of August 4, 1780 makes clear: "—it mortifies & humbles me to think, so fine a Taste—so classical a Genius—& so wonderful a monument of the Power of Divine Grace should exist within 5 Miles & I can't have the Honour nor Taste the pleasure of his friendship—."[75] In response to this plea, Newton, who was then living in London, finally agreed to make the introduction.

When he finally met him, Cowper recognized in "Taureau," as he playfully nicknamed him, an utterly charming and eccentric mixture of human foibles.

> A Dissenter, but a liberal one; a man of Letters and of Genius; master of a fine Imagination, or rather *not* master of it; an imagination, which when he finds himself in the company he loves and can confide in, runs away with him into such fields of speculation as amuse and enliven every other imagination that has the happiness to be of the party. At other times he has a tender and delicate sort of melancholy in his disposition, no less agreeable in its way. No men are better qualified for companions in such a world as this, than men of such a temperament. Every scene of life has two sides, a dark and a bright one, and the mind that has an equal mixture of melancholy and vivacity, is best of all qualified for the contemplation of either. It can be lively without levity, and pensive without dejection. Such a man is Mr. Bull. But he smokes tobacco—nothing is perfect.[76]

If Walter Bagot was the boy from Westminster who was most like Cowper, Bull was the friend in adult life in whom Cowper saw the clearest reflection of his own comic and tragic sides, of his own vivacity and melancholy. This depiction of William Bull is the finest "character" in all of Cowper's letters, and it is so because it is, in part, an unconscious self-portrait.

Cowper's affection for Bull even transcended his aversion to pipes and tobacco, which he had once castigated as "lascivious" and "pernicious."[77] As this delicate disquisition reveals, Cowper's love for his friend conquered such feelings: "My Greenhouse fronted with Myrtles, and where I hear nothing but the pattering of a fine shower and the sound of distant thunder, wants only the fumes of your pipe to make it perfectly delightfull. Tobacco was not known in the Golden age. So much the worse for the Golden age. This age of Iron or Lead would be unsupportable without it. . . ."[78]

7   When Cowper emerged from the depths which had overwhelmed him in 1773, he obviously could no longer devote himself to the religious preoccupations which had filled his life from 1765. His letters and poems became from 1779 his mainstay against depression, but from 1774 to 1778 it was his animals and his gardening which gave him solace in his battle to reenter a world from

which he felt perilously excluded. In each of these activities, there was an attempt to delineate nature, to give it order, to nurture it, and to take pleasure in proximity to that which is beautiful and needful—but not human. Cowper also took lessons in drawing from his "Michael Angelo,"[79] James Andrews, who paid him many compliments on his skill, and he became interested in travel literature. But the other two interests consumed much of his time.

Cowper as a Templar had kept a tame mouse in his chambers, and in 1774 he was delighted by the three hares—Puss, Tiney, and Bess—which some children gave him. An accomplished carpenter, he made the box in which the three lived, and he also constructed the small portal through which the hares were released into the parlor for "a thousand gambols"[80] on the carpet. In 1784, he wrote the *Gentleman's Magazine* to describe how he had come to be involved with these animals. A child of a neighbor received one for a present, and then grew weary of it. Cowper, "willing enough to take the prisoner under [his] protection" since he was "much indisposed both in mind and body, incapable of diverting [himself] either with company or books, and yet in a condition that made some diversions necessary . . . was glad of any thing that would engage [his] attention without fatiguing it."[81] In his letter, he also described in minute detail the personalities of his companions, lamenting the treatment they received from the unthinking huntsman: "he little knows what amiable creatures he persecutes, of what gratitude they are capable, how cheerful they are in their spirits, what enjoyment they have of life, and that, impressed as they seem with a peculiar dread of man, it is only because man gives them peculiar cause for it."[82] Cowper would later describe himself as "the stricken deer" and a "hunted hare," and there can be little doubt that the impulse to keep animals—in addition to the hares, there were the spaniels, Beau and Marquis, and the bulldog, Mungo—and the inclination to portray them in poetry and prose came from a remarkable sense of identification with their helplessness in the face of a hostile world. In caring for these creatures, Cowper was caring for himself, and in slaying the serpent (as described in *The Colubriad*) who threatens his cat and her kittens, he returns his rural paradise to its rightful order. Cowper, himself the prisoner, was able to write in such detail and with considerable feeling for domestic animals and their sometimes tragic existences because of the remarkable similarities he perceived between their fates and his own.

In his first letters (in May 1776) after the events which began in 1773, Cowper was concerned with his garden. He was mortified to discover that Joe Hill's gardener had got a start on him, "but let him be upon his guard, or I shall be too nimble for him another year."[83] Indeed, Cowper's garden became a recurrent theme in his letters: "Pray tell Mrs. Hill my Mimulus ringens, my Flower Fence, my Wild Olive and Silk Cotton are all well and thriving. As to the rest, the Day of their Sowing was the Day of their Burial."[84] Cowper became an expert grower of cantaloupes, cucumbers, and watermelons—he was also fascinated with the more exotic coconut and pineapple. All of Cowper's observations on gardening have the unmistakable air of authenticity, but a garden for him was also a symbolical representation of man's ability to care, protect, and foster:

> Much yet remains
> Unsung, and many cares are yet behind,
> And more laborious; cares on which depends
> Their vigour, injur'd soon, not soon restor'd.
> The soil must be renew'd, which, often wash'd,
> Loses its treasure of salubrious salts,
> And disappoints the roots; the slender roots
> Close interwoven, where they meet the vase,
> Must smooth be shorn away.
>   .   .   .   .
> Discharge but these kind offices, (and who
> Would spare, that loves them, offices like these?)
> Well they reward the toil.[85]

As an Adam very much unparadised and feeling the mark of Cain upon him, Cowper was still able to discharge his "kind offices." Although this self-contradictory man would lament his involvement with Olney, he was able in *The Task* to describe the countryside and its life—his extended garden—in all its complexity as "blest seclusion from a jarring world."[86] The world of retirement could not be perfect because nothing human is flawless, but in his best Miltonic manner he called forth its splendid possibilities:

> Retreat
> Cannot indeed to guilty man restore
> Lost innocence, or cancel follies past;
> But it has peace, and much secures the mind
> From all assaults of evil; proving still
> A faithful barrier, not o'erleaped with ease
> By vicious custom, raging uncontroll'd
> Abroad, and desolating public life.[87]

In tranquil, happy moments, Olney and its environs were paradise regained, but in other, darker moods, it was the scene of bitter inner turmoil. A resident of Olney recalled seeing him: "A sorrowful looking man and very particular in avoiding persons in his walks: —he would turn down any path that presented itself to avoid being seen."[88]

When he was taken to Norfolk in 1795, Cowper declared that it was impossible that he should reside in East Dereham because it was a market town. This fear was based on the assumption that East Dereham would be much like Olney, which became a prison for him because he was forced to participate in the town's daily life. Soon after Cowper and Mrs. Unwin left Olney for Weston in 1786, they learned that Orchard Side was in serious danger of collapsing: "Once since we left Olney I had occasion to call at our old dwelling, and never did I see so forlorn and woeful a spectacle; deserted of its inhabitants it seemed as if it could never be dwelt in for ever. The coldness of it, the dreariness and the dirt, made me think it no unapt resemblance of a soul that God has forsaken."[89] For Cowper, the building had become an emblem of his own "forlorn and woeful" heart.

Cowper arrived in Olney a convinced Evangelical, but he left there nineteen years later assured of his unending alienation from God. He came to the town to live a testimonial to God's overwhelming goodness and then became irrevocably convinced of God's hatred for himself. He ultimately saw Olney as a place of torment, but it was in this small community in rural Buckinghamshire that Cowper slowly came to a recognition of himself as a literary artist. Drawing, carpentry, animals, reading, and gardening became the focus of his world, and he started to write letters of surpassing beauty about his involvement with these concerns. He then renewed his poetic impulses, and by 1785—the year before he left Olney for the more aristocratic Weston Underwood and his dedication to Homer—this man of retreat was the best known living poet in England. He had retired to Olney, but the world would seek him out.

6
Poems (1782)

1   MARY UNWIN told Hayley that she was the
muse of *Poems by William Cowper, of the Inner Temple, Esq.* She
had "strongly solicited her Friend to devote his thoughts to Poetry,
of considerable extent, on his recovery from his very long fit of mental dejection, suggesting to him, at the same time, the first subject
of his Song, 'The Progress of Error!' "[1] However, Mrs. Unwin probably offered her advice only after Cowper from May 1779 had devoted himself to the composition of a number of short poems. Indeed, although Cowper's first volume of verse contains eight poems
of considerable length which satirically, prophetically, and often
sententiously examine the moral and social fabric of contemporary
England and find it wanting, it also comprises thirty-four occasional
poems which display a far more considerable range in subject and
dexterity. The impulses which led to *Poems* were of the "Lyric
kind," but those feelings were often at odds with Cowper's distrust,
as expressed in the moral satires, of art and artifact.

In May 1779, three months after the publication of *Olney Hymns*,
Cowper began a series of letters to William Unwin and Joseph Hill
which include poems. To Unwin, he confided, "You are my Mahog-
any Box with a Slit in the Lid of it, to which I Committ my Productions of the Lyric kind, in perfect Confidence that they are safe, &
will go no furthur."[2] *The Pine Apple & the Bee* became payment to
Hill for a gift, as he waggishly confessed: "I really have no Design
to Fiddle you out of more Fish, but if you should Esteem my Verses
worthy of such a price."[3] Poetical thoughts "that popp'd into" his
head became the most suitable vehicles "for the most vehement Expressions."[4]

By July 1780, Cowper's collaborator in the *Olney Hymns* had
written to express his dismay that these short poems were being dis-

patched to Unwin and not to him. Cowper assured Newton that these were mere "trifles."[5] Meanwhile, Newton had asked Cowper to write a poem which would attack Martin Madan's infamous *Thelyphthora or, a Treatise on Female Ruin, Considered on the Basis of the Divine Law.* Madan's tract, which appeared anonymously on May 31, 1780, argued that a man who takes a woman's virginity has, according to the Old Testament, married her, and is consequently responsible for her economic support. Madan was concerned with the spread of prostitution, and his work was an attempt to halt its growth. The book, however, was perceived as advocating polygamy. Newton, who tried to persuade Madan not to publish this book, was irritated when Madan refused to heed him. Cowper's initial reaction to this dispute between Newton and his cousin was wry: "I suppose [the book] might be properly render'd *Woman debauched;* to which I would add in the Dramatic stile, Or a bold stroke for a Wife! . . . it remains true, as it will for ever, that happiness cannot be found within the walls of a Seraglio."[6] As usual, Newton was insistent in his displeasure, but at first Cowper did not allow himself to be drawn. Newton's persistence finally had its effect, however, and in November Cowper mentioned to Unwin: "I am inform'd that Thelyphthora is at last Encounter'd by a Writer of Abilities equal to the Task. An Answer to that base:born Book was a grand Desideratum in the World of Literature."[7] Cowper then slyly—and misleadingly—referred Unwin to Samuel Badcock's review of *Thelyphthora* in the October–November 1780 issues of the *Monthly Review.* By the end of November, Cowper told Newton that his own rejoinder to Madan was almost finished: "Mrs. Unwin having suggested the Hint, I have added just as many Lines to my Poem lately mentioned, as to make up the whole Number 200."[8]

Cowper's first and separate publication since the halfpenny ballads of many years before was in Newton's hands by December 2 with the poet's admonition that Joseph Johnson, who had published the *Olney Hymns* the year before, was to preserve his "Muse immaculate, and not s[uffer her] to be injured by a Thelyphthorian mixture."[9] Cowper was also concerned that his identity not be leaked. He did not want his aunt, Mrs. Madan, to be offended, and he was still mindful of the kindness Martin had showed to him in the Temple seventeen years before. *Anti-Thelyphthora,* a mock-Spenserian allegory in which Madan, in the guise of the Quixotic "Sir Airy," is bested by "Sir Marmardan," alias Samuel Badcock, the critic, is a blend of censoriousness and humor, especially in its treatment of Sir Airy and his Dulcinea:

But Fate reserv'd Sir Airy to maintain
The wildest Project of her teeming Brain,
That Wedlock is not rig'rous as suppos'd,
But Man within a wider Pale inclos'd
May Rove at Will, where Appetite shall lead,
Free as the Lordly Bull that Ranges o'er the Mead.
That Forms and Rites are Tricks of Human Law,
As idle as the Chatt'ring of a Daw,
That lewd Incontinence and lawless Rape
Are Marriage in its true and proper Shape,
That man by Faith and Truth is made a Slave,
The Ring a Bauble, and the Priest a Knave.[10]

The poem was an amalgam of the subject matter which John Newton would approve and the sprightliness of the short poems which
Cowper had been composing since the middle of 1779. Although
the *Critical Review* dismissed the poem, Badcock was delighted
by it:

The heroes of the little tale are—Reader, pull off thy hat!—the
Rev. Martin Madan, and—put on thy hat again—*the Monthly
Review*. . . . We must do our Poet the justice to acknowledge,
that his *Tale* is the offspring of an elegant fancy, and we are
much obliged to him for the compliments he hath paid our
theological associate. . . . But we must not repeat *our own*
praise; for notwithstanding we have been called impudent, and
saucy, and *magisterial,* and all that, yet we are verily so modest
that we should blush to repeat all that hath been said about us.[11]

Badcock's good-natured praise obviously gave Cowper confidence,
and he soon began work in earnest on the first of the moral satires,
The Progress of Error, which he may well have begun before com-
mencing work on Sir Airy. In moving in this direction, Cowper was
certainly following the lead of John Newton, who had retained his
ascendancy as the mentor of Cowper's burgeoning literary talent.
In the wake of the poor sales of *Anti-Thelyphthora,* he advised the
would-be poet: "But I think your other pieces, according to the
sample of the progress of Error, will certainly find Readers &
Buyers."[12]

William Unwin, now the Rector of Stock in Essex, whom Cowper
had truthfully informed in August 1780 that he was making a "Collection [of short poems], not for the Public, but for Myself"[13] was
excluded from Cowper's decision to seek a popular audience for his

religious verse. Cowper did this even though he was able to tell Unwin at the time he was working on *The Progress of Error:* "You have an Ear for Music, and a Taste for Verse, which saves me the Trouble of pointing out with a Critical Nicety."[14] "Taste" and "Critical Nicety," usually important values to Cowper, became secondary considerations as work on the moral satires wore on.

2   When he wrote to Newton on December 21, 1780, Cowper enclosed "a long thought in verse,"[15] *Heroism,* which is concerned with the eruption of Mount Aetna from January to June 1780. Cowper obviously thought this sable effusion[16] on the vanity of human wishes would please Newton, and he promised to send *The Progress of Error,* which had been completed, and, in due course, *Truth.* "Don't be alarmed," he told Newton. "I ride Pegasus in a curb."[17] Earlier in the letter, Cowper assured Newton how important his approbation was to him: "when a judicious friend claps me on the back, I own I find it an encouragement."[18]

> While I am held in pursuit of pretty images, or a pretty way of expressing them, I forget every thing that is irksome, &, like a boy that plays truant, determine to avail myself of the present opportunity to be amused, & to put by the disagreeable recollection that I must after all, go home & be whipt again.[19]

Newton was not only to provide encouragement, but he was also to read each poem and give it his imprimatur. As well, he approached Joseph Johnson who, having served as Cowper's publisher twice before, agreed to the venture in May 1781.

Quite soon after he began the moral satires and well before Joseph Johnson's approbation, Cowper was concerned about publication. He warned Johnson in January 1781 that he had just completed *The Progress of Error,* which, when it eventually found its way into print, would not require the kind of meddling by the printer to which *Anti-Thelyphthora* had been subjected. Later that month, elated that Newton liked *The Progress of Error,* Cowper sent him some additional lines on Lord Chesterfield. He was too weary that day to transcribe his other poem, *Truth.* On February 4, Cowper was well into another poem, *Table Talk,* but *The Progress of Error* was worrying him. He wanted *Truth* to have precedence over it in the proposed collection, and, to Cowper's taste, the new poem, *Table Talk,* was the most topical and liveliest of the three. Although Cowper argued the importance of "some Connexion with the present day"[20] in his religious verse, it may well be that he already felt himself—however slightly—at odds with Newton's rigorous taste. He apologized for the exuberant tone of *Table Talk* when he told him on February 18, "I am merry that I may decoy people into my Company, and grave that they may be the better for it."[21]

By February 25, a fourth poem, *Expostulation,* was in progress, although Cowper was experiencing considerable difficulty in its writing. With the completion of that poem in early March, Cowper realized he had completed a publishable volume. He was inclined to cancel a passage in *The Progress of Error* which attacked Martin Madan, he wished *Table Talk* to be placed first in the collection, and he wanted Johnson to announce him by the style and title of "William Cowper Esqr. of the Inner Temple."[22] Cowper was especially obdurate on the placing of *Table Talk:* "one would wish at first setting out to catch the public by the Ear and hold them by it."[23] *Expostulation* was still causing problems. Nevertheless, the wily poet had many further thoughts on his new book:

> If therefore the three first [poems] are put into the Press, while I am spinning and weaving the last, the whole may perhaps be ready for Publication before the proper Season will be past. I mean at present that a few select smaller pieces, about 7 or 8 perhaps, the best I can find in a bookfull that I have by me, shall accompany them. All together they will furnish I should imagine a volume of tolerable bulk, that need not be indebted to an unreasonable breadth of Margin for the importance of its figure.[24]

As well as insisting on jurisdiction as to the manner in which his muse would make a public appearance, Cowper also felt publication was vital to his creativity: "And if I did not publish what I write, I could not interest myself sufficiently in my own Success to make an Amusement of it."[25] As well, poetry at this time had become the only diversion which could prevent the incessant "train of Melancholy thoughts."[26] For Cowper, poetry was an escape from emotion, but it was so in an essentially positive way. As Leon Edel has said of Henry James, Cowper's poetry was "a work of health and not of illness, a force for life and life-enhancement, not a mere anodyne or 'escape' or a symptom of neurosis."[27] Poetry offered Cowper not only the opportunity to reflect upon his unhappy existence but also the chance to distance himself from some of its most painful aspects. Art is not life, but artists who draw freely from their own lives often gain a mastery over "sable effusions."

Cowper's poetic mastery became more and more evident as he labored on *Poems*. Still, by April 1781, the final form this collection would take had not been decided upon. Newton felt that *Truth* was too acerbic for the "unenlighten'd Reader,"[28] and Cowper agreed to allow him to write an introduction to it, or to the entire volume. And *The Progress of Error* was again niggling Cowper, particularly the lines on Madan. Two weeks later, he considered inserting some further small pieces, "less calculated for Utility than Amusement," but he changed his mind. "If hereafter I should accumulate a sufficient Number of these Minutiæ to make a miscellaneous Volume, which is not impossible, I may perhaps collect and print them."[29] Cowper may well have seen such a volume as one which would not suit Newton's taste. Two days later, reasonably sure that Johnson would agree to publish, Cowper decided to use these 808 lines of verse as well as four translations from Vincent Bourne. "There are times when I cannot write, and the present is such a time; and were it not, I should yet prefer this method of swelling the Volume, to that of filling the Vacuity with one long-winded poem like the preceding."[30] Cowper had obviously begun to have serious doubts about the moral satires. Variety, he felt, however, would give relief to the reader and prevent weariness. Cowper's trepidations about the volume were eased after he decided for the inclusion of the short poems, and he was delighted when Johnson agreed to publish. As soon as the agreement had been concluded Cowper broke the news to Unwin and Hill. "I am in the press."[31]

If *Poems* had been "speedily" published as Cowper expected in May 1781, it would have been a comparatively slim book of just over 3,650 lines. The volume which was issued on March 1, 1782, runs to almost 7,000. Cowper appended only 134 lines to the miscellany of short poems, but he added 3,123 lines of moral satires (*Hope, Charity, Conversation,* and *Retirement*) to the 2,718 of the four earlier poems. The transformation of what would have been a relatively modest effort into a more substantial one was due principally to delays in the printing shop. Cowper's sense of having completed a volume spurred him on to plan a new one (in the way he had earlier thought of a collection of short verse), and he confided to Unwin: "Since I have begun to write long poems, I seem to turn up my Nose at the Idea of a short one."[32] Johnson had assured him that only collections—and not single poems such as *Anti-Thelyph-*

thora—sold well. *Hope,* which was to be part of Cowper's "second volume" was already well under way.

By May 21, when Cowper learned that publication of his book would be seriously delayed, he made Johnson's procrastination his own opportunity. He decided to add new poems to the four original moral satires in order to compensate for his "Methodist shoes" with "Sugar plumbs."[33] In early July, he planned to add only *Hope* and *Charity,* but by July 22 he was busily working on a seventh poem: "I am in the middle of an Affair called Conversation, which as Table-talk serves in the present volume by way of Introductory fiddle to the band that follows, I design shall perform the same Office in a second."[34] A fortnight later, Cowper offered Johnson a choice: he could have *Conversation* as the opening piece in a new collection or it could be the concluding moral satire to the volume in the press. At the same time that he wrote to Johnson, Cowper told Mrs. Newton that *Conversation* did not "bear the least resemblance to Table-talk, except that it is serio-comic like all the Rest."[35] Cowper's view of his enterprise had changed considerably since *The Progress of Error* had come into being. By August 25, Johnson had informed Cowper that he would take *Conversation* and that Cowper was not to be afraid of making the volume too large.

Cowper had begun *Retirement:* "My view in chusing that Subject is to direct [mankind] to the proper use of the opportunities it affords for the cultivation of Man's best Interests. . . . But all this is at present in Embryo."[36] This poem was completed in October and was printed as the final—eighth—moral satire. Although political circumstances would force Cowper to replace two of the short poems (*A Present for the Queen of France* and *To Sir Joshua Reynolds*) in December, the format of *Poems* had been established. At least, the selection of verse was complete. There were to be other serious problems before the volume appeared in March. However, in October 1781, Cowper looked back with justified self-assurance at the previous twelve months: "About this time twelvemonth I began with Antithelyphthora and have never allowed myself more than a fortnight's respite since. I reckon the volume will consist of about 8000 lines."[37]

3   Although Joseph Johnson had acted as Cowper's publisher twice before, *Poems* brought them, for the first time, into collaboration, and it was this encounter which set the pattern for the re-

mainder of their relationship. Johnson's extraordinary kindness to writers and his ability to bypass the demands of commerce in order to publish work to which he felt a strong commitment was celebrated by another of his authors, Maria Edgeworth:

> Wretches there are, their lucky stars who bless
> Whene'er they find a genius in distress;
> Who starve the bard, and stunt his growing Fame
> Lest they should pay the value for his name.
> But JOHNSON rais'd the drooping bard from Earth
> And fostered rising Genius from his birth:
> His lib'ral spirit a *Profession* made,
> Of what with vulgar souls is vulgar Trade.[38]

Cowper would have agreed with Edgeworth. Johnson showed himself a cordial, sometimes detached, and always critical and discriminating ally to him. In turn, Cowper, although he was to be irritated by the frequent delays in receiving proofs and was later to quarrel with Johnson about financial matters, appreciated the discernment and acumen Johnson always showed in seeing his books through the press.

Johnson, who migrated to London from Liverpool in 1754 at the age of fourteen, at which time he began his apprenticeship in the book trade, was established in St. Paul's Churchyard from August 1770, well before he first acted as Cowper's publisher in 1779. In addition to publishing controversial works by Wollstonecraft, Priestley, Paine, Malthus, and Beckford, among many others, Johnson was a committed Unitarian and many tracts by fellow members of that religion carry his imprint; he also had a keen interest in scientific treatises and some significant medical publications bear his name as publisher. As well, Johnson cultivated a special interest in writers from his native city: Newton's first book with Johnson was a collection of sermons written in Liverpool in 1760. It was this unlikely route that brought Cowper and Johnson together.

Cowper's initial reaction to Johnson was one of gratitude for agreeing to accept a volume of verse which might not be up to contemporary taste: "I was very much in doubt for some Weeks whether any Bookseller would be willing to subject himself to an Ambiguity that might prove very expensive in case of a bad Market. But Johnson has heroically set all peradventure at defiance, and takes the whole charge upon himself."[39] In doing so, Johnson held the copyright and any potential earnings. There was little likelihood that Joseph Johnson would derive a substantial profit, or any profit at all, from *Poems*. Did he feel himself under an obligation to a poet who had published with him before? Or did he see a potential in Cowper beyond this volume of verse? Had he been intrigued by the comic liveliness and satiric bite of *Anti-Thelyphthora?* Whatever his motivations, Johnson in March 1781, a month before he had definitely agreed to publish, insisted that Cowper's name should appear on the title page of *Poems*.

The author's desired anonymity having been cast aside and the terms of publication established, *Poems* was in the press that May, at which time Johnson decided he would prefer to postpone publication until winter, as he could not then issue the volume before the end of the London season. As we have seen, delay ultimately doubled the size of the volume, but it was also a constant source of irritation to Cowper. He complained to Unwin:

> If a Writer's friends have need of patience, how much more the Writer! You desire to see my Muse in public, and mine to gratify you, must both suffer the Mortification of delay. I expected that my Trumpeter would have inform'd the world by this time of all that is needfull for them to know upon such an Occasion, and that an advertizing Blast blown through every Newspaper, would have said, the Poet is coming! But Man, especially Man that writes verse, is born to disappointments, as surely as Printers and Booksellers are born to be the most dilatory and tedious of all Creatures.[40]

Delays in receiving proofs haunted Cowper throughout the long, tedious printing. Both Newton and Unwin were encouraged to press Johnson, and, toward the end of this process, Cowper confided to Newton his suspicions about Johnson: "I suspect that he gives a preference to others who engaged him not so early as myself, and that my distance from the Spot is used to my disadvantage."[41] However lax Johnson might have seemed about supplying "sheets," he was a rigorous examiner of what he was asked to set in type.

When Cowper became aware in late May that his volume would be substantially delayed, he altered the arrangement about the reading of proofs which he had made with Newton. At the time in April 1781 when publication had been agreed to and it seemed as if the book would appear imminently, Cowper had decided to allow Newton to correct the sheets for the press. The fair copies of the poems would be sent to Newton who would transmit them to Johnson; Johnson would send the proofs to Newton who would correct them and then return them to Johnson. Cowper wrote to Newton on May 21 to cancel this plan: "this leisurely proceeding being so favorable to my purpose, I have conceiv'd a design to save you the trouble of revising the proof, and that for two reasons. First because your time is precious, and mine is not so, and secondly because having written nothing of late that I do not retain memoritèr, it is impossible for the Alteration of a Word, or the least Inaccuracy to escape me."[42] Although Cowper was "a most inefficient proof-corrector and must take some part of the blame for the many errors which disfigure the first edition,"[43] Johnson's delay inadvertently breached the collaborative activities between Newton and Cowper which, up to this time, had been central to the execution of the volume. Newton demurred (he did correct the first sheet issued by Johnson), but Cowper insisted. Having disrupted Newton's role, Johnson proceeded to offer suggestions for improvements to the poems themselves. Johnson's displeasure at some lines was conveyed to Cowper by Newton, and the poet replied on July 7:

> I had rather submitt to Chastisement now, than be obliged to undergo it hereafter. If Johnson therefore will mark with a marginal Q, those Lines that He or His, object to, as not Sufficiently finished, I will willingly retouch them, or give a reason for my refusal. I shall moreover think myself obliged by any hints of that sort, as I do already to somebody who by running here and there two or three paragraphs into one, has very much improved the Arrangement of my matter.[44]

Although he was not always to agree with Johnson and was frequently unbudging, Cowper was ultimately grateful for his publisher's queries, suggestions, and complaints. His compliment to Johnson as the printing came to an end suggests the confidence he had in him: "I now reckon the book finished, and therefore once for all and very unfeignedly return you my thanks for the many usefull hints you have given me. And if I were to prefix an Advertisement to the Reader, would most willingly acknowledge my self indebted to my Bookseller, as my very judicious, and only Corrector."[45] Up to this time, Johnson had only accidentally disturbed the alliance between Newton and Cowper, but in February 1782 he was to take steps which would ultimately contribute to a drastic change in the relationship.

When it was agreed that Newton was no longer to serve as his

"Corrector" at the press, Cowper attempted to placate him. He had earlier allowed Newton to write a preface to *Truth* or to the entire collection, and in October he had been delighted with Newton's proposed appearance as "The Editor" of the volume: "I have told the public that I live upon the banks of the Ouse; that public is a great Simpleton if it does not know that you live in London; it will consequently know that I had need of the assistance of some friend in town, and that I could have recourse to nobody with more propriety than yourself."[46] Newton's plan to appear as editor seems to have been dropped as soon as Cowper gave his approbation, but, by October 22, Cowper had seen the draft of a preface to the entire collection. Although he approved the document, he nevertheless wanted Newton to emphasize the lighter or comic aspects of the collection, "for when I am jocular I do violence to myself, and am therefore pleased with your telling them in a civil way, that I play the fool to amuse them, not because I am one myself, but because I have a foolish world to deal with."[47]

Joseph Johnson, however, was not as easily pleased. He quite rightly found passages such as this inappropriate:

> It is very probable these Poems may come into the hands of some persons, in whom the sight of the Author's name will awaken a recollection of incidents and scenes which, through length of time, they had almost forgotten. They will be reminded of *one,* who was once the companion of their chosen hours, and who set out with them in early life, in the paths which lead to literary honours, to influence and affluence, with equal prospects of success. But he was suddenly and powerfully withdrawn from those pursuits, and he left them without regret; yet not till he had sufficient opportunity of counting the cost, and of knowing the value of what he gave up. If happiness could have been found in classical attainments, in an elegant taste, in the exertions of wit, fancy, and genius, and in the esteem and converse of such persons as in these respects were most congenial with himself, he would have been happy. But he was not. . . . But in due time, the cause of his disappointment was discovered to him—He had lived without God in the world.[48]

Although Newton's biographical comments are accurate and reflect the motives with which *The Progress of Error* and substantial parts of the other moral satires were taken up, they are presented in a

heavy, abrasive manner. Joseph Johnson printed the preface, and
he then had grave doubts about it. It was in a mood of agitated
concern that he wrote to Cowper on February 18:

> If I was to omit mentioning any circumstances that appeared to
> me likely to affect the sale of the Poems you would have just
> cause to blame me hereafter, and this must be my apology for
> what otherwise might be thought impertinence to you or want
> of respect for Mr. Newton. If there was not plenty of entertain-
> ment for poetical readers, whatever may be their religious Sen-
> timents, I should think it very candid & honest to prefix the
> preface you receive herewith, for I detest the practice of taking
> in the public under false pretences, but as I think few lovers of
> poetry, whether they have any religion or none, will find them-
> selves so much disappointed as to regret the loss of their five
> shillings, it appears to me wrong to insert a preface which has
> a direct tendency to prevent readers of very different Senti-
> ments from the writer of it, from turning over a single page, &
> which will infalibly prejudice the critics against the work be-
> fore they have read a line, & their judgment has no small in-
> fluence on the success of poetical composition. Those who are
> acquainted with Mr N's genius & worth & are also of his senti-
> ments [will] indeed be disposed to read & be benefitted, but I
> do not think this a sufficient motive for giving up the public
> at large by a preface which does not appear to me to be at all
> necessary. After having said thus much you will determine as
> you think proper & I shall think no more on the subject: but
> allow me to add that few men stand so high in my esteem as
> Mr Newton or have so much a share of my love.[49]

Cowper acted decisively when he received this letter. He agreed to
cancel the preface and took Johnson up on his offer to "negotiate
the matter" with Newton. In a letter of about February 24, Cowper diplomatically thanked Newton for writing the introduction,
and, without expressing a direct opinion, he suggested that Johnson's views should be weighed seriously. On March 7, Cowper still
did not know what resolution had been reached. A week later,
having heard that the preface was not to appear, he wrote to Newton. He attempted to console him on the suppression of the preface
which he asserted was "free from every thing that might with propriety expose it to the charge of Methodism, being guilty of no
offensive peculiarities, nor containing any of those obnoxious doc-

trines, at which the world is so apt to be angry. . . ."[50] Having expressed confidence in Newton, Cowper went on: "I have reason to be very much satisfied with my publisher."[51]

Although Cowper's friendship with Newton would survive, it had been badly damaged. Cowper would not again rely on Newton as his literary mentor. The doubts Cowper himself had had about possible twinges of Methodism in the moral satires were to move him in his next book in the direction of praising virtue while, at the same time, seeking to accommodate himself to public taste. The straitened religious vision of *Poems* was to be replaced in 1785 by a long poem of much more complexity and sophistication, and Cowper was to become more decisive about his poetical career.

However, as Cowper's career as a publishing poet began to emerge, he owed a great literary debt to Newton. In his canceled preface, Newton had written:

> At a time when hypothesis and conjecture in philosophy are so justly exploded, and little is considered as deserving the name of knowledge, which will not stand the test of experiment, the very use of the term *experimental* in religious concernments, is by too many unhappily rejected with disgust. But we well know, that they who affect to despise the inward feelings which religious persons speak of, and to treat them as enthusiasm and folly, have inward feelings of their own, which, though they would, they cannot suppress.[52]

Newton insisted that it was important to write about the actual experience of divine grace: philosophy had come to reject that which is merely defined in preference to that which can be actually felt, and religion must do the same. In this passage, Newton seized upon a central aspect of Cowper's poetry. The moral satires, for all their obvious indebtedness to classical and eighteenth-century precedents, describe the actual experience of faith, hope, and charity—they do not merely enumerate those qualities in an abstract manner. John D. Baird has put the matter well: "They are directed not toward rational conviction but to the creation of a state of mind on the part of the reader. [Cowper] expounds not what true believers believe—but the happy results of their believing it."[53]

Thus, the originality of the 1782 volume lies in its attempt to describe the actual experience of religious devotion. Most of the moral satires are ineffectual because the feelings explored are treated from far too general a vantage point. Cowper's artistry found its match in *The Task*, where he related God's intervention in his own life.* Although Cowper and Newton were doctrinally at odds by 1785, Cowper's long poem owes a great deal to precepts imbibed from Newton.

4   Despite Cowper's reservations about the direction his muse took after she had given birth to *The Progress of Error* and despite the incredible metamorphosis of *Poems* from what was originally intended to be a slender volume into a substantial book of 468 pages, the eight moral satires are extraordinarily uniform. In these poems, Cowper examines, from various perspectives, man's place in a world from which God has been excluded. Man has attempted to make this earth his paradise, but he has forgotten Milton's exhortation, delivered by Michael in *Paradise Lost,* that man in a fallen world must, to achieve salvation and any measure of happiness, create a paradise within. The poet in retreat from the corrupt luxury of the world, having secreted himself in the country where real introspection is possible, is the proper Miltonic poet-priest to speak to England in the 1780s, since he has heeded the words of the archangel. It is from this vantage point that the voice of the poet speaks in the moral satires.

Although they are vastly different in tone and complexity from Pope's *Essay on Man* and *Moral Essays,* Cowper's poems have many of the aims and methods of Pope's poems of fifty years before. Pope had avoided consideration of Christ and the Incarnation in his poems and had then gone on to examine the follies and stupidities of man's pride. Pope had considered the "Mighty Maze" of human existence, showed that it did indeed have a plan, and then castigated the deviants from the proper middle state of man and praised those resolute few, like Martha Blount, the Earl of Burlington, and the Earl of Bathurst, who clung to virtue. Cowper had his heroes too—people like Nathaniel Cotton, the Earl of Dartmouth, Robert Smith—who led virtuous lives in a debased world, and he attacked persons such as Lord Chesterfield and Martin Madan who led society astray. Cowper, however, lacked the powerful aphoristic and imagistic complexity Pope had brought to his philosophical examinations of man. He was also not at ease in writing satire and certainly felt a deep-seated antagonism to Pope:

---

* In the seemingly impersonal format of the *Olney Hymns,* Cowper had written of his troubled relationship with God; in the autobiographical formats provided by *Poems* and *The Task,* he wrote of his spiritual history with considerable discretion.

as harmony itself exact,
In verse well disciplin'd, complete, compact,
Gave virtue and morality a grace
That quite eclipsing pleasure's painted face,
Levied a tax of wonder and applause,
Ev'n on the fools that trampl'd on their laws.
But he (his musical finesse was such,
So nice his ear, so delicate his touch)
Made poetry a mere mechanic art,
And ev'ry warbler has his tune by heart.[54]

For the remainder of his career, especially when he began work on a rival translation of Homer, Cowper would see Pope as his antagonist, the writer he must surpass. Some of this rivalry is implicit in these lines from *Table Talk,* but Cowper in 1782 was on unsure footing in employing the dramatic, exhortative voice. He did not possess Pope's elegance of language, and, whereas Pope deliberately eliminated a personal God in his essentially traditional Christian poems, Cowper's God is everywhere present.

Cowper's hostility to Pope is also due to another deep chasm separating them. Pope had written with a great deal of assurance of his vision of man's place in the universe. Cowper did not inherently share such convictions: he found it more difficult than Pope to come to terms with man's—particularly his own—position in a fallen world. He was riddled with self-doubt, whereas Pope never expressed such trepidations. Ultimately, Pope's calm assurance deeply niggled Cowper. Pope spoke as one conversant with divinity; Cowper sometimes feared he was the outcast of God. Cowper's envy of Pope's majestic surety simply overwhelmed him, making the dead poet his spiritual enemy.

In addition, Cowper saw the heritage Pope had bestowed upon the poets of his generation as a sterile one, Cowper claiming his contemporaries served up poetry "as a cook serves a dead turkey, when she fastens the legs of it to a post, and draws out all the sinews. For this we may thank Pope; but unless we could imitate him in the closeness and compactness of his expression, as well as in the smoothness of his numbers, we had better drop the imitation, which serves no other purpose than to emasculate and weaken all we write.—Give me a manly, rough line, with a deal of meaning in it, rather than a whole poem full of musical periods. . . ."[55] For Cowper, the pursuit of a "manly rough line" was an effective way of escaping the emasculating specter of Pope.

Poems is ultimately a handbook of Evangelical doctrine. *Table Talk,* a dialogue between A and B, examines the nature of kingship and liberty. Cowper placed this poem first in the collection because the question and answer format excluded the controlling and directing voice of the earlier *Progress of Error* and the later moral satires. A is disappointed with the world he lives in but attempts to make peace with it; B, the more mature and wise person, is at pains to point out to him just how corrupt the world is. In many ways, this dialogue is between the youthful Cowper ("At Westminster . . . I was a poet too"[56]) and the older Cowper who is in retirement and writes a different type of poetry. Throughout *Table Talk,* there is a constant discussion about the place of art in the world of vanities. The contrast is between the utter simplicity of God's beneficent providence and the destructive complexity of all the works of man, including poetry. Cowper recognizes the necessity of a poetry which celebrates the works of God, but he is dangerously aware of how the pursuit of art frequently leads man away from his creator. His alter ego, B, recognizes the redemptive possibilities of art, and yet he fears that he will not achieve his proper end:

> in a Roman mouth, the graceful name
> Of prophet and of poet was the same,
> Hence British poets too the priesthood shar'd,
> And ev'ry hallow'd druid was a bard.
> But no prophetic fires to me belong,
> I play with syllables, and sport in song.[57]

The poem concludes with a stated preference for the work of the English versifiers of the Psalms, Sternhold and Hopkins, over the literary pretensions of "Butler's wit, Pope's numbers, Prior's ease." And B also laments, "Pity! Religion has so seldom found / A skilful guide into poetic ground."[58] The entire collection of 1782 examines various facets of Evangelical doctrine as embraced by Cowper, but it is also a series of poems in which he has set himself the task of "skilful guide."[59]

Employing the format of the traditional progress piece used with great success by, among others, Pope, Collins, and Gray earlier in the century, Cowper examines in his second poem (first in point of composition) the growth and development of error from a variety of perspectives, with comments on such diverse subjects as church-going, card playing, education, the grand tour, enthusiasm, and writers. The most uncompromising of the moral satires—

I am no preacher, let this hint suffice,
The cross once seen, is death to ev'ry vice:
Else he that hung there, suffer'd all his pain,
Bled, groan'd and agoniz'd, and died in vain.[60]

—it is also the one which is most antagonistic to art:

Ye pimps, who under virtue's fair pretence,
Steal to the closet of young innocence,
And teach her inexperienc'd yet and green,
To scribble as you scribble at fifteen.

. . . .
Oh that a verse had pow'r, and could command
Far, far away, these flesh-flies of the land.[61]

At the very outset of the poem, Cowper even doubts whether it is possible to compose a poem about the nature of error: "Sing muse (if such a theme, so dark, so long, / May find a muse to grace it with a song)."[62] The third, fifth, and sixth moral satires scrutinize truth, hope, and charity, respectively. In his discourses on the nature of these abstract qualities, Cowper again elaborates on the simplicity of God and the sophistication of wayward man: "Oh how unlike the complex works of man, / Heav'ns easy, artless, unincumber'd plan!"[63] These poems are not remarkable in their subject matter, but for the first time in this collection, some of Cowper's characteristic imagery and symbols are introduced. Like Pope, Cowper frequently employs images of sight or lack of it to characterize the presence or absence of moral goodness:

Suppose (when thought is warm and fancy flows,
What will not argument sometimes suppose)
An isle possess'd by creatures of our kind,
Endued with reason, yet by nature blind.
Let supposition lend her aid once more,
And land some grave optician on the shore,
He claps his lens, if haply they may see,
Close to the part where vision ought to be,
But finds that though his tubes assist the sight,
They cannot give it, or make darkness light.[64]

It is also in these poems that the imagery of the sea, the most dominant and evocative in his verse, again asserts itself:

Man, on the dubious waves of error toss'd,
His ship half founder'd and his compass lost,

Sees, far as human optics may command,
A sleeping fog, and fancies it dry land.[65]

His passions, like the wat'ry stores that sleep
Beneath the smiling surface of the deep,
Wait but the lashes of a wintry storm,
To frown and roar, and shake his feeble form.[66]

Cowper used the sea to explain his spiritual predicament, and in his later poetry and prose he resorted to it as the dominant metaphor to describe the harshness and bitterness of a savage God against one of his creatures, Cowper himself. In the moral satires and the early poetry, man is victim of the sea, but he is a willing victim who has determined and weighed his own perfidy. Cowper had not yet turned the metaphor completely against himself.

Truth, Hope, and *Charity* are rigorous in their presentation of standard Evangelical doctrine, so rigorous that Unwin complained to Cowper about his treatment of faith and good works in *Truth.* Cowper was uncompromising: ". . . I wrote that Poem on purpose to inculcate the eleemosynary Character of the Gospel, as a dispensation of Mercy in the most absolute Sense of the word, to the Exclusion of all claims of Merit on the part of the Receiver. Consequently to set the brand of Invalidity upon the Plea of Works, and to discover upon Scriptural ground the absurdity of that Notion which includes a Solecism in the very terms of it, that Man by Repentance and good works may deserve the Mercy of his Maker."[67] *Expostulation* begins with a question, "Why weeps the muse for England?,"[68] and, despite the poet's sorrow, at the corruption he uncovers, he finds it difficult to feel much compassion, especially when he considers that England has a portent of retribution in Israel, which earlier abandoned God's ways. The poem is a "warning song" which the poet feels "is sung in vain."[69] "What ails thee [England], restless as the waves that roar, / And fling their foam against thy chalky shore?"[70] The poet-prophet continues his meditations on art ("Rhet'ric is artifice, the work of man / And tricks and turns that fancy may devise, / Are far too mean for him that rules the skies"),[71] and he finally decides on the futility of his own art:

Muse, hang this harp upon yon aged beech,
Still murm'ring with the solemn truths I teach,
And while, at intervals, a cold blast sings
Through the dry leaves, and pants upon the strings,
My soul shall sigh in secret, and lament

A nation scourg'd, yet tardy to repent.
I know the warning song is sung in vain,
That few will hear, and fewer heed the strain.[72]

The homogeneous consistency of *Poems* is broken slightly only when the reader reaches *Conversation,* the seventh moral satire.

Although Cowper had warned Mrs. Newton that *Conversation* and *Table Talk* did not "bear the least resemblance"[73] to each other, despite the affinities in their titles, he asked Newton in writing the preface to link the two poems: "By the way—will it not be proper, as you have taken some notice of the modish dress I wear in Table-talk, to include Conversation in the same description, which is (the first half of it at least) the most airy of the two?"[74] As the writing of *Poems* continued, Cowper attempted to find a "modish dress" for his verse. It is in *Conversation* that these efforts first bear fruit. Whereas the other poems had meditated on corrupt human nature, pointed at the conflicts between human and divine history, and exhorted a sinful nation to repent, *Conversation* is a guide to the proper use of human discourse. Its tone is frequently like that of the earlier poems, but there is, as Cowper insists, at least in the first half of it, a movement in the direction of reconciliation with sinful city dwellers:

A tale should be judicious, clear, succinct,
The language plain, and incidents well-link'd,
Tell not as new what ev'ry body knows,
And new or old, still hasten to a close.[75]

The standards of good talk are also, of course, the standards of good poetry, although "Conversation in its better part, / May be esteemed a gift and not an art."[76] However, Cowper still betrays here the uneasiness toward art displayed in the earlier poems.

It is only in *Retirement,* the final moral satire, that the writer of *The Task* begins to emerge. This poem, in many ways a rehearsal for the later poem, possesses the greatest strength of all the moral satires because it is only here that Cowper's "modish dress" is worn with ease and the fear of art put aside. Although the other poems contain passing autobiographical references, it is in *Retirement* that we meet the poet in retreat, where, away from the burly-burly of urban society, he discovers his mind open and receptive to divine providence. Cowper's overriding conceit in *Retirement* is based upon the Marvellian paradox that in solitude the mind becomes most active. And it is in such a scene, where man is close to God, that the poet does not have to fear his artistry.

> Nature in all the various shapes she wears,
> . . . .
> All, all alike transport the glowing bard,
> Success in rhime his glory and reward.
> Oh nature! whose Elysian scenes disclose
> His bright perfections at whose word they rose,
> Next to that pow'r who form'd thee and sustains,
> Be thou the great inspirer of my strains.
> Still as I touch the lyre, do thou expand
> Thy genuine charms, and guide an artless hand.[77]

Those who abuse retirement or reject it are examined in the course of the poem, and Cowper is critical of Pope's portrayal of the country:

> And Cobham's groves and Windsor's green retreats,
> When Pope describes them, have a thousand sweets,
> He likes the country, but in truth must own,
> Most likes it, when he studies it in town.[78]

However, Cowper depicts the life of retreat with genuine ambivalence—a quality which is absent from the other moral satires—when he qualifies his view of country life toward the end of the poem:

> For solitude, however some may rave,
> Seeming a sanctuary, proves a grave,
> A sepulchre in which the living lie,
> Where all good qualities grow sick and die.
> I praise the Frenchman, his remark was shrew'd—
> How sweet, how passing sweet is solitude!
> But grant me still a friend in my retreat,
> Whom I may whisper, solitude is sweet.[79]

Cowper's ability in this poem to call up the virtues of retirement and then to modify those views with the admission that he does not really want complete solitude displays a distinct movement away from the relentlessly categorical viewpoint of God's good versus man's evil in the other moral satires, despite the "jocular" air of some passages in the other poems. Cowper's newfound ability to merge the worlds of God and man is reflected in the conclusion of *Retirement* where the poet's humility and justified sense of accomplishment in the song he sings are fused:

> Me poetry (or rather notes that aim
> Feebly and vainly at poetic fame)

Employs, shut out from more important views,
Fast by the banks of the slow-winding Ouse,
Content, if thus sequester'd I may raise
A monitor's, though not a poet's praise,
And while I teach an art too little known,
To close life wisely, may not waste my own.[80]

Retirement is the final poem in a series of eight experimental attempts to write a religious poetry, and, during the course of the writing of these poems, Cowper learned that to write a successful narrative poem he would have to rely on his own view of himself and his relationship to God. One of Cowper's principal strengths as a poet derives from his ability to write directly of the struggles and conflicts within his own life. *Retirement* is the only one of the moral satires to do this.

Many of the thirty-four lyrics which conclude the book were composed before *The Progress of Error,* and the voice of the poet in those poems, whether discoursing on a goldfinch, the burning of Lord Mansfield's library, Lord Thurlow, human frailty, or Boadicea, speaks in a direct, straightforward manner. In a very real sense, *Poems* ends where it begins. Cowper's instincts in 1779 were toward the lyrical mode of direct confrontation with natural objects; he began to fear such an approach as he began writing extended narratives, and *Retirement,* his first really successful long poem, returned him to "suitable Vehicle[s] for the most vehement Expression my Thoughts suggest to me."[81] In many ways, Cowper is a lyric poet—at his best in letters and short pieces of verse—who strayed into narrative poetry. *The Task's* finest moments are in brief, intense passages where the poet speaks directly of his finest subject: himself.

5   The reviews of *Poems* were mixed. Edmund Cartwright in the *Monthly Review* felt the collection introduced a poet of remarkable originality.

What Pope has remarked of women, may, by a very applicable parody, be said of the general run of modern poets, *Most poets have no character at all;* being, for the chief part, only echoes of those who have sung before them. For while not only their sentiments and diction are borrowed, but their very modes of thinking, as well as versification, are copied from the said models, discrimination of character must of course be scarcely perceptible. Confining themselves, like pack-horses, to the same beaten track and uniformity of pace, and, like them too, having their bells from the same shop, they go jingling along in uninterrupted unison with each other. This, however, is not the case with Mr. Cowper; he is a poet *sui generis*, for as his notes are peculiar to himself, he classes not with any known species of bards that have preceded him: his style of composition, as well as his modes of thinking, are entirely his own. The ideas, with which his mind seems to have been either endowed by nature, or to have been enriched by learning and reflection, as they lie in no regular order, so are they promiscuously brought forth as they accidentally present themselves.[82]

Although he was to have other sources of inspiration for writing in *The Task* a long narrative poem whose "ideas" appear to "lie in no regular order," Cowper may have found support for his approach in Cartwright's generous review. And he was pleased with the notice in the *Gentleman's Magazine*, which was probably written by John Duncombe: "We have perused, with great pleasure, both the serious and humorous pieces, the Latin and English, of which this collection consists. The author we know to have been a keen sportsman in the classic fields of Westminster, and was a coadjutor of the celebrated Mr. Town in *The Connoisseur*."[83] The reviewer then prints *An Adjudged Report* and a portion of *On the Burning of Lord Mansfield's Library*. Although he does not say as much, this reviewer may be indicating a preference for the short poems. The *London Magazine*, however, was very decided in its choice: "An entertaining collection upon a variety of subjects, temporary, moral, and satirical; composed with sound judgment, good taste, and no small share of wit and humour. *Table talk*, the *Progress of Error, Truth, Hope,* and *Charity,* are laboured pieces of considerable length, but the greatest part of the volume consists of lively sallies, called by the French *jeux d'esprit*. . . ."[84] The *Critical Review* asserted that "whilst the author avoids every thing that is ridiculous or contemptible, he, at the same time, never rises to any thing that we can commend or admire." That reviewer finishes with a lament:

> Towards the end of this volume are some little pieces of a lighter kind, which, after dragging through Mr. Cowper's long moral lectures, afforded us some relief. The fables of the Lily and the Rose, the Nightingale and Glow-worm, the Pine-apple and the Bee, with two or three others, are written with ease

and spirit. It is a pity that our author had not confined himself altogether to this species of poetry, without entering into a system of ethics, for which his genius seems but ill adapted.[85]

Cowper would modify his "genius" in his next volume, but in February 1782 he looked forward stoically to the publication of his book: "I sometimes feel such a perfect indifference with respect to the public opinion of my book, that I am ready to flatter myself no Censure of Reviewers or other Critical readers, would occasion me the smallest disturbance. But not feeling myself constantly possessed of this desirable apathy, I am sometimes apt to suspect that it is not altogether sincere."[86] The notice in the *Monthly Review* satisfied him, but he felt "Rather ashamed of having been at all dejected by the censure of the Critical Reviewers who certainly could not read without prejudice a book replete with opinions and doctrines to which they cannot subscribe."[87] The notices in the *London Magazine* and the *Gentleman's Magazine* "gratified"[88] him.

Perhaps the most important reflection Cowper made on his accomplishment in bringing *Poems* to fruition is contained in the letter he wrote to John Newton on November 7, 1781. There, he obliquely referred to his previous failures in public life:

> Had it [the writing of verse] been suggested to me as a practicable thing in better days, though I should have been glad to have found it so, many hindrances would have conspired to withold me from such an Enterprize. I should not have dared at that time of day to have committed my name to the public, and my reputation to the hazard of their Opinion. But it is otherwise with me now, I am more indifferent about what may touch me in that point than ever I was in my life. The stake that would Then have seemed important, now seems trivial, and it is of little consequence to me who no longer feel myself possessed of what I accounted infinitely more valuable, whether the world's verdict shall pronounce me a Poet, or an empty Pretender to the title.[89]

In *Table Talk*, Cowper also offered a poignant summation of his accomplishment in his first volume of verse:

> The nightingale may claim the topmost bough,
> While the poor grasshopper must chirp below.
> Like him unnotic'd, I, and such as I,
> Spread little wings, and rather skip than fly,
> Perch'd on the meagre produce of the land.[90]

Cowper's moral satires were the chirps of the grasshopper; he would begin to "fly" in 1785 with *The Task,* the poem which liberated his imagination and his ambition. Cowper often viewed himself as verbally as well as spiritually impoverished. He would never achieve spiritual restoration—even intermittently. He did learn, however, that the struggles within himself were proper subjects for poetry. In many of his finest poems and letters, Cowper produced art out of the "meagre produce" of his life. This was the battle he did win: his true subject was his own tormented heart.

As we have seen, Cowper's profession of writer from 1779 onwards was also a carefully selected refuge from depression: "Dejection of Spirits, which I suppose may have prevented many a man from becoming an Author, made me one. I find constant employment necessary, and therefore take care to be constantly employ'd. Manual occupations do not engage the mind sufficiently, as I know by experience, having tried many. But Composition especially of verse, absorbs it wholly."[91] As well, Cowper consciously linked his poetical activity to his mother, who was reputed to be a descendant of John Donne. He said to Mrs. Bodham: "There is in me, I believe, more of the Donne than of the Cowper."[92] He then went on to speak of his "natural temper" as an inheritance of his mother's "Good nature." "Add to all this, that I deal much in poetry as did our venerable ancestor the Dean of St. Paul's, and I think I shall have proved myself a Donne at all points."[93] Although Cowper's melancholia stemmed from the unresolved loss of his mother, his poetry provided him with a link to the Donne side of his ancestry and thus back to her. In his occupation as writer and the consequent release of creative energy, Cowper, to a significant extent, attempted to repair the psychic damage he had endured as a child of six.

In 1782, the "world's verdict" was neither overwhelmingly favorable nor crushingly unfavorable, but Cowper had commenced his career as an author in earnest, and, as he told Thomas Park in 1792, "It is a whim that has served me longest and best, and which will probably be my last."[94] He was perhaps wrong when he felt that in beginning work on the moral satires "he had stumbled upon some Subjects that had never before been poetically treated,"[95] but his experiments in narrative poetry allowed him, as that volume assumed its final form, to find his poetical voice, and he would not forget in the future that he had been praised for his ability to write "lively sallies." He would soon seek fresh worlds, and he would find them in the company of Lady Austen and William Unwin.

7
Lady Austen and William Unwin; Cowper's Letters

1   WHEN HE met her in 1781, Cowper was smitten by Lady Austen's extraordinary charm. Twenty-two years later, as Samuel Greatheed discovered, that power was still intact.

> A sudden explosion of the Countess's Wit needs not to be apprehended. I have only known it set at liberty by some familiarity of acquaintance, except provoked by something bizarre, which you [Hayley] are not capable of. Against her Eyes, I will warrant you safe, at least for the first rencontre; without the last 6 or 7 Years have, contrary to the course of nature, *increased* their influence. She is not, what I have often heard her call herself, the ugliest of all women, but her conversation is certainly more fascinating than her features.[1]

Lady Austen's personality was engaging, but touched with the desire for dominance. However, there was also a softer, more vulnerable side to her, of which Greatheed seems to have been unaware. A woman who claims she is "the ugliest of all women" may wish to appear immune from criticism, but such behavior sometimes masks a deeper sensitivity. This was true of Ann Austen. In her dealings with William Cowper, the enchanter became the enchanted, and she suffered cruelly.

Lady Austen was born Ann Richardson, daughter of John Richardson, an army agent who lived in Middlesex. In 1755, at the age of 19, she married Robert Austen, a man more than twice her age. Austen succeeded to the baronetcy in 1760 upon the death of his brother, and the couple departed for France three years afterward.

Before she left England, Lady Austen hired a waiting maid. The selection of Mistress Jenny would not usually be an event worthy of notice, but Lady Austen's conduct in this seemingly unimportant matter reveals something of her own view of herself: "among those who applied for the situation, was one who professed herself wholly unqualified for it, but earnestly desirous of going with her. When she made her appearance it was greatly against her, as she was far from handsome and very meanly dressed: but she told her story in so interesting a manner, that Lady Austen could not reject her."[2] Lady Austen saw in Mistress Jenny a reflection of herself, and in the mirror that displayed someone "far from handsome" but "interesting" obviously caught a glimpse of her own inner vitality.

It was probably after the signing of the Peace of Paris at the beginning of 1763 that Sir Robert and Lady Austen left for France, where they were to spend most of their married life. Rather than selecting the cosmopolitan haunts of society, they settled in Sancerre, a small town on the Loire, not far from Bourges. A peculiar characteristic of this village was that it sustained a little colony of Jacobite refugees. The beauty of the surroundings conjoined to the prospect of inexpensive living may have encouraged some of the exiles to invite their friends to join them there. Sir Robert was certainly old enough to have friends who had either sympathized or fought with Bonnie Prince Charlie during the rebellion of 1745, though he had been a loyal Captain in the Horseguards at that time. Whether invited or not, Sir Robert, suffering under the weight of a heavily mortgaged estate, no doubt saw the advantage of such a move. He and Lady Austen entertained no qualms about settling with the Jacobites and lived happily with them as neighbors and friends.

After four years in France, the Austens returned to England where Lady Austen began attending Evangelical meetings. She was soon on the road to conversion, and, when she went back to France in 1768, she took with her some Evangelical literature, including the works of the Reverend James Hervey, a favorite of Cowper's in 1766.

In 1771, Sir Robert and Lady Austen were in England again, living with Lady Austen's relatives. While staying with Lady Austen's brother, John Richardson, at Bramshott Place, Sir Robert grew ill and died on February 13, 1772, aged 64. Lady Austen remained with her brother until August of the following year when she decided to go to Bristol; in April 1773, she searched unsuccessfully for a house in the Olney region, where her sister lived. Less than a year later, possibly in June 1774, she went to Sancerre again, where she stayed until France entered the war with America against England in 1778, at which time she left to take up residence at Number 8, Queen Ann Street East in London.

Lady Austen's life in London over the next few years was spent frugally yet comfortably. She had to be careful with her money, as Sir Robert had not left her much in the way of property, portable or otherwise. Although her father had made her residual legatee in his will, legal difficulties had tied up the inheritance—difficulties which had still not been resolved by 1784.

The prospect of Lady Austen's visit to Clifton, in the summer of 1781, awakened a great deal of interest at Olney. No doubt, her sister, Mrs. Jones, the wife of the curate at Clifton,* had told of her pious sister's plan to visit the country while the dog days of midsummer raged in London. Cowper was able to report to John Newton, who had only just returned from visiting Olney, that "Lady Austen waiving all forms has paid us the first Visit, and not content with showing us that proof of her Respect, made handsome Apologies for her Intrusion. We return'd the Visit yesterday. She is a lively agreeable Woman, has seen much of the World and accounts it a great Simpleton as it is, she laughs and makes laugh, and keeps up a Conversation without seeming to labor at it."[3] Within a week, Cowper commemorated an expedition to the Spinney, "without one cross occurrence, or the least weariness of each other."[4] The joy of this new friendship was not simply his; Lady Austen was equally enamored of Cowper and Mrs. Unwin, and by the third week of August 1781, eight years after her first house hunt there, had determined to settle at Olney.

Earlier, Lady Austen had thrown herself into London society. Yet she could turn her back on it and majestically discount the world "a great Simpleton." Cowper was taken with the "degree of compassion in her composition," but from the beginning of the

---

* Lady Austen evidently disliked her brother-in-law, Thomas Jones, formerly a barber, who had become some sort of spiritual apprentice to Newton at Olney. (Jones was earlier expelled from St. Edmund Hall, Oxford, in 1768 for methodistical practices.) Jones was Martha Green's second husband, whom she probably met through the Earl of Peterborough. Lady Austen may have been averse to Jones's lowly origins, or she may have been dismayed by the circumstances of her sister's marriage to him. Newton, who performed the marriage on May 15, 1778, suggests that there was at least the hint of a scandal: "We all went early to Clifton, & after breakfast I terminated the long anxious embarrassment between Mr. —— and Mrs. —— by marriage. They then walked hither [Olney], & set off in 2 Chaises—the new couple to Bristol." (Newton diary, entry for May 15, 1778, MS formerly owned by Miss C. M. Bull.)

relationship he perhaps sensed his ultimate alienation from her: "a person that has seen much of the world and understands it well, has high spirits, a lively fancy and great readiness of Conversation, introduces a sprightliness into such a Scene as this, which if it was peacefull before, is not the worse for being a little enlivened."[5] Cowper eventually found Lady Austen's "sprightliness" irritating, but in the summer of 1781 surface misgivings can be discerned only intermittently. In his rhyming letter to Newton, there seems a sub-conscious wish that the picnic in the Spinney will be put off: ". . . we had better by far, stay where we are."[6] But all in all, Cowper was happy with his new friend. She was a worthy intellectual companion, who forced him to be merry in spite of himself.

When she returned to London in November, Lady Austen had trouble adjusting to London life. She missed Cowper. Without, it would seem, any tangible reality on which to base her aspirations, Lady Austen began to imagine a new and more intimate direction in her relationship with him. Cowper wrote her in December with "glowing heart," speculating on what their friendship might bring:

> This page of Providence, quite new,
> And now just opening to our view,
> Employs our present thoughts and pains,
> To guess, and spell, what it contains.[7]

Nevertheless, Lady Austen remained insecure. She was not in Olney, where Mary Unwin reigned, and Mary was beginning to become jealous of Ann's hold over Cowper. Lady Austen's anxiety made her deeply sensitive to any hint from Cowper, and she undoubtedly in-timated in her letters to him that she would have liked the relation-ship to become one in which marriage was a possibility. Cowper noticed this disturbing trend, just after the beginning of January:

> This sort of intercourse [by letter] had not been long main-tained, before I discovered by some slight intimations of it, that she had conceived displeasure at somewhat I had writ-ten . . . Conscious of none but the most upright and inoffen-sive intentions, I yet apologized for the passage in question, and the flaw was healed again. Our correspondence after this proceeded smoothly for a considerable time, but at length hav-ing had repeated occasion to observe that she expressed a sort of romantic idea of our merits, and built such expectations of felicity upon our friendship, as we were sure that nothing hu-man could possibly answer, I wrote to remind her that we were

mortal, to recommend it to her not to think more highly of us than the subject would warrant, and intimating that when we embellish a creature with colors taken from our own fancy, and so adorned, admire and praise it beyond its real merits, we make it an Idol, and have nothing to expect in the end but that it will deceive our hopes, and that we shall derive nothing from it but a painful conviction of our error.[8]

Lady Austen's overtures must have been strong to merit such a reprimand. She took "mortal Offence"[9] at Cowper's retreat from her advances. She felt that she had opened her heart only to have it betrayed. Her immediate reaction was of anger, and she wrote him a letter which he felt he "could by no means reply to."[10] Cowper told Unwin on March 7, 1782, that Lady Austen's outrage was "absolutely incompatible with the pleasures of real friendship. She is exceedingly sensible, has great quickness of parts, and an uncommon fluency of expression, but her vivacity was sometimes Too much for us; occasionally perhaps it might refresh and revive us, but it more frequently exhausted us, neither your Mother nor I being in that respect at all a match for her."[11] When Cowper learned that Lady Austen was to return to Buckinghamshire in the summer of 1782, he characterized her as a representative of jaded London society about to invade his retirement in order to entice him to "cast off the simplicity of our plain and artless demeanour."[12]

Yet it would seem that both Cowper and Lady Austen hoped for a renewal of the friendship. Lady Austen made various signs that she was willing to open negotiations not much more than a month after the break, when she sent Cowper three pairs of worked ruffles, which she had earlier promised him. When Unwin visited Lady Austen, possibly in late February, she spoke in loving terms of Cowper and Mrs. Unwin, hinting perhaps that Cowper should take the first step toward a reconciliation. Cowper stood firm. He made it clear that the ruffles were not to be considered a peace offering, but he sent her a copy of *Poems* because he likewise had promised a gift before the fracas had erupted. In spite of the rigidity he expressed in his letter to Unwin of March 7, 1782,[13] he made it clear that the lady should make the first move: "But after all, it does not entirely depend upon us, whether our former Intimacy shall take place again or not. . . . I suspect a little by her sending the ruffles, and by the terms in which she spoke of us to you, that some overtures on her part are to be looked for."[14] Cowper only then intimated that he had perhaps been less than generous in his description of

Lady Austen, whom Unwin had consequently seen at a "disadvantage." Finally, Lady Austen wrote to Cowper at the beginning of July and visited with him and Mrs. Unwin soon afterwards. She "seized the first opportunity," he told Unwin, "to embrace your mother with tears of the tenderest affection, and I, of course, am satisfied. We were all a little awkward at first, but now are as easy as ever."[15] Two weeks later, Lady Austen made a brief trip to London to dispose of the remainder of the lease on her London house. A fortnight later, she was back in Clifton to await the day of her move to the Olney Vicarage.

August was wet and cold. Heavy rains deluged the road between Clifton and Olney, rendering it impassable. As soon as the waters became fordable, Lady Austen visited Orchard Side. Cowper confided in Unwin: "Lady Austen's behaviour to us ever since her return to Clifton has been such as to engage our affections to her more than ever."[16] But Lady Austen's retirement was not to be spent so pleasantly. On Thursday, August 23, having come to Olney to attend the Reverend Scott's evening lecture, she suffered an attack of "bilious Cholic" and was brought to Orchard Side, where she was put to bed. Although she was much better the next day, she was seized on Saturday evening by a "Hysteric fit," which, as Cowper noted, had been "accompanied with most of the symptoms of the most violent fits of that sort I have ever seen."[17] The spell passed within an hour, and she was soon asleep. Sunday was spent enjoyably, and Lady Austen felt well enough to return to Clifton on Monday.

Lady Austen had virtually been refused by Cowper the previous January, and it must have seemed to her then that he did not care if the relationship was renewed. She remained resentful, but, at the same time, she wanted her love to be returned. The "bilious Cholic" may have been induced by her wish to be closer to Cowper and to gain his attention, and the fit of hysterics by horror at her own weakness in being drawn helplessly into an impossible situation.

One night, soon after her return to Clifton, a band of thieves attempted to enter the Jones residence while the curate was in London. The ladies of the house, "worn out with continual watching and repeated alarms, were at last prevailed upon to take refuge"[18] at Orchard Side. When Mr. Jones returned from London, he took Mrs. Jones and her daughter with him back to Clifton, but Lady Austen stayed on, her "Spirits having been too much disturbed to be capable of repose in a place where she had been so much terrified."[19] She did not return to Clifton but waited for the Vicarage to be ready. Again, there can be discerned in this incident Lady Austen's obsessional wish to be with Cowper.

Lady Austen moved into the Vicarage in early October. From this time until May 1784, Cowper, Mary Unwin, and Lady Austen spent every day but Sunday together. Cowper rose early and breakfasted until ten o'clock. He would then compose or write letters until his morning visit to Lady Austen at eleven. After this he would walk, sometimes accompanied by one or other of the ladies until it was time for the midday meal which was taken alternately at the Vicarage and Orchard Side. The three did not part company until ten or eleven at night. Cowper spent his afternoons by the fireside winding thread and his evenings listening to Lady Austen at the harpsichord, while he and Mrs. Unwin engaged in games of battledore and shuttlecock. When the music and games had been put aside, he would read aloud to his small audience.

Equilibrium had been regained. Lady Austen was the muse of *John Gilpin* and *The Task,* and yet, perhaps unaware, Cowper began to view her far differently than he could any sister.

> The star that beams on Anna's breast
>   Conceals her William's hair,
> 'Twas lately sever'd from the rest
>   To be promoted there.
> The heart that beats beneath that star
>   Is William's, well I know;
> A nobler prize and richer far
>   Than India could bestow.[20]

Cowper seemed to have enjoyed the "constant Engagement" which his life had become through Lady Austen, but in commenting on his task of winding thread, he says: "—thus did Hercules, and thus probably did Samson."[21] Despite the air of joviality here, Cowper may well be expressing the fear that a sexual attachment might, as in the instances of Hercules or Samson, subject him to the destructive powers of a woman. Much earlier, Thea had become a Delilah whose powers he feared, and Ann Austen's urbanity must have reminded him of the Theadora Cowper with whom he had once been dangerously entranced.

In February 1783, Cowper told Newton that he was "well in body but with a mind that would wear out a frame of adamant."[22] His condition worsened at the beginning of September when he developed a fever which seems to have aggravated his feelings of dejection. By the end of the month, the fever had disappeared and with it the more overburdening aspects of despair. Inspired by his new-found vigor and by Lady Austen, he began *The Task* the following month. All went well until February 1784 when Cowper simply could not work. He had begun to resent Lady Austen's demands on his time, and he told Newton that he did not have many opportunities to compose, "Sunday being the only day in the week which we spend alone."[23] As he later told Lady Hesketh, "sometimes I had not opportunity to write more than 3 lines at a Sitting."[24] Lady Austen, sensing Cowper's reluctance to make a commitment to her, demanded more of his time. In venting her chagrin, she became obdurate and hostile toward Mary Unwin: "she entertained no small contempt and aversion to her; and frequently indulged her unequalled turn for satire at Mrs. U——'s expense, sometimes in her company, but oftener in Mr. C——'s. . . . He has acknowledged to me [Samuel Greatheed] that Lady A——'s flow of spirits, and talent of ridicule, rendered their intercourse frequently uneasy, and always of precarious comfort or duration."[25] By the beginning of 1784, Cowper's retirement was a troubled one, where it had become virtually impossible for him to write poetry. In March, he withheld some of his time from the ladies. Finally, in May, Lady Austen left Olney for Bath. She went, Cowper claimed, because of "ill-health," but she may well have gone away in order to force him to make a decision about the future. However, it was really Cowper who withdrew from Lady Austen in 1783—just as he had retreated from marriage to Thea in 1763 and to Mary Unwin in 1773.

Letters between the two were maintained for a time, but the friendship had been broken completely by July 12, as a letter to William Unwin of that date reveals:

> You are going to Bristol. A Lady, not long since our very near neighbour, is probably there. She *was* there very lately. If you should chance to fall into her company, remember if you please that we found the connexion on some accounts an inconvenient one; that we do not wish to renew it, and conduct yourself accordingly. A character with which we spend all our time should be made on purpose for us. Too much or too little of any single ingredient, spoils all. In the instance in question, the dissimilitude was too great not to be felt continually, and consequently made our intercourse unpleasant. We have reason however to believe that she has given up all thoughts of a Return to Olney.[26]

The circumstances here are much the same as they were in 1781. The separation had again been effected through a letter; there was the same claim of incompatibility, though this time it seems to be based on "intercourse unpleasant"; Unwin was again placed in the thankless role of intermediary.

Lady Austen admitted to Hayley that she had sent Cowper a letter in which she claimed she was willing to devote her life and fortune to him.[27] Cowper undoubtedly responded in 1784 with a reproof—against indecorous advances—similar to the one he had delivered three years earlier. He did not seem to feel that his conduct had been in any way flirtatious. In effect, Lady Austen forced his hand twice and lost on both occasions. She realized the hopelessness of the situation, and she did not approach Cowper again. Lady Austen returned to Clifton at the end of 1785 where she remained until 1790. Her air of defiance allowed her to return to the scene of her failed romance. In 1790, Lady Austen settled in London, where she ultimately married Count Claude Tardiff du Granger, a French nobleman and poet, on July 16, 1796.

There can be little doubt that Mary Unwin, in her quiet but powerful way, played some role in both breaches with Lady Austen, but exactly what her part was in these instances is difficult to determine. Greatheed suggests that she had become "apprehensive . . . that some ideas were formed of a permanent union between her two companions" and that "at her request Mr. C. drop'd all Correspondence with Lady A—— upon her removal."[28] If Mrs. Unwin had been fearful of Lady Austen's ability to entice Cowper away from her and acted decisively, she was to meet the following year a similar but much stronger adversary in Lady Hesketh.

2   In 1781, Lady Austen brought about a vital change in Cowper's life. Although Evangelical, she was from the great Babylon of London, and Cowper responded eagerly to his new muse and her tidings of the outside world. Earlier, during the last stages in the composition of *Poems,* he had moved away from the moral rigors of most of the poems in that collection. When he had begun work on his first volume, Cowper excluded Unwin from knowledge of the proceedings and had told him of the book only when it was at the press. As he completed work on *Poems,* he had become alienated from Newton, and Joseph Johnson's desire to cancel the preface further shook his confidence in him.

The person to whom Cowper turned for assistance in seeing *The Task* through the press was, like Newton, an ordained priest of the Evangelical persuasion, and he was in his religious and moral up-bringing very much his mother's son. Despite this, Unwin was a considerably more worldly person than his mother or John Newton, and Cowper's movement toward him and Lady Austen bespeaks a considerable expansion at that time in his view of himself as a man and as a writer. In his life of retreat, Cowper began searching out some of the remnants he had left behind when he had departed from London in 1763, and in these two friendships he returned in-directly, but nevertheless decisively, to the world he had abandoned.

During the domestic turmoil which had ensued after he had in-troduced Cowper into his family's household in 1765, William Un-win had doubtless sided with Cowper against his own father, and he sought to be a worthy son to the man who became his adopted parent. From the outset of his friendship with Unwin, Cowper was impressed by his candor: "To my inexpressible joy I found him one whose notions of religion were spiritual and lively. . . . We opened our hearts to each other at the first interview." It was William Un-win who had "engaged" Cowper in conversation that day—even though he had been told that Cowper "rather declined society than sought it." As Cowper said, Unwin had "nothing in his heart that [made] it necessary for him to keep it barred and bolted."[29] Wil-liam Wilberforce, the abolitionist, expressed similar feelings when he remarked that his heart opened "involuntarily"[30] to Unwin's charm.

At Cambridge, Unwin had formed so many important connec-tions that, as early as 1769, he could tell Newton: "I have so many old acquaintances and Engagements of one sort or other when I am in town [London] that I seldom make new ones unless acciden-tally."[31] His friends included, besides Wilberforce, Robert Smith the banker, and Henry Thornton, John's son. All these men were Evangelical reformers dedicated to the abolition of slavery. How-ever, largely because of the strong and advanced convictions he held on penal, social, and political reform, Unwin experienced from the outset at Stock, Essex, in 1769 great difficulty in dealing with parishioners. The young priest who had gained a substantial reputation at Comberton with his sermons reflected somberly at the beginning of his stay in Essex:

My parishioners by report are extremely ignorant—to such a de-gree that I shall find it expedient to begin from the very foundations. . . . To me it indeed appears that the common people of the serious sort are generally very shallow in Knowledge of a religious kind for want of having the first principles of things more largely laid before them. . . . I am sometimes fearful of not being able to instruct them in any thing—but I hope the Almighty will be my Helper & his Holy Spirit the Director of all my purposes![32]

Unfortunately, although Unwin rightly saw himself as a person "intently" dedicated to divine truth whose behavior was accompanied by becoming "modesty,"[33] his demeanor was often forbidding. His progressive views and haughty behavior certainly proved a disastrous combination at Stock, leading to constant bickering with his congregation. For some reason, the charm that had captivated Cowper and Wilberforce was completely absent in the Rector's dealings with his truculent flock.

Raising money was always particularly troublesome for Unwin, and in the various financial difficulties which plagued him—obviously a frequent theme in his now-lost correspondence with Cowper—a true reflection of how the parish viewed its Rector can be discerned. In September 1779, Cowper jocularly advised his young friend to become a glazier that he might save money and make himself popular. In December, at tithing time, Unwin was terrified that he would not be able to extract money from his congregation. Cowper reassured him, "Your Delicacy makes you groan under that which other Men never Feel, or Feel but Slightly."[34] In 1780, Cowper treated the over-sensitive young man's problems facetiously:

> This priest he merry is and blithe
>   Three Quarters of the Year,
> But oh it cuts him like a Scythe
>   When Tything Time draws near.[35]

However, Cowper urged Unwin the following year to make a stand in the face of dilapidations and threatened lawsuits: "It is high time you should consult your own peace of mind, and not suffer the insatiable Demands and unreasonable Expectations of other men, to be a Source of unhappiness to yourself. You have lived long enough in the world to know that it swarms with people who are always ready to take advantage of the Generosity of such men as yourself."[36]

Cowper, who often experienced considerable difficulty in making his own demands known, became insistent in his advice to Unwin:

"it is weakness to be the willing Dupe of Artifice."[37] He sensed Unwin's need of constant reassurance and provided it: "I know no better Shield to guard you . . . than what you are already furnished with, a clear and an unoffended Conscience."[38] As well, Cowper was always ready to advise Unwin on such diverse matters as young John Unwin's education or the composition of poetry. Despite the demands that Unwin made upon him, Cowper was at ease with him, and he could, for example, be tartly frank with him about the vocation of poet: "I have no more Right to the Name of a Poet, than a Maker of Mousetraps has to That of an Engineer. . . . Such a Talent in Verse as mine, is like a Child's Rattle, very entertaining to the Trifler that uses it, and very disagreeable to all beside."[39] Only in letters to Unwin could Cowper speak in whimsical self-abnegation of his early "Trifles." Indeed, as Cowper's self-confidence in his verse increased markedly during the latter stages of the preparation of *Poems,* he was able to deepen this relationship and ultimately appoint Unwin his "Authorship's go-between with Johnson."

Unwin likely reminded Cowper of his brother, who had a similar career at Cambridge, and he must have seen himself at times as the secure older brother guiding the younger one. He offered Unwin advice which he himself, as a younger man, would have liked to have received and acted upon. Despite his difficulties, Unwin made his way in a world from which Cowper had departed, and his words of counsel to Unwin are often admonitions to himself about assertiveness and aggressiveness which were never taken.

For his part, Unwin played the role of the dutiful son or younger brother, and he gladly acted as Cowper's envoy to Ashley Cowper, Maria Cowper, Lady Austen, and, later, Lady Hesketh, who aptly characterized him as "that very amiable Sensible Ingenious Learned Willy."[40] He sent books to his mentor at Olney, thus helping him to become more and more aware of the London literary world of the 1780s. Cowper's initial impulse toward verse in 1779 began with Unwin, and his heightened perception of himself is reflected in his ability to offer advice and consolation to Unwin, who was the first of a series of young men (Samuel Rose, John Johnson, Thomas Lawrence, James Hurdis) who were devoted to Cowper and to whom he acted in a beneficent, paternal—sometimes fraternal—way. These men admired Cowper's genius, and he was remarkably unconstrained in his dealings with them. The reserve that Cowper sometimes showed to women was absent in these friendships. His generosity was unleashed, and his youthful vivacity was rekindled.

The friendship with Unwin remained constant during all the

difficulties with Lady Austen; it was only to falter from October 1785 when Cowper, obsessed with Lady Hesketh, became perfunctory in his letters to Unwin.* Cowper's fear of domination ultimately unbalanced his relationship with Lady Austen, but in exercising his controlling hand with Unwin he displayed restraint and selflessness.

3   Cowper's impulses as a poet in 1779 were of the "Lyric kind," and William Unwin was the chief recipient of the delicious trifles which are the first evidence of Cowper's emergence as a poet in search of public approbation. In a similar way, Cowper from 1778 to 1780 perfected in his correspondence with his younger friend the artful simplicity, candor, and spontaneity which are the hallmarks of his finest letters.

Much earlier, Cowper had written jubilant, sprightly missives to Walter Bagot, Chase Price, and John Duncombe. On January 11, 1759, he facetiously told John Duncombe that he would be disappointed to discover that his friend had "Altered" his "Stile": "you never could write or Speak good English in your Life, which is so true, that it were vain to denie it, but your Language has always been more Entertaining than the best English I ever met with. I shall be sorry to receive a Letter from you in more Elegant Phrase than usual."[41] As we have seen, Cowper's letters from 1763 to 1778 are, unfortunately, replete with Evangelical phraseology. He complained to his aunt, Mrs. Madan, on January 15, 1768, that his barren spiritual state left him nothing to write about:

> I put off writing to you from day to day in hopes, that I shall find a subject in my own experience that may make it worth your while to hear from me. . . . But blessed be the Lord. Our anchor of hope is fastened on good ground, not in our own righteousness, but in that of Jesus: and every view of our own unworthiness is sanctified to us, and becomes a solid blessing if it drives us closer to our only refuge. Since I wrote the above, I have been taking a walk, and from my going out, to my coming in, I have been mourning over (I am afraid I ought to say

---

* Cowper had a tendency to "play favourites" in his friendships, and there is usually a principal correspondent (John Newton from 1779 to 1781, William Unwin from 1781 to 1785, Lady Hesketh from 1785 to 1791, William Hayley from 1792 to 1793) who is made privy to thoughts and feelings from which others are excluded.

repining at) my great insensibility. I began with these reflections soon after I rose this morning, and my attempt to write
to you has furnished me with additional evidences of it. I pro-
fess myself a servant of God, I am writing to a servant of God,
and about the things of God, and yet can hardly get forward so
as to fill my paper.[42]

From 1778, Cowper was eager to "fill his paper," and he returned
to the values which can be seen in his letters from 1750 to 1763. It
had been a long, fifteen-year hiatus in the composition of beautiful
letters, and all of Cowper's best ones display a propensity to speak
freely. However, Cowper was usually diffident and awkward in conversation. In his letters, he talked unaffectedly of the people, places,
and events which shaped his life.

Nevertheless, Cowper was deeply aware of the process of writing
letters. He made this reflection in April 1783: "When one has a
Letter to write there is nothing more usefull than to make a Beginning. In the first place, because unless it be begun, there is no
good reason to hope that it will ever be ended."[43] In a similar,
offhand vein, he wrote William Unwin on February 27, 1780: "As
you are pleased to Desire my Letters, I am the more pleased with
Writing them. Though at the same time I must needs testify my
Surprize that you should think them worth receiving, as I seldom
send one that I think favorably of myself."[44] In a self-ironical aside,
he went on: ". . . though Men of ordinary Talents may be highly
satisfied with their own Productions, Men of true Genius never
are."[45] Although he could write humorously and with irony of his
own letters, Cowper could be a severe judge of the talents of others
in the same enterprise. He was particularly hostile to Pope, a "disgusting" letter writer, "who seems to have thought that unless a
Sentence was well turned, and every Period pointed with some Conceit, it was not worth the Carriage. Accordingly he is to me, except
in very few Instances, the most disagreeable Maker of Epistles that
ever I met with."[46] For Cowper, the standard of poetry was obviously not the standard of letter writing.

What, then, was for Cowper agreeable letter writing? He provides an answer of sorts in a letter to Unwin of February 27, 1780:
"Alas! what can I do with my Wit? I have not enough to do great
things with. . . . I must do with it as I do with my Linnet, I keep
him for the most part in a Cage, but now & then set open the Door
that he may whisk about the Room a little, & then shut him up
again."[47] If one cultivates a "Whisking Wit," one must be con-

cerned with those thoughts that come "uppermost."[48] As he averred to Lady Hesketh, "method . . . is never more out of its place than in a letter."[49] He also claimed "A Letter is Written, as a Conversation is maintained, or a Journey perform'd, not by preconcerted, or premeditated Means, by a new Contrivance, or an Invention never heard of before, but merely by maintaining a Progress, and resolving as a Postillion does, having once Set out, never to Stop 'till we reach the appointed End. If a Man may Talk without thinking, why may he not Write upon the same Terms?"[50] He later said it was important not to write without thinking "but always without premeditation."[51] As a consequence of this, thoughts that passed through his head when he was not writing became the subject of my letters. He also admitted that a "Dearth of Materials is very apt to betray one into a Trifling Strain, in spite of all one's Endeavours to be Serious."[52]

Nevertheless, there is more "method" in Cowper's letters than he wishes to acknowledge. For example, he habitually begins a letter with a humorous or incidental observation, moves to his proper subject in the second paragraph, and then returns to the ephemeral in a subsequent paragraph. Of course, many letter writers consciously or unconsciously do the same (the etiquette of letters is that of polite conversation). Another method—one Cowper is largely unaware of—is his tailoring of his letters to his recipient's requirements and personality. There are duty letters to Joe Hill and Margaret King; pious missives to John and Mary Newton, Maria Cowper, and Judith Madan; and vibrant, lively letters to William Unwin and Harriot Hesketh. Again, all letter writers tend to frame their letters according to the expectations of the recipient.

This obvious truth can be pushed a little further to explain the emergence of Cowper as a great letter writer: his finest ones—as a youth and as a middle-aged man—are those in which he attempts to match the vitality of a cosmopolitan recipient's world. Montaigne said: "Speech belongs half to the speaker, half to the listener."[53] This observation is particularly true of letters, and in the most vivacious of them—to use Montaigne's tennis metaphor[54]—Cowper serves his best to those who are from the world he left as a young man. There is a sense of competition at work: Cowper has to summon up his best in order to capture the attention and favor of his elegant, learned friends. From 1778, he wanted to regain his past, and he first regained it in the letters—and lyrics—to William Unwin. In so doing, he opened the door to his "Whisking Wit."

8
The Task (1785)

1   COWPER GAVE his muse a slight rest after the publication of *Poems* in March 1782, but later that year he embarked on two projects. In July 1782, William Bull handed Cowper a copy of the verse of Jeanne Marie Bouvier de la Motte Guyon, the French mystic, and Cowper readily agreed to Bull's suggestion that he translate some of the poems into English. On an October evening in the same year, Lady Austen told Cowper the story of John Gilpin, and Cowper, according to John Johnson, "versified [it] in bed, and presented [it] to her next morning in the shape of a ballad."[1] The gulf between the two subjects is not as vast as first appears. In his rendition of the Frenchwoman's Quietistic writings, Cowper chooses to ignore the more sensational aspects of the soul's utter dependency upon God, and *John Gilpin,* in which the hero never does achieve a holiday, has a somber and tragic air despite its comic tone. Cowper frequently blends the homorous and the tragic in his work, or he attempts to modify rigid and seemingly intransigent views.

Cowper had reservations about Madame Guyon from the beginning of the enterprise, and, as he told Unwin, he was not "her passionate admirer."[2] Nevertheless, Cowper found the routine of translating enjoyable, and by September he had become more hospitable to the Frenchwoman: "the strain of simple and unaffected Piety in the original, is sweet beyond expression. She sings like an Angel, and for that very reason has found but few Admirers."[3] By October 27, the translation was finished but not completely transcribed. John Gilpin had entered Cowper's thoughts at about this time, and he did not refer again to his efforts as a translator until he wrote to Bull in August 1783: "I have made fair copies of all the pieces I have produced upon this last occasion, and will put them into your hands when we meet."[4] Cowper likely presented Bull with some translated poems in the autumn of 1782 and with another batch the following summer. Unwin was hostile to Madame Guyon's fatalistic view of the soul's relationship to God, and on September 7, 1783, Cowper felt called upon to defend her. However, he was hesitant: he obviously thought Madame Guyon's intimacy with God was too familiar and fulsome, and yet he found elements of religious zeal which appealed to him. He frequently felt that God had cast him aside, whereas Madame Guyon was too self-assured about her union with the divine:

> There is a mixture of Evil in every thing we do, indulgence encourages us to encroach, and while we exercise the rights of Children, we become Childish. Here I think is the point in which my Authoress failed, and here it is that I have particularly guarded my translation. Not afraid of representing her as dealing with God familiarly, but foolishly, irreverently and without due attention to his Majesty, of which she is sometimes guilty. A wonderfull fault for such a woman to fall into, who spent her life in the contemplation of his glory, who seems to have been always impressed with a sense of it, and sometimes quite absorbed in the views she had of it.[5]

Although Cowper felt awe in the presence of a person who could speak with such supreme self-assurance of the continual presence of divine benignity, there is no reason to disbelieve Bull's disclaimer (in the preface which appeared when the translations were published in 1801): "To infer that the peculiarities of Madame Guion's theological sentiments, were adopted either by Mr. C. or by the Editor, would be almost as absurd as to suppose the inimitable Translator of Homer to have been a pagan."[6] Bull undoubtedly captured Cowper's sentiments perfectly in the next sentence: "He reverenced her piety, admired her genius, and judged that several of her poems would be read with pleasure and edification by serious and candid persons."[7]

The insistence in Madame Guyon on the necessity of finite man to surrender himself voluntarily to divine omnipotence—

> Yield to the Lord, with simple heart,
> All that thou hast, and all thou art;
> Renounce all strength but strength divine,
> And peace shall be for ever thine:—
> Behold the path which I have trod,
> My path, 'till I go home to God.[8]

—receives an antipodal treatment in *John Gilpin* where man is shown to be helpless in the face of nature. Madame Guyon celebrated the happy circumstance in which man can abandon himself to supernatural forces, whereas John Gilpin is the victim of those forces. God's omnipotence in both poems remains constant, but that force can be seen as kindly and gentle or overweening and malicious. Gilpin is snatched away by the horse ("That trot became a gallop soon, / In spite of curb and rein"),[9] who removes him from the company of his wife and the celebration of their anniversary. Gilpin's efforts to curb the horse prove futile, and he cannot dismount until the horse has returned him to where the ride began. The circularity of the poem, the manner in which Gilpin becomes the victim of the "snorting beast,"[10] and the depiction of the ruined holiday give an ominous mood to what is in tone an amusing ballad. Toward the end of the poem, Mrs. Gilpin hands a youth half a crown to stop the horse:

> The youth did ride, and soon did meet
>   John coming back amain;
> Whom in a trice he tried to stop,
>   By catching at his rein;
>
> But, not performing what he meant,
>   And gladly would have done,
> The frighted steed he frighted more,
>   And made him faster run.[11]

Despite kindly intentions, Mrs. Gilpin and the youth make things more difficult for Gilpin, and this is an emblematical representation of Cowper's deepest fears about the futility of human compassion when compared to the scorn of God.

In the fall of 1782, Cowper was still a full year away from beginning work on *The Task*, but his "Whisking Wit" had gone in two directions and come back successful. The Guyon translations are simple, elegant renditions from the French, and the melancholy which lies behind *John Gilpin* discreetly suggested. The sophistication which emerged in *Retirement* had been nurtured.

2   As work on *Poems* reached its conclusion in November 1781, Cowper quite accurately predicted another volume of verse: "A French Author I was reading last night—says, he that has written, will write again. If the Critics do not set their foot upon the first

Egg that I have laid, and crush it, I shall probably verify his observation."[12] In the same letter, Cowper makes a boast which explains some of the shortcomings in the first volume:

> I reckon it among my principal advantages as a composer of verses, that I have not read an English poet these thirteen years, and but One these twenty years. Imitation even of the best models is my Aversion. It is servile and mechanical, a trick that has enabled many to usurp the name of Author, who could not have written at all, if they had not written upon the pattern of some body indeed original. But when the Ear and the taste have been much accustomed to the manner of others, it is almost impossible to avoid it, and we imitate in spite of ourselves, just in proportion as we admire.[13]

Cowper's "Aversion" to reading the work of other English poets in 1781 was part of his withdrawal from the world.

During the late 1770s and early 1780s, the travels of Captain Cook had held Cowper's absorbed attention, and even in 1784 he looked forward to "taking my last trip with a voyager whose memory I respect so much."[14] Like many Englishmen of his time, he was fascinated with the hazardous journeys and exotic landscapes which Cook and his colleagues had visited, and his imagination, which was always stimulated by the sea, was receptive to Cook's accounts. In 1782, however, Cowper began to look to other writers for enjoyment and emulation.

Cowper had always retained his literary interests during the 1760s and 1770s, but such predilections had been for him rather suspect during the height of his Evangelical fervor. On the advent of his appearance in print, a newly awakened, sometimes virulent, critical sensibility began to appear. Robert Lowth's verses were "so good that had I been present when he spoke them, I should have trembled for the *Boy,* lest the *Man* should disappoint the hopes such early genius had given birth to."[15] The Earl of Clarendon's history was held up next to Catharine Macaulay's: "see Charles's face drawn by Clarendon and it is an handsome Pourtrait; see it more justly exhibited by Mrs. McAulay, and it is deformed to a degree that shocks us."[16] Joseph Milner's *Gibbon's Account of Christianity Considered, with Some Strictures on Hume's Dialogues on Natural Religion* gave Cowper "great pleasure as a sensible, just and temperate piece of argument. I only regret that having it in his power to be perfectly correct in his expression, he should suffer any inaccuracies to escape him."[17] The notice of Thomas Newton's

Works in the February and March 1783 issues of the *Monthly Review* called up especially hostile sentiments on contemporary writing as he saw himself as a "very supercilious Reader of most modern writers. Either I dislike the subject, or the manner of treating it, the stile is affected, or the matter is disgusting."[18] William Robertson and Edward Gibbon, he felt, were affected. "In every line of theirs, I see nothing else. They disgust me always—Robertson with his pomp and his Strut, and Gibbons with his finical and French manner."[19] Henry Swinburne's *Travels in the Two Sicilies* proved to be a disappointment: "I found the Author, for so well informed a man, the dullest writer I remember to have encounter'd."[20] Hugh Blair was damned: "But Oh the sterility of that man's fancy, if indeed he has any such faculty belonging to him."[21] He was suspicious of David Hume: "He is the Pope of thousands as blind and as presumptuous as himself. God certainly infatuates those who will not see."[22] The self-esteem Cowper had gained with the publication of *Poems* can be discerned in these reflections on contemporary writers, and as his confidence and critical strictures expanded, he became less resistant to the influence of other writers.

In May 1779 when Cowper's "Productions of the Lyric kind" had begun, his first effort had been a translation of Prior's ode, *The Merchant, to Conceal his Treasure*, into Latin. In January 1782, when he was anxiously awaiting the release of his own volume, he was deeply angry at Samuel Johnson's treatment of Prior:

> [Johnson] must endeavour to convince the world, that their favourite authors have more faults than they are aware of, and such as they have never suspected. Having marked out a writer universally esteemed, whom he finds it for that very reason, convenient to depreciate and traduce, he will overlook some of his beauties, he will faintly praise others, and in such a manner as to make thousands, more modest though quite as judicious as himself, question whether they are beauties at all. Can there be a stronger illustration of all that I have said, than the severity of Johnson's remarks upon Prior, I might have said the injustice?[23]

Cowper was scornful of Johnson's disdain for Prior's "mythological" love verses and his dismissal of *Henry and Emma* as a "dull and tedious dialogue, which excites neither esteem for the man nor tenderness for the woman."[24] On two scores, however, Cowper was especially upset: he claimed that Johnson had ignored *Solomon on the Vanity of Human Wishes* (Johnson did treat the poem), and he was irritated with what he took to be Johnson's attack on Prior's "familiar stile," which "of all stiles [is] the most difficult to succeed in. To make verse speak the language of prose, without being prosaic, to marshall the words of it in such an order, as they might naturally take in falling from the lips of an extemporary speaker, yet without meanness; harmoniously, elegantly, and without seeming to displace a syllable for the sake of the rhyme, is one of the most arduous tasks a poet can undertake."[25] Although Cowper goes on to speak of Prior's versification as "a very uninteresting subject," he knew full well that in *Poems* he had attempted to "make verse speak the language of prose, without being prosaic." He had unconsciously imitated Prior, and he feared the consequences. He was concerned about *Solomon* because the form and subject matter of that poem are similar to many passages in the moral satires. Prior's Solomon in his commentaries on Knowledge (book 1), Pleasure (book 2), and Power (book 3) discourses at length on the vanity of human wishes as practiced in the world, and he offers his reflections in a prophetic voice which "upon the whole, resolves to submit [its] Enquiries and Anxieties to the Will of [the] Creator."[26] Cowper obviously had a great deal of admiration for Prior, but there was the unsettling fear that what Johnson disliked about Prior would be his grounds for dismissing the as-yet-unpublished *Poems*.*

If Prior was the poet from earlier in the century whom Cowper attempted to emulate and whose literary career served in many ways as a model for his own, James Beattie was the contemporary writer with whom he had the most in common. At the time he was translating Madame Guyon and before writing *Gilpin*, Cowper asked Unwin to send him Beattie's latest volume (probably the fourth edition of *Poems on Several Occasions*):

> Doctor Beattie's is a respectable character. I account him a man of sense, a Philosopher, a Scholar, a person of distinguished Genius, and a good Writer. I believe him too, though with less spiritual light than is generally supposed requisite, a Christian. With a profound Reverence for the Scripture, with great zeal and ability to inforce the belief of it, both which he exerts with the candor and good-manners of a Gentleman, he seems well entitled to that allowance, and to deny it him, would impeach one's own right to the appellation.[27]

* Johnson did not review *Poems*. See *Letters* 2, 520 and n. 1 (Cowper to Newton, September 18, 1781).

When he was halfway through the writing of *The Task* in March 1784, Cowper took up *Dissertations Moral and Critical,* which had appeared the previous year. Before he read the book, Cowper was sure he would be pleased, and he mentioned that the extracts from *The Minstrel* which he had seen earlier had intrigued him. A fortnight later, Cowper was ecstatic about *Dissertations:*

> The only Author I have seen whose critical and philosophical researches are diversified and embellished by a poetical imagination, that makes even the driest subject and the leanest, a feast for an Epicure in books. He is so much at his ease too, that his own character appears in every page, and, which is very rare, we see not only the writer but the man. And that man so gentle, so well-temper'd, so happy in his religion, and so humane in his philosophy, that it is necessary to love him if one has the least sense of what is lovely.[28]

Cowper insisted that Unwin obtain a copy of *The Minstrel* for him, and he was delighted with it. "Beattie is become my favorite Author of all the moderns. He is so amiable I long to know him."[29]

An enormously popular poem, *The Minstrel* was first published in 1771 (book 1) and 1774 (book 2; two-book edition, 1775). The narrator relates the gradually unfolding poetic consciousness of another bard, Edwin. "The design was, to trace the progress of a Poetical Genius, born in a rude age, from the first dawning of fancy and reason, till that period at which he may be supposed capable of appearing in the world as A MINSTREL. . . ."[30] The "visionary boy" who is entranced by the sublimity of the landscapes evoked in book 1 is instructed by a hermit in book 2, who warns him against an undue emphasis on "Fancy." Edwin follows this advice, and he embraces "Science" or "Philosophy" ("The influence of the Philosophick Spirit, in humanizing the mind, and preparing it for intellectual exertion and delicate pleasure . . .").[31] Edwin, as the poem concludes, has been "taught to modulate the artful strain" and he has learned a via media between "Fancy" and "Philosophy."[32] Cowper would have been impressed with the depiction of a conflict which is so central to his own verse, but he would have been especially moved by the hermit's commendation of some aspects of man in society:

> Ah, what avails it to have traced the springs,
> That whirl of empire the stupendous wheel!
> Ah, what have I to do with conquering kings,

Hands drench'd in blood, and breasts begirt with steel!
To those, whom Nature taught to think and feel,
Heroes, alas! are things of small concern.[33]

The lesson that Edwin learns, that the imagination must be tempered by adhering to the exterior discipline of nature, was one that
Keats in *The Fall of Hyperion* and Byron in *Childe Harold*—as
well as Cowper—imbibed from *The Minstrel*.

Cowper would have found the sentiments in Beattie's *Retirement*
(1758) congenial. In that poem, the "pensive youth" recalls the devotion he once had to rural solitude and asks to be taken back ("O
take the wanderer home!").

For me no more the path invites
Ambition loves to tread;
No more I climb those toilsome heights
By guileful Hope misled;
Leaps my fond fluttering heart no more
To Mirth's enlivening strain;
For present pleasure soon is o'er,
And all the past is vain.[34]

Although Beattie is much more even-tempered and less zealous in
his commendation of withdrawal than Cowper, his verse anticipates
a great deal of the praise of retreat found in *Retirement* and *The
Task*. In book 4 (*The Winter Evening*) of *The Task*, the poet celebrates the sanctuary of his sitting room:

Now stir the fire, and close the shutters fast,
Let fall the curtains, wheel the sofa round,
And, while the bubbling and loud-hissing urn
Throws up a steamy column, and the cups,
That cheer but not inebriate, wait on each,
So let us welcome peaceful ev'ning in.[35]

In *The Triumph of Melancholy*, the speaker contemplates a very
similar pleasure:

Now when fierce Winter arm'd with wasteful power
Heaves the wild deep that thunders from afar,
How sweet to sit in this sequester'd bower,
To hear, and but to hear, the mingling war!

Ambition here displays no gilded toy
That tempts on desperate wing the soul to rise,

Nor Pleasure's flower-embroider'd paths decoy,
Nor Anguish lurks in Grandeur's gay disguise.[36]

Beattie's versification would not have been up to Cowper's Miltonic taste, and in his poem, *The Hares*, Beattie is more concerned with allegorical implications than with precise attempts to depict animals. Cowper may have simply discovered in Beattie confirmation of his own poetic incentives. In *Dissertations Moral and Critical,* he certainly found critical approbation of the form *The Task* was taking in March 1784.

Earlier, in *Conversation,* Cowper anticipated the apparently loose structure of *The Task* when he praised "Digression":

Though such continual zigzags in a book,
Such drunken reelings, have an aukward look,
And I had rather creep to what is true,
Than rove and stagger with no mark in view,
Yet to consult a little, seem'd no crime,
The freakish humour of the present time.
But now, to gather up what seems dispers'd,
And touch the subject I design'd at first . . .[37]

David Hartley in his monumental *Observations on Man* (1749) had celebrated "continual zigzags." According to him, the mind operates solely through associations, which are really modified sense impressions, and through these associations builds from simple to complex mental states. In Proposition 91 (part 1), Hartley presents his theory of the imagination: "The Recurrence of Ideas, especially visible and audible ones, in a vivid manner, but without any regard to the Order observed in past Facts, is ascribed to the Power of Imagination. . . . Now here we may observe, that every succeeding Thought is the Result either of some new Impression, or of an Association with the preceding."[38] Hartley lists many elements that induce aesthetic pleasure and shows how they are united into a complex of feelings: for example, he writes of the great pleasure in rural scenes, saying that the individual sights and smells mix with each other; he concludes that the combination of these associated ideas is the source of delight in nature's beauty. Cowper was obviously aware of associationist principles when he wrote *Conversation* and *The Task,* but it is difficult to know the precise way in which he became aware of this important theory. One of the sections, however, which would have pleased him in Beattie's *Dissertations* was his chapter *Of the Association of Ideas:*

The human soul is essentially active; and none of our faculties are more restless, than this of Imagination, which operates in sleep, as well as when we are awake. While we listen to a discourse, or read a book, how often, in spite of all our care, does the fancy wander, and present thoughts quite different from those we would keep in view! That energy, which lays a restraint upon the fancy, by fixing the mind on one particular object, or set of objects, is called Attention: and most people know, that the continued exercise of it is accompanied with difficulty, and something of intellectual weariness. Whereas, when, without attending to any one particular idea, we give full scope to our thoughts, and permit them to shift, as Imagination or accident shall determine, a state of mind which is called a Reverie; we are conscious of something like mental relaxation; while one idea brings in another, which gives way to a third, and that in its turn is succeeded by others. . . .[39]

Beattie's distinction between "Attention" and "Reverie" is essentially Hartleian, and he then goes on to speak particularly of the poetical manipulation of "Reverie":

If contrast were not a natural bond of union among ideas, we should not be so much pleased with it in works of fancy. But in fact, we find, that poets and other artists, whose aim is to give pleasure, are all studious of it. Homer frequently interrupts the description of a battle, with a similitude taken from still life or from rural affairs: and in this he has been imitated by succeeding poets; who have also, after his example, in the contrivance of characters, opposed the violent to the gentle, the cunning to the generous, and the proud to the humble; and, in the arrangement of their fable, diversified events by a like artifice. . . . On all these occasions we are pleased with the variety; and we are also pleased with the opposition, because it makes the variety more observable and surprising, and suits that propensity of human mind, of associating contraries, or passing from one extreme to another.[40]

Although Cowper's commitment to associationism as a literary device predated his reading of *Dissertations*, he discovered in Beattie a prominent critic and poet who was in accord with literary principles which might seem suspect to some. He also would have found in *Dissertations* a strong conviction that the sublime, although obviously evoked by awesome spectacles from nature, could be awakened by "any great and good affection, as piety"; as well, the Psalms contained "the most magnificent descriptions that the soul of man can comprehend."[41] Even domestic subjects could be made sublime when there was an allusion to a grand object, and the sublime did not always have to be "accompanied with sonorous expression, or a pomp of images."[42] And Cowper would have been especially reassured to hear: "Poetry is also sublime, when it describes in a lively manner the visible effects of any of those passions that give elevation to the character."[43]

Despite the affinity with Beattie that Cowper discerned in the year before he wrote *The Task* and which he affirmed halfway through its composition, it is difficult to know if Beattie influenced the design of Cowper's long poem or if Cowper simply found in Beattie a fellow writer with similar propensities. Cowper made a clear statement on this matter: "For though the Art of Writing and composing was never much my study, I did not find that they [Beattie and Blair] had any great news to tell me. They have assisted me in putting my own observations into some method, but have not suggested many of which I was not by some means or other, previously apprized."[44] However, Cowper was always reluctant to admit that any writer, with the exception of Milton, had "suggested" anything to him. In this instance, he likely protests too much.

If Cowper's readings in Beattie and Prior stimulated him and helped to confirm the direction he was pursuing, the poet whom Cowper hoped to emulate in *The Task* was John Milton. Cowper's anger at Samuel Johnson for the way in which he treated Prior was matched by his contempt at the way Milton was depicted by the same writer. Johnson "talks something about the unfitness of the English Language for Blank Verse, & how apt it is, in the Mouth of some Readers to degenerate into Declamation. Oh! I could thresh his old Jacket 'till I made his Pension Jingle in his Pocket."[45]

Cowper's anger at Johnson also arises from his own strong sense of identification with Milton. For much of his life, Cowper viewed himself as a man disinherited by God, as a person crippled by an overwhelming sense of damnation. However, Milton's obvious disability—his blindness—had been transformed into a strength, as in the invocations to "holy Light" in book 3 and to Urania in book 7 of *Paradise Lost:*

> Taught by the heavenly Muse to venture down
> The dark descent, and up to reascend,
> Though hard and rare: thee I revisit safe,

And feel thy sovereign vital lamp; but thou
Revisit'st not these eyes, that roll in vain
To find thy piercing ray, and find no dawn;
So thick a drop serene hath quenched their orbs,
Or dim suffusion veiled.[46]

More safe I sing with mortal voice, unchanged
To hoarse or mute, though fallen on evil days,
On evil days though fallen, and evil tongues;
In darkness, and with dangers compassed round,
And solitude; yet not alone, while thou
Visit'st my slumbers nightly . . .[47]

In these two passages, Milton reminds his readers that although he is physically blind, he feels called upon to illuminate the spiritual condition of mankind. The irony is that he who has been robbed of sight becomes the appropriate person to discourse on inner light. Indeed, the poet seems to suggest that his disability has made him the most likely person to speak of such things. This aspect of Milton's existence obviously appealed to Cowper, and he hoped his experience, harrowing as it was, of spiritual darkness would enable him, in turn, to write of the possibility of spiritual rebirth. In imitating Milton, he hoped that what was dark in himself would be illuminated.[48]

Surprisingly, Cowper was silent about the composition of *The Task* when he began working on it in October 1783 (he does not talk about the poem in the extant correspondence until February 1784), but, from the outset, the Miltonic mode was central. He assumed that his great task would be to write a poem about a corrupt individual—himself—who wanders back into the garden and finds salvation. Such thoughts preoccupied him, and he saw *The Task* as a continuation of *Paradise Lost*. Since Cowper now envisioned his career as a poet to be a dedication to the poet-priest calling of Milton, it was incumbent upon him to abandon heroic couplets and to go back to the verse form of the great seventeenth-century poem. Having renounced the sententious manner of most of the moral satires, he would also be employing a verse form susceptible to a much greater diversification.[49] These considerations must have weighed heavily with Cowper as he began work on the poem, despite the facetious tone he adopted when commenting on the genesis of the poem in its first verse paragraph—"The theme though humble, yet august and proud / Th'occasion—for the Fair commands the song"[50]—and in his letter to Lady Hesketh of January

16, 1786: "I began the 'Task,'—for [Lady Austen] gave me the Sofa for a subject."[51]

3   When Cowper did mention his progress in writing *The Task,* it was in a letter of dismay to Bull of February 22, 1784, at which time he had completed four books and a portion of the fifth. "When the sixth is finished the work is accomplished. But if I may judge by my present inability that period is at a considerable distance."[52] By August, the poem was "ended but not finish'd."[53] It was in this month that Cowper began assiduously seeking Unwin's advice about the poem. Only in these letters can the author of *The Task* be seen preparing his book for the press.

Cowper's initial request to Unwin concerned clothing worn in London society, especially "upon the subject of male rumps cork'd."[54] Unwin, unfortunately, could not discover any information on this matter, and Cowper discarded the passage in question. He was in haste in October to finish the transcript of the poem for Joseph Johnson, and he sent Unwin portions of it for correction (he was especially concerned about the pointing of the blank verse). In his letter of October 10, 1784, Cowper made some candid remarks to Unwin on the scope and structure of *The Task*. He reflected on the necessity of employing satire, especially in book 2: "I can write nothing without aiming at least at usefullness."[55] He averred that all his descriptions were taken from nature; they were "delineations of the heart. . . . from my own experience. . . . I have imitated nobody."[56] He then went on to talk about the "plan" of his poem: "If the work cannot boast a regular plan (in which respect however I do not think it altogether indefensible) it may yet boast, that the reflections are naturally suggested always by the preceding passage, and that except the 5th. book which is rather of a political aspect, the whole has one tendency. To discountenance the modern enthusiasm after a London Life, and to recommend rural ease and leisure as friendly to the cause of piety and virtue."[57]

It was at about this time that the manuscript (transmitted by Unwin who was inserting corrections) was submitted to Joseph Johnson. Unwin's support at this crucial time was invaluable: "Your letter has relieved me from some anxiety. . . . I have faith in your judgment, and an implicit confidence in the Sincerity of your approbation."[58] Although there was still the possibility on October 20 that Johnson might refuse the manuscript, an agreement to publish was reached by the end of the month (Johnson consented to this venture, which was undertaken at his own risk, without seeing a line, Cowper claimed in 1791; as before, Cowper received no payment for the volume).

Finally, Cowper wrote to Newton to break the news. After commenting on the heroism of the Sandwich Islanders and reviewing Knox's essays, Cowper arrived at the real purpose of his letter in a seemingly offhand way in his final paragraph: "I am again at Johnson's; in the shape of a Poem in blank verse; consisting of Six books, and called the Task. I began it about this time Twelvemonth. . . . I mentioned it not sooner, because almost to the last I was doubtfull whether I should ever bring it to a conclusion."[59] As Cowper had expected,[60] his old friend was deeply distressed that the new book had been written without his being informed. Newton was also angry that Unwin had replaced him as intermediary with the publisher. When Newton had earlier complained in July 1780 that Unwin, and not he, was the recipient of some verse, Cowper had rejoined: "Mr. Unwin himself would not be affronted if I was to tell him that there is this difference between him and Mr. Newton: That the latter is already an Apostle while He himself is only undergoing the business of Incubation with a hope that he may be hatched in time. When my Muse comes forth arrayed in sables, at least in a robe of graver cast, I make no scruple to direct her to [you] at Hoxton."[61]

During the composition of *The Task*, Cowper decided to cast off those "sables," and his conflicting statements to Newton and Unwin regarding that poem delineate the changes that had taken place within him. On November 27, 1784, he told Newton: "The subject of [*The Task*] I am sure will please you, and . . . I have admitted into my description no images but what are scriptural."[62] A month earlier, he had assured Unwin that all his images were from nature: "Not one of them second-handed."[63] To Newton he claimed his principal purpose was to allure the reader into "what may profit him,"[64] but to Unwin he had rehearsed a strategy of throwing the religious parts "towards the end of it."[65]

In John Newton, *The Task* faced its harshest critic. Newton knew full well that Cowper was being duplicitous, and his objections to the poem were unyielding. Those strictures were directed at Cowper even before Newton saw the poem. In his answer to Cowper's letter of October 30, Newton objected to the title and to the use of blank verse. In his response, Cowper agreed to send a "Copy of the Advertisement," "an Argument, or a Summary of the Contents of each book," and an "Extract."[66] In his description of the poem,

Cowper managed to make *The Task* seem like just another long moral satire: "My principal purpose is to allure the Reader by character, by scenery, by imagery and such poetical embellishments, to the Reading of what may profit him. Subordinately to this, to combat that predilection in favor of a Metropolis that beggars and exhausts the Country by evacuating it of all its principal Inhabitants. And collaterally and as far as is consistent with this double Intention, to have a stroke at Vice, Vanity and folly wherever I find them."[67] Newton did not defer in the face of this letter. On December 11, Cowper responded to another series of objections: "As to the Title, I take it to be the best that is to be had. It is not possible that a book including such a variety of subjects, and in which no particular one is predominant, should find a title adapted to them all. In such a case, it seemed almost necessary to accommodate the name to the incident that gave birth to the poem. Nor does it appear to me, that because I performed more than my task, therefore the Task is not a suitable Title."[68] Newton was still not satisfied by Christmas of 1784, but Cowper was able to offer a conciliatory wish: "I am however willing to hope that when the Volume shall cast itself at your feet, you will be in some measure reconciled to the name it bears. . . ."[69] Cowper concluded his remarks on the poem by agreeing with Newton: "enough . . . of a subject very unworthy of so much consideration."[70] Only in April 1785 did Newton bestow his reluctant consent to publication.

Although Cowper underwent a great deal of difficulty with Newton regarding *The Task,* he found his working relationship with Joseph Johnson considerably eased this time. He received his first set of proofs in the third week of January 1785, and he returned the last proof on May 31. However, Cowper was once more agitated during the printing. At several points, he thought that Johnson was moving too slowly; he was certainly impatient on June 25 when he told Newton: "I know not what Johnson is about, neither do I now enquire. It will be a month to-morrow since I return'd him the last proof."[71] He complained again about Johnson being "dilatory" on June 29, but the book was published at the beginning of July.

As Cowper, now the author of a second published volume, awaited the reviews of his book, he ruminated on the reasons which had led him to publish again. In a nonchalant mood, he speculated on how he had merged the serious and the humorous in the new volume: "A serious poem is like a Swan, it flies heavily, and never far. But a Jest has the wings of a Swallow that never tire and that carry it into every nook and corner."[72] To Hill and Newton he repeated what he had said about *Poems* in 1781 and 1782: "Despair made amusement necessary, and I found poetry the most agreeable amusement."[73] And he sadly reflected on what he conceived to be his imperviousness to potentially hostile criticism: "The view that I have had of myself for many years has been so truely humiliating, that I think the praises of all mankind could not hurt me."[74]

After he had finished work on *The Task,* Cowper considered additions to the volume. In October 1782, he had begun *Tirocinium,* a long poem on education which he had laid aside when it had reached 200 lines. On October 20, 1784, he told Unwin that he had resumed work on the poem, which would not be shorter than 700 or 800 lines (the poem reached 922). "It turns on the question whether an Education at School or at Home be preferrable, and I shall give the preference to the latter. I mean that it shall pursue the track of the former [*The Task*], that is to say, that it shall visit Stock in its way to publication. My design also is to Inscribe it to you; but you must see it first."[75] Unwin, of course, was delighted with the poem, which is an elaboration of many of the sentiments which Cowper had expressed in letters of September 7 and October 5, 1780, concerning John Unwin's schooling. Joseph Johnson accepted the poem readily. A month later, Cowper sent another poem to Unwin: "You will find also an Epistle to Joseph Hill Esqr. which I wrote on Wedn'sday last. A tribute so due that I must have disgraced myself had I not pay'd it. He ever serves me in all that he can, though he has not seen me these 20 years."[76] Whereas Newton and Unwin had been publicly affirmed as the mentors in *Poems* (and the poem to Unwin perhaps only accidentally gaining the important, final position in that volume), Cowper in his second volume dedicated a poem of substantial length to Unwin, and he celebrated another friend in another poem. Newton was displeased by his obvious exclusion. Cowper did not consider for the moment that Hill might be offended by unsolicited publicity and by being mentioned favorably at the expense of the Lord Chancellor.

The final poem to find a place in the new collection was *John Gilpin.* In October 1784, Cowper admitted to Unwin that he would like to see that poem in the volume: "The Critical Reviewers charged me with *an attempt* at humour. John having been more celebrated upon the score of his humour than most pieces that have appeared in modern days, may serve to exonerate me from the imputation."[77] It was upon this score that Cowper had not been without "thoughts of adding John Gilpin at the tail of all."[78] Twelve days later, he was delighted at the prospect of claiming the anonymous *Gilpin* for his own and to "mend him," especially to rework the "quaint and old-fashioned"[79] language. It now seemed that *John* would appear, but Cowper was startled when Johnson wrote in the spring to inquire if Cowper had any improvements to the poem, for "to print only the Original again, would be to publish what has been hackney'd in ev'ry Magazine. . . ."[80] He replied that he had only two or three small variations. He sent these corrections (there were in fact thirty-five) and then assumed *John* would not appear. Johnson, however, had decided to allow *John Gilpin*, with its revisions, to stand at the end of the new volume. Cowper was surprised when *John* arrived in the last set of proofs. He speculated that with or without *John* the book might not be a success, since Johnson did not seem especially interested in advertising it.

4   The autobiographical elements in *The Task* have often been noted. Cowper portrayed his retreat from the world ("I was the stricken deer . . ."), his recovery from mental distress, his conversion to Evangelicalism, and his search for a suitable rural locale, with appropriate companionship, far removed from London and its concerns. As important, however, is the way in which the other poems in the collection give balance and support to the events described in the long poem. In *Tirocinium*, there are clearly autobiographical recollections of cruelty experienced by Cowper as a young boy (as described in *Adelphi*), and an element lurking behind this poem is Cowper's desire to have been removed from such an environment. Although Cowper justly celebrated Hill's compassion and kindness despite their separation from each other for twenty years, he also cast scorn on two school friends from London—Colman and Thurlow—who had abandoned him. In all three poems, there is the celebration of the constant and unswerving (the country, an education at home, Joseph Hill) in opposition to the vain and fickle (London, public schools, Colman and Thurlow). If these poems are read as an autobiographical collection, Cowper may be seen as the distressed schoolboy (of *Tirocinium*) who seeks comfort in a London life and makes friendships with some successful people (*Epistle*), ultimately collapses there, and seeks retreat in the country (*The Task*). The fourth poem in the collection does not fit directly into an autobiographical mold; however, in *Gilpin*, Cowper's ability to present the darker side of human nature in a humorous way finds its finest expression, and the ability to speak solemn thoughts in a

more sophisticated manner than he had been able to do in *Poems* was a central preoccupation of Cowper's artistry from 1782 onward.

If the shorter poems supplement the autobiographical portions of *The Task,* they do so in relatively unobtrusive ways. *The Task* itself is a poem in which Cowper meditates on the perpetual conflict between reality and art, and he finally arrives at a precarious balance between the two. Although the "task" is, at various times, to write an amusing poem, to justify his choice of life, to compare city and country life, to recommend rural solitude, to satirize London and its inhabitants, it is also to find the poetic mode which will allow Cowper to be creative *and* to serve God. Cowper remains distrustful of art, but he now presents this in a vision of uneasy conflict, rather than simple cavil. In one of the great set pieces of the poem, he compares the ice palace of Catherine the Great to a simple waterfall in rural Buckinghamshire. Despite his disclaimer, Cowper's evocation of the watery chasm is a powerful evocation of a natural phenomenon in which the domestic reaches true sublimity:

> On the flood,
> Indurated and fixt, the snowy weight
> Lies undissolv'd; while silently beneath,
> And unperceiv'd, the current steals away.
> Not so where, scornful of a check, it leaps
> The mill-dam, dashes on the restless wheel,
> And wantons in the pebbly gulph below:
> No frost can bind it there; its utmost force
> Can but arrest the light and smoky mist
> That in its fall the liquid sheet throws wide.
> And see where it has hung th'embroider'd banks
> With forms so various, that no pow'rs of art,
> The pencil or the pen, may trace the scene!
> . . . .
> Thus nature works as if to mock at art,
> And in defiance of her rival pow'rs;
> By these fortuitous and random strokes
> Performing such inimitable feats
> As she with all the rules can never reach.[81]

Cowper's very lines here contradict his assertion that no pen "may trace the scene": in these skillful lines about the impossibility of art, he attains it. Cowper also achieves his intention of describing the limitations of art when he juxtaposes the landscape in Bucks with Catherine's "marble of the glassy wave":

once a stream,
And soon to slide into a stream again.
Alas! 'twas but a mortifying stroke
Of undesign'd severity, that glanc'd
(Made by a monarch) on her own estate,
On human grandeur and the courts of kings.
'Twas transient in its nature, as in show
'Twas durable: as worthless, as it seem'd
Intrinsically precious; to the foot
Treach'rous and false; it smil'd, and it was cold.[82]

In *Poems,* Cowper had made assertions about the discrepancy between art and true spiritual reality, but those claims had been stated in a frequently cumbersome, didactic way; in *The Task,* he was able to evoke that conflict in passages of remarkable descriptive force in which the struggle between evanescent glory and the power of nature is fully dramatized. Nevertheless, there are two voices in the poem. Cowper the would-be satirist of such poems as *The Progress of Error* speaks of public vice, and Cowper the confessional poet speaks of private virtue.[83]

Nevertheless, the sureness of Cowper's more personal voice in *The Task* allows him to range much further than in his previous verse, even *Retirement.* In book 1, he surveys the countryside below him: "Now roves the eye; / And, posted on this speculative height, / Exults in its command."[84] The entire poem, despite the discrepancy in the voices, is written from the perspective of one who has assumed a position of authority and is intent on pressing his advantage. It is in such a state of mind that the various walks in the poem are taken. The walks are real ones, but they are also metaphors for the poem itself, defining the ways in which the task will be performed. With its connotation of leisure, the "walk" suggests what kind of a "task" it will be: rambling, casual, and circumambient. The "walk" is also a symbol of Cowper's choice of "laborious ease"[85] as his mode of life.

However, Cowper did not achieve a completely integrated vision of the conflicts between the country and the city, freedom and profligacy, peace and war, God's wisdom and man's partial knowledge. The poem is ultimately about the attempt of an individual to understand the ambivalences of life and to write about them, an effort—because of man's finite capabilities—which is doomed at the outset. However, in his *Pilgrim's Progress,* Cowper joins together those things which he had once thought intolerably disjointed. His

"wand'ring muse," which is at first unsettled ("Roving as I rove, /
Where shall I find an end, or how proceed?")[86] and painting every
"idle thing / That fancy finds in her excursive flights,"[87] is ultimately able to perceive the intricacy of the world—the fear of being
tainted has decreased markedly. At the end of book 3, the poet at
last comes to terms with London:

> Oh thou, resort and mart of all the earth,
> Chequer'd with all complexions of mankind,
> And spotted with all crimes; in whom I see
> Much that I love, and more that I admire,
> And all that I abhor; thou freckled fair,
> That pleasest and yet shock'st me, I can laugh
> And I can weep, can hope, and can despond,
> Feel wrath and pity, when I think on thee![88]

Cowper's newfound acceptance of the contraries of human existence allows him to transform the wreath which Adam unconsciously
dropped to the ground in book 9 of *Paradise Lost* into sacred verse;
he is now able to unite divine providence and artifact together in
an appropriate song:

> It shall not grieve me, then, that once, when call'd
> To dress a Sofa with the flow'rs of verse,
> I play'd awhile, obedient to the fair,
> With that light task; but soon, to please her more,
> Whom flow'rs alone I knew would little please,
> Let fall th'unfinish'd wreath, and rov'd for fruit;
> Rov'd far, and gather'd much: some harsh, 'tis true,
> Pick'd from the thorns and briers of reproof,
> But wholesome, well-digested; grateful some
> To palates that can taste immortal truth;
> Insipid else, and sure to be despis'd.
> But all is in his hand whose praise I seek.[89]

For Cowper, "warfare is within," and *The Task* is an attempt to ex-
ternalize conflicts, to dramatize them, and to place them side by
side. In the end, discord remains, but there has been at least the attempt to justify the ways of God to late eighteenth-century man.

In *The Task*, Cowper presents salvation for himself as a distinct
possibility. This is poetic license. His sense of worthlessness and deep-
seated unhappiness continued unabated. Cowper's artistry sometimes
mastered such feelings. He was thus able to delineate the differ-
ences between art and nature, but he did not understand the con-

tradictions within his own being. And he could not conquer the hostile forces which haunted him.

5   *The Task* was immediately greeted by the critics as a master-piece. Cowper was gratified by the notice in the *Critical Review* of October 1785 which he modestly called a "handsome escape, so far at least, out of the paws of the Critics."[90] Although he had some reservations, that reviewer felt that the volume was "superior to any that has lately fallen into our hands. We here meet with no affected prettiness of style, no glaring epithets, which modern writers so industriously accumulate. . . ."[91] He did feel, however, that the transitions were "in many places happily contrived: in others, too abrupt and desultory."[92] In November, the *New London Magazine* ("The Poem throughout is a well-written ingenious performance"),[93] the *London Chronicle* ("The superiority of nature's works to the imitations of art is . . . pointed out, and the wearisomeness of what is commonly called a life of pleasure, much in the manner of Young, strongly delineated"),[94] and the *European Magazine* ("upon the whole [Cowper] is possessed of more originality of thought, more genuine satire and solid argument, than falls to the share of most of our modern Juvenals")[95] bestowed generous praise upon the volume. The latter journal (as well as the *Chronicle*) compared Cowper to Edward Young: "a kind of gloom, however, pervades the whole work, tho' sometimes a gleam of sunshine breaks thro' when it is least expected. His colouring partakes . . . of the *sombre* stile of Young's *Night Thoughts*."[96]

Cowper had to wait a bit longer for the reviews in the *Gentleman's Magazine* (December 1785, January 1786, March 1786), the *New Review* (January 1786), and the *Monthly Review* (June 1786). The anonymous reviewer in the *Gentleman's Magazine* was pleased by the diversity of *The Task:* he found the books "all miscellaneous and introducing a variety of amusement and instruction, much humour and pleasantry being occasionally blended, but, on the whole, the grave and serious, the moral and religious, prevail, and have the principal end in view. Seldom have we seen the *utile* and the *dulce* so agreeably united; and yet so numerous and digressional are the subjects, that we cannot regularly give an epitome. . . ."[97] Paul Henry Maty in the *New Review* worried that the voice of the poet in *The Task* seemed "now and then a little fretful, a little partial to his own ways of thinking, and a little contemptuous to science," but he conceded "these are small blemishes in a work in general very good."[98] It was left to Samuel Badcock in the *Monthly Review* to worry about the apparent lack of unity in the poem (a charge which haunts the poem to this day):

> The great defect of the present poem is a want of unity of design. It is composed of reflections that seem independent of one another; and there is no *particular* subject either discussed or aimed at.
>
> An imagination like Mr. Cowper's is not to be controuled and confined within the bounds that criticism prescribes. We cannot, however, avoid remarking, that his muse sometimes passes too suddenly from grave and serious remonstrance to irony and ridicule. The heart that is *harrowed* and alarmed in one line, is not prepared to smile in the next.[99]

Despite his reservations, Badcock admitted that "the defects of this poem bear a very small proportion to its beauties:—and its beauties are of no common account."[100]

Despite some negative strictures, *The Task* was an overwhelming critical success; as well, it remained the most widely read poetical text in England until about 1800.[101] It was also an enormously influential poem, its most important offspring being *The Prelude*.[102] As Wordsworth recognized, *The Task* was the first significant autobiographical narrative poem in the English language; *Paradise Lost*, to which Wordsworth was also indebted, is only intermittently autobiographical, whereas all the reflections in *The Task* are part of a comprehensive spiritual autobiography. Indeed, one of the reasons why Cowper's poem is sometimes badly focused is that he had no precedent in English verse upon which to draw in designing and writing the story of his life. In many ways, Cowper bestowed a precious gift on Wordsworth: a long narrative poem from which the younger poet could discern the problems inherent in writing autobiographical verse. Cowper's *Task* was, to a large extent, the tradition from which Wordsworth's individual talent in *The Prelude* flowed.

Cowper's influence on the Romantic movement can also be seen in his treatment of the sublime. The poets of mid-century had been concerned with the rhetorical sublime, which aims to move the reader by the use of bold and imaginative language; these poets (Collins, the Wartons, and Gray) imitated the Milton of *L'Allegro* and *Il Penseroso*, who was consciously concerned in these poems with the methodology to be employed in evoking strong feelings. Cowper was interested in the religious sublime, as we have seen, and he was able to evoke poetry of genuine compassion and emotion from ordinary subject matter; Cowper's Milton was the poet of *Paradise Lost* who could summon up sublime feelings in describing a wide variety of circumstances, ranging from the perfidy of Satan to the simple domestic pleasures of Adam and Eve before the Fall.[103] Cowper's willingness to make his own humble life of retirement the occasion of sublimity helped to legitimatize Wordsworth's recreation of the intensely felt "spots of time" from his childhood, adolescence, and young manhood.

Cowper presented the Romantics with yet another legacy. *The Task* is written in forceful, virile diction, his speaking voice in his long poem being remarkably clear and straightforward. The poets of mid-century in their devotion to Milton had frequently allowed themselves to be encumbered by what was, even by 1730, a slightly obscure diction and syntax; although Cowper, in obvious imitation of Milton, employed blank verse, the tempo and modulation of *The Task* are conversational, often reminiscent of the poet's finest letters. In their attempt to write poetry in the "real language of men in a state of vivid sensation,"[104] Wordsworth and Coleridge had an obvious precedent in Cowper's long poem. Indeed, Wordsworth saw *The Task* as a "composite order" of the "Lyrical," "Idyllium," and "Didactic."[105]

The Task was revolutionary in yet another way. Pope's poetry had been, in the very best sense of the word, humanistic. He had been concerned to describe and analyze the fullest potentials of which man was capable and, in some of his poems, he had shown man's inability to reach those heights. In the 1730s, however, Collins's poetry ushered in a new concern: he and the Wartons investigated the nature of poetic sensibility and the difficulties inherent in attempting to write poetry in the shadow of Pope, and, especially, Milton. Collins's is a poetry of process, not product, in which the "I" monitors its ability or inability to write effective poetry. In *Poems,* as we have seen, Cowper was interested in such issues, but in *The Task,* he broke through the barriers which had previously inhibited his immediate predecessors. Through his use of Milton and his own conversational tone, he largely eschewed the problem of what to write by telling of his own life. His "product" is himself and the "process" of salvation is intimately described.

Ultimately, *The Task* is a poem of enormous vigor. In it, Cowper wrote simply and directly of what he knew best: his own contrary heart. However, having confessed the secrets of that heart, he had vanquished the need to write his own verse. He told Newton in

January 1787 that many of his friends had urged him to continue "in the way of Original poetry": "But I can truely say that it was order'd otherwise; not by me, but by the Providence that governs all my thoughts and directs my intentions as he pleases . . . Extreme distress of spirit at last drove me . . . to translate for amusement."[106] In some ways, translation is a passive activity, and it might seem that the submissive portion of Cowper's personality manifested itself in the Homer project. This is not so. One of the great ironies of Cowper's literary career is that all his energies as a writer were unleashed when he abandoned his concern for the domestic sublime, as seen in *The Task*, and pursued its heroic, epic counterpart in his translations of Homer. Having lost his fear of art, he was free to dedicate himself to literary artistry.

9
Lady Hesketh

1   ON OCTOBER 12, 1785, Cowper came down to breakfast and found a letter from Harriot Hesketh, perhaps the most important letter he was ever to receive. The cousins had exchanged letters last in 1767, eighteen years before, and earlier in 1763, Cowper had chosen not to accept an invitation from Sir Thomas and Lady Hesketh to live with them. Although Lady Hesketh's extended absences from England from 1769 onward and her preoccupations as a widow in England from 1778 help to explain the breach, there can be little doubt that the cousins had been in serious disagreement in 1767 about religious matters. Lady Hesketh disliked "extremely" the "methodistical Cant"[1] with which she felt Cowper's letters of this period were filled. Despite the "sincere Affection"[2] on both sides, the cousins drifted apart, and Cowper had been cut off from a relative and friend with whom he had shared many happy times.

When she wrote in 1785, Lady Hesketh reminded her cousin of the joys of their past friendship: "Will you not be surprised my dear cousin, at receiving a letter at this distant period from an old correspondent and a still older Friend? one who tho' she has long ceased to be the former, can never cease to be the latter, nor can ever forget the happy hours and years of friendly intercourse which she formerly enjoyed with her valuable Friend. . . ."[3] Many years later, in 1798, Lady Hesketh provided Samuel Greatheed with the motivation behind her letter: "I ceased writing . . . with great reluctance & having the misfortune to lose an affectionate Husband, after a three years illness, which engross'd my whole Time and thoughts, my early Friend was for a while—*not forgot indeed*—but neglected. When my Spirits had a little recovered the Shock of this loss and that of my dear Mother I renewed my enquirys after my . . . friend

& companion—and being told his health was much restord I haz-
arded a letter to Him . . ."[4] In her letter, Lady Hesketh mentioned
Sir Thomas's death, and her great admiration for some of Cowper's
verse, particularly *John Gilpin*. As well, she provided news of Ashley and Theadora: "you know both my Father and Sister never
were fond of company, and I think this has increased greatly upon
him lately, even more I believe than even my Sister finds Pleasant
as he does not wish to see even his nearest relations. . . ."[5] The
letter also contains a very extended description of the delights of
Margate: "I never was at Margate before, and was Vastly pleased
with it, 'tis so different from the generality of seacoasts, which seldom afford any view but sea and Sky, that I was quite delighted to
enjoy so fine a view of the Ocean, accompanied by every other
beauty that makes an *inland* prospect delightful. I think I hardly
ever saw any Country more highly cultivated than the Isle of
Thanet. There is such a profusion of Corn, beans, and clover, that
the Air is perfumed with the two latter in the highest degree. I
walked from morning to Night and found myself so comfortable
there. . . ."[6] This passage, similar in its precision of detail and language to Cowper's, reveals something of the affinity of the cousins.
Although he partook a great deal in the melancholia of Ashley and
Theadora and, like them, wished to abandon the cares of the
world, the vibrancy and cordiality that Lady Hesketh expressed in
her letter had been a very real part of Cowper's personality as a
young man in the London of the 1750s and early 1760s. This is why
he could truly say to his cousin: "We are all grown young again,
and the days that I thought I should see no more, are actually return'd."[7]

During his period of religious preoccupation from 1763 to 1773,
Cowper was not interested in the London world he had abandoned,
and, despite his real affection for many of his former friends, his
fear of being corrupted by them and his feeling that he had lost all
interest in their activities had made him disdainful. In October
1785, the author of two successful volumes of verse was more sympathetic to the charms of a world he still did not wish to reenter,
when he answered Lady Hesketh's letter with warmth and cordiality:

> . . . truely [I can boast] of an affection for you that neither
> years nor interrupted intercourse have at all abated. I need
> only recollect how much I valued you once, and with how
> much cause, immediately to feel a revival of the same value; if

that can be said to revive, which at the most has only been
dormant for want of employment. But I slander it when I say
that it has slept. A thousand times have I recollected a thousand scenes in which our two selves have formed the whole of
the Drama, with the greatest pleasure; at times too when I had
no reason to suppose that I should ever hear from you
again. . . . The hours that I have spent with you were among
the pleasantest of my former days, and are therefore chronicled
in my mind so deeply as to fear no erasure.[8]

In this letter, Cowper tells of his life at Olney, describes the health
of his pets, Puss, Marquis, and Mungo, and comments on the care
and devotion that Mrs. Unwin has given him. He mentions that
he is delighted at the news of Ashley's good health. Of course, he
avoids referring to Theadora directly: "Happy for the most part,
are parents who have daughters. Daughters are not apt to outlive
their natural affections . . . I rejoice particularly in my Uncle's
felicity who has three female descendents from his little person,
who leave him nothing to wish for upon that head."[9] Although he
was willing, even anxious, to resume his correspondence with Harriot Hesketh and wished to share the details of his life with her, he
seems in this letter to have politely but firmly indicated that he did
not wish to talk of the all too painful memory of Theadora and lost
possibilities.

2   The woman who wrote to Cowper in the fall of 1785 and
who more than any other person returned her cousin to the concerns of the refined and genteel London society in which she moved
and which he had once known well had, since her husband's death
seven years previously, lived in comfortable, if somewhat reduced,
circumstances. According to his will, Sir Thomas left his wife the
yearly sum of £800.[10] Although neither Sir Thomas's will nor codi-
cil mentions it, Lady Hesketh must have retained control of the
house in Charles Street, which Sir Thomas purchased in 1775. In
November 1779, she was anxious to let that house and find other
lodging: "[I] am very desirous of getting into a smaller House, have
not however as yet heard of a Tenant for mine. I hope I shall, as I
really think it one of the best Houses in London for a single Man,
or Woman, of large fortune—or for a Man & his Wife—but it is a
House of too much pretention for my Income . . ."[11] By April

1780,[12] she was at New Norfolk Street in the "smaller House" she desired. Although Lady Hesketh always praised her husband's "bountifull kindness" which had "provided for [her] equally above [her] deserts, and *expectations*,"[13] her letters testify to the fact she was very well aware of the limits of her income, limits within which she always endeavored to live. In 1798, she offered John Johnson unsolicited advice in pecuniary matters: "I believe I do not owe a shilling in the world except what I shall pay to-morrow morning in my weekly books and tho' by this means one cannot possess much money one has the comfort of knowing it is *all ones own* which otherwise it could not be you know . . ."[14]

Lady Hesketh's life was divided among various places—London, Cheltenham, Clifton, Bath, Twickenham. Her life at Bath and Clifton is reminiscent of the descriptions of Bath Jane Austen conjures up in *Northanger Abbey* and *Persuasion*, and Lady Hesketh's existence seems to have been devoted to the "regular duties" of the society in those novels: ". . . shops were to be visited; some new part of town to be looked at; and the Pump-room to be attended, where they paraded up and down for an hour, looking at every body and speaking to no one."[15] In fact, she felt Bath a *"vraie paradis terrestre"*: "At all seasons indeed no place can be so amusing as Bath and all Entertainments lye in so small a Compass and are to be got at with so much ease, and for so little cost and without the expense of late Hours, that I never am here that I don't wonder that people live anywhere else. The town is so uncommonly beautiful and the country about it so charming."[16]

Lady Hesketh was interested "in the company of clever, well-informed people, who have a great deal of conversation."[17] Although the evidence is scanty, it would seem that she was well known in the world of letters before she became renowned as Cowper's relative and confidante. When she met her in 1780, Fanny Burney was impressed: "Lady Hesketh made us a very long, sociable, and friendly visit before our departure, in which she appeared to much advantage, with respect to conversation, abilities, and good breeding."[18] Twelve years later, Fanny reiterated her admiration for Lady Hesketh, but she also put her finger on a very real aspect of Harriot's demeanor: "I began, or rather returned, a new visiting acquaintance in Lady Hesketh, whom I have long and often met at other houses. She is a well-informed, well-bred, sensible woman; somewhat too precise and stiff, but other wise agreeable."[19] Mrs. Thrale, who classified Lady Hesketh in 1780 as one of the

three "Women I *like* the best in the World,"[20] also attempted to
define that quality in Lady Hesketh's personality which made others
become defensive:

> Dear Lady Hesketh! . . . She is: so round, so sweet, so plump,
> so polished; so red, so white,—every Quality of a Naples Wash-
> Ball. with more Beauty than almost any body, as much Wit as
> many a body; and six Times the Quantity of polite Literature—
> Belles Lettres as we call 'em; Lady Hesketh is wholly neglected
> by the Men:—why is that? if it were Age that stopt her Prog-
> ress—*Volontierre;* but many as old are caress'd, admired, &
> follow'd: I never can find out what that Woman does to keep
> the people from adoring her.[21]

The quality of personality which repelled others was the amazingly
opinionated views which Harriot Hesketh possessed on most subjects and which she would express forthrightly and sometimes bel-
ligerently. This was an aspect of her own personality that she recognized: "I am afraid you will think me *very troublesome,* & very
Impertinent, and indeed I feel that I have long been both . . . but
having thus acquir'd a *decided* Character, I believe I have nothing
to do but to keep *up to it.*"[22] ". . . I too often give way to an Im-
petuosity of Temper, which I [am] sensible never does any good to
those I wish to serve, and cannot fail to be in every way detrimental
to myself; I shall only adde on this subject, that it is difficult to see
what I see, and keep within the bounds of that moderation which
I nevertheless feel is required of me . . ."[23] Harriot Hesketh held
especially strong opinions on social class and politics (she was an
ardent Tory), on the monarchy (which she adored beyond the point
of idolatry), and her family (whose reputation she attempted to protect at all costs and by all means).

Politics was a topic on which the cousins managed to quarrel.
Cowper greatly admired the revolution in France—although he
wanted it to remain there. He disliked Tom Paine, but he often espoused radical causes in his letters. Cowper's Whig sentiments were
thus never really in accord with Lady Hesketh's political philosophy, and the cousins chided each other when discussing such issues.
"I used to argue with him sometimes, and this merely to divert both
myself, and Him, yet I love liberty as well as he did."[24] In the same
letter, Harriot went on to express her opinions of democracy and
republicanism in more candid words: "I shall always consider the
People (exactly so call'd) as proper to be placed in the same Class,
with *Fire,* and *Water,*—admirable Servants, but very bad Masters."[25]

Despite arguments with Cowper on such subjects, she had a real confidence in the conservativeness of his political judgment: "and I know his way of thinking (*Whig* as I own he was) too well to believe he wou'd have committed to the Press any thing that could reflect on the Character of the Executive Power."[26]

George III and his family were a source of endless fascination for Lady Hesketh. She was particularly disturbed by the reports and rumors surrounding the King's illness in 1788 and the speculation that he would possibly be forced to abdicate. Her visit to Weymouth in 1799 was notable because the Royal Family was staying there: "my whole time was taken up in looking at the Royal Family who were parading under my window half a dozen times a day and you . . . will readily imagine the pleasure it gave me to see the dear King so *well* and so *happy*."[27] Five years later, she received the great pleasure of having her "well-known Loyalty" rewarded in a most flattering manner:

> I can only say that they have *realiz'd* all the Sanguine ideas I entertain'd, of their *extreme* goodness, & Graciousness! that from the moment they saw me their flattering attentions have never relaxd, that I have been in one week at two Balls, to one of which (given by his Majesty) He invited me himself; at Concerts, & Tea parties, at the Lodge, where I really receiv'd ev'ry honor in their power to bestow, & vastly more than I cou'd deserve—but nothing amidst all these gay doings was so truly flattering and gratifying to me, as the Queen's allowing me to pass near 3 hours Tete-a-Tete with her in her Dressing room on Thursday last; to *me* the time pass'd away insensibly, and She possesses in so Superior a degree the Art of putting people at their Ease, that in spite of the extreme Respect I entertain for her, I was not sensible of any Embarrassment, and I know no person (Equally a Stranger to me) with whom I could have pass'd so much time so agreably.[28]

Lady Hesketh's devotion to the Royal Family was further enhanced when Princess Amelia showed her the traveling case where her favorite books were placed. In addition to Milton, Edward Young, and William Mason, there were two volumes of Cowper which the Princess showed to Lady Hesketh stating, "and here above all, is my favrite Cowper."[29]

Lady Hesketh was very concerned with the place of the Cowper family in society, and she once upbraided Hayley for daring to suggest that the Cowpers had established themselves through trade: "I feel myself led to mention one more Circumstance which I rather think must arise from some mistake, I mean that you speak of our family as being descended from the *Mercantile Line;* . . . tho. I entertain a due Respect (as every English woman ought) for the Character of a *British Merchant,* I would not claim an Affinity with them to which I do not know that I have any title . . ."[30] Despite her impatience with her sisters, Theodora and Charlotte, she always made a point of not allowing altercations within the family to become public. She deliberately concealed the history of Theodora's various confinements for mental illness. She was also careful not to discuss her estrangement from her sister, Elizabeth Croft, whom she would not visit even when they were both staying at Bath or Clifton. In fact, the only "family connection" whose alienation from her she did freely discuss was Sir Thomas's mother, Martha Chetwynd: "I made a point to pay her a Visit . . . , I was so lucky as not to find her at home, and was out when she came to me, and so the thing rests, I did not think it at all Incumbent upon me to renew my visits to a Person of her unhappy character . . ."[31] After Cowper's death, Lady Hesketh was concerned to control as much as she could any publications concerned with him, and this led to quarrels with both Samuel Greatheed and William Hayley.

There were two people in her life upon whom Lady Hesketh bestowed unmixed devotion and esteem—her husband and her cousin, William Cowper. With these two men, the austerity and reserve with which she treated all others was absent.

Mrs. Thrale was certainly impressed with the care Lady Hesketh bestowed upon her dying husband, and she relates an amusing yet touching incident:

> When Sir Thomas Hesketh was dying his Wits were affected, & he rambled a good deal of Delirious Stuff—his Lady kneeling by the Bedside trying to keep up his Spirits said She was sure he would recover—Nonsense (says he) Harriott! how can you talk so?—For shame, she replied gaily *"Je parle comme un Livre;"* "yes, reply'd the dying Man—*et moi je reponds comme un Livre ferme."*[32]

Lady Hesketh herself, in a letter of 1775 at the beginning of Sir Thomas's fatal illness, reveals some of the discomfort she has endured: "I wish it was in my power to give you a more favourable account of Sir Thomas's health, but I think he remains much as you left him, which is not by any means a desirable State, as to myself, I believe I should Recover my health, were it possible for my Mind to be at Ease, but that is impossible In a Situation so truly alarming as mine."[33]

As an elderly woman in 1804, she recollected for Hayley the carefree and reckless times she and Sir Thomas had shared at the outset of their marriage:

> I pass'd, at the very early period of my life, much time at Southampton, I cannot say when I was a Girl, because I was a married woman—but before I was Twenty, and as I was then at least as Gay as I was *young*, I dearsay these good people, thought us very wild Neighbours; I know I shou'd not like such now neither did they then . . . I us'd to walk about in a White & Silver Short Sack and Petticoat! not because I was a Bride for I had been married some years only as an *agreable Deshabille,* & by way of wearing out my wedding garment &— could such a figure appear *now,* it would be thought to have escaped from Bedlam, and indeed I can always laugh when I think of anything so ridiculous & extraordinary.[34]

This passage in its sprightly, self-mocking humor evokes the happy times the couple had spent together in their early married life. Unfortunately, there are few surviving documents to chart the course of the Hesketh marriage. The couple were in Naples from 1768/9 until 1775; they probably made their home there because the climate suited Sir Thomas's precarious health.

3   In the year before her death, Lady Hesketh confessed to Hayley that her attachment as a young girl to Cowper had been amatory:

> I have repeatedly told her [Theadora], I thought it her glory [the attachment between herself and Cowper], & I am sure I should have felt it to be mine, had his attachment been to me!; at five and twenty there may be a natural & a graceful Shiness on such occasions, but surely it is one of the priviledges & the Comfort of advanc'd Life, to be entitled to speak ones Sentiments, & to our own predilections: whether I have more pride, or less delicasy than others of my Sex I know not, but I really think there was no period of *my Life* in which I should not have gloried in being known to the whole World, as the decided Choice of *Such* a *Heart as Cowper's!*[35]

Lady Hesketh's envy of the attachment between Cowper and Theadora might help to explain some of the resentment she felt against her sibling ("this strange sister of mine," "perverse sister").[36] Although she was always ready to defend or justify Thea's bizarre conduct to the outside world, she nevertheless could privately express great dismay at her erratic behavior: ". . . since we cannot new make people, we must have them as they are, and content ourselves with being truly concern'd, when in the hand of the unskilful, Cordials become Poisons."[37] In the same letter, she makes a direct contrast between herself and her sister: ". . . she seldom loves to pitch her Tent *long* in one spot; & in this she differs much from me, who take root wherever chance happens to fling me."[38]

When Lady Hesketh, then, resumed her correspondence with Cowper in 1785, she did not simply pay heed to the needs of a charming and tender cousin of whom she was fond; she was also resuming a relationship which in her youth could have led to marriage. There can be little doubt that her devotion to her cousin was an encompassing one. She had known him as a charming and witty beau in the London of the 1750s; she was obviously concerned about his intense periods of depression, and she may have wished to be in a position to direct his poetic efforts.

4   It was with unmitigated joy that Cowper received Lady Hesketh's letter. He had long been separated from the society into which he had been born and in which he had lived for the first thirty-one years of his life. He had thrust his hand out to that world in his two volumes of verse, and he sometimes received news of former friends and acquaintances from Joseph Hill, but Lady Hesketh's missive inaugurated a more direct involvement with the past. Her rich and varied gossip provided him with a view of a world which he regarded with hostile eyes but whose enticements nevertheless attracted him. She could tell him of the follies of former friends or of their triumphs; she could advise him on the attitudes of polite society; she could offer guidance as to how his name and reputation as a poet should be presented to the sometimes harshly critical world of letters. Cowper could have gathered much of this information from his newspaper or the *Gentleman's Magazine,* but his cousin catered to his interests, and she gave him all the news he wished in letters of warmth and affection. The letters of Lady Hesketh also reminded Cowper that he had not been forgotten by a person with whom the happiest hours of his youth had been spent. He did not associate Harriot Hesketh with the pangs and anguish of his love for Theadora, and she had not been directly

involved in the events surrounding his collapse in 1763. She could remind him of the very finest moments of his past, and she must have reminded him that those moments of intense happiness were real—that they had happened to him—and he saw her as the augur of new possibilities of renewal in his life. Although Cowper's feelings for Lady Hesketh were intense and deep, they did not consist of an elaborate amalgam of varied response: she was merely his dearly beloved, gentle cousin who was concerned about his welfare and who would do everything in her power to assist him.

Cowper's "unspeakable pleasure in being still beloved"[39] by Lady Hesketh is reflected in the letters he sent to her from October 1785 until her arrival at Olney on June 21, 1786, seven months after the renewal of their friendship. Harriot's primary concern was his financial and material welfare; he wrote, "I know you thoroughly and the liberality of your disposition; and have that consummate confidence in the sincerity of your wish to serve me, that delivers me from all aukward constraint, and from all fear of trespassing by acceptance."[40] Lady Hesketh showered her cousin with a variety of gifts (a Solander case, toothbrushes, chiffoniers, books, port), and Cowper who could in turn give only an occasional fowl or rabbit sent her his most beautiful and eloquently phrased letters in payment. She was his "coz," his "dear coz," his "dearest cousin," his "dearest coz," his "dearest Cozwoz," and in a moment of exuberance, his "dearest Cuzzy-wuzzy."[41] From the outset of the renewal of their friendship, she revived within him all the latent forces of benignity and good feeling which one sometimes finds in the verse and in the letters to Unwin. So steeped was Cowper in his devotion to her that he could both truly and artfully say to her: "I love you my cousin . . . my very roses smell of thee."[42]

In his letters in the autumn and winter of 1785–86, Cowper revealed the tremendous challenges and difficulties facing a would-be translator of Homer, and Lady Hesketh became involved in Cowper's somewhat complex negotiations with Joseph Johnson and General Cowper regarding the specimen proposal. He told of his life at Olney, of his severe depression in 1773. He confided to her how poetry had become his "therapy"[43] against his ever-threatening melancholia. He also asked Lady Hesketh to thank "Anonymous" for his letters and his gifts, particularly the magnificent desk which arrived on December 7.[44] In his letters, Cowper always refers to "Anonymous" as masculine, but it is likely he realized that Theadora was the source of these mysterious missives and gifts: "Anonymous is come again; —may God bless him, whosoever he be . . .

I . . . know nothing of anonymous, but that I love him heartily and with most abundant cause."⁴⁵ Cowper was also enchanted with the tortoiseshell snuffbox from the same source with the "portraits" of Tiney, Puss, and Bess: "the most elegant Compliment that ever Poet was honour'd with."⁴⁶ Bemusedly, he told his cousin in January 1786: "I am become the wonder of the Post Office in this town. They never sent so many letters to London in their lives."⁴⁷

It was early in February 1786 that Lady Hesketh told Cowper she would like to visit him and Mrs. Unwin at Olney. Cowper's response was immediate: "I have been impatient to tell you that I am impatient to see you again."⁴⁸ Cowper's letters to Lady Hesketh from February 9, 1786, until June 12, 1786, are filled with delighted expectation at such a meeting: "And will it not be one of the most extraordinary æras of my extraordinary life?"⁴⁹ However, there were many difficulties to overcome before Lady Hesketh arrived in Olney on June 21.

Cowper and Mrs. Unwin assumed at first that Lady Hesketh and at least part of her entourage would stay with them: "Talk not of an Inn, mention it not for your life."⁵⁰ Lady Hesketh did not wish to stay at Orchard Side (she probably did not want to put Cowper and Mrs. Unwin to any expense) and there ensued various attempts to find a suitable location for Harriot, her lady's maid, Mrs. Eaton, Cookee, and Samuel. There was the possibility of staying at Judith Rubathon's house directly opposite Orchard Side, and Maurice Smith's house was also considered. It was Mrs. Smith, however, who finally suggested the solution to all the difficulties concerning housing: "Lady H. is to have all the vicarage, except two rooms, at the rate of ten guineas a year; and Maurice will furnish it for five guineas from June to November, inclusive."⁵¹ Not only was there the vexing question of where Lady Hesketh was to stay, there was also a great deal of difficulty as to when she would arrive. She told Cowper in February that she would visit him in early June; in early April, she suggested that she postpone the visit until August. Lady Hesketh relented on the proposed delay but said she could not arrive in Olney until June 15 because of an expected visit from the Earl Cowper early in the month. Harriot ultimately arrived a week later than the fifteenth of June because of difficulty in renting a suitable coach by the middle of that month.

Lady Hesketh's fussiness concerning the housing at Olney and her various delays were at least in part caused by some shyness about seeing her cousin after so many years. The usually timid poet did not feel any such trepidation, and he remonstrated with her: "Ah!

my Cousin, you begin already to fear and quake. What a hero am I, compared with you. I have no fears of *you*. On the contrary, am bold as a lion."[52] Nine days before she arrived, he told Lady Hesketh, "When I wake in the night, I feel my spirits the lighter because you are coming."[53] In February 1786, he had anticipated their reunion in a dream of great vividness: "About three nights since I dreamed that, sitting in our summer-house, I saw you coming towards me. *With inexpressible pleasure I sprang to meet you, caught you in my arms, and said,—Oh my precious, precious cousin, may God make me thankful that I see thy face again!*"[54] However, as he confessed to William Unwin: "Her first appearance was too much for me. My Spirits, instead of being greatly raised as I had inadvertently supposed they would be, broke down with me under the pressure of too much joy, and left me flat, or rather melancholy throughout the day to a degree that was mortifying to myself and alarming to her."[55]

Despite the false start, Lady Hesketh's visit at Olney from June 21 until mid-November, a stay of approximately five months, was a time of undisputed joy for Cowper. The cousins recollected their past times together; they discussed Cowper's two volumes of verse and all the intricacies of the Homer translation and its subscription list; Cowper frankly related his periods of severe depression, and he told her of his meeting with Theadora in 1763. It was a time of frank and intimate discussion, but it was also a time of high spirits. "She pleases every body, and is pleased in her turn with every thing she finds at Olney; is always cheerful and sweet temper'd, and knows no pleasure equal to that of communicating pleasure to us and all around her."[56]

Early during her stay at Olney, Lady Hesketh provided Theadora with an account of an evening spent with Cowper and Mrs. Unwin at the Vicarage:

> It proving a wet evening, we had no temptation to walk, but continued sitting comfortably round one dining-table without stirring till after supper. Our friend delights in a large table and a large chair; there are two of the latter comforts in my parlour. I am sorry to say that he and I always spread ourselves out in them, leaving poor Mrs. Unwin to find all the comfort she can in a small one, half as high again as ours, and considerably harder than marble. However, she protests it is what she likes, that she prefers a high chair to a low one, and a hard to a soft one; and I hope she is sincere; indeed I am persuaded

she is. Her constant employment is knitting stockings, which she does with the finest needles I ever saw, and very nice they are (the stockings I mean). Our cousin has not for many years worn any other than those of her manufacture. She knits silk, cotton, and worsted. She sits knitting on one side of the table in her spectacles, and he on the other reading to her (when he is not employed in *writing*) in his.[57]

Lady Hesketh had been very concerned before her arrival at Olney about Mrs. Unwin, and she had asked Cowper for precise information on the nature of their friendship: "Your question, your natural, well warranted, and most reasonable question concerning me and Mrs. Unwin, shall be answered at large when we meet. But to Mrs. Unwin I refer you for that answer; she is most desirous to give you a most explicit one. I have a history, my dear, belonging to me, which I am not the proper person to relate. You have heard somewhat of it, —as much as it was possible for me to write; but that *somewhat* bears a most inconsiderable proportion to the whole."[58]

When Lady Hesketh and Mrs. Unwin finally did meet, Mrs. Unwin doubtlessly reassured Lady Hesketh that the "engagement" had been firmly broken off and that she and Cowper lived as mother and son. In the same letter in which she spoke of an evening at the Vicarage, Lady Hesketh gave an extensive and glowing portrait of Mary Unwin:

She is very far from grave; on the contrary, she is cheerful and gay, and laughs *de bon coeur* upon the smallest provocation. Amidst all the little Puritanical words, which fall from her *de temps en temps,* she seems to have by nature a great fund of gaiety—great, indeed, must it have been, not to have been totally overcome by the close confinement in which she has lived, and the anxiety she must have undergone for one whom she certainly loves as well as one human being can love another. I will not say she idolizes him, because that she would think wrong, but she certainly seems to possess the truest regard and affection for this excellent creature, and as I before said, has, in the most literal sense of those words, no will, or shadow or inclination, but what is *his.* My account of Mrs. Unwin may seem, perhaps to you, on comparing my letters, contradictory; but when you consider that I began to write at the moment, at the first moment that I saw her, you will not wonder. Her character develops itself by degrees; and though I

might lead you to suppose her grave and melancholy, she is
not so by any means. When she speaks upon grave subjects she
does express herself with a Puritanical tone, and in Puritanical
expressions, but on all other subjects she seems to have a great
disposition to cheerfulness and mirth; and, indeed, had she
not, she could not have gone through all she has. I must say,
too, that she seems to be very well read in the English poets, as
appears by several little questions which she makes from time
to time, and has a true taste for what is excellent in that way.
There is something truly affectionate and sincere in her manner. No one can express more heartily than she does her joy to
have me at Olney; and as this must be for his sake, it is an
additional proof of her regard and esteem for him.[59]

In 1786, Mary Unwin was not yet the "enchantress" or "the Old
Lady," but someone, like herself, completely devoted to Cowper:
"As to her, she does seem, in *real truth,* to have no will left on
earth but for his good, and literally no will but *his.*"[60] Having
been satisfied soon after her arrival at Olney that the friendship
between Cowper and Mrs. Unwin was of the highest integrity,
Harriot turned her hand to practical affairs.

Within three weeks of her stay at Olney, she had arranged for
Cowper's limited resources to be augmented. After looking about
Olney and having settled these difficulties, Lady Hesketh decided
it was time that he be exposed to cultivated people such as herself.
There were also excursions to nearby Gayhurst and other places of
interest by Lady Hesketh's coach. The sedentary habits of Cowper
and Mrs. Unwin were transformed to such an extent that a pious
neighbor in Olney wrote to Newton to complain. Newton relayed
the censure back to Cowper in a letter to Mary Unwin and evidently passed on some words of his own on worldly living. As we
have seen, the poet responded angrily.[61] In addition to encouraging
Cowper in what might have seemed "dissipation" to some of his
neighbors and friends, Lady Hesketh suggested Cowper abandon
Olney in favor of the more rustic and secluded charms of Weston Underwood. He himself had first hinted at such a change
shortly before Lady Hesketh's arrival at Olney in 1786. He mentioned encountering Mrs. Throckmorton and Teresa, her sister-in-
law, and the ensuing discussion about a house at Weston "at present empty. It is a very good one, infinitely superior to ours. When
we drank chocolate with them, they both expressed their ardent
desire that we would take it, wishing much to have us for nearer

neighbours. We could not accept this offer for reasons that we could not give; it is unfurnished and we have no furniture fit for it, nor should find it very convenient to purchase such as it deserves."62 When she was settled at Olney and had been charmed by the Throckmortons, despite their Roman Catholicism and Whig leanings, Lady Hesketh was anxious that her cousin be placed in such a comfortable house with the prospect of becoming friendlier with the aristocratic family: "I wish he could, with ease to himself, see as much of them as possible: for I am sure a little variety of company, and a little cheerful society, is necessary to him."63 By August 31, the move had been arranged.

After a visit which had included good talk, discussions of the translation of Homer, and improved arrangements regarding Cowper's financial status as well as the prospect of moving to a much larger and more pleasant house, Lady Hesketh left Olney in November 1786. In his first letter to her after her departure, Cowper implored her to visit again: "I will not begin already to teaze you upon that subject, but Mrs. U remembers to have heard from your own lips that you hate London in the Spring. Perhaps therefore by that time you may be glad to escape from a scene which will be every day growing more disagreeable, that you may enjoy the comforts of the Lodge."64

When Cowper related to William Unwin in July 1786 the jubilant welcome that had been bestowed upon Lady Hesketh when she arrived at Olney ("I am fond of the sound of Bells, but was never more pleased with those of Olney, than when they rang her into her new habitation"),65 he was justifiably pleased by the enormous compliment which had been paid to his cousin. The town of Olney had recognized her place both in the world and in her cousin's esteem. For the remainder of his life, she would continue to act as his confidante and trusted advisor; she would pay further visits to him at Weston; she would take a large part of the responsibility for his welfare until his death in 1800. In the great sorrows that were to engulf him in the near future (the death of William Unwin in December 1786) and in the years to come (Mrs. Unwin's illness and death; the move to Norfolk), she continued her watchful support. Although she was proud to be known as Cowper's cousin and was to act in a haughty manner in regard to his reputation, she was a loyal friend, and she was careful not to betray that trust. Her relationship with Cowper was similar to Lady Austen's in that both women transported the concerns of the feared metropolis of London into Cowper's confined world of Olney; both women reminded him of the society which he had fled, and yet they also summoned up for him the finest aspects of that civilization. If Lady Austen is the muse of *The Task*, Lady Hesketh is the muse of the letters, for it is in his elegantly contrived and honestly expressed letters to her that the fullest force and vitality of his prose is found. Although Lady Hesketh's role as muse was not public, it was very real, and Cowper's most beautiful letters are suffused with his affection for her.

1   COWPER MADE daily forays to Weston as early
as August 1784, when he told William Unwin that he and Mary
found "in those agreeable bowers such amusement as leaves us but
little room to regret that we can go no farther."[1] It is a short distance, less than a mile, from Olney to Weston, but they are vastly
different places. The pent-up, drab town gives way to a flat, idyllic
landscape which quickly ascends to a high ridge overlooking the
Ouse. This is the setting of Weston Underwood, which is a cluster
of houses built into the terrain. The "superior beauties" of Weston
made it for Cowper "our pleasantest retreat of all."[2]

The exquisite natural charm of Weston was graced by the presence of the Throckmorton family. Cowper had known of the Squire
of Weston and his family well before 1784, but it was not until May
of that year when he and Mrs. Unwin attended by invitation an
attempt to "throw off a Balloon at Mr. Throckmorton's"[3] that any
sort of relationship began. Cowper, knowing that the recusant family had been subject to affronts because of their religion, was especially cordial on this occasion. Further invitations to witness the
launchings (or attempted launchings) of new balloons followed,
but in September, Cowper, somewhat disappointedly, described the
friendship as "most perfectly polite" and "in statû quo,"[4] although
he had been given a key to the family garden. John Throckmorton
was certainly pleased by a compliment which had been paid to him
in *The Task* (1, 252–65), and he circulated some subscription proposals for the translation of Homer; however, cordiality was transformed into friendship when the Throckmortons, who lived at
Weston Hall but who owned nearby Weston Lodge, urged Cowper
and Mrs. Unwin to rent the latter. Harriot Hesketh prompted the
move, and in May 1786 Cowper was delighted when he heard

Throckmorton wanted to be on a more intimate footing. The eager pursuit of the company of Cowper and Mary, the shared sensitivity toward animals,[5] and the ability of the Throckmortons to joke about their Roman Catholicism contributed to the graceful and pleasant ease which remained throughout the friendship. When they moved to Weston, Cowper and Mrs. Unwin found that the good nature and conviviality of their landlords increased immeasurably. In August, three months before the move, Cowper's reserve had worn off, and he and Throckmorton looked forward to winter evening conversations—Mrs. Throckmorton had even volunteered to transcribe the Homer for him. In December, he was able to tell Harriot Hesketh that all his great expectations had been met.

Of distinguished recusant stock, the Throckmortons had been associated with Weston Underwood from 1446 when Margaret, the daughter of Robert Olney, married Thomas Throckmorton, of Coughton, Warwickshire. Cowper's Mr. Throckmorton was John Courtenay Throckmorton, who was to succeed in 1791 to the estate and baronetcy of his grandfather, Sir Robert (John's father had died in 1767, predeceasing his own father), and to leave Weston at that time for Buckland House, Berkshire; John had married in 1782 Maria, daughter of Thomas Giffard of Chillington Hall, Staffordshire. Weston Hall after 1792 was occupied by George, John's brother, who was also known to Cowper. He and Mrs. Unwin were especially fond of George's wife, Catharine, daughter of Thomas Stapleton of Carlton, Yorkshire. Another good friend at Weston Hall was the Throckmortons' chaplain, the Reverend William Gregson; the "padre" was a companionable person, and he, as well as Maria and George Throckmorton, copied portions of the translation of Homer.

The physical setting of Weston was ravishing, and the residents at the Lodge were the type of people of whose company Cowper— and Mrs. Unwin—had been long deprived at Olney. The Throckmortons and their associates were fitting companions for a man who now saw himself as a committed writer and who, through his subscription scheme, was at the age of fifty-five about to launch himself on the world as a professional man of letters. Harriot Hesketh and John Newton had reservations about Cowper's contacts with Roman Catholics; but, in his friendship with the recusants, who were suspect in the neighborhood because of their religious convictions and, as a result, cut off from local society, Cowper moved back to the type of company and mode of living from which he had long been disengaged. Lady Hesketh initiated this change in 1785 and

1786, but it was to be in daily companionship with the Throck-mortons that it was lived.

Weston Hall consisted of a quadrangle enclosing a court; the north or Queen Anne front, the principal one, faced the park and had been built in 1710. The stables were at right angles to this entrance, and the rest of the exterior was partly in Queen Anne style and partly Elizabethan. The house had probably been begun at the end of the fifteenth century; it contained the trapdoors and hidden rooms which were a feature of many Roman Catholic houses in the sixteenth century. The park belonging to the Hall, seventy-five acres in extent, had varied and extensive views over the Ouse and the surrounding land. The grounds at Weston had been laid out for the Throckmortons by "Capability" Brown. Although Cowper somewhat sardonically termed Brown "Th'omnipotent magician" at the end of book 3 of *The Task*, he earlier in book 1 evoked his work at Weston:

> And now, with nerves new-brac'd and spirits cheer'd,
> We tread the wilderness, whose well-roll'd walks,
> With curvature of slow and easy sweep—
> Deception innocent—give ample space
> To narrow bounds.[6]

Within the Wilderness were the Alcove, the hexagon with three open sides built in 1753, the Gothic Temple, the avenue of lime trees, and the Rustic Bridge. There were similar—if not as carefully planned—delights to be found at the Ho-brook, a diminutive stream that crossed the road halfway from Olney to Weston, which led to the First Spinnie (called the Shrubbery in Cowper's poem), the Moss-house, the field which gave a splendid view of the Peasant's Nest (a picturesque thatch-roofed cottage), the Second Spinnie, and the Chestnut Avenue of the Park. Cowper had explored all these places well before the move to Weston (they are all celebrated in *The Task*), but it must have been an especial pleasure in 1786 to live among them.

Weston Lodge, Cowper's home, stood halfway up the street of Weston Underwood among the stone-built and thatched cottages of which the village primarily consisted. It was a good-sized seventeenth-century building of stone with a tiled roof, with a small garden in front and a larger one at the back. A low wall and railings separated it from the street. At Olney, Cowper had lived in a house which fronted and was a part of the market square; in the countrified atmosphere of Weston, his house was clearly demarcated from the road. Cowper's removal to Weston represented not only a change in status but also a symbolic withdrawal to Parnassian splendor.

2   There were other pleasant neighbors at Weston: the Reverend John Buchanan, who lived a few doors away, and John Higgins, who was only eighteen when Cowper moved to Weston. Buchanan, the curate of nearby Ravenstone, was of a similar temperament to Cowper in his possession "in a scene of rustic privacy, [of] extensive scholarship, . . . gentleness of manners, and . . . a contemplative dignity of mind";[7] it was he who suggested that Cowper write a poem on the four ages of man, and Cowper wrote him in 1795 one of his last extant letters. When Cowper learned that young Johnny Higgins could repeat many of his poems by heart, he invited him to tea, and this began a friendship to which Higgins later "reverted with affectionate delight and excusable pride."[8] In 1792, he inherited the estate of Turvey Abbey, several miles away, and left Weston. Higgins's admiration for Cowper, however, was unflagging, and he cherished a collection of relics of the poet (he wore his shoe buckles constantly).

It was, nevertheless, the cultivation, breeding, and youthfulness of the Throckmortons which captivated Cowper, and he became deeply involved in the activities of that family. John Courtenay Throckmorton's involvement with Charles James Fox, his sympathy with the Prince of Wales, and his membership on the Catholic Committee would not have endeared him to Cowper, but Cowper was able to put these matters aside in the interests of friendship. The Throckmortons were suitable companions for a man who worked all day at Troy, and they were to shore him up time and again in the next five years, but even their good offices did not prevent Cowper from suffering a major depression early in 1787.

Moving house can be an unsettling experience, and the removal to Weston may have contributed to Cowper's sinking spirits: he had expected a great deal from the move, perhaps too much, and at first he had thought he had indeed escaped the prison of Olney; depression may have invaded him when he came to realize, two months afterward, that, despite the much more pleasant circumstances of his life, he still had to battle the same antagonistic inner forces. It was, however, his double loss in 1786 that overwhelmed him.

Cowper had come to depend on Harriot Hesketh and had eagerly looked forward to her visit; that visit had been a success, but she had then returned to her London life. The event, however, which deeply impressed itself on him was the sudden death of William Unwin at Winchester on November 29, 1786, while visiting Henry Thornton. Cowper was strangely reticent about Unwin's death in his letters; he dwelt on it at length only in his letter to Lady Hesketh of December 4. There, he lamented Unwin, who had "attained to an Age when, if they are at any time useful, men become most useful to their families, their friends, and the world."[9] Cowper's statement is a severely restricted, not callous, tribute to the man he had seen as both a son and a brother. As always, he avoided exploration of the causes of his distress.

During the first six months of 1787, Cowper lost a great deal of weight. By July 5, 1787, he was somewhat fatter, although Harriot Hesketh was concerned: "I am griev'd to hear he looks so thin, but 'tis impossible he should do otherwise after all he has gone through. Mrs. Unwin's last three or four letters give me the strongest hopes of his recovery."[10] This extreme bout, although of relatively short duration, probably followed the course of the depressions of 1763 and 1773, with psychotic interludes and suicide attempts. The *Universal Review* in 1890 claimed "it was Mrs. Unwin's hand which actually cut the rope when, for the second or third time in his life, Cowper attempted suicide in 1787."[11]

3   As Cowper emerged from his confinement in 1787, one of the first persons to whom he wrote was Samuel Rose. Earlier, in January 1787, Rose had called on Cowper at Weston. Like Unwin, he was of frail constitution (he was to die at the age of thirty-seven in 1804), and his admiration for Cowper was much like that which Unwin had earlier bestowed. It may be that this visit awakened in Cowper dormant memories of the twenty-one-year-old William Unwin he had met at Huntingdon in 1765. In any event, Cowper eagerly encouraged the friendship:

I have not yet taken up the pen again, except to write to you. The little taste that I have had of your company, and your kindness in finding me out, make me wish, that we were nearer neighbours, and that there were not so great a disparity in our years; that is to say, not that you were older, but that I were younger. Could we have met in early life, I flatter myself that we might have been more intimate, than now we are likely to be. But you shall not find me slow to cultivate such a measure of your regard, as your friends of your own age can spare me.[12]

This intrepid young man was the son of William Rose, who kept a highly regarded school at Chiswick. Samuel graduated from the University of Glasgow in 1787, entered Lincoln's Inn, and was called to the Bar in 1796. While a student at Glasgow, he had lodged with William Richardson, a man of strong literary interests, and it was Richardson and some of Rose's professors at Glasgow who commissioned him to call on Cowper to pay their compliments. Although Rose never acted as a go-between with Joseph Johnson in the way William Unwin had done for *The Task,* he was to place his legal abilities at Cowper's disposal and to negotiate the financial arrangements for the translation of Homer. Rose later edited the minor works of Goldsmith, compiled two volumes of law reports, and contributed to the *Monthly Review.* His most famous client was William Blake, whom he represented at his trial for sedition at Chichester in 1803. Although his health was precarious and he had been quite ill a number of times, there is a legend that he caught a cold at Chichester, while defending Blake, from which he never recovered.[13] Harriot Hesketh had thought the profession of lawyer too arduous for him, and she was surprised to hear of his marriage in 1790 to Sarah, daughter of William Farr, the distinguished physician: "He came to take leave of me. I well remember [his] saying he was going to the West of England for Change of Air as he was not in good health—at that time he appeared to me to be *Dying!* & never did I expect to see him again! but in a few weeks he return'd equally the Shadow of Himself, but brisk & in Spirits, and told me he was going to be married! nothing ever astonish'd me more!"[14]

Another friend from the Weston years was Margaret King, the daughter of the Reverend Hans Deveille, Vicar of Saling and Felsted in Essex. She had married in 1752 the Reverend John King, Rector of Pertenhall, Bedfordshire. King—who had been with Cowper at Westminster—matriculated at Balliol College, Oxford, and was later a Fellow of King's College, Cambridge. Although Cowper was pleased to hear from the wife of a former school fellow, she also wrote as a friend of his late brother, whom she had probably known when he was a student at Felsted when her father was the Vicar there: "A Letter from a lady who was once intimate with my Brother, could not fail of being most acceptable to me."[15] Cowper's letter to her of February 12, 1788—the first of twenty-eight extant letters to Mrs. King—began a series of somewhat formal, moralizing missives to his brother's friend.

4   The Weston years from mid-1787 until 1791 were largely devoted to Homeric—at times, seemingly Herculean—tasks, but Cowper also managed to fulfill two other part-time occupations as book reviewer and occasional versifier of original verse. These were productions of the left hand, but necessary occupations for a man whose entire waking life was devoted to literature and the pursuit of reputation.

Ten of the eleven reviews which Cowper wrote for Joseph Johnson's *Analytical Review* appeared in 1789 and 1790. Lady Hesketh thought the reviewing of books was unworthy of her cousin's status as an important poet and translator, and he admittedly found the "Reviewing business . . . too much an interruption of [his] main concern."[16] Although he had taken on these pieces to accommodate his publisher who required competent reviews for his magazine, he regarded his involvement as something of a nuisance; they provide, nevertheless, fascinating evidence of what William Cowper perceived to be the laws of literature and his own place in that world as legislator.

Cowper, as we have seen, could be stern in assessing the work of other writers. In his letter to Unwin of January 5, 1782, he made his feelings about Samuel Johnson explicit: "I admire Johnson as a man of great Erudition, and Sense, but when he sets himself up for a Judge of Writers upon the Subject of Love, a passion which I suppose he never felt in his life, he might as well think himself qualified to pronounce upon a treatise of Horsemanship or the Art of Fortification."[17] Comments like this show a capacity for severity which Cowper excised in any writing intended for publication—whether in the satirical verse of 1782 or in his book reviews.

In these reviews, however, Cowper aptly mixes praise and blame; he can be deliciously sarcastic, and he even jokes about suicide when remonstrating against the phrase, *"To finish life before that life expires"* from *Poetical Essays* by a "young Gentleman of Hertford College, Oxford": "The line distinguished by italics is a very alarming one, especially considering that it is written by a lover mourning the death of his mistress. His tutor should watch him narrowly, and his bed-maker should every night take care to secure his garters";[18] he shows a fastidious care for language: ". . . it appears to us properly part of a reviewer's province to mount guard on the language of authors . . . convinced as we are that our language will never cease to be charged with barbarism and impurity, unless men of talents and of letters will condescend to be strictly grammatical";[19] above all, the reviews are the work of a man who is a practicing poet and who reads the work of others to assess technical as well as thematic mastery.

The work of Joel Barlow (*The Vision of Columbus*) and Timothy Dwight (*The Conquest of Canäan*) appealed to Cowper, and he advised young Englishmen to take note that these two poems, "respectable works both, and on well-chosen subjects, are the productions of two *young* Americans."[20] He felt there was "more good sense . . . than good poetry"[21] in the anonymous *Essay on Sensibility*, which he attacked for its problems in versification. Joseph Champion's translation of *The Poems of Ferdosi* did not appeal because he did not think the subject matter ("the imperial annals of Persia") of much interest, but it did lead to an interesting reflection: "Poetry can give grace to monsters; there is hardly any subject so deformed in itself, but verse has charms that can recommend it to our contemplation."[22] Cowper must have seen immediately a resemblance between himself and G. N. Heerkens who wrote *The Friesland Birds:* "The author informs us in his preface, that finding it necessary during the troubles with which Holland has been agitated, to disengage himself from scenes of active life and to retire to his native place in the country, he there amused himself with the composition in verse of the history of such birds as were most common in Friesland."[23] Heerkens in exile identified himself with Ovid, and those allusions are not lost on Cowper, for he recognized a kindred spirit in Heerkens when he commended his accounts of the birds as "minute, philosophical, and we doubt not, given with exact fidelity."[24] However, Cowper's most enthusiastic praise was given to Erasmus Darwin, who displayed a "strong romantic imagination":

His descriptions themselves are luminous as language selected with the finest taste can make them, and meet the eye with a boldness of projection unattainable by any hand but that of a master. . . . All his flowers undergo a change, not a simple one, but each into as many persons, male and female, as there are symptoms of either sex in their formation. For it is on their sexuality that he has built his poem. Reversing the Metamorphoses of Ovid, who transformed persons, human and divine, into trees and flowers, he calls them (as he says in his proem) from their vegetable mansions to their original animality again. He endues them with human passions and propensities; they manifest all the variety of feelings to which amorous inclination subjects its votaries, but always with a strict attention on the poet's part to the discoveries which philosophy has made among them.[25]

In a passage such as this, Cowper's learning, his precise control of language, his ability to deal directly with an author's concerns, and his generosity to fellow poets are evident. The reviews may have seemed hack work to him and to others, but in those pieces many of Cowper's governing literary concerns are reflected in his meditations on a wide variety of poetry.

Cowper also managed during the Weston years to compose occasional lyrics which reflect his ability to be exact as well as philosophical in his own observations of nature. There is the saga of his spaniel, Beau, in *The Dog and the Water-Lily* and the gentle attack on Rousseau, *Pairing Time Anticipated, A Fable,* which begins: "I shall not ask Jean Jacques Rousseau, / If birds confabulate or no, / 'Tis clear that they were always able / To hold discourse, at least, in fable."[26] *On the Death of Mrs. Throckmorton's Bullfinch* is very much in the mode of Gray's *Elegy on the Death of a Favourite Cat,* although darker, and the reader is meant to participate fully in the mythic world which the poet summons up at the end of the poem:

> Maria weeps—the Muses mourn—
> So, when by Bacchanalians torn,
>   On Thracian Hebrus' side
> The tree-enchanter Orpheus fell;
> His head alone remain'd to tell
>   The cruel death he died.[27]

Cowper's last long poem, *Yardley Oak,* was written in 1791, and there he draws a comparison between the oak which survives and the "oracle"—himself—whose death is nigh. However, Cowper would not have devoted himself to original verse while at work on the translation of Homer if specific requests had not been made to him for three types of verse: the poems for the Northampton Bills of Mortality, the anti-slavery poems, and the poems on the King's recovery.

Cowper told Lady Hesketh in a letter of November 27, 1787,

how he came to be pressed into service as a verse writer for the
Northampton Bills:

> On Monday Morning last, Sam brought me word into the study
> that a man was in the kitchen who desired to speak with me.
> I order'd him in. A plain decent elderly figure made its appear-
> ance, and being desired to sit, spoke as follows. Sir, I am Clerk
> of the Parish of All Saints in Northampton. Brother of Mr. Cox
> the Upholst'rer. It is customary for the person in my office to
> annex to a Bill of Mortality which he publishes at Christmas,
> a Copy of Verses. You would do me a great favour, Sir, if you
> would furnish me with one.[28]

Cowper demurred at first, suggesting alternatives which had not
escaped Mr. Cox, but when he realized the man had walked all the
way to Weston to present his request, he agreed to supply the desired poem. The six ballad-style poems (1787, 1788, 1789, 1790,
1792, 1793) which Cowper eventually contributed for the annual
bills make the same point: "No present health can health insure /
For yet an hour to come; / No med'cine, though it often cure, /
Can always balk the tomb."[29]

Cowper in *Charity* and *The Task* had expressed his antipathy to
slavery, but early in 1788, Lady Hesketh had intimated that he
should write a poem specifically against it. Having heard that Hannah More was about to publish such a work, Cowper declined the
suggestion. However, in March 1788, Lady Balgonie, John Thornton's daughter, had written to Newton asking him to intercede
with Cowper to compose abolitionist ballads which could be sung
in the streets, and complying with her request, Cowper composed
The Negro's Complaint and *Sweet Meat Has Sour Sauce*, both
completed by March 21; *The Morning Dream* was finished shortly
afterward. These three poems, specifically indited for the Committee for the Abolition of the Slave Trade, are strongly conceived,
dramatic descriptions of the horrors of slavery. The setting at sea,
the sense of deprivation and separation, and the castaway ambience
of *The Negro's Complaint* display the strong similarity Cowper
saw between his plight and that of the slaves:

> Forc'd from home, and all its pleasures,
>   Afric's coast I left forlorn;
> To increase a stranger's treasures,
>   O'er the raging billows borne.
> Men from England bought and sold me,

Paid my price in paltry gold;
But, though theirs they have enroll'd me,
Minds are never to be sold.[30]

There is also a hint of disguised autobiography in Cowper's poems celebrating George III's recovery from (alleged) madness.

The King's mental stability had declined considerably in the autumn of 1788, and on November 5 he had become delirious and assaulted the Prince of Wales. There was talk in late 1788 and early 1789 of forming a Regency, and Cowper was gratified to see in the court circulars in February that the King was recovering. Cowper wrote a poem—now lost—in January 1789 in which he looked forward to the King's approaching return of good health. It was in March 1789, after the King had resumed his normal duties, that Cowper composed *Annus Memorabilis 1789* and *The Queen's Nocturnal Visit* at the suggestion of that ardent monarchist, Harriot Hesketh. On June 25, 1789, the King went to Weymouth in the hope that the sea air would further improve his health, and Cowper responded to a dispatch dated July 11 with a short poem celebrating the report that sea bathing had indeed proved beneficial. Although William Cowper held Whig principles, he had the greatest respect for monarchy. Nevertheless, the King's seemingly miraculous recovery from mental affliction must have acted as the real incentive on Cowper's part in composing this particular group of poems.

5   By 1790, Cowper was totally immersed in his translation of Homer when another interruption to his busy schedule intervened. He had in the past five years established strong ties with Harriot Hesketh, Margaret King, Samuel Rose, and the Throckmortons. Each of these friendships had re-created important aspects of his past. In January 1790, however, Cowper had not been in touch with his mother's family for twenty-seven years.

On a January evening when Cowper was at dinner at the Throckmortons, Kitch, the gardener, arrived from Olney with a message from a stranger who had just arrived on the London coach. Mrs. Unwin sent Kitch back to town with a message saying that Mr. Cowper was at the Hall and would reply in the morning. When Cowper returned to the Lodge just after ten, he was disconcerted to discover the billet on the study table. "Who in the world can it be,

and what does he want?"[31] The letter somewhat pompously and
stiltedly introduced its twenty-one year old author: "J. Johnson, a
grandson of the Rev. R. Donne, late of Catfield, in Norfolk, is just
arrived at Olney, and with the greatest pleasure will pay his respects to Mr. Cowper in the morning, if he may be allowed that
happiness. Mr. Johnson reflects with satisfaction on being so near
a gentleman whom he has long had the greatest desire to see, and
for which sole purpose his journey to Olney has been so long premeditated."[32] Cowper was not delighted by this intrusion, and, as
he said to Mrs. Unwin, he was not quite sure what his feelings
were: "He may be a grandson of my uncle Roger, for aught I know;
but he may also be a butcher-like man, the very sight of whom will
be enough to kill me."[33]

Cowper went to bed and spent a night of "unremitted watching"
and "most fearful forebodings."[34] When he rose in the morning, he
wrote a polite note ("A grandson of my uncle Roger cannot be but
welcome")[35] inviting Johnny to stay at the Lodge as long as he
wished, and he gave the message to Sam Roberts to deliver. Whatever Cowper's apprehensions had been before his cousin's arrival,
they were dispelled immediately when he met the small, slight man
from Norfolk, and recognized in him at once "a shred of my own
mother."[36] Cowper asked about Johnny's mother and Castres Donne,
and Johnny told him that his mother had died in 1770, when he
was a year old, and that the mourning garb he wore attested to the
death the year before of his uncle. Johnny went on to assure Cowper that his once-beloved cousins, Elizabeth Hewitt, Harriot Balls,
and Anne Bodham, were well. Cowper's ruminations on this mixture of welcome and unhappy news were interrupted by Mrs. Unwin who told him that his morning "stint" of Homer awaited him.

The translator retired from the room, and Johnny had the opportunity to talk with Mrs. Unwin and to hear from her the story
of the poet's life with her at Huntingdon, Olney, and Weston. This
conversation had gone on for some time when Mrs. Unwin reminded Johnny that Cowper would soon be taking his morning
walk and that he would be invited to accompany him. When Cowper and Johnny with Beau, the spaniel, left the Lodge that first
time together, they made an extended tour of the environs: the
Park, the Grove, the Hall, the Colonnade, and the Wilderness. In
future walks, Cowper would often speak little or not at all, but on
this January morning, he described the sights of Weston in detail
and at the end of the walk he pointed to the Greenhouse, which he

said had been at a happier time his consecrated bower. They quietly left the Greenhouse, passed through the Grove, and returned to the Lodge.

Cowper, as he was quick to tell Harriot, immediately conceived a great affection for "the wild boy Johnson"[37]: "There is a simplicity in his character that charms me, and the more because it is so great a rarity. Humour he certainly has, and of the most agreeable kind. . . . He has a countenance which with all the sweetness of temper that it expresses, expresses also a mind much given to reflection and an understanding that in due time will know how to show itself to advantage."[38] Cowper intuitively knew that Johnny's high spirits and exuberance were real, but he also perceived the deep melancholic strain in his temperament.

John's father, also John Johnson, a tanner by profession, had been married three times. He first married Mary Bacon and by her had a daughter Sarah; the name of his second wife is unknown, but she was the mother of Hannah Maria and Anne. Catherine Donne, Johnny's mother, was his third wife. In 1790, Johnny's mother had been dead for twenty years and his father for five. His older sister by two years, Catharine, the only other child from his father's final marriage, was his closest friend. Johnny also visited with and wrote frequently to his Donne aunts, to whom he was attached. Nevertheless, he felt an emotional lack, which manifested itself in an inordinate concern with ancestry and family connections. Certainly, by the time he was a scholar at Gonville and Caius, Cambridge, he had become devoted to the study of pedigree. He was excessively conscious, and ashamed, that his father, although prosperous, had been a tradesman of a very humble kind, and in 1790, Johnny was a young man in search of a new father, whose cultivation and sophistication matched his own aspirations to literary accomplishment.

Earlier at Dereham, Johnny had known Sir John Fenn, the antiquary and editor of the Paston letters, who was able to trace the Donne line back to Thomas Howard, first Duke of Norfolk. This led Johnny to approach Charles Howard, eleventh Duke of Norfolk, in 1789. At that meeting, the Duke, impressed by Johnny's sincerity and interest in poetry, intimated that he celebrate in verse Audley-End, his seat near Saffron Walden. The resulting poem, a hackneyed pastoral eclogue vaguely reminiscent of Theocritus and Spenser, accompanied Johnny on his first visit to Weston, and he claimed that *Audley End* had been written by the Duke of Norfolk. Cowper began to criticize the poem severely until the expression on Johnny's face revealed the lie.

This incident shows not only Johnny's interest in poetry but also, unfortunately, his lack of ability as a writer. It displays likewise his snobbery and his desire to impress. Undoubtedly, there was a great deal of pretentiousness in his character: in a short span of time, he sought out two distinguished relatives, hoping in each case to ingratiate himself. Nevertheless, Cowper immediately accepted Johnny as a son, and he conferred his wholehearted approval on his mercurial young cousin.

Although many of the extraordinary changes in Johnny's life as a result of his involvement with his elderly cousin were some years ahead, his friendship with Cowper from the outset deepened and strengthened his character. When he decided that he must meet his celebrated relative, no one could tell him where he lived. They had simply lost sight of him. Johnny decided that Cowper's publisher was the likely person to inquire of his whereabouts, and so he took the stage to London and turned up at Joseph Johnson's door. Johnson was both befuddled and amused by the young man's request, but he was also touched by his sincerity and eagerness. He quickly ascertained that Johnny had never been to London before. He gave the youth from Norfolk a room for the night and put him on the coach for Olney the next morning. This young man showed real ingenuity in contriving to meet Cowper, just as two days before he had charmed Joseph Johnson.

Despite Cowper's refusal to take part in any church activities, Johnny's friendship with him also inspirited his determination to choose a career in the church, and the influence of James Bean and Samuel Greatheed, both of whom he met through Cowper, deepened his Evangelical interests. By June 1790—six months after they had met—Johnny had decided to abandon his mathematical studies at Cambridge, and he sought Cowper's advice, which was unflinching:

> You never pleased me more than when you told me you had abandoned your mathematical pursuits. It grieved me to think that you were wasting your time and doing perhaps irreparable injury to your constitution merely to gain a little Cambridge fame, not worth your having.[39]

> Life is too short to afford time even for serious trifles. Pursue what you know to be attainable, make truth your object and

your studies will make you a wise man. Let your Divinity, if I may advise, be the Divinity of the glorious Reformation.[40]

Cowper had offered such unequivocal counsel only to one other person, William Unwin, and it is a measure of his devotion to Johnny that he could speak with such frankness so soon after meeting him. Acting on Cowper's advice, Johnny decided to prepare for the ministry by reading for a degree in civil law, and he thus came under the sway of one of the great Cambridge Evangelicals, Joseph Jowett, a Fellow of Trinity Hall.

During his first visit to Weston, Johnny transcribed portions of the translation of Homer, and he went on further walks with his cousin. He spent a pleasant week in Buckinghamshire before going back to London, where he visited with some Donne cousins and called upon Samuel Rose and Lady Hesketh. Harriot was delighted to make Johnny's acquaintance, realizing that the young man from Norfolk could be a useful coadjutor to herself in caring for their cousin. When he arrived back in Norfolk, Johnny told his aunts, Harriot Balls and Anne Bodham, of his encounter with their famous cousin. Mrs. Bodham was so pleased to hear news of her old playmate that in February 1790 she sent him one of her most treasured possessions, the miniature of his mother by Heins.

In turn, Cowper was entranced with Johnny, and he responded warmly and enthusiastically to the prospect of reviving ties with his mother's county and with childhood friends. He was deeply touched when the portrait arrived, as his letter to "Rose" amply shows:

> Whom I thought wither'd and fallen from the stalk but who I find are still alive, nothing could give me greater pleasure than to know it and to learn it from yourself. I loved you dearly when you were a child and love you not a jot the less for having ceased to be so. Every creature that bears any affinity to my own mother is dear to me, and you, the daughter of her brother, are but one remove distant from her; I love you therefore and love you much, both for her sake and for your own.[41]

Cowper's restoration to his mother's family through Johnny came in the midst of his wearying Homeric activities and uplifted him during that formidable venture.

11
Homer: The Heroic Task

1   COWPER'S TRANSLATION into English blank verse of the *Iliad* and *Odyssey* was the most complex literary project in which he ever became involved. Up to the publication of *The Task* in 1785, Cowper had been a gentleman who wrote verses for publication, but with Homer he frequently saw himself as a professional writer dedicated to fame and royalties. Although he referred occasionally in his extant correspondence to his habits as a composer of verse from 1779 to 1784,[1] the letters from late 1785 to 1791[2] are concerned with little more than the translation of Homer and provide the only extended view we have of Cowper the literary craftsman at work. And in those letters, a very determined, frequently passionate, and often aggressive William Cowper comes into being.

In Cowper's eyes, his Homer was the great undertaking of his life, and he became obsessively involved with every aspect of it. In going back to Milton as his obvious predecessor in English blank verse, he was also attempting to forge a literary identity as if Pope had not existed. Cowper's efforts as a translator were to provide him with a great deal of stress and, ultimately, as far as the reviewers were concerned, only a modicum of success. However, Cowper's Homer, in its attempt to redefine the heroic sublime in a manner substantially different from Pope ("the Sublime of Homer, in the hands of Pope, becomes bloated and tumid . . .")[3], is an important document in late eighteenth-century aesthetics.

After completing work on *The Task* in 1784, Cowper felt that he had taken his abilities as a writer of original verse as far as they could go. Yet, he had to live up to the high expectations he had aroused in others and in himself. He did not turn to Homer casually. As a boy at Westminster, he had been steeped in the classics, and the *Iliad* and *Odyssey* stood at the core of his education, as they did for his peers. In 1757, Cowper told a friend: "I would recommend it to you, now that you have made yourself almost a Master of the Paradise lost, to read the Iliad & the Odyssey in their Original Languages."[4] Behind the great English epic loomed Homer. There was a continuity from one to the other. Samuel Johnson had spoken for the majority of educated Englishmen in declaring that Milton owes reverence "to [Homer's] vigour and amplitude of mind to which all generations must be indebted for the art of poetical narration, for the texture of the fable, the variation of incidents, the interposition of dialogue, and all the stratagems that surprise and enchain attention."[5] As such, Homer was perceived as the source and root of poetic energy.

However, in becoming an Evangelical Christian, Cowper had entered quite a different tradition, one which fundamentally opposed devotion to the classics. In *Adelphi,* John Cowper recalled ironically the way in which he had placed a whole life's literary exertions within the Christian framework: "At the age of fourteen or thereabouts, they sent me to a public school where I learned more Latin and more Greek, and last of all to this place where I have been learning more Latin and Greek still. Now, has not this been a blessed life and much to the glory of God?"[6] This may be the way in which the life of a Cambridge don was blessed, but the irony of John Cowper's last words, his sense of wasted time, outweighs that possibility. Christian faith often displaced Homer and the ethos which set such high value on him. Cowper had made this discovery in 1763–1764; his brother, six years later. Unlike John, he had to live with the consequences of his new commitment. By 1784, this had become no easy task for a person with a growing sense of his own creative abilities.

With an increasing desire to write at the outset of the 1780s, Cowper's interest in Homer reawakened. To William Unwin, he made the following request in the autumn of 1780: "If you could meet with a Second Hand Virgil, Ditto Homer, both Iliad & Odyssey, together with a Clavis, for I have no Lexicon, & all tolerably cheap, I shall be obliged to you if you will make the Purchase."[7] Apparently, he did receive an edition of Homer's works, though not from Unwin but from Thomas Jones, Lady Austen's brother-in-law.

This rediscovered fascination with the great literature of the past continued to be counterbalanced by Cowper's awareness of the deeper truths of salvation, which seemed often inaccessible to him.

In attempting to embrace Christian dogma, Cowper looked to John Newton, and he frequently condemned his own secular literary predilections when writing to him: "When you married I was 18 years of age, and had just left Westminster School. At that time I valued a man according to his proficiency & Taste in classical literature. . . ."[8] However, even at the time he wrote this letter, Cowper's attention was turning back to the gentlemanly values of poetry he had been raised to espouse. To Newton, he had been able to justify *The Task* as a work—although addressed to all levels of society—deeply concerned with moral and religious issues. Homer could not be similarly defended. Cowper's commencement of work on the *Iliad* in 1784 was yet another secret that was kept from Newton.

In fact, Cowper did not mention his translation of Homer to Newton until December 3, 1785, almost a year after he had commenced work on it. Carefully, he stressed that this project was but another stage in his personal literary therapy. As well, Cowper assured his old friend that the *Iliad* evoked none of the intense self-consciousness of his spiritual failings that *Poems* and *The Task* had done, and provided for him a refreshing escape into creative activity. He emphasized to Newton the value of this project in keeping him out of the depths of depression. He suggested that he had taken on the work of translation not so much from confidence in his abilities as from a sense of his own vulnerability and how it might best be shielded.

Nevertheless, Cowper did not allow this simple view of his purpose to remain unqualified. It was merely the first of a number of reasons, implied rather than stated in the letter to Newton, for his desire to translate "pagan" epics: "Homer, in point of purity is a most blameless writer, and though he was not an enlighten'd man has interspersed many great and valuable truths throughout both his poems."[9] Of all Cowper's correspondents, Newton was the one with whom he was most reluctant to discuss Homer. Even at the end of almost six years' work in 1791, the poet could tell him that Homer "was never worth my meddling with, but as an amusement he was to be invaluable."[10] At that time, Cowper again stressed the fundamental morality of Homer, thus binding together the twin ends of pleasure and proper instruction.[11] What Cowper kept hidden from Newton as time went on was his growing social ambition, his interest in establishing his place as a spokesman for polite society, and his desire to renew links with friends and relatives from whom he had been cut off. Homer was the common property of the world he had rejected, and, in tackling the translation of the two epics, Cowper was sure to receive the attention of that world.

Filled with hopes of success, Cowper at times could actually embrace the bustling world of high society and assert his place in it by virtue of his poetic accomplishments; however, the possibility of failure led him back to himself and to a sense of his translating work as having a purpose separate from that existence. Either way, in success or failure, he had a role to play as a translator of Homer. Given his awareness of the personal necessity of his creative work, Cowper refused to accommodate himself to Newton's religiosity or to Lady Hesketh's longing for social recognition. The central impulse was simply the desire to write.

Nevertheless, the translation of the *Iliad* and *Odyssey* was to become the culmination of Cowper's poetic career, and, in the process, a major aim of his parallel "career" as a letter writer was attained as never before. During the period from 1785 to 1791, he managed to reestablish many old friendships and give them new life in the course of his preparations for publication. As he became increasingly involved in the process of raising subscriptions to the work, he turned, inevitably, to the friends of his youth at Westminster and the Middle and Inner Temples. Perhaps his greatest personal triumph in the period was the regaining of active correspondences with Walter Bagot, George Colman, Clotworthy Rowley, Robert Smith, Edward Thurlow, and others. These were not all lasting relationships, nor were they generally motivated by more than the desire to gain support and assistance from influential people, but more than once this superficial aim led to the discovery of a surviving affection, a shared stock of memories that could bring happiness and strength to him.

2   Cowper's initial interest in Homer's poetry seems to have been accompanied by a dissatisfaction with Pope's translations, which he had first read with a friend at school: "We compared Pope with his original all the way. The result was a discovery, that there is hardly the thing in the world of which Pope was so entirely destitute, as a taste for Homer."[12] (Strangely, Cowper never seems to have taken into account that Pope's ideals [as stated in his *Preface* to the *Iliad*] as a translator were remarkably similar to his own. In fact, despite the multiplicity of references to Pope's translation in his correspondence, Cowper never once refers to Pope's *Preface*. At some level,

Cowper must have realized that his aims were virtually identical with Pope's, the two poets differing in their methods of execution.) Nevertheless, in 1782, Cowper renewed his sense of rivalry with Pope at Lady Austen's instigation: "Mr. C frequently reading Homer for his own Amusement, and Pope's translation for that of the Ladies, sometimes complained severely of the dissimilitude, and wished that some person would make a more faithful copy of the Original. 'Why do you not do it yourself,' said Lady A. 'who else is so capable of the undertaking?' "[13] As the idea matured in Cowper's mind, it centered on the desire to outdo Pope. One of the earliest public expressions of this sense of rivalry came in an essay submitted by Cowper under the pseudonymn "Alethes" to the August 1785 issue of the *Gentleman's Magazine*. In a sharply critical attack on Pope's loose yet elegant version, he elaborated on his major complaint that it was "tinged with affectation." He duly acknowledged his predecessor's technical virtuosity, but extended this into an expressed awareness that Pope's greatest strength became a liability in translating Homer:

> Pope was a most excellent rhymist: this is to say, he had the happiest talent at accommodating his sense to his rhyming occasions. Formerly, to discover homotonous words in a language abounding with them like ours, is a task that would puzzle no man competently acquainted with it. But for such accommodation, as I have mentioned, when an author is to be translated, there is little room. The sense is already determined. Rhyme, therefore, must, in many cases, occasion, even to the most expert in the art, an almost unavoidable necessity to depart from the meaning of the original.[14]

In the quick, nervous movements of this last sentence, Cowper reveals the basic issue: Pope's Homer is not Homer at all, even though as a translator "he is thought by thousands ignorantly to have succeeded." Against Pope's grace and melody Cowper sets fidelity to the thoughts and diction of the original. A new conception of the role of the translator is thus opposed to Samuel Johnson's celebration of Pope as having translated "for his own age and his own nation."[15]

Cowper located much loss of sublimity in the choice of meter Pope had made and accordingly extended his argument against rhyme in a translation of such magnitude as necessarily involving a "violation of Homer's sense";[16] "instead of Homer in the graceful habit of his age and nation, we have Homer in a straight waistcoat."[17] Pope's mode of expression, unnaturally forced and poised at the best of times, distorts the appearance of Homer, said Cowper. From stylistic considerations in the "Alethes" essay, he moved to an analysis of the more fundamental distortions Pope had perpetrated on his original: "The Iliad and the Odyssey, in his hands, have no more of the air of antiquity than if he had himself invented them."[18] The end result of Pope's desire to ornament Homer with rhyme, elegant diction, and picturesque scenes had been to smother him. Cowper concluded his essay with the particularly cutting remark: "Pope resembles Homer just as Homer resembled himself when he was dead. His figure and his features might be found, but their animation was all departed."[19]

Despite the animadversions of John Dennis and Samuel Say, many readers had been especially taken with the "painting" of Homer by Pope. Among these admirers was Lady Hesketh. She defended Pope's elaborate versions of such set pieces as the night simile in book 8 of the *Iliad* (lines 685–708 in Pope's translation) in writing to her cousin, who tartly directed her attention to the artificiality in which she had so long delighted:

> The next opportunity you have, observe the face of the country by Moonlight; then tell me if the verdure be at all yellowish, and the hills only tipt with silver. You will find au contraire that the green leaves are as green as ever, and that when the Moon is so high as to shine upon the valleys the hills are cover'd with her light. I have made the remark myself particularly with a view to the passage in question. In truth my Dear I am no snarler. But when a man professes to paint Nature he must not give me Yellow for Green, nor a *tip* when I have a right to the whole. I admire Pope as much as any man that lives, but I will have a twitch at his laurel when he attempts to impose upon me. These misrepresentations of the matter are not found in Homer.[20]

Cowper thus made clear his alliance with those writers who would have the translator be as true as possible to the original, rather than introduce excessive art of his own devising. According to this view, Pope's transgression had been his pride in his own artistry, which had caused him to obscure or falsify information as recorded by Homer.

Cowper set himself a double task in planning to write an authentic version of Homer that was at the same time a fine blank verse poem. At his most diffident, he could still say of the work

that "a Translation, properly so called, of Homer, is notwithstanding what Pope has done, a Desideratum in the English language."[21]
It was to be an attempt rendered more arduous by Cowper's determination to work in blank verse, a form he was convinced was
the most natural and suitable counterpart in English to the Greek
hexameter.

The argument that the epic, by virtue of its episodic structure,
cannot be rendered in such a demanding verse form was made by
Samuel Johnson in his discussion of *Paradise Lost* in his *Life of
Milton*. Johnson argued that rhyme cannot "ever be safely spared
but where the subject is liable to support itself."[22] Though Cowper
found the couplet too restrictive for his purposes, Johnson condemned the Miltonic style as prosaic when not handled by its master. Indeed, Cowper was to encounter this argument again and again
during his career as Homer's translator.

Cowper felt he was eminently qualified to render the relaxed
tone of voice of Homer into English, considering his success in this
mode of expression in *The Task*. Other special qualities of Homer
that appealed to him were that writer's powers of precise observation and memorable description: "accordingly, when he describes
nature, whether in man or in animal, or whether nature inanimate,
you may always trust him for the most consummate fidelity. It is his
great glory that he omits no striking part of his subject, and that he
never inserts a tittle that does not belong to it."[23] As a translator,
Cowper saw his goal to be the emulation of Homer's own ease and
fidelity, in order to be as faithful to his original as Homer himself
had been to nature.

3   In the flyleaf of his Greek text of the *Odyssey*, Cowper noted
in 1790 that "My Translation of the Iliad I began on the twenty
first day of November in the year 1784." However, his earliest surviving mention of the project occurs in a letter to William Unwin
of July 28–29, 1785, in which he remarked, "I am proceeding in my
translation velis et remis omnibus nervis as Hudibras has it."[24]
After eleven months of intense work, Cowper was ready to admit
taking his new project seriously, and even then only to his closest
friends. He had not begun with any fixed plan, but as he realized
the magnitude of the job he became increasingly ambitious. On
November 9, he revealed his intentions to Lady Hesketh, adding,
"It is a great Secret, that you must not whisper even to your Cat."[25]
With the onset of November and the broaching of the news to Har-

riot Hesketh, the long silence came to a sudden end. It was decided that printed proposals for the translations would be circulated in order to gain support for them. Lady Hesketh had assured the poet that she would "further my Subscription, with a readiness and warmth that leaves me no doubt that my Proposals will be circulated far as she can drive them."[26]

Under this method of publication, the author and his agents were responsible for the advance sales of the book, and a bookseller was contracted, usually on a commission of a certain percentage of funds received in the subscription. In return, the bookseller agreed to arrange all the practical details of publication, such as printing and binding, and to oversee the process of printing itself. The major attraction of this method for Cowper was that it gave him a chance to test his popularity, especially among those wealthy, important, or knowledgeable enough to be interested in keeping abreast of the latest literary trends. The success of a subscription, however, depended principally on two factors: the trustworthiness of the publisher and the persistence of the subscription raisers.

Cowper was fortunate in both these respects, but especially the latter. Lady Hesketh had already expressed her willingness to work on his behalf, and Walter Bagot, who visited him twice between November 23 and 28, 1785, "engaged himself and all his connexions"[27] to the same task. Bagot's efforts toward raising the subscription were matched by the part he would come to play as Cowper's most learned correspondent, who was able to produce Latin epigrams on contemporary events and to discuss matters of Homeric lore and scholarship. In addition, he was generous. His first pledge of support came with a draft for twenty pounds, and he was not remiss in following this with further sums of money.

Though still somewhat cautious, Cowper was beginning to feel optimistic about the possibilities growing out of his latest poetic work. By December 1785, he could confide to Lady Hesketh that although "not naturally addicted to much rashness in making conclusions favourable to myself, I have a certain lightness of heart upon the subject, that encourages me to hope."[28] And he was ready by December 7 to put his proposal for the translation before the public as soon as possible. Joseph Johnson soon advised the poet not to attempt to offer his work by subscription, as it was no longer a popular method of gaining an audience. Cowper refused, all the same, to deal with his publisher on any other terms, despite Johnson's declaration that "he could make me such offers as he believed I should approve."[29] To Walter Bagot, the poet indicated that he had committed himself irrevocably to the subscription, "having indeed made at that very time such advances toward the execution of my own plan, by calling aloud for the aid of all who had aid to lend, as could not decently be retracted."[30]

With the assistance of the politician and philanthropist Robert Smith, and of John Thornton, Cowper was well on the way by mid-December toward gaining subscriptions in government and mercantile circles. In addition, by the end of December, he had begun to renew contact with old friends and colleagues from Westminster and the Temples, many of whom had attained positions of considerable importance. Among these were Colman and Thurlow. Although his bitterness at having been snubbed by these two men in 1782 was still strong, he decided to approach them: "I have gulp'd and swallow'd, and I have written to the Chancellor, and I have written Colman; I now bring them both to a fair test."[31]

Cowper salved his pride with the consideration that on such occasions "a man sets every wheel in motion,"[32] but Colman's response was to prove worth the effort.[33] Thurlow did not contact Cowper directly until after the translation was published in 1791. His silence was rapidly forgotten, however, in the accumulation of support for the project from a number of Cowper's past acquaintances.

With this growing interest in his work on Homer, Cowper was glad to receive by the end of December Joseph Johnson's agreement to work according to his terms. The publisher recommended that the *Iliad* and *Odyssey* be offered "in two large Quartos," and he advised that the poet call for "a 3 guinea Subscription, which, he added, would at the rate of 500 Subscribers bring . . . in more than 1000£ clear."[34] Cowper, despite his occasional bursts of irritation with Johnson, was convinced that the publisher's suggestion was a good one. By January 15, however, the poet's confidence in the salability of his work had for some reason sunk. He told Bagot that the common paper edition would be two guineas (the price that appeared in the printed proposals which are dated February 10, 1786). Perhaps Johnson had had second thoughts about the size of the readership willing to commit money to such a project; perhaps it was General Spencer Cowper, the poet's cousin, whose interest had recently been awakened in the Homer work, and whose caution would on several future occasions affect the course the work would take. Earlier, Spencer had disowned his cousin; in 1791, he became an anxious taskmaster who feared that his temperamental relative would bring disgrace down upon the Cowper family by rushing the translation into print.

4   By the end of December 1785, Cowper had received from Johnson a printed proof of the *Proposals* and was at work assembling a roster of those who had agreed to distribute the pamphlet; he also compiled a list of potential subscribers. On December 31, however, a suggestion was made to him that he should include an example of his translation with the *Proposals*, a suggestion which he was inclined to reject with contempt, snorting, "When I deal in Wine, Cloth, Cheese I will give Samples, but of Verse, never."[35] He was by now anxious to charge ahead, and he was unwilling to see further conditions and impediments placed in the way of his rapid course toward publication. Besides, this proposition implied a lack of respect for his already established name as a writer of verse. Cowper was planning an idealized schedule leading up to publication, one which allowed for no delays or misunderstandings; he was not to escape from this tendency to underestimate the amount of time or effort it would take to bring his work into print despite the six years of delay and difficulty that lay ahead.

Cowper's sanguine mood was not shared wholeheartedly by some of his assistants in the project. Lady Hesketh, for instance, was beginning to have second thoughts about her cousin's abilities to cope singlehandedly with such an immense undertaking. He hastened to reassure her: "I understand Homer as well as I understand Chevy Chase. And if I do not prove it soon, call me Coxcomb for ever."[36] Lady Hesketh was not the only one anxious to ensure that Cowper would not act rashly in his determination to publish his new work. "Anonymous" would eventually express similar fears, and in mid-January 1786, General Cowper took up the call for a specimen of the *Iliad* translation, probably from the same motive. With this request coming from such an august member of the family, the poet relented from his earlier refusal to provide an example of his work for the *Proposals*. He sent the General a passage of 107 lines from the last book of the *Iliad*, comprising part of the interview between Priam and Achilles (corresponding to book 24, lines 599–716, in the first edition of the translation).

Somewhat subdued, perhaps, by his military cousin's concern, Cowper was beginning to reconsider his wish for haste in readying the *Iliad* for publication. The General's correspondence with Cowper has not survived, but he must have succeeded at this time, as Lady Hesketh had not, in convincing the poet of the risks he ran in challenging Pope as the English Homer, risks which were not to be taken lightly.

Cowper sensed his temerity in competing openly with the poet generally conceded to be the greatest of the century. He defended the price of his subscription by comparing his own moderate price to Pope's exorbitant one, and such a comparison led inevitably to considerations of more intrinsic value: "You may say . . . It is well—but do you place yourself on a level with Pope? I answer, or rather, *should* answer—By no means. Not as a poet. But as a Translator of Homer if I did not expect and believe that I should even surpass him, why have I meddled with this matter at all? If I confess inferiority, I reprobate my own undertaking."[37] With this admission of disillusioned, realistic commitment, Cowper became better equipped to deal with the doubts of others. Although he freely admitted to an unwillingness to accept advice, which he ascribed to a "principle of shame-facedness,"[38] he did not react to this self-discovery by going to the other extreme of submitting himself uncritically to the directions of his two strong-willed cousins. He was equally candid in revealing to Lady Hesketh that his reluctance to provide a sample of his work in the *Proposals* had simply been due to uncertainty when faced suddenly with the actual fact of publication: "I do tremble at the thought, and so tremble at it that I could not bear to send out a specimen, because, by doing so, I should appear in public a good deal sooner that I had purposed."[39] The approaching realization of his ambitions understandably abashed Cowper, yet he was not willing to escape responsibility either by giving up entirely or by handing control of all aspects of preparation beyond actual composition over to the General. Cowper understood that he had to retain confidence in his own judgment for the project to be his own. Even in acquiescing on the question of the specimen passage, he insisted that external pressure could be harmful to the preparation of the verse itself.

By January 16, a revised copy of the specimen passage had been sent to General Cowper for him to peruse and then to deliver to Joseph Johnson. Within a few days, however, the poet wrote directly to his publisher, asking him to append a lengthy note to the excerpt, offering an interpretation of it. This miniature essay may have been intended by Cowper as an example of his own critical acumen, in order to put off any doubt of his scholarly competence for the undertaking.

The matter of the *Proposals* was not yet resolved. Johnson returned the specimen to Cowper before the month of January was out, when further corrections appended in an unknown hand. Though Cowper was not to learn his name until March, this new reader was the artist Henry Fuseli, who now resided permanently in London.

Fuseli was at that time employed on a casual basis by Johnson as a reader and reviewer. Among many other accomplishments, he was an extremely knowledgeable classical scholar. Johnson showed the acerbic Fuseli the freshly arrived passage of Cowper's *Iliad,* the artist rapidly noted a few points which he felt were in need of improvement, and Johnson then returned the specimen to its author.[40]

Cowper may have been impressed with the judgment of his unknown revisor, but this new setback was a shock and a disappointment to him. Immediately after he received the copy, he set about writing a reply to Johnson that would gracefully register the full range of his surprise: "I am delighted with taste, judgment, and learning, that discover themselves in the strictures of your friend, and will submit my translation to them with all my heart. I have only to wish, that he would treat me with as much lenity as he can afford, and on his compliance with that preliminary request promise, that I will entertain his remarks with all the respect, to which I doubt not, that they will be entitled."[41] Clearly, Johnson had recommended that Fuseli continue to play a part in the revision of future installments of the translation. As Cowper sardonically remarked to Lady Hesketh a few days later, this nameless reader had proved to be a "very clever fellow . . . one who I promise you will not spare for severity of animadversion where he shall find occasion."[42] Faced with this new hurdle, the poet proceeded once more to readjust his timetable. Having finished the first draft of the *Iliad* by mid-January, he began to revise it, always conscious that "time is likely to be precious, and consequently any delay that is not absolutely necessary, as much as possible to be avoided."[43] The date of completion was receding into a conjectural future.

Meanwhile, further complications had arisen. Despite Cowper's injunction that she not ask "the Magi" to overlook his translation, Lady Hesketh had contacted the editor of the *New Review,* Paul Henry Maty, requesting that he read and give his opinion of Cowper's recently published volume of verse, with a view to getting him to mention the Homer project, and ultimately to review the specimen passage, in his journal. Possibly disguising a certain exasperation at his cousin's forwardness, Cowper wrote to her about her zeal in promoting his translation: "If Dr. Maty applied to you for permission to mention my Homer in his next Review, it is plainly enough to be seen that from you he received, or by your means, my last publication. . . . Neither the asperity of a critic professed, nor the frowns of a whole university whom I have censured, have any terrors for you, where you apprehend my interest is concerned."[44]

Lady Hesketh responded to this gentle teasing by urging Cowper to send Maty the revised manuscript of the first book of the *Iliad*. In complying with her request, the poet realized that to gain this formidable critic's support for his work would be a major coup.

With Fuseli awaiting the return of the specimen passage to Johnson, and Maty expecting the arrival of book 1 of the *Iliad*, an increasing amount of pressure was being brought to bear on Cowper. Despite the lingering doubts in his abilities expressed from time to time by his cousins and Joseph Johnson, or perhaps in defiance of these influences, Cowper rallied himself with praise and encouragement that had recently come his way.

Even so, Cowper subjected his exemplary passage to yet another series of adjustments, probably as a result of a new batch of criticisms—a "multitude of . . . strictures"[45]—prepared by Fuseli. This final revision took place on the very eve of printing. By now, Cowper's initial blaze of enthusiasm had cooled, not so much from personal misgivings as from disgust with the repeated efforts necessary to make his work conform to the expectations of his anxious circle of onlookers. On February 11, annoyance at his coworkers' lack of faith in his poetic instincts finally overcame him, and he gave vent to his feelings to Lady Hesketh:

> The vexation, the perplexity that attend a multiplicity of Criticisms by various persons, many of which are sure to be futile, many of them ill-founded, and some of them contradictory to others, is inconceivable unless by the Author whose ill fated work happens to be the subject of them. . . . I speak thus, my Dear, after having just escaped from such a storm of trouble occasioned by endless remarks, hints, suggestions and objections as drove me almost to despair, and to the very edge of a resolution to drop my undertaking for ever.[46]

Though wearied and disillusioned, Cowper had learned to listen more objectively to the advice of his little squadron of readers. A day or so before writing the above letter to Lady Hesketh, he had sent a thoroughly revised copy of the specimen passage to her to be conveyed to Dr. Maty and then back to himself in readiness to be sent at last to Johnson to be printed. Together with the *Proposals* and *Specimen*, Cowper prepared a brief and precisely worded advertisement, in which, rejecting the advice of yet another interested party, Joseph Hill, he had decided to skirt the question of his challenge to Pope's translation. He realized that in such a place, "The only proper part for me is not to know that such a man as Pope has ever existed."[47]

Cowper had intended to send the freshly completed revision of book 1 and the first half of book 2 of the *Iliad* to Lady Hesketh on February 15 so that she could deliver it to Dr. Maty; but, apparently, General Cowper was not willing to see the translation move into the path of public scrutiny just yet. By the end of the month, he had written back to the poet to express serious misgivings about the work. "Our dear friend, the General," Cowper informed Lady Hesketh, "in his last letter mortified me not a little."[48] The General felt such a great work should be handled carefully and patiently—made worthy of Cowper. If the General's worries that the translation was being rushed were well founded, Cowper felt, "I appear to have made shipwreck of my hopes at once."[49] However, having somewhat more faith in himself than his cousins had, he was ready within a week to let Fuseli see the beginning of the translation, as the General had in fact previously urged him to do. Maty, however, was not to read the translation until a third reworking had taken place.

5   Meanwhile, Lady Hesketh was taking the opportunity to express some of her own reservations about Cowper's style. She hinted that he would be seen by many readers, especially those unfamiliar with the original, to have sacrificed elegance to simplicity and rugged energy. In fact, Cowper had already addressed this criticism in answering his publisher's objections: "To translate an author of such great antiquity into English purely modern appears to me an absurdity. Hardly anything has hurt Pope's translation more. I have therefore thrown the language of mine somewhat backward. . . ."[50] Cowper saw himself in the initial stage of his translation as having made a judicious choice between ancient and modern in creating a suitable epic diction. He had been employing such a compromise from the very start of his work on Homer, and, as he indicated in a letter of December 1784 to John Newton, the question of the proper language inevitably led to larger questions of style and originality: "Milton's manner was peculiar; so is Thomson's. He that should write like either of them, would in my judgment, deserve the name of a Copyist, but not of a Poet."[51]

Though he had declared his independence from the "fine Organ"[52] of Milton's voice, Cowper was drawn inexorably closer to the patterns of that voice in his efforts to provide an English Homer that would stand at the opposite end of the spectrum from Pope's. Pope, he declared, "has written a great deal of very musical and sweet verse in his translation of Homer, but his verse is not universally such; on the contrary, it is often lame, feeble and flat."[53] One device initially favored by Cowper in his progress toward synthesizing a "nervous, plain, natural"[54]* language equivalent to Homer's own, was a reliance on elisions to resolve the metrical pattern of the blank verse line. So great was this reliance that it was pounced upon by Lady Hesketh and Joseph Johnson. The poet's response to such criticism was to reiterate his confidence in his method.

Cowper also stood firm on the question of meter, which he had endeavored to modify beyond the limits of grace and smoothness approved of by his immediate circle of readers. Significantly, it was once again to Milton that he turned in justification of his procedure: "With respect to those lines, which are said to be prosaic, if

* Cowper's assertion here is part of an important debate in the eighteenth century concerning the conflicting claims of a "plain" and "natural" style versus one which is excessively sophisticated. The ballad was frequently a staging ground of this quarrel, as in Addison's defense of "Chevy Chase." Addison, a writer whom Cowper greatly admired, had, in *Spectators* 70 and 74, promoted that ballad on grounds similar to Cowper's defense of his approach to Homer:

> I know nothing which more shews the essential and inherent Perfection of Simplicity of Thought, above that which I call the Gothick Manner in Writing, than this, that the first pleases all Kinds of Palates, and the latter only such as have formed to themselves a wrong artificial Taste upon little fanciful Authors and Writers of Epigram. *Homer, Virgil,* or *Milton,* so far as the Language of their Poems is understood, will please a Reader of plain common Sense. . . . an ordinary Song or Ballad that is the Delight of the Common People, cannot fail to please all such Readers as are not unqualified for the Entertainment by their Affectation or Ignorance; and the Reason is plain, because the same Paintings of Nature which recommend it to the most ordinary Reader, will appear beautiful to the most refined (*Spectator,* no. 70 [May 21, 1711], vol. 1, ed. Donald F. Bond [Oxford: Clarendon Press, 1965], 297–98).

The ballad's cause was taken up later in the century by Bishop Percy in 1765: "In a polished age, like the present, I am sensible that many of these reliques of antiquity will require great allowances to be made for them. Yet have they, for the most part, a pleasing simplicity, and many artless graces, which in the opinion of no mean critics have been thought to compensate for the want of higher beauties, and, if they do not dazzle the imagination, are frequently found to interest the heart." ("Introduction" to *Reliques of Ancient English Poetry* [1765] as cited by Alan Bold, *The Ballad* [London: Methuen, 1979], 9.) Thus, in his defense of his approach to Homer, Cowper is agreeing with Addison that Homer is a writer of "Perfection of Simplicity of Thought," and, by implication, he is relegating Pope's translation to the affected "Gothick Manner" attacked by Addison. Cowper's Homer is a poet of "pleasing simplicity" and "artless graces."

indeed they be such, I will undertake to show no small number, that are equally such in the sublimest parts of the Paradise Lost."[55] Cowper's desire for metrical roughness to obtrude itself at key moments of his work was not quelled in future revisions, although the trend of those revisions was towards polishing and regularizing. And Fuseli, who perhaps came to read the work with greater care than anyone save Cowper himself, wrote of the published translation that Cowper had "often adopted or imitated the discords of Milton, as his flow of verse."[56] The remark was not meant to be wholly disapproving.

Cowper's vigorous defense and rationalization in 1785 and 1786 of devices that were intended after all to please the reader ultimately gave way. By March 1786, he was still receiving suggestions, especially from Lady Hesketh, about the translation in general and the elisions and metrical roughness in particular, and in replying to her, he conceded that he may have originally taken too radical a stance on the issue and was ready to mend the offending verses: "I do not indeed absolutely covenant, promise and agree that I will discard *all* my Elisions, but I hereby bind myself to dismiss *as many* of them as without sacrificing energy to sound, I can."[57] Obviously, Cowper had become more pragmatic. As he summed up the matter to Lady Hesketh, "I am most willing to conform myself to your very sensible observation, that it is necessary if we would please, to consult the Taste of our own day."[58]

6   The poet dutifully set about modifying his translation, in accord with his cousin's wish, that he "allow to *The* his whole dimensions, wheresoever it can possibly be done."[59] On March 20, he was able to inform her that he had achieved a workable compromise. During this debate with Lady Hesketh, Cowper kept at the work of revision; having sent off to her the remainder of book 2 and books 3 to 5, he asked her to send the manuscript directly to the General, who would in turn pass it on to Fuseli. But this complex arrangement did not work. The manuscript never reached Fuseli, for the General looked it over and sent it back to Cowper for further preliminary revisions. By mid-March, still no word had been heard from Fuseli about the first book, except for the vague remark, relayed to the poet by Johnson, that "he is very much pleased with what he has seen."[60] In answer to Lady Hesketh's request that the manuscript should be shown to yet another critic friend of hers, Cowper could only state that he was still waiting for Fuseli's reply.

By April 3, he had at last received back his first book of the *Iliad*, annotated by Fuseli, and on that day he decided to send the re-revised text of books 2 to 5 along the usual route via Lady Hesketh and the General, ultimately to reach Fuseli. As Cowper informed Lady Hesketh, "I am a good child. I send you, I suppose, above two thousand lines, and not two hundred in the whole of the first translation. In fact, I am making a new translation, and find that the work will be much a gainer by it."[61]

The prospect of getting the manuscript of book 1 into Dr. Maty's hands was by now dimmer than ever. With the long-awaited arrival of Fuseli's criticisms, Cowper set about on new revisions of the book, which as a result was not ready to be sent off again to the General until as late as April 24. Cowper's bypassing of Lady Hesketh at that time was intentional. As he admitted to her, the General himself "would not suffer me to send it to you my Dear, lest you should post it away to Maty at once."[62]

Cowper did not hear of the fate of his printed *Proposals* until the end of April (although they had been in circulation ever since he had returned the specimen passage from its final revision for printing, probably sometime between February 11 and the end of that month). The date on the first page of the *Proposals* is February 10, 1786, which suggests that the *Specimen* was put through the press several days later than the *Proposals* proper.

The little pamphlet was also published in the March issue of Maty's *New Review*, together with a brief introductory note by Maty himself that turned out to be a strange mixture of grudging praise and vague condemnation. Lady Hesketh, not eager to reveal the disappointing contents of this notice, managed to keep the news of its appearance from Cowper for well over a month. Not until May 1 did he hear about it, and even then only by hearsay in a letter from William Bull. The poet's initial reaction was bewilderment, as he was still unable to ascertain the actual state of affairs, but almost immediately the situation was made clear to him. The General, less fearful for Cowper's loss of equanimity than Lady Hesketh, had sent him a copy of the review, along with an anonymous "Squib" written in support of Maty's strictures, which had appeared in the Monday, May 1, issue of a London newspaper, the *Public Advertiser*. This unpleasant package arrived a week after Bull's letter mentioning the matter. Cowper felt betrayed.

Luckily, a highly encouraging letter from George Colman arrived on May 16, which provided a positive balance to keep Cowper from falling into despondency. Colman had read Maty's review with displeasure and was eager to offer more constructive remarks on the style of the *Specimen,* an annotated copy of which he included in his communication to Cowper. In the introductory note to his comments, Colman strongly supported blank verse as the best possible medium in the English language for Homer. Colman drew particular attention in his notes to the petulance Maty had exhibited, especially in his reading of the lines, "draw the hand / Close to my lips, the hand that slew my son" (corresponding to *Iliad* 24, lines 634–35 of Cowper's translation). A "detestable modern repetition"[63] Maty had called this. Colman responded, "I have not the Original Line but don't know why Maty objects to this expression."[64] Cowper was sufficiently encouraged by this to declare to Lady Hesketh, "I could easily alter it, but the case standing thus, I do not know whether my proud stomach will condescend so low. I rather feel disinclined to it."[65]

However, Colman also commented on Cowper's extensive use of elisions, which he, like Lady Hesketh, saw as a flaw in the work. Roused already, and having been made all too aware of this particular blemish to wish to take full responsibility for it all over again, the poet told her that he "altered and altered 'till at last [he] did not care how [he] altered."[66]

Bolstered by Colman's judicious encouragement and urged on by the General, Cowper set about answering the letter by "T. S." in the *Public Advertiser.* His reply was printed in that newspaper's May 16 issue and was signed "A Well-Wisher to the New Translation." In this letter, Cowper vigorously defended his choice of blank verse as appropriate for what he considered to be Homer's abundance of "ornament." The exalted and sublime subject had been couched in a rich variety of textures of sound and diction by Homer, and it deserved, Cowper asserted, to be rendered into the English metrical form most capable to match such richness and contain such sublimity. "T. S." had stated that "The English Couplet is very well calculated to express the versification of Homer,"[67] but Cowper flatly denied this. He pointed out that the fastidiousness and formal rigidity of the couplet form tended to express tidy, elegant thoughts, such as were foreign to Homer.

The elisions, Cowper suggested, were an outward sign of his desire to synthesize a diction more suitable for Homer than Pope's imposition of modern graces. As he had come to accept, though, he could not get closer to Homer by writing in a consciously archaic mode. In doing so, he was merely cutting himself off from his audience. Near the end of his labors, looking back on his long search for the best diction for his translation, Cowper would write in 1790: "I knew that there was a stile somewhere, could I but find it, in which Homer ought to be render'd and which alone would suit him."[68]

Cowper's annoyance with the critical reception of his *Proposals* gradually subsided, and by the middle of May 1786, having discussed the matter with Mary Unwin, he had come to accept Lady Hesketh's interpretation of Maty's attack on his work: "We both think it highly probable that you suggest the true cause of his displeasure when you suppose him mortified at not having had a part of the translation laid before him, 'ere the Specimen was published."[69] But the episode had left its mark. Cowper became profoundly aware of his vulnerability to praise or blame and of the wide arc he could quickly swing between joy and despair, as external circumstances changed.

In engaging and persisting in an undertaking that would place him under intense critical scrutiny at every step, Cowper had moved beyond the superficial view of his poetic self, made to John Newton, as conjuring away the spirits of depression with the easy delights of verse composition. That picture had fit the writer of *John Gilpin* or *The Task* but would not do for the translator of the *Iliad* and *Odyssey*. Whatever Cowper's motives in beginning to dally with Homer in 1784, his ensuing adversities and growing awareness of the immensity of the undertaking had led him to a deeper sense of artistic commitment than he had felt before. Fresh from doing masked battle with "T. S." and Maty in the *Public Advertiser,* he stated to Lady Hesketh that "I am not ashamed to confess that having commenced as an Author, I am most ardently desirous to succeed as such. *I have, what perhaps you little suspect me of, in my nature an infinite share of ambition.*"[70]

Cowper was particularly fortunate in his great undertaking in having a reader as knowledgeable as Henry Fuseli. The Swiss artist challenged him to realize his sense of ambition and urged him to put that ambition to precise and practical use. As a result, Cowper pursued his ideal of the closest possible translation. The first book of the *Iliad* had been returned by Fuseli by the end of March, carefully annotated; shortly thereafter, the remaining portion of the translation up to the end of book 5 was sent to him. Overshadowed as this ongoing dialogue of revision was by the squabble in print over the *Proposals,* Cowper was yet engaged through the month of May in a double and sometimes triple procedure of drafting out, reworking, and reworking again. Simultaneously, it seems, he prepared sections for General Cowper to deliver to Fuseli, revised the work sent back from that reader, and, especially in his work on the early books, he immediately went through the section involved once again. By May 20, Cowper had readied book 6 for Fuseli, and was already halfway through a first redrafting of book 7. These were probably sent off early in June, during which the poet worked concurrently on incorporating the suggestions of Fuseli into the third, fourth, and fifth books, and on a preliminary recasting of book 8. These tasks were finished by July 18, on which day Cowper received by way of the General the annotated texts of the books Fuseli had meanwhile been examining. The poet sent his completed second draft of book 8 to London about four days later.

Cowper was by now well set in the routine of his project. His work schedule from day to day had been established during the previous winter, and he had described it then to Lady Hesketh, perhaps in order to allay her fears that he was overworking: "My task that I assign myself is to translate forty lines a day; if they pass off easily I sometimes make them fifty, but never abate any part of the allotted number. Perhaps I am occupied an hour and a half, perhaps three hours; but generally between two and three. This, you see, is labour that can hurt no man; and what I have translated in the morning, in the evening I transcribe."[71] By the summer, Cowper's pace intensified. As he wrote in a brief note to Joseph Hill, "Homer is urgent. Much is done, but much remains undone, and no School-boy is more attentive to the performance of his daily task than I."[72] From three hours at most in the morning and a leisurely copying out in the evening, the poet's time at work each day grew substantially and the afternoons were soon taken over by Homer.

7   Cowper's sense of creative urgency may well have been largely due, at least in the initial stages of revision, to Fuseli's presence at his shoulder, overseeing every word he produced. Explaining the significance of Fuseli's perspective on the work, he wrote to Walter Bagot that "Experience has convinced me that other eyes than my own are necessary, in order that so long and arduous a task may be finished as it ought, and may neither discredit me, nor mortify and disappoint my friends."[73] As in 1782 and 1785, Cowper was afraid that his work would embarrass himself as well as his friends and relatives.

The sharp eye and sharper pen of Fuseli may have seemed necessary, but they were rarely a source of pleasure for Cowper. Writing

again to Bagot, he elaborated on his respect for the man and justified the important role he was taking in the preparation of the
translation, but did so somewhat ruefully: "I do not wonder at the
judgment that you form of Fuseli a foreigner: but you may assure
yourself that, foreigner as he is, he has an exquisite taste in English
Verse. The man is all fire, an Enthusiast in the highest degree on
the subject of Homer, and has given me more than once a jog when
I have been inclined to Nap with my author."[74] Henry Fuseli was
not hired by Johnson to assist with this project, but rather engaged
himself "for his amusement,"[75] as Cowper put it. However, his interest in Homer was far from that of a dilettante. He read the translation with great care, comparing it at every step with the Greek original, and wherever pertinent, suggesting readings closer or cleaner
than ones Cowper had adopted. He was a relentless critic of sloppy
translations and feeble expressions, and Cowper trusted his judgment and consistently followed his recommendations.

Fuseli demanded, for example, that Cowper render Homer's epithets and titles as faithfully as possible and stressed from the very
beginning of his revision "what appears to me the constant practice
of Homer, when talking of the gods, that He never saves words nor
ever clips their titles."[76] Clarifying this statement shortly after, he
added, "In translating Epithets I should prefer that they are derived
from some quality of body or mind. We have passed [several epi-
thets] without notice; and now we translate what is obscure to the
Scholar and conveys no idea whatever to the common Reader."[77]
The last part of this remark came in specific response to Cowper's
rendering of "Ægis-bearing Jove." In the first printed edition, Cowper refused to abandon this title but provided a footnote for it. In
general, he was faithful to such titles, even in excess of what Fuseli
advised.

The Swiss artist also sought precision in the translator's manipulation of diction, and he castigated Cowper for what he saw as inappropriate English counterparts of the original. Having considered
Cowper's initial rendition of lines 125 and 126 of book 1 ("his
form / And gesture all disturb'd"), Fuseli responded, "I am sensible that the strength of the greek [sic] is beyond all Translation; but
something nearer and stronger, and of less tautology with the 'troubled mien' of the foregoing line might be substituted."[78]

Another important aspect of the work particularly studied by Fuseli was Cowper's attention, or lack of it, to the mechanics of translation. Commenting on unnecessary compression of the original at
one point, he dryly remarked, "here is, what perhaps no other

translation can boast of—two greek lines rendered by a single English one. . . . not the kind of conciseness I wish to see."[79] Fuseli's more wide-ranging comments were aimed at the preservation of Homer from the "importunities of impatient Blank verse."[80] Wherever Cowper deviated from the Greek, his reader pulled him up short. For example, he called attention to Cowper's elegant detail at book 2, line 725, of the printed edition ("Cyparissa veiled / With broad redundance of funereal shades"):[81] "I do not dislike this—I can even applaud it—but do not let us call it Translation."[82]

Continually, Fuseli demanded better things of Cowper, asking at length, "does the Translator imagine he improves upon his original, by confining himself in a vague manner to the general sense of passages . . . without the least attention to their detail? what is it then we are to have of Homer, more in this version than in any other?"[83] Cowper was to be permitted no looseness of expression, especially after his published declaration to make a "just representation" of Homer in his *Proposals:* "it is curious to hear the Translator boast of an exclusive attachment to the peculiarities of stile and the primitiveness of Homer's expression; whilst he either passes heedless over or without mercy mows down every Caracteristic of diction & figure."[84] In effect, Cowper was being driven ever further from vestiges of Augustan decorum in Fuseli's caustic annotations, along the path originally envisaged by himself to be the right way to approach Homer most closely.

Fuseli was not unwilling to praise Cowper from time to time, yet he made his most perceptive and rewarding insights in terms of neither praise nor condemnation, but in enthusiastic advice and encouragement, as shown in his response to Cowper's early rendition of book 3, line 404, "eyes that glare hostility and hate": "as in Painting one colour is purer & brighter than two and two than three—So in Poetry, whatever Image can be conveyed in one word, will impress itself stronger than that which calls to its assistance two or more."[85] On the other hand, Fuseli could on occasion overstep himself, provoking Cowper to scribble annoyed rejoinders beside comments that seemed especially unjust. Thus, when his lines "wealth / boundless and like an overflowing flood" (equivalent to book 2, line 805), which Fuseli had termed a "prosed" imitation of Milton, were returned to him, he wrote beside them that "I do not account it prose."[86] Fuseli wrote an extensive note on what he saw as the translator's misreading of Homer, in line 970 of book 2 as printed: " 'Polytes posting abroad' is a mere contrivance of the Translators; his swiftness is not mentioned by Homer because he posted from the assembly to the tomb of Aisyetes, but as a reason why he ventured on a post so near the Ennemi."[87] To which Cowper, thoroughly irritated, could only reply: "posted means stationed in this place, my man of other countrys."[88] All the same, the line was to be altered to "Polites . . . posted was abroad."[89]

Despite Fuseli's asperity as a critic, Cowper greatly appreciated his freely given assistance, as he acknowledged in a letter to Joseph Johnson in July 1786. Writing about the quality of the annotations to the *Iliad* up to book 8, he stated that the more he proceeded through them, the more convinced he became of their value. Cowper expressed his gratitude to Fuseli in his *Preface* to the published translation. At the end of that short essay, he declared with candor that "To his classical taste and just discernment I have been indebted for the discovery of many blemishes in my own work, and of beauties, which would otherwise have escaped me, in the original."[90]

During the summer of 1786, prodded by Fuseli, Cowper worked toward a more precise conception of the art of translation. He had begun to realize that there may have been some truth in the claim of his critic "T. S." that "blank verse degenerates into mere prose, when it is not kept up by strong images and bold metaphors."[91] With this new sense of the task remaining ahead, Cowper was finally ready to assert a greater independence and responsibility toward his translation than Fuseli had previously allowed him. Writing to Joseph Johnson at the beginning of September, he indicated that, being convinced of the justness of Fuseli's demands, he would "attempt at least to conform to them."[92]

When summer drew toward autumn, Cowper's pace relaxed, as did Fuseli's. The eighth book of the *Iliad* had been sent to General Cowper to be delivered to Fuseli around July 21, but by the beginning of September, the Swiss artist still had not finished with it. Through those weeks, Cowper had been revising the first seven books yet again and, as he informed Johnson, he had "not yet begun the ninth, but shall in a day or two; and will send it as soon as finished."[93] By October, book 9 was completed in a draft ready for Fuseli, and was sent off to General Cowper shortly thereafter. However, a mishap befell the manuscript on its way by boat down the Thames to London: "You have not heard I suppose that the ninth book of my Translation is at the bottom of the Thames. But it is even so. A storm overtook it on its way to Kingston, and it sank together with the whole cargo of the boat in which it was a passenger. Not figuratively foreshowing, I hope, by its submersion, the fate of all the rest."⁹⁴ The manuscript, freshly copied out by Lady Hesketh and well protected in a box constructed by Cowper himself, was apparently recovered from the river and returned to its owner. In what state it was returned is not recorded. The poet would later put an interpretation on the event very different from his doubtful prognostication at the time of the accident. Writing to Lady Hesketh some years later, he alluded to the event, asking, "may not I . . . consider the marvellous recovery of my lost book from the bottom of the Thames as typical of its future prosperity?"⁹⁵

With the onset of winter, Cowper began to work more regularly. He revised the first eleven books of his initial translation, and was well into the twelfth by the time he and Mary Unwin moved to Weston on November 15. The increase of activity seems to have initially spurred him on rather than delayed him in his work on Homer, and his new proximity to the Throckmortons was an additional incentive to his efforts. Following the example of Lady Hesketh, members of that family began to offer their assistance in transcribing Cowper's work into fair copies.

Amidst all this activity and optimism, William Unwin died on November 29, 1786. While engaged in adapting the freshly returned book 9 to Fuseli's criticisms, the poet began by December 9 to sense the approach of depression. Two days later he wrote to Lady Hesketh, attempting to shrug off the forbidding symptoms: "The cloud that I mentioned to you, my cousin, has passed away, or perhaps the skirts of it may still hang over me."⁹⁶ For a while, he was able to keep his sense of doom at bay. The verve and enthusiasm with which he looked forward to the approaching phases of his work equaled his continuing, scrupulous care in revising what had already been translated. The General had been sent the latest revision of the first eight books of the *Iliad*, just as he had earlier been receiving the corrected books as they emerged from Fuseli. After perusing this final draft, he wrote back to Cowper, earnestly telling him "that in the 8 first books which I have sent him he still finds alterations and amendments necessary."⁹⁷ But this potentially dismaying news gave Cowper no visible hardship. He told Lady Hesketh, he was "equally persuaded"⁹⁸ of the necessity of yet another revision of the eight books.

From about January 7 onward, symptoms of emotional stress began to assert themselves and to affect the progress of the translation. All Cowper's expressions of confidence came to an abrupt halt. A silence fell, not to be broken until June, and through the summer months of 1787 he rested. By the end of August he could write that "My health and spirits are considerably improved, and I once more associate with my neighbours."[99] Even so, he was far from ready to take up translating, as he suffered yet from vertigo and severe headaches.

8   The lengthy interruption of Cowper's activities with the translation meant once and for all that his visionary schedule of preparation for publishing, made the previous spring, was no longer feasible. In March 1786, when the end of the project had seemed to be close, he had enthusiastically said to William Unwin, "I am bound to print as soon as 300 shall have subscribed, and consequently have not an hour to spare."[100] The combined efforts of his friends at soliciting subscriptions was proving the target of 300 to be accessible. Walter Bagot in particular had succeeded in obtaining the Earl of Uxbridge, Lord Harrowby, and an old school friend, Frederic Vane; Lady Hesketh was in the process of recruiting members of the elite social circle at Mrs. Montagu's salon; the attention of such prominent Evangelicals as William Wilberforce and the Earl of Dartmouth had been gained; Cowper himself succeeded in distributing thirty-three subscription papers among friends and relatives, twelve of which papers he had given to John Throckmorton to circulate; and even William Bull had promptly "sent me names that will do honour to my list of subscribers."[101] In addition, Robert Smith had made a useful suggestion: advertisements for the Homer should be bound up with editions of Cowper's two volumes of verse.

The momentum of the drive for subscriptions was greatly diminished by the lengthy indisposition of the translator, but this was not the only aspect of the project that suffered a setback in the spring and summer of 1787. The chain of correspondence between Cowper and Fuseli, via General Cowper and Joseph Johnson, fell apart, and would never again operate as smoothly as it had done in the past. Even more seriously, Cowper's emergence from his mental and emotional collapse made him aware of the lost time. His confidence in his abilities was severely dented and would take time to mend.

Joseph Johnson, worried that Cowper's convalescence might extend indefinitely, wrote to him about renewing work on the translation as early as June 1787, but it was some months before Cowper himself was ready to proceed, and, accordingly, he did not reply until October to his publisher's queries. Cowper also admitted to

Samuel Rose that his previous technical fluency had not been restored to him. While he prepared himself for the business of composition, close friends were expressing doubts about the value and
even the safety of doing so. But feeling anew his sense of commitment to Homer, Cowper was inclined to dismiss such fears. In writing to Lady Hesketh, he sought to alleviate her concern and indicated that he was once again calm and in control.

Recalling his personal defense of poetry making as an activity
designed to lure himself out of depression, Cowper was suggesting
an important reason why Lady Hesketh should not condemn his
work as dangerous to his precarious emotional equilibrium. The
defense did not end there, however. In the same letter to his cousin,
Cowper went on to reawaken his old sense of rivalry with his
"predecessor": "I compliment myself with a persuasion that I have
more heroic valour, of the passive kind at least, than he had,—perhaps than any man; it would be strange had I not, after so much
exercise."[102] Cowper's heroism, if not like that of Achilles, bore
some resemblance to the fortitude of Ulysses, the survivor. He was
at least occasionally able to move beyond immediate problems and
difficulties and place his trials and anxieties as a translator into a
larger existential frame. He could subordinate such anxieties to the
overriding purpose of completing the work at hand. Thus, this
sense of purpose was of vital importance to him. In a lighter mood,
he responded to Joseph Hill's advice that he "abstain" from Homer:
"I might as well advise him to abstain from parchment."[103]

With the onset of December, Cowper established himself once
more into a routine of work, writing as before to Walter Bagot
about the technical difficulties of translating Homer, and eagerly
inquiring to another correspondent about the present location of
his manuscript containing books 12 and 13, which had been sent to
Johnson before his collapse. Although he sometimes saw his labor
as "endless," Cowper also freely admitted that "I am neither weary
of it, nor even wish to arrive soon at the conclusion."[104] If the work
was frequently frustrating and time-consuming, its eventual completion seemed to him to present a "tremendous Vacuum" of far
more unpleasant aspect. But that "dreaded consummation seems
yet at a distance."[105]

Cowper may well have felt that as long as there was Homer there
was life for him. Certainly the prospect of future labors on the
project seemed to revive and refresh him at this time. He was de-
lightedly obsessed with the intricate problems his translation en-
tailed, expressing his pleasure in a vibrant series of letters.

Above all, Cowper was intent on reestablishing, not only for his correspondents but for himself, his sense of dedication. By January 5, 1788, his first thirteen books of the *Iliad* had been revised in the light of Fuseli's comments, sent to London again, and returned again to Weston with the news that they were ready to be printed. Nevertheless, Cowper would not accept this finality: "I am now revising them again by the light of my own critical taper, and make more alterations than at the first."[106] With his creative powers once again flowing freely, Cowper began to feel himself somewhat restricted by the monumental job, as he excused his lack of time for "the pretty little vagaries,"[107] the brief verse confections that Lady Hesketh and others longed for him to produce.

Indeed, Cowper had begun to feel a comradeship for Homer. He hoped to get beyond the barrier of the centuries and to make Homer's poetry live for very personal reasons, as he spontaneously exclaimed to Samuel Rose: "What would I give that he were living now, and within my reach! I of all men living have the best excuse for indulging such a wish unreasonable as it may seem, for I have no doubt that the fire of his eye and the smile upon his lips would put me now and then in possession of his full meaning more effectually than any Commentator."[108] Translating thus was becoming an act of friendship for Cowper, who with justifiable pride treasured the unique intimacy and vitality of his contact with the poetry of the long-dead Homer.

Indeed, by means of Homer, Cowper had created and revived many friendships. Admirers wrote to him and were enlisted in the corps of subscription hunters. Such was Walter Churchey, a Welsh attorney and aspiring poetaster. Cowper grimaced at his verse, but he warmly appreciated his assistance. Similarly, the flamboyant Clotworthy Rowley, once Cowper's neighbor and comrade at the Inner Temple and now Member for Downpatrick in the Irish Parliament, had written to the poet in February 1788 and received in turn a full account of the progress of the translation. And some months later, Cowper reestablished ties with Martin Madan, on the basis of their mutual interest in the translation of classical literature. Madan, now a sick man, had just completed and published his translation of Juvenal and Persius, and Cowper wrote to him in June 1789 to describe his own labors and to pay his respects to one who had aided him many years before.

Underlying these strengthening bonds of friendship, however, there remained for Cowper an unappeasable sense of emptiness. Depression had been mastered, not expelled. Alluding to his uneasy feelings, he confided to Margaret King at the beginning of March 1788 that "In the Depths of it I wrote the Task and the Volume which preceded it, and in the same Deeps am now Translating Homer."[109] But the toil went on, and Cowper's own efforts were made easier by his copyists, particularly Mary Unwin and George Throckmorton.

Johnson and Fuseli were not proving so eager to move ahead with their part of the undertaking. With March drawing to a close, Cowper needed to hear promptly from Fuseli, who was then in possession of a fresh revisal of books 12 and 13, in order that he could send him an initial revision of the next three books. Distraught by the delay, he at last sent to London a fair copy of the first four books of the *Iliad* on or about April 2.

Cowper wished to get the potentially lengthy business of printing underway as soon as possible, and he fretted at Fuseli's lack of cooperation. Cowper asked Johnson to begin printing, since eleven books were ready. Johnson replied that "he never knew a work sent to the Printer before finish'd, but the Author repented of it, it being impossible to contrive the plan with any certainty."[110] Cowper accepted this judgment and proceeded with the work of revision, not without occasional snorts of exasperation at his subject matter: "We admire that in an Antient for which we should send a modern Bard to Bedlam."[111] By May 24, he had reached book 19 in his revised translation, and a month later he was at work on book 21. By the end of August, Cowper was on the verge of completing the penultimate book, and still grumbling that he "being advanced so far could easily keep before the Printers, were they to begin to morrow."[112] September 23 saw the end of the first revision of the *Iliad,* but his satisfaction with this achievement was tempered by an awareness of what still lay ahead.

Though his progress was occasionally punctuated by this kind of outburst against the lack of relevance of "these two long stories,"[113] Cowper nevertheless proceeded quickly into the *Odyssey.* By December, Fuseli by his increasing tardiness revealed his lack of enthusiasm for his ongoing role as Cowper's principal revisor, and so the poet tactfully released him from any sense of obligation by informing Johnson that the Swiss artist had "found the revisal of my translation a burthen, which he could not conveniently bear."[114] Despite Fuseli's increasing detachment, or perhaps because of it, Cowper worked his way rapidly through the first version of the *Odyssey,* reaching book 16 by April 20, 1789. The pace of work remained quick during that summer, so much so that Cowper apologized for his slowness in replying to correspondents.

The translation had already been a long race, but it was far from over yet. Cowper indulged in wishful thinking when in mid-August he reckoned on another "half a year's work before me."[115] New Year's Day 1790 came, and he was "still thrumming Homer's lyre."[116] The process of translation had grown no easier as his critical insight and translating skill increased. If anything, it had become more intense: ". . . it cost me all the morning yesterday, and all the evening, to translate a single simile to my mind."[117] Cowper's daily routine focused entirely upon the translation. "Homer in the morning and Homer in the evening, as constant as the day goes round."[118]

With the *Odyssey* nearing completion, Joseph Johnson once more persuaded his Swiss friend to continue helping with the revision of the drafts. Fuseli's renewed efforts were generally of the most cursory nature, and by autumn he had given up for good. He wrote to a friend: "I heartily wish with you that Cowper had trusted to his own legs instead of a pair of stilts to fame: and this I wish as much for my own sake as for his; for I am deadly sick of revising his foul linen."[119] Cowper's response to the news of Fuseli's "resignation" was to touch gently on the matter of his uncooperativeness during recent months: "It grieves me, that after all, I am obliged to go into public without the whole advantage of Mr. Fuseli's judicious strictures. My only consolation is, that I have not forfeited them by my own impatience."[120]

By February 1, 1790, the *Odyssey* (completed in its first draft the previous summer) had been revised from beginning to end, and the poet had returned to the *Iliad*, having checked and revised that poem up to its fifteenth book. Once again he was peering hopefully into the future. "When the Iliad has had the revisal which I am now giving it, I shall give the whole one more, in which I shall find but little to do, and then throw myself into the hands of the Public."[121] Also during February, John Johnson began to play a role in the preparation of the fair copy, taking on the duties of amanuensis and working on a first fair copy of the *Odyssey* in tandem with Lady Hesketh. As March drew to a close, Cowper, having completed his corrections to the *Iliad*, asked for the *Odyssey* manuscript on which his two cousins had been employed. Lady Hesketh's delay in sending the manuscript which was in her keeping caused Cowper to start all over again his reading through and tidying up of the *Iliad*.

Cowper was compelled to proceed in this manner from more than sheer boredom. He had recently submitted books 1 and 2 of the *Iliad* to Lady Hesketh so that she could pass them on, as she had asked to do, to Mrs. Caroline Howe, "a great Critic of your sex" as the poet termed her, and "mistress of more tongues than a few."[122] Caroline Howe was a noted intellectual and a friend of Mrs. Montagu, at whose home Lady Hesketh probably met her. Notwithstanding Mrs. Howe's return of the manuscript to Lady Hesketh with praise and admiration for Cowper's work, it did not reach the poet's own hands until April 30, more than a month later. This further delay was incidental in Cowper's eyes, for by now the end of six years' work was in sight.

Spring passed into summer, and Lady Hesketh's and John Johnson's clean transcript of the *Odyssey* grew black in the last work of revision. Cowper looked forward in July to the approaching visit of John Johnson: "I shall find employment for you, having made already some part of the fair copy of the Odyssey, a foul one. I am revising it for the last time, and spare nothing that I can mend. The Iliad is finish'd."[123] Just over a month later, on September 4, he announced to Joseph Hill, "My Homer is finished, goes to London on Wednesday and in a few days will be in the Press. It will not be long before I shall make my bargain with Johnson for the Copy."[124] The completed manuscript was too valuable to allow it to go the regular way of delivery by stagecoach to London. Cowper did not wish for any further disasters in transit. Fortunately, John Johnson was on hand to perform the duty of courier, and he departed with the completed copy on September 8.

12
Homer: Final Preparations,
The Quarrel with Johnson, Reviews

1   As SOON as Johnny had left for London, Cowper eagerly anticipated the arrival of proofs. In the intervening time, he completed some of the subsidiary material to the translation, most important of which was the *Preface*. In this brief essay, he pulled together many years of thought on the proper relationship of the translator to his original, and of the special significance of his own work on Homer. He wrote his argument in a style that is only slightly more formal than that of his familiar letters, choosing to proceed in an apparently casual and associative way, reminiscent of Dryden's easy manner in *Preface to Fables Ancient and Modern*. Cowper's aim in his *Preface* was to assert his own poetic function in relation to the august company of Homer and Milton, just as Dryden had understandably laid claim to a similar position a hundred years earlier. Both poets saw themselves as revivers and restorers of the vigor of the classical tradition, and they spoke of their work as continuations of that tradition, not as culminations.

For Cowper, however, the fulfillment of this noble aim would be more difficult than it had been for the earlier poet-translators. Despite the support of several influential literary figures, he could expect to be attacked by those convinced that Pope's version was the ideal one. In calling into question many obsolete but still-cherished notions about what Homer and the epic were really about, he was setting forth concepts that would seem radical to many. In particular, he claimed to have found the ideal balance between exactness and ornament in blank verse, that form of "greatest difficulty . . . that calls for the most artificial management in its construction."[1] Thus, the *Preface* was Cowper's public statement of how he conceived of the challenge he had set himself. It provided a calm and realistic estimate of his attempts to meet the often impossibly high ideal of a translation that is at once inspired and exact.

Cowper set forth in the *Preface* the twin virtues of fidelity and poetic vitality which he had always seen to be the crucial qualities of a worthwhile translation of Homer. In the course of the essay, these virtues tend to merge and blend, so that at times he seems to be working toward a theory not merely of translation, but, by implication, of poetry as a whole. As he admitted, he was discussing more an ideal of poetic re-creation than the ways in which he had come to attain that ideal.

From both stances, as poet and as translator, Cowper was determined to assert that blank verse was the ideal metrical form. Thus, he stressed that the essential qualities of Homer's verse were energy and harmony, and, claimed Cowper, the English poet is blessed with a metrical and verbal treasury as rich as Homer's. Milton had provided the supreme example of how the poetic potential of English could be realized.[2] In fact, that poet became for Cowper the supreme exponent in the language of the grand epic style, Cowper's vigorous advocacy of blank verse being based on his conviction that in order to get a taste of the living Homer, the poet-translator must express himself in the Miltonic voice, for there was something in the very nature of that voice, abstracted from the sense it expressed, that was the essence of epic. In much the same vein, Samuel Johnson had said of the *Iliad* that "you could not read it without the pleasure of verse."[3] Cowper agreed: "A translator of Homer, therefore, seems directed by Homer himself to the use of blank verse, as to that alone in which he can be rendered with any tolerable representation of his manner in this particular."[4]

In his *Preface,* Cowper also declared that he had remained faithful to every detail of the narrative line in his original: "I have omitted nothing; I have invented nothing."[5] Further, he had tried to match the range of his vocabulary to Homer's, as he attempted to match the richness of Homer's meter. In the translation, he was compelled to make use of whole categories of terminology and diction that had not been considered proper for Pope's epics. In fact, Cowper was to be lashed by his critics for a looseness of language that could allow even a god to speak in a moment of stress like a "Chelsea pensioner."[6]

Ultimately, Cowper's chosen meter was not flexible. As Matthew Arnold put it, "between Cowper and Homer . . . there is interposed the mist of Cowper's elaborate Miltonic manner, entirely alien to the flowing rapidity of Homer."[7] In a sense, Cowper's conception was impossible to put into practice: "I can only pretend to have endeavoured it."[8] However, Cowper had hoped to escape this dilemma by following the example of Milton.

2   The *Preface* did not take long to complete. It was finished within five days of the dispatch of the manuscript of the translation to London on September 8. Only eight days had passed since the manuscript had left when Cowper wrote nervously to Clotworthy Rowley: "My copy has been some weeks in Town, yet have I but this moment received the second proof-sheet."[9] Through the following months, Cowper's sense of urgency did not dissolve into acceptance of the printers' routine. By the end of October, though, he sought to calm himself with the knowledge that at least some kind of steady pace had been established. But a month later, Cowper was chafing again. Experiencing what must have seemed to him excruciating delay, Cowper threw himself into the chore of proofreading: "To this business I give myself with an assiduity and attention truly admirable—, and set an example which, if other poets could be apprized of it, they would do well to follow. Miscarriages in Authorship I am persuaded are as often to be ascribed to want of pains-taking as want of ability, and it shall for ever be an axiom with me, that, let a writer's ability be what it may, he has never done his best 'till he has done the same thing five times over."[10]

In the case of the *Iliad* in particular, "five times" was an understatement. Even in December 1790, Cowper was recasting whole passages (such as book 10, lines 674–83) before returning the proofs to the printers. He admitted that his sense of commitment to the work was becoming obsessional: "The truth is, that I could, more easily perhaps, satisfy the majority of readers, than I can satisfy myself."[11] Still searching for "a better spur than I master to prick the printer forward," Cowper fell prey at Christmas to what he termed "a nervous fever."[12] As a result, he attempted to reassert a more objective attitude toward the process, an attempt which was perhaps made easier by the establishment of a more satisfactory printing routine.

Meanwhile, Joseph Johnson, acting on the advice of Cowper himself, had been doing his own proofreading with assistance from a scholarly printer friend, Deodatus Bye. He wrote Cowper in early February warning him that the translation of the *Odyssey* was not up to the level of finish of the *Iliad*. In his desire to get ready quickly, Cowper had not revised the work sufficiently. Cowper had to agree. As had happened before, a newly copied manuscript was darkened with "a thousand alterations," but now there was no time for another copy to be made, printing of the *Odyssey* having begun by the end of February.[13] On Sunday, March 6, 1791, Cowper wrote: "I have within these two days given the very last stroke of my pen to my long Translation, and what will be my next career I know not."[14]

Future plans could not properly be addressed as long as the printing dragged on, however. And as it was, the publication date had been moved back to the end of May, for by March 19, Cowper had only received proofs up to book 6 of the *Odyssey*. If anything, the rate of production worsened in April, five sheets a week trickling into his hands. He deputized Samuel Rose to ask Johnson "when he thinks the Town will adjourn to the Country, and when we are likely to publish."[15] Easter festivities proved a further block: "These holiday times are very unfavourable to the Printer's progress. He and all his dæmons are employed in making themselves merry, and me sad, for I mourn at ev'ry hindrance."[16] The pace picked up in May. As Cowper learned on the 22nd of that month, the printing of the *Odyssey* was to be completed in four days.

Only the subsidiary material remained to be run through the press: the *Preface,* the dedicatory inscriptions (of the *Iliad* to Earl Cowper, the *Odyssey* to the Countess Dowager Spencer), and the pseudo-Homeric burlesque epic, *The Battle of the Frogs and the Mice,* which Cowper may well have worked on in the winter or spring from sheer energy and boredom, although he defended its place with the two great epics to John Johnson by stating that it was a "poem of much honour," adding that "I found the translation of it very amusing."[17] He had kept work on this trifle a secret for fear that friends and relatives might object to its inclusion as "a measure more bountiful than prudent."[18]

3   Together with the subsidiary items was the crucially important final draft of the *List of Subscribers,* which, Cowper stated, "can hardly be got ready and sent too soon."[19] This list had expanded well beyond the original limit of three hundred subscriptions, set by Cowper in agreement with his publisher for the February 1786 printing of the *Proposals;* in fact, he had seemed well on the way toward that goal as early as February 1788, at which time he told Rowley that he could already "boast of a very good"[20] response. Six weeks later he wrote to Lady Hesketh, expressing the

same vague optimism: "What is the state of the Subscription I know not nor am at all able to conjecture, but I suppose it is such as may vindicate such a noble enterprize as that of going to Press immediately, from the imputation of rashness."[21] Cowper's ignorance of the exact status of his list was understandable, given the fact that so many people were working for him in raising subscriptions, each with a different degree of success. The submitted pledges quietly accumulated at Johnson's shop in St. Paul's Churchyard and at the shops of Johnson's agents in the business, J. Walter at Charing Cross and J. Debrett in Piccadilly.

An initial cause of the growth of the subscription was the increasing interest of Cowper's own large and distinguished family in the outcome of his efforts. General Cowper was able to reach the more aristocratic Cowpers and their friends, and his son Henry was equally willing to contact colleagues and acquaintances in political and legal circles. By the spring of 1788, Henry had given the poet cause to expect "upwards of thirty Right Honourable names,"[22] with many more to come during the approaching session of Parliament. Indeed, as Clerk Assistant to the House of Lords, Henry Cowper was admirably placed to make such catches. He seems to have succeeded where the translator himself had not, for example, in having the "address"[23] to win the attention of the Lord Chancellor, Edward Thurlow, for the Homer project and to gain his pledge to subscribe.

On September 16, 1790, Cowper had an opportunity to examine a relatively complete subscription list sent him by Joseph Johnson. Characteristically, he scanned it first to discover the names of friends. As he said in a letter written that night to Rowley, "I cannot help considering my subscription as a sort of test of their constancy who formerly professed a kindness for me. They in whom a spark of that kindness survives will hardly fail to discover it on such an occasion, and seeing the affair in this light, I feel myself a little grieved and hurt that some names which old friendship gave me a right to expect, are not to be found in my catalogue."[24] And in acknowledging Joseph Hill's aid in gaining subscriptions, Cowper gave way once more to the unavoidable feelings of disappointment which the list inspired: "It is an illustrious catalogue in respect of rank and title, but methinks I should have liked it as well had it been more numerous."[25]

It transpired that forty-five names had been omitted from the list by Joseph Johnson's copyist, and so Cowper could afford to regain something of his sanguine mood regarding public support. As well, support in obtaining subscriptions was beginning to come from new sources. Mrs. King's cousin, the Reverend Thomas Martyn, Professor of Botany at Cambridge and an admirer of Cowper's poetry, subscribed early in 1789 and was subsequently helpful in attracting the attention of the "Cambridge Critics" toward the Homer project. Cambridge was also the center for John Johnson's highly successful activities as a subscription raiser, which began at the end of 1790 with the winning of support from King's as well as from individuals at the university. Meanwhile, Cowper's more distant correspondents had begun to respond. Admirers, such as Walter Churchey, wrote to him and were enlisted in the corps of subscription hunters. Rowley in Ireland had garnered sixteen pledges, and Henry Mackenzie had begun to gain support from the northern libraries and universities, including, by the end of January 1791, the Advocates Library and the University of Edinburgh. By the end of February, all the Scottish universities had subscribed.

A new, up-to-date issue of the *Proposals* was separately printed at the end of January 1791, together with a first printed edition of the *List of Subscribers*. The *Proposals* and the *List* were "annext to the Analytical Review" for February, and to the *Gentleman's Magazine* for the same month. This printed *List* still did not include all the subscriptions, probably because of Rowley's "procrastinating moods"[26] in not sending off the names of his Irish subscribers on time. The 1791 edition of the *Proposals* commenced with the same list of conditions as its 1786 predecessor, only augmented by two new items which stressed the impending appearance of the work and removed the ceiling of three hundred subscriptions. The appended roster of subscribers, incomplete as it was, consisted of 270 names: 317 copies had been ordered, 106 of which were to be on fine paper. The appearance of this new issue of the *Proposals* gave a boost to the drive for yet more subscriptions and to Cowper's hopes.

John Johnson's resourcefulness was having especially positive effects on both the author and the list. Even before the publication of the 1791 *Proposals,* he had been making advertising placards, mounting the advertisement from the *Proposals* on boards, and posting them in public places in Cambridge. He had sent one such poster to Cowper, who was suitably impressed and passed it on to Samuel Greatheed in Newport Pagnell "to catch as many gudgeons there as will bite."[27] Johnny then suggested "that it might not be amiss to advertize the work at Merryl's the bookseller. I acquiesced in the measure, and at his return [to Cambridge] he pasted me on a board and hung me in the shop, as it has proved in the event, much to my emolument."[28] In addition to Cambridge connections, many of Johnny's relations and friends in Norfolk were added to the list.

In contrast to Cambridge, Oxford was barren territory. The Oxford colleges chose to ignore the subscription entirely, an event Cowper had foreseen at the time the second *Proposals* were printed:

> Should the Oxonians bestow none of their notice on me on this occasion, it will happen singularly enough that as Pope received all his university-honours in the subscription way from Oxford, and none at all from Cambridge, so I shall have received all mine from Cambridge and none from Oxford. . . . I understand that on whatsoever occasion either of those learned bodies thinks fit to move, the other always makes it a point to sit still. Thus proving its superiority.[29]

Only three Oxford names appeared in the 1791 publication of the *List*. John Throckmorton's efforts to interest the college libraries had been rebuffed with the claim "That it is a Rule with *Them*, never to subscribe to any thing."[30]

A revision of the *List* sent to Cowper in late March showed substantial gains over the printed version of the previous month, eighty-three names having been added, including those of the Scottish and Irish subscribers that had arrived too late for the press. Five hundred ninety-seven copies had been subscribed for, of which 175 were on fine paper. Cowper's total roster of 498 names came satisfyingly close to Pope's 600, as he noted to Samuel Rose. To obtain this victory, however, the whole process had cost a lot of time and energy. The complexities of organizing and keeping track of the efforts of all his agents led Cowper at last to declare, "I shall be glad for your sake when the Subscription Books are all sent to their proper homes, and hereby promise never to publish more in that way."[31]

4   The success of the subscription list was soured by an acrimonious squabble over the distribution of profits that took place between Cowper and his publisher immediately following the publication of the translations on July 1, 1791. Since their initial negotiations in December 1785, the matter had not been seriously raised again until the text had reached the printers. Discussing his plans with Joseph Hill on September 4, 1790, Cowper had mentioned that "It will not be long before I shall make my bargain with Johnson for the Copy, and then, once in my life I shall have money with

which to purchase Stock instead of selling it."[32] A week or so later it occurred to the poet to write to Samuel Rose, to request his professional advice should any difficulty emerge in the final negotiations.

In the spring of 1791, Cowper still anticipated a trouble-free transaction with his publisher, considering that a bond of amicable trust united them as it had done in the past. By the end of April, he had received from Johnson an offer to purchase the copyright and had "graciously consented to sell it to him."[33] However, he felt wary about the final terms of the agreement that was to be decided, as he intimated in writing to Rose: "He promised me, when I began the work, to deal as liberally with me as any man of his trade could possibly do, and I wish for more reasons than one that he may keep his word, but especially for your sake, because in that case he will give you no trouble."[34] On the eve of publication, however, Johnson still had not seen fit to inform his client of his proposal.

Johnson did not wait much longer before suggesting what he saw as a fair distribution of the profits. On July 3, two days after publication, Cowper received a note containing his publisher's offer and he was deeply distressed:

> Do you mean that the whole Subscription money, both first and second payment shall be yours, except the Sums beyond the price of a copy? Out of this money to pay the Printer &c and take the Remainder as your own?

> This seems, by the manner in which your proposals are expressed, to be the purport of them, and yet I cannot believe it to be so. Because in that case I should have no other reward of my labours other than the Thousand pounds which you propose to give for the copy right.[35]

Cowper's initial bewilderment passed away as he took careful stock of his financial position. Methodically, he set forth the situation to Rose three days following his receipt of Johnson's letter. He was no longer leaving the calculations to somebody else:

> The case therefore stands thus—The whole subscription money, exclusive of extras, will amount of £1144—The unsubscribed copies being 200 will sell at the advanced price that he proposes for £500 more. These sums together make £1644.

> With this money he means to pay the expences of the first edition—viz—£600. And with this money he means to pay me

£1000 for my copy right. When he has so done £44 will remain in his pocket.

This to me has much the appearance of giving me nothing for my copy, or rather it has the appearance of being paid £44 for accepting it.[36]

Clearly a misunderstanding had developed out of the exchange of letters between author and publisher made at the end of April. Cowper seems to have thought that he would be paid for his copyright in addition to receiving the net profit from the subscription money. Johnson, on the other hand, saw the payment for the copyright and the net profit from the subscription as one and the same. Considering that there was some confusion, Cowper wrote more cautiously to Rose on the day after his first letter, commenting further on what Johnson obviously had considered to be a fair offer. By this time, however, Johnson had already made a second proposal, having been startled into action, perhaps, by Cowper's vehemence. This second, generous proposition, as the poet soon informed Lady Hesketh, was "to pay all expences and to give me a £1000 next Midsummer, leaving the copy-right still in my hands."[37] This suggestion became the basis of the agreement.

Whatever the financial losses on either side, the dispute between Cowper and Johnson cast a shadow over what should have been a triumphant moment in Cowper's career as a poet. In the week following the appearance of his Homer, Cowper's spirits sank. This was not merely due to a feeling of anticlimax after years of preparation and hope. The trouble with Johnson had taken its toll. As Cowper told Joseph Hill, "It was irksome to me . . . to feel myself on the edge of a quarrel with a man who has not corresponded with me merely as a Trader in my commodity, but familiarly and almost as a friend."[38]

William Cowper had spent six years working on his translation of Homer's two great epics. During that time he had given a great many reasons for having chosen such a project, instead of applying his creative powers—then at their height—to original work. He had justified with care and precision his particular approach to Homer's poetry and had created a language and a manner which he considered to be faithful to the original, in the tradition of Milton's variegation and elaboration of diction and meter. Ultimately, Cowper's work on Homer had been a labor of love, an act of friendship. Not only did Cowper make new friends and rediscover old ones in the course of those six years, but he established a personal sense of affinity with the Greek poet. Homer himself had come to live in the lines of the *Iliad* and the *Odyssey*. It was thus especially unpleasant that the last moment of a long process toward publication of the translation should have been marred by the rupture of an excellent working friendship over a relatively small disagreement. As we have seen, Cowper was inordinately dependent on the largess of others, and, in this instance, he had fantasized that the Homer, as in the case of Pope, would bring him a substantial financial reward. He was distressed when this design was unexpectedly frustrated. However, Cowper's monetary advisers, Hill and Rose, thought their friend acted with propriety, and it must be remembered that Cowper had heretofore not received payment of any kind for any of his published work, including *The Task*.[39] Nevertheless, taken by itself, Johnson's offer had been a munificent one, and once again, Cowper's great—and unrealistic—expectations had not been met.

5   Critics did not wait long after the appearance in print of Cowper's Homer to express their misgivings, together with some praise. The earliest of these was Edward Thurlow who, first in correspondence with Henry Cowper and then directly with the poet, stressed that Cowper's choice of meter contributed little to the translation. Thurlow translated the speech of Achilles to Phoenix into rhyme (*Iliad* 9, 758–72, in Cowper's translation), and the passage involved was conveyed to Cowper, so that by the middle of August he was ready to respond to the Lord Chancellor. In his letter to Thurlow, Cowper diplomatically but firmly reiterated his assertion that rhyme had become merely an ornament, impeding all efforts to achieve exactitude in translation:

> I allow your Lordship's version of this speech of Achilles to be very close and closer much than mine. And to say truth, I should like a whole Iliad render'd according to that sample better far than Pope's; because it is Homer and nothing but Homer. But I believe that should either your Lordship or I give them burnish and elevation, your lines would be found, in measure as they acquired stateliness, to have lost the merit of fidelity. In which case nothing more would be done than Pope has done already.[40]

Writing again to Thurlow on August 22, Cowper offered his own couplet version of the passage in question and affirmed that this form was incompatible with the requirements of poetic translation:

"I have not treacherously departed from my pattern, that I might seem to give some proof of the justness of my own opinion, but have fairly and honestly adhered as closely to it as I could."[41] Thurlow was duly persuaded by Cowper and endorsed his rejection of rhyme. As the poet exclaimed to Lady Hesketh, "Such is the candour of a wise man and a real scholar. I would to heaven that all prejudiced persons were like him!"[42] Of course, not all Cowper's critics could be won over in this manner, and several of them were far more determined than Thurlow to examine the implications of his approach to translation.

The first installment of what would turn out to be an extended analysis of Cowper's Homer appeared in the September 1791 issue of the *Gentleman's Magazine*. Its author followed Cowper in singling out energy and harmony as the two essential qualities of the Homeric style, and he examined Cowper's work to determine whether it revealed them. Underlying this reviewer's praise for details in the translation was the complaint that Cowper's "commendable desire of retaining the strength of his original has made him less attentive to that sweetness and melody which the Greek language possesses above all others, but of which our own is sufficiently capable."[43]

Cowper was delighted yet disturbed by the attention given to his work, being sensitive to the poise maintained between praise and blame in this article. By the time of its fourth installment in the December issue, the tone of the reviewer's comments had become increasingly positive. "Should he continue to sweeten at this rate, as he proceeds," Cowper said, "I know not what will become of all the little modesty I have left."[44] But by the final installment, in June, the balance had swung against Cowper. The reviewer claimed that Cowper's attempt to present the most exact replica of his original was fundamentally inadequate. Cowper had undertaken a project, he claimed, which was quite unsuitable for his particular strengths and weaknesses.

This sense of Cowper's failure to live up to his readers' expectations was echoed by John Parsons in an essay published anonymously in the *Monthly Review* for August 1792 and reprinted in the *English Review* later that year. Parsons objected to Cowper's literalness but approved of his choice of blank verse: "If Mr. Cowper has employed it with less success than we expected, his failure may be ascribed to that quixotical spirit, which has impelled him to engage in a contest in which victory affords few laurels, and ridicule exasperates defeat."[45]

In an article published in the *Critical Review* for March 1792, yet another anonymous reviewer made far more sweeping condemnations of Cowper's Homer, going so far as to declare that "Had his intention been merely to preserve the sense of the Grecian bard, we are inclined to think that a liberal prose translation would have preserved it in periods no less musical than the present."[46] In a second installment published the next month, he harkened back to the strictures made by "T. S." six years earlier against the *Specimen* of the translation. In essence, this reviewer faulted Cowper as Cowper had done Pope. The chosen mode of expression, he declared, had proved too artificial and inflexible. Like Parsons, this reader was inclined to dismiss Cowper's Homer as a noble failure, or even as a regrettable waste of considerable talent and energy: "We heartily wish, if it would have yielded equal amusement, that he had dedicated those hours to original composition; we should then have followed him with more satisfaction."[47]

These reviewers all stressed that Cowper had failed because his concept of his undertaking contained a basic contradiction: exactness and inspiration could never be comfortably reconciled. What particularly bothered these critics was Cowper's insistence that his version was intended as an honest and faithful mirror of the original. In response to this claim, stated in the *Preface,* they hunted diligently for distortions in that mirror.

The intentionally negative thrust of these three notices was countered in January 1793 in an article written by Henry Fuseli and published in Joseph Johnson's own *Analytical Review.* Under the initials "Z. Z.," Fuseli set out to provide a more thoroughgoing and objective examination of Cowper's achievement than his predecessors had offered. Certainly no one was more qualified to provide this kind of authoritative statement than Fuseli, who had come to understand Cowper's ideals of poetic translation and who had even taken a significant role in the shaping of those ideals.

One of Fuseli's main purposes was to define carefully what was meant by fidelity of translation in Cowper's work on Homer. This concept, maligned by all of Cowper's earlier reviewers, is seen by Fuseli to be essential for the preservation of the spirit of the epic:

> When we consider the magnificent end of epic poetry, to write for all times and all races, to treat of what will always exist and always be understood, the puny laws of local decorum and fluctuating fashions, by which the omission or modification of certain habits and customs, natural but obsolete, is prescribed,

cannot come into consideration. . . . He [Cowper] neither "attempts to soften or refine away" the energy of passages relative to the theology of primitive ages, or fraught with allegoric images of the phenomena of nature, though they might provoke the smile of the effeminate, and of the sophists of his day. This is the first and most essential part of the fidelity prescribed to a translator, and this Mr. C. has so far scrupulously observed, that he must be allowed to have given us more of Homer, and added less of his own, than all his predecessors; and this he has done with that simplicity, that purity of manner, which we consider are the second requisite of translation.[48]

The translator who would prune away particulars of time and place is himself bound within the scope of his own milieu, with its own equally artificial and ephemeral concepts of decorum. Fuseli concentrates here upon the apparently less valuable material in Homer's narratives, in order to present a new concept of decorum, one less bound to the social and aesthetic expectations of the audience than to the integrity of the work itself.

This justification and clarification of Cowper's central artistic concerns in translating Homer is qualified, however, by Fuseli's comments on Cowper's frequently inappropriate mode of expression:

> The chief trespass of our translator's style, and it will be found to imply a trespass against his fidelity and simplicity, is no doubt the intemperate use of inversion, ungraceful in itself, contrary to the idiom of his language, and what is still worse, subversive of perspicuity, than which no quality more distinguishes Homer from all other writers.[49]

In the effort to create a suitably epic voice, Cowper had subjected the natural order of English syntax to unnecessary distortions. As the reviewer for the *Critical Review* also noted, the imposing example of Milton's bold deviation from the common track had led the translator into numerous inexcusable stylistic complexities. Mode of expression had tended to come unstuck from the clear narrative flow which it should embody. Cowper had merely exchanged Pope's ornament for Milton's. The weakness of Cowper's Homer, according to Fuseli, was not in its conception, as earlier reviewers had declared, but in its execution. He saw the immense effort made by Cowper to come to terms with his original as flawed, not wasted, energy.

Cowper began making minor alterations, leading toward a to-tally new version, less than a month after the publication of the first edition. He reworked passages for the remainder of his life. And, finally, in 1797, prodded by John Johnson, he set about revis-ing the work for the last time. This renewed activity, if such it can be called, began as an effort to shake off the lethargic depression that had by then engulfed him.

Meanwhile, in the autumn of 1791, Cowper, looking about for a new project, decided to edit Milton's poems. This undertaking, al-though it was to prove abortive, was his fourth major literary proj-ect since 1779, and the culmination of his career as a man of letters. In *Poems,* he had found the format he had used for his confession of faith inadequate; he had turned to blank verse in *The Task* to write a poem about a man who remains in the garden and attempts to find a paradise within. From 1785 to 1791, he employed Mil-tonic means to unravel Homer's heroic sublime. It was thus appro-priate that he should decide to edit the verse of the English poet whose literary successor he had become.

13
Milton and William the Second

1   COWPER DID not rest for long after completing work on Homer. His reading of the proofs of the *Odyssey* was finished at the end of May 1791, and the printed proposals for his edition of Milton are dated September 1, 1791. In August 1790, Joseph Johnson had decided to publish a "Milton Gallery" which would rival Boydell's *Shakespeare Gallery*. Fuseli was to undertake most of the paintings, and the engravings done from his work would be accompanied by an edition of the poetry. A year later, Johnson approached Cowper concerning this venture. The first of Cowper's extant letters to mention this matter is that of September 6, 1791, to Bagot. Cowper was ecstatic.

> I am on the brink of a new literary engagement, and of a kind with which I ever meddled before. A magnificent edition of Milton's works (I mean his poetical ones) is about to be published in the Boydel stile, with notes; Fuseli, the Painter, and your humble servant, the Editor. Thus I shall have pass'd through the three gradations of authorship, Poet, Translator, and Critic. Wish me success in this last capacity.[1]

Cowper had evidently been concerned about extending his career in such a direction, and he sought the advice of Samuel Teedon, the Olney schoolmaster, who was, we shall see, gradually assuming more and more importance in his life. Teedon told Cowper that his project had God's approbation. With this assurance, he was able to begin work.

Cowper was certainly well-qualified as poet and translator to render Milton's Latin and Italian poems into English, but he did not have the books at hand to "select notes from others, and to write original notes,"[2] and he was never particularly concerned in the proofreading of his own poetry with establishing a correct text. When he agreed to Johnson's proposal, the only edition of Milton Cowper possessed was the seventh edition (1770) in two volumes of Thomas Newton's edition of *Paradise Lost.*[3] On September 14, nevertheless, Cowper assured Rose: "You, who know how necessary it is to me to be employed, will be glad to hear that I have been called to a new literary engagement."[4]

There was something desperate in Cowper's decision to proceed with the Milton. His years as a translator of Homer had been so busy that he had often not had the time to be unduly concerned about many of his inner struggles, and it was for such therapeutic reasons that he probably welcomed the opportunity to become involved in the Milton project. As well, this venture offered Cowper the opportunity to become directly involved with Milton's forceful, dynamic personality. However, his interest soon waned. On October 30, he was still favorably disposed to the project, although he was now irritated with Milton's elegies; he felt their versification "equal to the best of Ovid" but found the subject matter "too puerile."[5] On November 16, he described the proposed edition as "pompous,"[6] and three weeks later he seemed willing to disengage himself if that were possible. "As to Milton, the die is cast. I am engaged, have bargain'd with Johnson and cannot recede. I should otherwise have been glad to do as you [Bagot] advise, to make the translation of his Latin and Italian, part of another volume."[7] Five days later, he told James Hurdis that he would have been better employed had he stuck to "original work rather than . . . translation."[8] He persevered with the project, however, and by February 19, 1792, had completed the Latin poems and, three weeks later, the Italian ones. The commentary, halted in May by Mrs. Unwin's ill health, was never completed. "Days, weeks and months escape me and nothing is done,"[9] he told Joseph Johnson on July 8, and by the end of the year his regret at having been involved in the "Milton Gallery" was complete: "How often do I wish in the course of every day that I could be employed once more in poetry, and how often, of course, that this Miltonic trap had never caught me!"[10] The energy and devotion that Cowper had been able to give to Homer had vanished, domestic circumstances impinging mercilessly on his work. He had feared from the outset, with good reason, that this was a task for which he was not suited. He was ultimately delighted to hear from Joseph Johnson at the end of 1793 that the project had been shelved.

Excerpts from Cowper's translation of the Italian and Latin po-

ems were first published in Hayley's *Life of Milton* in 1794 and
again in 1796. But the greater portion of them remained unpublished until they appeared, with Cowper's commentary on *Paradise
Lost,* in 1808, edited by Hayley. In addition to five "complimentary
pieces" to Milton by various Italian authors, Cowper translated five
sonnets and one canzone from the Italian into English; as well as
the seven elegies, he rendered fourteen epigrams and miscellaneous
poems from Latin into English. If the Miltonic translations do not
constitute a considerable body of work, they have the merit of being
elegant renditions of the originals. In the course of this work, Cowper prepared two fragmentary sets of remarks on Milton. As well as
the commentary on books 1 through 3 of *Paradise Lost,* Cowper
also made a series of intriguing pencil notes on Johnson's *Life of
Milton.*

Cowper had been irritated in 1779 when he had first read Samuel
Johnson's treatment of Prior and Milton, and he expressed himself
forcefully on the subject in letters to Unwin. When he began work
on his own commentary twelve years later, he obtained (possibly
from Joseph Johnson) a four-volume edition of *The Lives of the
Poets.* Cowper entered comments sporadically in volumes 2 through
4 (a total of seven minor entries), but there are almost fifty notes in
volume 1 to the *Life of Milton.* Where Johnson says, "I cannot but
remark a kind of respect, perhaps unconsciously, paid to this great
man by his biographers,"[11] Cowper adds: "They have all paid him
more than you."[12] When Johnson condemns the use of blank verse,
Cowper remonstrates, "Did you ever write Blank Verse yourself?"[13]
In speaking of *Lycidas,* Johnson claims "Passion plucks no berries
from the myrtle and ivy,"[14] and Cowper rejoins: "but poetry does."[15]
Johnson felt that "Milton never learned the art of doing little
things with grace";[16] Cowper adds his assessment: "I thought his
Elegies were lusciously elegant."[17] In much of his career as a writer
of original verse and later as a translator of Homer, Cowper had
continually kept Pope before him as the opponent he would have
to best. The pencil annotation reveals that Samuel Johnson's antagonistic comments were his target in the Milton project.

In his commentary on *Paradise Lost,* Cowper pays close attention
to the felicities of blank verse as employed by Milton. Choosing the
manner of a practicing poet discussing the technical successes and
failures of a colleague, he offers his opinions on the virtuosity of
various passages. In his note to "As when from mountain tops"
from line 488 of book 2, he says:

The reader loses half the beauty of this charming simile, who does not give particular attention to the numbers. There is a majesty in them not often equalled, and never surpassed even by this great poet himself; the movement is uncommonly slow; an effect produced by means already hinted at, the assemblage of a greater proportion of long syllables than usual. The pauses are also managed with great skill and judgment; while the clouds rise, and the heavens gather blackness, they fall in those parts of the verse, where they retard the reader most, and thus become expressive of the solemnity of the subject; but in the latter part of the simile, where the sun breaks out, and the scene brightens, they are so disposed as to allow the verse an easier, and less interrupted flow, more suited to the cheerfulness of the occasion.[18]

Cowper also greatly admired Milton's use of "suppressed force":[19] "he addresses himself to the performance of great things, but makes no great exertion in doing it; a sure sign of uncommon vigor."[20] The fifty pages (in the 1808 edition) of Miltonic commentary are written in clear and precise language, and, although Cowper does not reveal any new directions for Miltonic criticism, he does provide a succinct testimonial to the English poet he most admired. The last three pages of that work are devoted to line 341 of book 3 ("God shall be all in all"):

Man, in the beginning, is placed in a probationary state, and made the arbiter of his own destiny. By his own fault he forfeits happiness both for himself and for his descendents. But mercy interposes for his restoration. That mercy is represented as perfectly free, as vouchsafed to the most unworthy; to creatures so entirely dead in sin, as to be destitute even of a sense of their need of it, and consequently too stupid ever to ask it.[21]

At this point in *Paradise Lost,* God the Father, in commending Christ's decision to assume human flesh, looks forward to a new "heaven and earth," after the attonement has been accomplished, "wherein the just shall dwell, / And after all their tribulations long / See golden days, fruitful of golden deeds, / With joy and love triumphing, and fair truth" (book 3, lines 335–38). It is under such circumstances that God's prophecy, taken over by Milton from St. Paul in 1 Corinthians 15:28, will be fulfilled: "When all things shall be subdued unto him, then shall the Son also himself be subject unto him that put all things under him, that God may be all in all."

However, Cowper did not think that he would participate in the "golden days" envisioned by Milton's God, and his conviction that he would not be saved but would exist forever in a state of damnation must have been uppermost in his mind when he wrote this. This poignant reminder of the apparent discrepancy by which God's mercy was bestowed on others and yet withheld from him must have been crucial in bringing the remarks on *Paradise Lost* to an abrupt termination.

Despite his abandonment of his new project, Cowper obviously perceived Milton as a spiritual father. He was delighted in February 1793 when Milton visited him in a dream: "He was very gravely but very neatly attired in the fashion of his day, and had a countenance which fill'd me with those feelings that an affectionate child has for a beloved father."[22] One side of Cowper's Miltonic heritage was a conviction instilled from 1763 that he was an outcast very much like Milton's vengeful Satan who proclaims "Which way I fly is hell; my self am hell."[23] Cowper saw his imaginary encounter with Milton in 1793 as an assurance that he did not contain such evil within himself.

2   If his Milton project brought Cowper a great deal of discomfort and frustration, it was responsible for a letter from William Hayley (dated February 7, 1792) which reached him rather belatedly on March 17. Since early 1792, Boydell and Nicol had been planning a rival illustrated *edition de luxe* to Joseph Johnson's Fuseli-Cowper project. George Romney was to provide the illustrations, and Hayley had agreed to write a life of Milton to accompany the engravings. A newspaper report claiming that Cowper and Hayley were rivals in writing lives of Milton prompted Hayley to write to Cowper, whose admirer he had been for some time.

> Though I resisted my desire of professing myself your friend, that I might not disturb you with intrusive familiarity, I cannot resist a desire equally affectionate, of disclaiming an idea which I am told is imputed to me, of considering myself, on a recent occasion, as an antagonist to you. . . . When I first heard of your intention, I was apprehensive that we might undesignedly thwart each other; but on seeing your proposals, I am agreeably persuaded, that our respective labours will be far from clashing. . . .[24]

Hayley sent his letter to Cowper at Joseph Johnson's, and it remained in London for almost six weeks before someone thought to send it on to Weston. Cowper was dismayed that Johnson had been so careless about transmitting the missive, and he answered Hayley on the day he received it. "What must you think of a man who could leave so valuable a favour almost six weeks unacknowledged?"[25] His letter was warm and frank: "I rejoice that you are employed to do justice to the character of a man, perhaps the chief of all who have ever done honour to our country, and whose very name I reverence. Here we shall not clash or interfere with each other, for a Life of Milton is no part of my bargain. In short we will cope with each other in nothing but that affection which you avow for me, unworthy of it as I am, and which your character and writings and especially your kind letter have begotten in my heart for you."[26] Two days after he had responded, Cowper mentioned to Lady Throckmorton Hayley's "handsome" and "affectionate" letter, and he was relieved that there was no rivalry between himself and Hayley. "Had there been any, I am verily persuaded that Hayley would have beat me hollow."[27]

The person who approached Cowper in February and who would be the last of the close friends Cowper made was one of the best known men-of-letters of the last part of the eighteenth century. William Hayley, poet, essayist, dramatist, patron, was the second son of Thomas Hayley and his wife, Mary Yates, of Chichester. He went to Eton in 1757 and in 1763 entered Trinity College, Cambridge, which he left in 1767 without taking a degree. He was admitted to the Middle Temple (an experience he shared with Cowper) in 1766. In 1769, he married Eliza Ball, the daughter of the Very Reverend Thomas Ball, Dean of Chichester. Eliza, who was five years younger than her husband, was of an unstable mental condition, and her father had been opposed to the match. The couple finally parted in 1789, but before that time the alliance between the two was precarious, and there had been long intervals of separation. Thomas Alphonso, Hayley's child, was the son of a Miss Betts, a housemaid at Hayley's house at Eartham, although any relationship between her and Hayley seems to have been over by the time of Tom's birth in 1780. There was a polite fiction that Eliza was the mother of Tom, and Tom perhaps was not informed of the identity of his real mother. In 1774, Hayley had settled at his family home at Eartham, Sussex, and it was to this place that many of his literary and artistic friends were summoned for long visits.

Hayley began his publishing career with *Ode on the Birth of the Prince of Wales*, which appeared in 1762, and which was reprinted in the *Gentleman's Magazine* the next year. Shortly after his marriage, he wrote a play, *The Afflicted Father,* and composed a number of celebratory epistles (including the *Epistle on Painting* in 1777 to Romney, and *Essay on History* in 1780 to Gibbon), but his first real success came with *The Triumphs of Temper* (1781; eleven London editions by 1817). *A Philosophical, Historical, and Moral Essay on Old Maids* (1785) brought him notoriety.

When Hayley wrote in 1792, he was, like Cowper, a celebrity. He was a kindly man, but he was excitable and flamboyant, and he surrounded himself with people who were, like himself, devoted to literature and art. It has become fashionable to see Hayley as a cultivated hanger-on, a man of no talent who wanted to be involved with the genuinely gifted. Horace Walpole's view of Hayley has often been taken as the correct measure of him: ". . . if you love incense, he has fumigated you like a flitch of bacon. . . . For Mr. Hayley himself, though he chants in good tune, and has now and then pretty lines amongst several both prosaic and obscure, he has, I think, no genius, no fire and not a grain of *originality*. . . ."[28] Walpole is just in his assessment of Hayley's literary gifts, although the historian William Robertson told Gibbon in 1781 how impressed he was by Hayley: "His poetry has more merit than that of most of his contemporaries; but his Whiggism is so bigotted, and his Christianity so fierce, that he almost disgusts one with two very good things."[29] The denigration of Hayley, then and now, as a serious writer is justified; but in his own time, he was a famous, if controversial figure, whom George Romney, Charlotte Smith (until they quarreled), Edward Gibbon, John Flaxman, William Cowper, and William Blake (until their celebrated dispute) admired and even cultivated. Within the context of the 1790s, Hayley was not simply a lionizer or a person whose sense of importance was established only by being in the company of the great. He was a well-known writer who sought out the best-known artistic people of his generation. He himself recognized the limits of his own talent; in 1792, he opined that his beams were shorn and if they had been "shorn like a sheep's coat . . . they would not have made a golden fleece large enough to have loaded a mouse."[30] Above all, Hayley was the Man of Sentiment par excellence.

Up to the receipt of Hayley's letter, Cowper had shown little interest in his writings. In April 1786, he mentioned that there was "much truth"[31] in an expression translated by Hayley, but the previous year he had seemed indifferent to Lady Hesketh's recommendation: "I have read Extracts from Hayley's works in the Review, and have admired some of them, but I know that he has published now and then a performance which I have no curiosity to be better acquainted with than I am already."[32] Cowper's detachment was irrevocably overcome soon after his correspondence with Hayley began.

Hayley was an effusive correspondent, and Cowper was certainly enraptured enough on March 24 (seven days after he first wrote to him) to begin his letter with "dear friend," and he assured Hayley that although he had "never 'till now address'd with [such a salutation] any of my correspondents in the beginning of our intercourse, with you I am sure that I may use it safely."[33] In his postscript, Cowper invited Hayley to Weston. It was impossible not to be susceptible to a fellow writer who assured you: "as to Genius, I declare by the Almighty Giver of it, I esteem your poetical *Powers* far above those, that I ever thought myself possess'd of in my vainer days—."[34] Cowper was responding to sincere declarations, however excessive they may have been.

By April 15, Hayley had become "Brother" as well as "Friend," and two weeks later Cowper was bursting with expectation of the fast approaching visit: "Mrs. Unwin says to me—Take care of yourself—William the second is coming."[35] Cowper, still embroiled in the Milton project at this time, was anxious to discuss their mutual "idol" and to castigate Samuel Johnson: "Oh That Johnson! How does every page of his on the subject, ay, almost every paragraph kindle my indignation!"[36]

From the time he had left London until Hayley's arrival in 1792, Cowper had not had a friendship which began, and which was largely maintained, through literature. In 1792, this was a vital consideration. Cowper was feeling bereft after he completed the translation of Homer, and when Hayley approached him he responded warmly.

Cowper was also intrigued with this claim by Hayley about the vicissitudes he had endured: "I flatter myself I possess *one advantage over you,* which it will gratify me to *hear you confess*—I mean the advantage of having endur'd *calamaties,* which even your Imagination, powerful and sublime as it is, *could not reach.*"[37] Cowper was gratified to have "bewitched" a "brethren"[38] in suffering; he undoubtedly felt he had found a kindred spirit in morbidity. Hayley's vigor was also fascinating:

> this William the second is coming with a *spirit so imperious*
> that he would carry off not only your Mary, but your Castle,
> your Garden and even your River Ouse with its Poet, if He

could transport all this radiant Spoil to enrich his favourite scenes of the South. There's an Invader for you!—what were your Norman Williams to this?[39]

Hayley also promised Cowper to "drive that depressive spirit of Melancholy you once mention'd, to such a distance from you, that it shall have no chance of invading you again."[40] For many reasons, then, Cowper eagerly awaited Hayley's arrival on May 15.

The visit went well at first. Mrs. Unwin's precarious health had stabilized, and Cowper felt he had formed a friendship which would make the connection between Hayley and himself "an edifying example to all future poets."[41] Hayley was also delighted: "My brother bard is one of the most interesting creatures in the world, from the powerful united influence of rare genius and singular misfortunes, with the additional charm of mild and engaging manners. . . . As to myself, I feel I have now the thing I most wanted—a congenial poetical spirit, willing to join with me in the most social and friendly cultivation of an art dear to us both, and particularly dear to us as the cement of friendship."[42]

Hayley's stay at Weston would by any reckoning have been the beginning of an important friendship, but events took a turn on May 22 to make it an event of even more far-reaching consequences. When Hayley and Cowper returned from their walk that afternoon, they were met by a neighbor, Samuel Greatheed, at the door of the Lodge with the dismaying news that Mary Unwin had suffered a stroke. Cowper rushed into the house to see her. A little while later, Hayley encountered Cowper in the passage as he was leaving Mrs. Unwin's bedroom, and Cowper shrieked: "There is a wall of separation between me and my God."[43] According to Hayley, he defiantly countered him: "So there is, my friend, but I can inform you, I am the most resolute mortal on earth for pulling down old walls, and by the living God I will not leave a stone standing in the wall you speak of."[44] Startled, and comforted by his friend's strong words, Cowper examined Hayley's "Features intently for a few moments; and, then, taking [his] Hand most cordially, said, 'I believe you.' "[45] Two days later, Cowper told Lady Hesketh that during the crisis it had been fortunate "that of all men living the man most qualified to assist and comfort me, is here."[46] Hayley not only provided moral support but also, and this was a vital consideration, he attempted to find a practical solution to the problem.

At Eartham, Hayley employed an electrical machine in medical emergencies. This device produced static electricity by the friction of rubber against a revolving glass cylinder. The cylinder was moved by hand, which required an assistant, since the person in charge of the mechanism was employed in passing the spark produced by the machine through the patient's body. After making inquiries of the whereabouts locally of such a device, Hayley learned, amazingly, that the Socket family, who lived nearby, had one. Mr. Socket was in London, but his wife lent the machine and the services of her son, Thomas.* Hayley used the machine on Mrs. Unwin, and he wrote to his friend, William Austin, a London physician, for suitable medicine. Under this regimen, Mrs. Unwin improved, and, on May 26, Cowper was pleased to tell Lady Hesketh that Mary had recovered "a little strength and a little power of utterance."[47] The right side of her body had been affected, but she had regained the use of her right hand four days after the attack, although she still had no control over her right foot. "Our good Samaritan Hayley has been all in all to us on this very afflictive occasion."[48]

Hayley's friendship became for Cowper, in a relatively short time, an encompassing one. He was the physician who had miraculously breathed new life into Mary Unwin. He was a well-known author with whom he could discuss his works as with an equal; he was anxious to alleviate his friend's melancholy; he was eager to help him in any practical way (Hayley's plan to obtain a pension for Cowper was launched during this visit); he wanted to be Cowper's spiritual father. Blake would later despise Hayley for persistent interference, but Cowper welcomed such intrusions. When Cowper told Lady Hesketh of Hayley's assistance—"He glows with benevolence to all men, but burns for my service with a zeal for which you will adore him"[49]—he was expressing the completeness of the relationship as he experienced it. By June 1792, the two men wrote to each other with an alacrity which Cowper said "all but youthful lovers must despair to imitate."[50] Later that month, Cowper asserted that Hayley "interests himself as much in my welfare as if he were not only my brother-bard, but my brother in truth, the son of my own mother."[51] Hayley was also the Robin "Red-breast" who, in a dream, crept into Cowper's bosom: "I never in my waking hours felt a tenderer love for any thing than I felt for the little animal in my sleep."[52]

* Thomas, fourteen at this time, was invited by Hayley to Eartham to tutor his son, Thomas Alphonso, and, in due course, the young man was introduced to Lord Sheffield and Lord Egremont. He subsequently attended Exeter College, Oxford, was ordained a priest in the Church of England, and held three livings at the time of his death in 1859.

Cowper even confessed to Hayley "what intense affection He had preserved [for Thea] thro his troubled Life."[53] The seemingly limitless "zeal," love, and intimacy he discovered in his friendship with Hayley led Cowper in August 1792 to undertake the extraordinary—for him—pilgrimage to Eartham.

3   Hayley left Weston on Friday, June 1, ten days after Mary Unwin's stroke. Cowper's first letter to Hayley was written on June 3, and the possibility of a visit to Eartham is mentioned there. Two days later, Cowper was immensely relieved to be able to tell Hayley Mrs. Unwin was progressing well, and a day later he told Lady Hesketh, "she walked from the stair-head through my chamber to her own, leaning only on one arm, and stepping rather less like an infant."[54] Although Cowper refused on June 7 an offer from Walter Bagot to visit Blithfield, he accepted an invitation twelve days later on behalf of Mary and himself to Eartham. At that time, he was of the opinion that July, when there would be "more long days before us,"[55] would be preferable to August. On June 21, he told Lady Hesketh that his acceptance of the offer was open to doubt. He likely did this because she had made a counter offer to receive Cowper and Mrs. Unwin in London. The remainder of June and most of July passed without further negotiations, but on July 20, Cowper had determined to make the trip to Eartham if Mary Unwin were well enough, and on the twenty-first he told Lady Hesketh that the matter was almost concluded: "We have not even yet determined absolutely on our journey to Eartham, but shall I believe in 2 or 3 days decide in favour of it." The thousand "Lions, monsters and giants"[56] that Cowper fantasized would block his way would vanish, he felt, if he confronted them. The next day he wrote to Hayley to announce that the "important affair" had been decided and "we are coming."[57] Cowper was confident on June 22 because he had just heard from Teedon that God had given approbation to the visit.

Cowper had to be skillful in his negotiations so as not to offend Walter Bagot, or, especially, Harriot Hesketh.* In fact, Lady Hesketh had good reason to be disturbed by the closing comments in Cowper's letter to her of June 11: "Hayley tells me you begin to be jealous of him, lest I should love him more than I love you, and bids me say that should I do so, you in revenge must love Him more

---

* Harriot Balls and Kate Johnson had visited Weston the previous summer, and Cowper had strongly intimated at that time that he might repay the visit in 1792.

than I do."[58] Jealousy was an emotion Cowper sometimes aroused in others, and it was a state of mind to which Harriot was extraordinarily prone.

Even after he had decided to take the trip, Cowper was haunted by "spiritual hounds"[59] which invaded his sleep and made the 120-mile journey seem an extraordinary obstacle. At the outset of the journey, Cowper wrote anxiously to Newton on July 30: "You may imagine that we who have been resident on one spot so many years, do not engage in such an enterprize without some anxiety";[60] he recalled later in that letter that, as the journey to Eartham became more and more a reality, the "comforts that I had received under your ministry in better days all rush'd upon my recollection, and, during two or three transient moments, seem'd to be in a degree renew'd."[61]

Cowper, Mrs. Unwin, John Johnson, Sam Roberts and his wife, and Beau left Weston on Wednesday, August 1, and stayed that evening at the Mitre at Barnet, which was noisy and rowdy according to Cowper. Samuel Rose, who had joined the party that evening, traveled back to London with them. From there, the group went to Kingston and met General Cowper, whom Cowper did not recognize—he had not seen him for thirty years—although he "guess'd him."[62] The final stop before Eartham was at Ripley. Cowper found this last stage of the journey taxing, and he was daunted by the "tremendous height of the Sussex hills in comparison with which all that I have seen elsewhere are dwarfs."[63] The party finally arrived at Hayley's on the afternoon of August 3.

In 1743, Hayley's father had negotiated the purchase of a small estate at Eartham, near Chichester, "a sequestered spot, peculiarly embellished by nature."[64] Since the original house was in ruins, the new owner built a small villa, which in Hayley's time was remarkably small in comparison to the far larger and more imposing house later erected around it. Cowper was delighted with the warm welcome bestowed on him and with the house and its environs:

> Here we are, in the most elegant mansion, that I have ever inhabited, and surrounded by the most delightful pleasure grounds, that I have ever seen. . . . It shall suffice me to say, that they occupy three sides of a hill, which, in Buckinghamshire, might well pass for a mountain, and from the summit of which is beheld a most magnificent landscape, bounded by the sea, and in one part of it by the Isle of Wight, which may also

be seen plainly from the window of the library, in which I am writing.[65]

Cowper's pleasure in his surroundings was enhanced by Mary Unwin's remarkable improvement—even after an arduous journey—and by the opportunity to work with Hayley. Mrs. Unwin was treated with the electrical machine every evening and was drawn about the estate in her chair twice a day by Thomas Alphonso Hayley and Thomas Socket. The two poets scrutinized and discussed each other's Miltonic work, and they began a joint translation of Andreini's *Adamo*. Hayley also confided in Cowper about his marital difficulties when Eliza threatened to join the group at Eartham.

The company also included George Romney and Charlotte Smith. Romney was of a habitually melancholic cast of mind—he and Cowper immediately sensed their similarity of spirits. The artist, who made his crayon portrait of Cowper during this visit, told his son John that Cowper was "a most excellent man,"[66] and he described the routine that Cowper, Hayley, and Mrs. Smith followed:

> She and the two poets were employed every morning from eight o'clock till twelve in writing, when they had a luncheon, and walked an hour; they then wrote again till they dressed for dinner. After dinner they were employed in translating an Italian play on the subject of Satan; about twenty lines was the number every day. After that they walked, or played at Coits; then tea, and after that they read till supper time.[67]

Charlotte Smith was writing *The Old Manor House,* and either Hayley or Cowper would read her day's productions to the assembled company in the evening. "Cowper repeatedly declared, that he knew no man, among his early associates in literature, who could have composed so rapidly and so well."[68] Despite her popularity as a writer by 1792, Mrs. Smith's financial position was precarious, and she was constantly preoccupied with the plights of her many children. When they met at Eartham, the two well-known writers recognized in each other a shared response to the vanity of human wishes. In the following year, she dedicated her poem, *The Emigrants,* to the poet who wrote with such "force, clearness, and sublimity."[69]

The visit went well except for the intrusion of James Hurdis. Hurdis, who was educated at the prebendal school at Chichester, St. Mary Hall, Oxford, and Magdalen College, Oxford, had been appointed curate at Burwash, Sussex, in 1785. In 1788, he had published his first collection of poetry, *The Village Curate,* a deliberate imitation of Cowper's style. Joseph Johnson sent the manuscript of Hurdis's second work, a long poem entitled *Adriano; or the First of June,* to Cowper for his opinion in the same year. Cowper undertook a painstakingly detailed criticism of the poem, which did not appear until 1790. At Johnson's instigation, Cowper also revised Hurdis's tragedy, *Sir Thomas More.* Having learned of Cowper's involvement in his work, Hurdis wrote to him on February 26, 1791, inaugurating a correspondence which lasted several years. When the Homer was published, Hurdis sent him numerous packets containing corrections and parallel passages from other translations. In November 1793, Hurdis was to be appointed Professor of Poetry at Oxford, and Cowper would be involved in securing him the requisite number of votes.

In August 1792, however, "broken-hearted for the loss of his favorite sister lately dead,"[70] Hurdis had written to Cowper at Weston. When the reforwarded letter reached Eartham, it drew copious tears from the assembled company, who invited Hurdis to join them. Although the description that Cowper gave of Hurdis to Lady Hesketh is restrained, this meeting was deeply troubling to him and to Mary Unwin: "He is gentle in his manners and delicate in his person, resembling our poor friend Unwin both in face and figure more than any one I have ever seen. But he has not, at least he has not at present, his vivacity."[71]

Despite Hurdis's melancholy presence, Hayley, Romney, Mrs. Smith, and Cowper provided convincing accounts of a genuinely relaxed and convivial August and early September at Eartham. However, John Johnson, who far more than Hurdis acted as the replacement of William Unwin in Cowper's life, left a vastly different version of the stay at Eartham. By the summer of 1792, Johnny was suspicious of Hayley's hold over Cowper. He was also upset because Hayley wanted Cowper to live with him at Eartham in the event of Mrs. Unwin's death. He also knew that Cowper viewed Hayley as an equal and himself as a son.

Whatever his motivations, Johnny drew for his sister, Kate, a picture of life at Eartham vastly unlike that to be found in any other participant's chronicle. On August 19, he gave a glowing report of the visit, and even speculated that Cowper would stay there until after Christmas. By September 3, however, he claimed that Cowper found the *"melancholy wildness"*[72] of Eartham more than he could bear, and Hayley, "although kindest of creatures"[73] had traits to which Cowper simply could not reconcile himself: "in the first place he has *put away his wife,* and keeps a woman in the house, by whom he had little Tom Hayley—this woman whose name is *Mary Cockerell* is the veryest skin-flint that the world ever bore."[74] Johnny went on to describe the stale bread, sour beer, and almost raw beef of which the menu at Eartham consisted; the rare roasts would have been particularly offensive to Mrs. Unwin and Cowper because they liked their "food cooked almost 'till it will shake to pieces."[75] "Hayley's constitution cannot bear a fire, and therefore he used to make my poor Cousin sit shivering in a great raw Library . . . till he almost got an ague."[76] The venetian blinds in the library were always drawn because Hayley detested natural light, whereas Cowper craved it. When Johnny was transcribing Cowper's revised translations of Milton's Latin and Italian poems, he was "shocked to see some of the *bold* and *forcible* language of our dear Bard, crossed out, and supplemented by some *flimsy, tinsel* lines of his Brother Poet . . ."[77] Johnny provided Lady Hesketh with a similar account, and she zealously confirmed his feelings: "I have long known in a degree that turn of Mind of our friend Hayley, and fear'd that on a nearer acquaintance it wou'd be too conspicuous to our dear Cousin for him to take that Comfort in his Society, that I sincerely wish'd him to do in that of one who had shewn him such uncommon marks of friendship and affection."[78] Hayley's *"Infidel"* principles were too much for Cowper, Lady Hesketh assured herself and Johnny. But Cowper probably did not share such views of Hayley. He obviously blinded himself to many of his friend's frailties. As well, he may not have been as sensitive to them as the jealous Johnny.

The return to Weston began on Monday, September 17. To avoid the pain of saying "Adieu under our roof,"[79] Hayley, Tom Hayley, and Tom Socket marched through a heavy rain in the North Wood, at the outskirts of Eartham, and waited there to give a last salutation to the two carriages that conveyed Cowper and Mrs. Unwin away. Cowper and his party stayed at the Sun at Kingston on the evening of the eighteenth and went to dinner from there at General Cowper's house at Ham. This meeting was a success, although Cowper and the General disagreed about Lord Thurlow. Cowper asserted that his old friend was by nature tenderhearted, whereas the General, rightly, could not agree. He told Cowper: "I have always set him down as bearish and hard-hearted."[80] The party left Kingston early on the morning of September 19, went to Samuel Rose's house in London where they took chocolate, and were then accompanied by Rose as far as St. Albans.

There were no remarkable occurrences on the way home. However, Edward Williams, the Welsh poet, was invited to Rose's home while Cowper was there:

> Small & pleasant company. One man sat in the corner of fireplace, not talking, but listening habitually. Williams, who was then regarded as a Jacobin, feared he might be a government spy. The group talked on various topics, among them Welsh literature and bards. When the company broke up, Rose took Williams aside & told him the man was Cowper, "who, having heard of his acquirements, was desirous of knowing him; but now the opportunity had arrived, the nervously sensitive poet was unable to encounter either an introduction, or any active share in the conversation; though he had evidently been an attentive listener, and Mr. Rose said was certainly much interested."[81]

Williams's portrait of Cowper as a "nervously sensitive" but "attentive listener" captures perfectly the demeanor of the poet in public from the time of his departure from London in 1763. "In the dark, and in a storm,"[82] Cowper and Mrs. Unwin arrived back at Weston on the evening of the nineteenth.

14
Trouble at Weston (1792–1795)

1   WHEN COWPER returned to Weston in September 1792, his home was no longer a sanctuary. Weston Lodge became his new prison," the *miserable* house in which I have suffered such a world of anguish." And he saw himself as "the most unpitied, the most unprotected, and the most unacknowledg'd Outcast of the human race."[1] Although Cowper had in various ways (chiefly through his work as poet and translator) been able to stave off the moments of intense depression for significant periods from 1779, his ability to conquer such forces declined rapidly as soon as he returned from Sussex. Mary Unwin's health continued to worsen, and Cowper's creativity—his refuge from despair—had abated.

Samuel Teedon, whom Cowper had known for years and who had been giving him advice from about 1791, became the mentor of his increasingly straitened existence. Although the two men were never friends, Cowper came to rely on Teedon's powers of divination, and he anxiously sought his advice on his fluctuating spiritual fortunes. Teedon had settled at Olney in 1775 at John Newton's instigation, and he had promoted the relationship between Teedon and "Esquire" and "Madame." Teedon, who resided in a cottage at the junction of Dagnell and High streets, was the Olney schoolmaster. He lived with Eusebius Killingworth and his mother Elizabeth ("Mammy"). Eusebius, or "Worthy" as Cowper called him, helped his cousin teach and also bound books for a living. Another inhabitant of the cottage was Polly Taylor, who called Teedon her cousin, although the townspeople of Olney assumed she was his daughter. Teedon had probably been educated for the Church, for he could read the Testament in Latin and Greek, and he had some knowledge of French. According to John Johnson, who met him

during his first visit to Weston in 1790, Teedon had been a tradesman at Bedford before arriving at Olney: "Shorn of his felt, the felt
his hands had wrought, / He wash'd those hands of trade, and Olney
sought."[2]

Cowper's attitude toward Teedon was distinctly hostile up to
1785: "He is the most obsequious, the most formal, the most pe-
dantic of all creatures. So civil that it would be cruel to affront him,
and so troublesome that it is impossible to bear him. Being possessed of a little Latin, he seldom uses a word that is not derived
from that language, and being a bigot to propriety of pronuncia-
tion, studiously and constantly lays the accent upon the wrong syllable. I think that Sheridan would adore him."[3] However, Cowper's
change of heart was discernible as early as October 5, 1787, when
he told Lady Hesketh: "The poor man has gratitude if he has not
wit, and in the possession of that one good quality has a sufficient
recommendation."[4] From about 1790, Cowper allowed Teedon a
yearly allowance (paid quarterly) of £30, a great deal of money to
the impoverished schoolmaster. In his turn, Teedon bestowed elaborate compliments and furnished supernatural prognostication. In
the 1760s and 1770s, Newton, in a relatively straightforward way,
had assured Cowper of his salvation, but the poet had become more
emotionally distraught in the 1790s, at which time he acquired a
confidant of more theatrical propensities.

Teedon's penchant for interpreting the spiritual state of her
cousin caused Lady Hesketh to describe him years later as "that
odd enthusiastic fanatical."[5] As John Johnson remembered, his appearance was especially droll:

> His hat, Mambresno's helmet, as to shape,
> And as to stuff, of beaver hats the ape.
> His locks as oily as door-locks should be,
> And as uncrushing as the middle key;
> Jet-black besides, and shadowing still more
> The Hindoo honours, that his visage bore;
> His length of visage, in which either cheek
> The fellow seemed internally to seek.
> Meanwhile, two busy eye-brows, and beneath
> . . . .
> Each pair intent to hit with riming bow;
> O'er the long nose the longer chin below;
> No rivals fearing in his lips, too thin
> Ever to dream that Teedon had a chin.[6]

Although Johnny shared Lady Hesketh's sentiments on most matters and obviously perceived the ludicrous side of Teedon, he also
saw him as a man who was a "compound of no common grace."[7]
This was the part of Teedon's nature to which Cowper responded
eagerly in 1792 and 1793.

The confidences (often summations of dreams) which Cowper
bestowed on Teedon were devoted to Cowper's perception of God's
irrevocable hatred of himself. The voices in those dreams were ac-
cusatory: Cowper had committed awful crimes for which a severe
penalty would be exacted. In one, he saw his own "everlasting
martyrdom in fire": "Dream'd that in a state of the most unsupportable misery I look'd through the window of a strange room
being all alone, and saw preparations making for my execution."[8]
In the 1780s, Cowper had learned to cope with the awesome depressions which frequently invaded his existence. His conviction of
his inherent depravity was contradicted by his poetry and the public response to it. In the years of the moral satires, *The Task,* and
the translations of Homer, he had been able to keep the self-hatred
at bay. However, his sense of complete worthlessness and continual
persecution were persistent. He had managed to push such feelings
aside, not conquer them. In the autumn of 1792, he fell victim to
those forces.

Samuel Teedon communed frequently with God, believing himself especially favored; through dreams and voices—"notices" he
called them—God revealed His divine will to him, and Cowper began to look to Teedon as an intermediary between God and himself. Teedon embraced his appointment with zeal and frequently
walked to Weston to relay auspicious news, continually urging the
"Esquire" to pray and have faith in God's ultimate benevolence: "I
went over after dinner to Madam, met the Esquire who gave a most
dreadful account of the state of his mind &c."[9] In spite of the importance with which Cowper invested Teedon, there was always a
gulf between them. Sometimes, much to his consternation, Teedon
met with a cold reception at the Lodge (Mrs. Unwin felt that
Teedon raised expectations concerning Cowper's eventual reconciliation with God that simply could not be fulfilled), and at least
twice she threatened to cancel his quarterage: "I went to receive my
pay & Mrs. U. informed me for the future I was to receive only 26
instead of 30. I was much discomposed &c. She said if I could do
better I was at liberty; she could dispose of it &c."[10] It was his despair that Cowper bestowed upon Teedon, and Teedon, in the manner of a spiritual alchemist, attempted to convert damnation into

salvation. In his letters to his friends, Cowper endeavored to "keep melancholy out of them as much as I can, that I may, if possible, by assuming a less gloomy air deceive even myself, and by feigning with a continuance improve the fiction into a reality."[11] It was only to Teedon, whom he held at a distance, that he could confide his frequent sense of damnation.

Indeed, Cowper's dreams of 1792 reveal that the pious part of his personality was persecuted by an inner voice which sought to destroy this kindly person. He often felt the active presence of this enemy: "I heard a word in the year 86, which has been a stone of stumbling to me ever since. It was this—I will promise you any thing."[12] This inner voice* of self-hatred told Cowper that salvation was at hand, but it also hinted that this was only a device for inducing a sense of false security. If the voice which sometimes promised salvation was not to be trusted, it is obvious that no friend or acquaintance could be successful in convincing him of his basic goodness and ultimate salvation. Cowper, however, continually sought from Teedon the reassurances he would never believe, and Teedon willingly provided them. Cowper once described himself to Teedon as "Tantalus, surrounded with plenty yet famished. If God designed that I should eat, would he not enable me to do so?"[13] Cowper felt that Teedon was in touch with the mysterious, seemingly contradictory God who promised salvation and then, maliciously, withdrew it, and Teedon became the only refuge he could find: "Could I feed on the bread which seems to be intended for me, it is so plentifully imparted to you that I should feel no want."[14] Teedon anxiously sought to palliate Cowper's distress. He did not, however, tend to provide direct responses to his dreams. When Cowper told him of the nightmare in which he had foreseen an "everlasting martyrdom in the fire,"[15] Teedon countered with this vision:

> Now my dear Sir, let me give this encouragement to you, for I besought the Lord with lively faith to shine in like manner on you, to dissipate your darkness and heal your wounded spirits . . . it was crowned with a lively confirmation from these words, *"For I will turn their mourning into joy, I will comfort them and make them rejoice, from their sorrow."* I most earn-

---

* In letters and in conversation, Cowper referred both to a "voice" and to "voices." At times, he perceived the voice or voices as Satanic; some references indicate that the voice(s) were spoken by a duplicitous God.

estly beg you will, dear Sir, persevere . . . And I doubt not
but divine light will follow.[16]

Cowper had many doubts. His letters to Teedon (seventy-two in
all) are mirrors reflecting his agonized face, denuded of hope and
contorted with the expectation of damnation. The discrepancy between the depressive reality which Cowper endured and the blithe
assurances of comfort which Teedon offered eventually made him
angry: "It would be better with poor me, if being the subject of
so many of your manifestations . . . I were made in some small
degree at least partaker of the comfort of them."[17] By January 1793,
Cowper's antagonism had grown. He became convinced that God
was tormenting him through Teedon and that the notices concerning Mary's health, the Milton project, and his own salvation were
lies: "having been assured that though they are indeed from God,
so far from being designed as comforts to me, to me they are re-
proaches, biting sarcasms, sharp strokes of Irony, in short the dead-
liest arrows to be found in the quiver of the Almighty."[18]

Cowper maintained the correspondence with Teedon, but he no
longer saw him as a mediator. He became useful only as someone
to whom Cowper could confess the pent-up agonies torturing him
from within, and the poet realized that despite Teedon's interces-
sions, his "imagination [was] left free to create an endless train of
horrible phantoms with which it terrifies itself, and which are, some
of them perhaps, more to be dreaded than the reality."[19]

2   Despite the constant depression which engulfed him, Cowper
attempted to work on his various projects: the preparation of the
Milton edition, the revision of the translations of Homer, and the
"Four Ages," the topic suggested to him in 1791 by his clerical
neighbor, John Buchanan. In November 1792, Cowper told Rose
how onerous the Milton had become: "it seems to me that a consciousness of that unperform'd engagement has no small share in
disqualifying me for the performance of it, by depressing my spirits
to a degree that they would not otherwise sink to."[20] The previous
month he told Harriot Hesketh that all his aspirations, so decisively marshaled for Homer, had deserted him. Hamlet-like, he said:
"Ambition I have none left, no not a spark; Fame has lost all her
charms . . ."[21] By December, he confided to Teedon that the edition had become a "mountain on [his] shoulders," and "it seems to

me that if the new year brings with it no favorable change for me, either in outward circumstances or mental qualification, I must at last relinquish him."[22] A year later, in December 1793, Cowper permanently "suspended" his Miltonic labors. "I am now busy in transcribing the alterations of Homer, having finished the whole revisal. I must then write a new preface, which done, I shall endeavor immediately to descant on the four ages."[23]

Cowper apparently did not complete his transcription of Homeric variants at the end of 1793 (Samuel Rose had negotiated an octavo edition of 750 copies with Joseph Johnson, and Cowper had hoped to reach a wider class of readers who could not afford quartos). He had begun work on *The Four Ages* in May 1791, dropped work on it, after several attempts, a month later, and in June 1793 had hoped, when "his hands [were] free,"[24] to work on it again. In July, Hayley suggested that "The Four Ages" be written jointly by Cowper and himself, and illustrated by two artists, probably Flaxman and Romney, and Cowper seemed pleased at the prospect of the "projected quadruple alliance."[25] He promised, as soon as circumstances permitted, to contribute to such a venture. He did not work on the poem in either June or December of 1793, and apparently wrote no more until March 11, 1799; however, at that time, "he merely corrected a few lines, adding two or three more, and declined to proceed."[26]

Samuel Rose assumed a more important role in Cowper's life at this time. He acted as a legal and financial adviser, and he served as Cowper's go-between with Joseph Johnson. Joseph Hill continued to oversee some of Cowper's financial interests, but Rose handled the important financial transactions with Johnson. He had been consulted in 1791 concerning the £1,000 plus retained copyright for the Homer, and it was he who in 1793 suggested an octavo format for the translation. He also arranged for Cowper to receive the profits from the fifth edition of 1793 of his two volumes of verse. In June 1793, the young Richard Phillips wrote to Cowper from Leicester that he was in serious difficulty for having sold copies of Tom Paine's *Rights of Man,* and he beseeched Cowper to compose a "Sonnet or Song or any thing in the poetical way"[27] which might assist his cause. Cowper was touched by Phillips's plea and composed the requisite sonnet. When Rose expressed the view that such a move would be "inexpedient, perhaps even dangerous," Cowper deferred, as he told Phillips, to his friend, "an able lawyer, and in party-matters a man of great moderation."[28]

Another young man who continued to be of considerable assistance was John Johnson. Johnny in 1793 was curate of the two parishes of Yaxham and Welborne, whose Rector was old and ailing. It was difficult for him to visit Weston, although he managed at times to do so by securing the services of a stand-in at Yaxham. In June 1793, he presented Cowper with what he thought, mistakenly, was an antique bust of Homer, and, in gratitude, Cowper composed the sonnet which begins, "Kinsman belov'd, and as a son, by me!"

Three months later, Johnny arranged yet another gift to relieve Cowper's depressed spirits. He knew his cousin craved a sundial, and he arranged for the delivery of one, which Sam Roberts installed on September 4. Before leaving for his walk on that day, Cowper had deplored his lack of such an instrument.

> My complaint was long, and lasted till having turned into the grass walk we reached the new building at the end of it, where we sat awhile and reposed ourselves. In a few minutes we returned by the way we came, when what think you was my astonishment to see what I had not seen before, though I had passed close by it, a smart sun-dial mounted on a smart stone pedestal? I assure you it seem'd the effect of conjuration.[29]

Cowper was convinced that Sam, without orders, had taken it upon himself to acquire the dial, but he soon informed Cowper of the donor's identity.

Another diversion in the autumn of 1793 was provided by yet another young man, Thomas Lawrence, who at the age of twenty-four, but already well on his way to fame (he had been invited in 1792 to paint George III), accepted an invitation from his friend, Samuel Rose, to paint the well-known poet of Weston. Cowper was much taken by Lawrence's friendliness and gentility and was distressed when the painter returned to London. "I am too old," Cowper told him, "to be very hasty in forming new connexions: but short as our acquaintance has been, to you I have the courage to say, that my heart and my door will always be gladly open to you."[30]

William Hayley also endeavored to comfort Cowper, and his main effort in that direction was his attempt to gain for the poet a royal pension. Hayley had begun work on this venture soon after his first visit to Weston, and it "became the most darling Project of [his] sanguine Spirit."[31] Hayley decided that Thurlow was the most likely person to bring such an enterprise to fruition, and through a series of elaborate maneuvers he obtained a set of Cowper's poems owned by one of Thurlow's daughters. After requesting from the young lady the loan of her set of verse, he inscribed upon a blank leaf a poem in which he beseeched the "Ingenuous Girl" to restore "The Friendship of their youth"[32] between the Lord Chancellor and Weston recluse. Thurlow was not well at the time and did not wish to see Hayley, but persistence won out: Hayley was invited to breakfast at the Chancellor's house in Great Ormond Street on June 8, 1792. Lord Kenyon, as well as Thurlow, was present for the interview at which Hayley suggested that George III should bestow a pension on Cowper "as an act of personal thanksgiving & Gratitude towards Heaven, for having restor'd [him] from that mental Malady by which this wonderful & most interesting poet had been periodically afflicted."[33] Although both law lords were noncommittal about success in such a difficult undertaking, Hayley wrote to Cowper on the following day saying that he was convinced that "your old Friend Thurlow will accomplish it if possible—."[34] After this meeting with Hayley, Thurlow, however, remained silent. He did not answer further letters from Hayley, showing no interest in Hayley's proposal that he renew his friendship with Cowper at Eartham in the summer of 1792.

In December 1792, Hayley composed a letter to William Pitt, the Prime Minister, in which he broached the matter of the pension, and this letter was delivered by William Huskisson in January to an officer of the Treasury. The seal to the letter remained unbroken in June 1793, when Hayley demanded the return of the letter and posted the missive directly to Pitt. He received no reply. Hayley again approached Thurlow, who suggested that Lord Spencer's intervention might be helpful or that Hayley might send a letter directly to Pitt (Hayley had not mentioned the unanswered letter). Hayley approached Pitt once again and received an interview on November 29, at which the Prime Minister agreed in principle to a pension. Hayley had hoped for written confirmation soon after the meeting, but none came. In desperation, he wrote to Pitt on February 27, 1794, and he heard soon after that Lord Spencer was said to be working on the matter. The news arrived at Weston on April 23, 1794, that the poet's pension of £300 a year awaited only royal sanction. By that time the success of "the darling project" had no noticeable effect on Cowper.

Despite his constant state of depression, Cowper rallied at the beginning of 1793, and he was able to tell Hayley he had been worried about him: "Sometimes I thought that you were extremely ill, and once or twice heard, you may guess from what quarter, that you were dead."[35] Cowper's fears for Hayley were more than likely reflections of his own fears about himself, but the complete retreat within that was to engulf him at the end of 1793 was not yet at hand. He was still able at this time to be concerned about someone other than himself and Mrs. Unwin. In the summer of 1793, he gardened and erected a pedestal for the bust of Homer, and he saw his horticultural achievements, as he had years before, as a refuge from despair. By January 1794, however, he was completely entrenched in his long, massive battle against the inner enemy, and, despite the outstretched hands of Lady Hesketh, John Johnson, and William Hayley, he never emerged again, even for a short period, as victor.

3   Since her initial visit to Cowper in Buckinghamshire in 1786, Lady Hesketh had paid four visits to Weston (October 1788 to mid-January 1789; mid-July 1789 to mid-November 1789; late September 1790 to early February 1791; autumn 1791 to March 1792) before she arrived in November 1793 for a stay of twenty-one months. Her own health at this time was poor, and she was deeply concerned about the increasing morbidity of her cousin. She wanted to do everything in her power to ease his burdens and to make his existence more tolerable. Lady Hesketh's visits before 1793 had been in relatively serene circumstances, the duration of the visits being under her control. When she arrived in the autumn of 1793, she came to take charge, not to visit, and she wandered into a situation where it was extraordinarily difficult to escape a sense of foreboding and doom. Lady Hesketh had asked Cowper when he wanted her to visit, and the poet had told her that he would prefer "the depth of winter . . . [f]or then it is that . . . I have most need of a cordial."[36]

Lady Hesketh soon found herself an unwilling witness to life at Weston Lodge. Although she lamented Cowper's plight and talked of ways in which he could be made better, she came to see Mary Unwin as the malevolent persecutor of her cousin. Lady Hesketh had always entertained suspicions of Mary Unwin, as Cowper's casual remark to his cousin in 1786 makes clear: "But do not suppose, my Dear, that Mrs. U. will be present at our first interview. You and I will have our clash of passions in the parlour, and when that is over we will all three drink tea."[37] During her visit in 1786, Lady Hesketh, as we have seen, decided she admired Mary Unwin, although she was acutely aware of Mary Unwin's power over her cousin, and she wisely chose to act as a friend toward her. If she considered continuing in the same way in 1793, her resolve soon broke down. She quickly came to see Mary Unwin as the "En-chantress"[38] and "Sycorax."[39] She also found it difficult to be "Stew-ard, Treasurer, Secretary &c &c &c"[40] to the household, and she was troubled by her suspicion that "hypocrisy had more to do with [Mrs. Unwin's] constitution than folks were in general aware of."[41] She became convinced that the "sooner it pleased God to remove the old woman from his side the better it would be on all ac-counts."[42] Any hint of separation from Cowper bothered Mrs. Un-win, who told Harriot that "if the *Angel Gabriel* was to [try to] persuade her to let him leave her *she would not comply!!*"[43] Lady Hesketh's obstinacy now found its match in Mary Unwin who was quite prepared to fight her. It was in a state of desolation that she appealed in January 1794 to Johnny for assistance:

> Mrs Unwin is not worse than she was, at least I think not, but, *our dearest Cousin* is so *very Low in spirrits* that it almost Dis-tracts me to see him, & I do not know a human Being the sight of whom is likely to be pleasing except yourself; you my dear Sir can be usefull to us on a *thousand* accounts, & Situated as I am—find myself (tho' I do all I can) unable to sustain *alone,* the whole weight of this excellent Creatures heavy affliction, the rather as it is unhappily of a sort that is not in my power to remove.[44]

It was undoubtedly Lady Hesketh's sense of helplessness that led her to become preoccupied with Mrs. Unwin. In her wish to allevi-ate Cowper's condition and sensing her inability to do so, she came to believe that if Mary Unwin died or was physically removed (to live with her daughter, Susanna Powley) there would be a remark-able change in Cowper. In her desperation, Mary Unwin became the focus of resentment, and Lady Hesketh's frequently politic be-havior began to disappear.

When she observed the supposedly very weak Mrs. Unwin sitting with her head held forward, Lady Hesketh baited her: "I should fancy Madam that keeping your head so *extremely high* must be painfull to you."[45] Cowper remarked that the silent Mrs. Unwin could not do otherwise with her cold, but Harriot rejoined: "Bless me . . . that is very extraordinary! it must require a deal of *Strength* to sit in that manner, and 'tis an *uncommon* effect of a *Cold.*"[46] Mary Unwin won the battle by rigidly holding her head upright until dinner was announced. Lady Hesketh was glad to tell Samuel Greatheed, who was favorably disposed toward Mrs. Unwin, that even Cowper could become severely irritated by Mary's "torment": he "often sits for an hour together alone in his bed chamber, professedly (as he constantly informs her) to be out of hearing of the many disagreeable things she says . . ."[47]

In August 1794, Johnny had taken a teapot from the Lodge to be repaired, but instead he exchanged it for a new one. Characteristically, he had forgotten that the old teapot was Mrs. Unwin's. His mistake led to a heated quarrel between Lady Hesketh and her opponent, as Harriot told Johnny:

> the pains you so ingeniously took to mark it for our dear Cousin's *own property,* gave me double pleasure, and seem'd I thought to gratify our poor Cousin himself—the effect it had on a *certain Lady* however was I believe very different. . . . I call'd out "Oh What a beautifull Tea-Pot!—well Johnny has *indeed* done the thing handsomely! I think I never in my life saw a handsomer or a more elegant thing of the kind!" She instantly roar'd out "is it *Solid* Silver? are you sure it is *real Solid Silver?* mine was silver"—"Indeed, Madam, I do not know, Plated things look sometimes very handsome and 'tis so large, one might almost *suppose* it was not, only Johnny is the *last* man on Earth who would take a Silver Pot, & return a Plated, unless you had order'd him to do so." Our dear Cousin, then said, "No No, it is Silver, very plainly, besides, here is the Hall mark. to which She *with a Grunt,* "oh you'r *sure* 'tis Silver, very well." I then proceeded in my admirations, and explanations, of this dear delightful Tea Pot . . .

Lady Hesketh pointed out to Cowper that his coat of arms was engraved on the pot, and Mrs. Unwin became disgruntled when she learned that it was the Cowper, and not the Unwin, crest on the vessel. Lady Hesketh then asked her "What has my Cousin to do with ye *Unwin crest?*" Mrs. Unwin explained that the other teapot was hers.

> oh says I, our kind Johnny never thought of that I *dear* say, & Mr Cowper added speaking to her, Pho Pho, what does that signify between you & me? she hemm'd & grunted again, and at last said—Well, I'm very glad Mr Johnson has sent it to you my man, very glad, and, as she repeated this, at different intervals thro' the whole Evening I gather'd from that the Inference that she was *not glad at all.*[48]

Lady Hesketh was obviously delighted at being able to tell Johnny an amusing story at Mary Unwin's expense, but in the telling of her tale she revealed a great deal of her own insensitivity to Mary Unwin, who did own the original teapot. She also displayed her willingness to act in a provocative manner toward her in Cowper's presence. Lady Hesketh must have been sparing on many occasions in her resentment, but she found frequent occasion to display antagonism toward Mary Unwin by her caustic behavior toward "Miss Hannekin," Mary Unwin's niece.*

Hannah Wilson had been at Olney from at least May 1780, and Cowper and Mrs. Unwin looked upon her as their ward. Although he does not refer to her very often in his letters, Cowper eventually

---

* According to Thomas Wright, Hannah Wilson was the daughter of Dick Colman's wife, Patty Wilson, who had previously been married to a Mr. Wilson, and Patty Wilson was the natural daughter of Mr. Cawthorne, Mrs. Unwin's father. Although Cowper and Mrs. Unwin were deeply interested in the plight of the poor of Olney, it is unlikely that they would have gone to so much trouble concerning Hannah if she was not a blood relation of Mrs. Unwin. Lady Hesketh, who after Mary Unwin's death refers to Hannah as Mrs. Powley's cousin, disapproved of Hannah from the time she was introduced to her in 1786, when she was twelve years old: "at that time she had no visible employment but going errands, and tho.' it was then very early days, I more than once took advantage of the kindness and esteem Mrs. Unwin professed for me, to remonstrate against the Impropriety of this poor girl being always in the Street, where she appear'd to me to be engag'd from morning till night, in playing with all the dirty boys in Olney . . ." (Lady Hesketh to John Newton, June 20, 1795, MS Bull). Lady Hesketh discussed Hannah with William Unwin in 1786, and he "seem'd to regret his mother's blind indulgence, which he thought even in those early days must tend to the ruin of the Being she seem'd to Idolize . . ." (Lady Hesketh to John Newton, June 20, 1795, MS Bull). In 1795, after Hannah had journeyed to Norfolk with Cowper and Mrs. Unwin, she was apprenticed for three years, presumably to a dressmaker or milliner, in Norwich, and by 1798 was serving as a journeywoman to the same person.

In 1799, Lady Hesketh had heard that "H.R." [Hannah Wilson] had gotten into a "sad scrape." However, Robert Southey was told in 1836 by a clergyman from Lincoln about a lawyer there by the name of Robinson who at "one time . . . had forsaken the law & entered the army. He came back with a wife & resumed his profession, having met with her, it was understood, in Ireland; but no one thought her an Irishwoman. She was very beautiful, both in face & person; but tho civil, & even bewitching, she was evidently underbred, & of no great abilities. As long as he lived, it was a mystery as to who she was; but as he was a gentlemanlike man, she got on well enough, not visiting much on account of their large family. This was the period when I knew her; perhaps she was then 40. She retained much of her beauty,—a brilliant, sunny sort of look, with an odd lively manner, which would have been I dare say, captivating enough in a girl. At her husband's death, a clever young man came to settle his affairs & succeed to his business. He lived with the widow & family a year or two, & wormed out of her that she had been brought up by Mrs Unwin & Cowper . . ." (Robert Southey to W. B. Donne, July 6, 1836, MS formerly Mrs. Augusta Donne).

saw her as something of a nuisance, who was a source of concern to both himself and Mrs. Unwin. This had not been quite so in 1784, as he told Newton: "We are agreeably disappointed in Hannah. We feared that through a natural deficiency of understanding, we should always find her an incumbrance. But she has suddenly brightened up, and being put into such little offices as she is capable of, executes them with an expertness and alacrity at which we wonder. She has an exceeding good temper, and bids fair to discover more Sense than we suspected would ever fall to her lot."[49] At the age of fourteen in 1788, she appeared to Cowper as "a very good girl,"[50] but there is an edge of anxiety in his remark to Hayley in July 1792: "Poor Hannah was very ill last night, so as to occasion much anxiety to Mrs. Unwin, but a few grains of Dr. James ['s Powders] have done her much good. We are going to send her for a year to Stratford School, where she will be taught such things as will qualify her when we are dead and gone to get her own living."[51] Any reservations Cowper felt, however, were slight compared to Lady Hesketh's remonstrances against her.

Hannah's flirtatious behavior offended Lady Hesketh. As she told Johnny in the midst of her preparations to go to Weston in 1793, she had been uneasy about her handsome servant "who might be unable to stand the fire of Miss Hannah's bright eyes."[52] Lady Hesketh's other concern, however, was that Cowper had to associate with Hannah: "I was told by somebody, I know not by whom, that She now always dines with Mrs U & Cowper, if so, she must either do so when I am there or be banish'd on my account, & neither plan would suit me at all—'tis in truth a *Sad Scrape* that Mrs. U: has drawn him into, for certainly a girl bred up in the Streets, & in ye Kitchin cannot be a proper Companion for Mr. Cowper!"[53] Lady Hesketh felt that Mrs. Unwin, the "Enchantress," had in turn been bewitched by Hannah, who was her "Idol." She also felt that Hannah, as well as Mrs. Unwin, was an unfit companion for her cousin: "—had our good well meaning Friend Mrs Unwin, educated her *purposely* for the purposes of Prostitution, she need only have done exactly what she did! poor Soul she never said, or did anything that was not exactly calculated to nurse up the seed of vanity, and idleness which nature had planted in her disposition, and when those qualitys are attended by *Povorty*, one need not be a witch to discover the natural Consequences, especially when a pretty Face & Figure are thrown into the Composition—."[54] Hannah's extravagance was another matter that worried Lady Hesketh, and in July 1795 she confiscated a white satin turban cap which Hannah had

ordered at Bedford; she presented the hat through Johnny to Catharine Johnson:

> [Lady Hesketh] could not help being extremely astonished at
> the impudence of this little extravagant bitch—for she makes
> no doubt but it is exactly the same kind of cap that my Lady
> Jersey brought down for the Princess of Wales on her mar-
> riage—Miss Hannah had ordered, moreover, a plume of white
> feathers which were to come to 5 *Guineas*—but Lady H. stop
> them *in time*.[55]

Hannah's deportment was undoubtedly inappropriate, and she did
not properly carry out her domestic duties at the Lodge. However,
the sharpness of Lady Hesketh's response to what was obviously
annoying conduct must be challenged.

In advanced middle age—she was sixty in 1793, only nine years
younger than Mary Unwin—Lady Hesketh was obsessed with Cowper, "the Saintly Creature" as she sometimes called him. She wanted
to be able to do something to relieve his melancholy, and, like
everyone else in 1793, she could do nothing. It was perhaps natural
that she turned her attention to Mary Unwin and, through her, to
Hannah. If these two women and difficulties associated with them
could be disposed of, her cousin would be better—or so she rea-
soned. There was an extraordinary reluctance on her part to see
that Cowper's psychological difficulties were lodged within himself
and were not the direct responsibility of either Mary Unwin or
Hannah. In the awesome circumstance that overtook her in 1793,
Lady Hesketh sought scapegoats. She did not like to be reminded
by Cowper that Mary was the person "in whom thou knowest that
I live and have my Being far more than in Him from whom I received that Being."[56]

Since Cowper wrote only twenty-two extant letters from 1794
until his death six years later, the overwhelming proportion of
evidence concerning his last two years at Weston (as well as the
time in Norfolk) is contained in the massive Lady Hesketh–John
Johnson and Lady Hesketh–William Hayley correspondences. Although none of these people were deliberately mendacious, they all
had special interests to protect: Lady Hesketh wanted to be the
most important Cowper relative to her cousin; John Johnson was
determined to be the closest Donne connection; William Hayley
desired to be the poet's great literary friend. In a very real sense, all
three people had played important restorative roles in Cowper's life
and were deeply upset when all their efforts went askew. Thus

Mary Unwin became the focus of their combined resentments—
they did not wish to admit that there was an unresolvable dilemma
in Cowper's personality which could not be mended by outside
help. As well, both Johnny and Hayley were awed by Lady
Hesketh and were thus natural allies with her against Mrs. Unwin. There can be little doubt that Mary Unwin was a tiresome,
pertinacious woman in her last years, and Cowper's devotion to
her and his fear that she might die obviously made his depression worse. However, when Hayley met Mrs. Unwin for the first
time in 1792, he characterized her as "a good, sensible, & pleasing
old woman *about 70*. . . . This most rare and excellent female
Friend nursed Him thro many calamitous years of mental darkness
& dejection, & is now most providentially rewarded by seeing the
object of her unwearied Care not only restored to reason & Comfort, but blest with Mental Faculties, whose strength & Lustre must
render his name immortal—"[57]

In any assessment of Cowper's final years at Weston, it must be
borne in mind that the available evidence gives only one side of
the story from a distorted angle and that no document survives to
tell the tale from the viewpoint of the "Enchantress," who, pace
Lady Hesketh, was not without social and literary refinement, and
who, moreover, was the freely chosen companion of her cousin's
life.

4   Cowper's fantasy of being destroyed by some nameless outward force continued: "the Terrors of being carried away, & being
Torn *to* pieces, seem to agitate him as much as ever . . ."[58] In his
last two years at Weston, he looked "like a Ghost"[59]; his legs were
"wasted away—and his poor hands [were] nothing but skin and
bone."[60] Concern about his physical as well as mental condition
prompted Hayley to write to Thurlow, who approached Francis
Willis, the celebrated clergyman who had attended George III in
1788 during his first attack of "madness." In May 1794, Lady Hesketh left Hayley in charge of the household at Weston and went
briefly to Greatford near Stamford in Lincolnshire where she visited with Dr. Willis to give him an account of Cowper's condition.
According to her, Willis felt that separation from Mary Unwin
would be the best cure for Cowper. When Lady Hesketh explained
that she could not effect such a remedy, he gave her some prescrip-
tions and a list of regulations.

Since Cowper did not wish to take the medicine Dr. Willis suggested and was loath to follow his advice, Lady Hesketh was "obliged to introduce a young man," Richard Buston, whom Dr. Willis sent along and whom Cowper saw *"now & then."*[61] Cowper listened to the young man and did, in his presence, what he asked, although he would not, in the matter of his health, attend to Lady Hesketh. A month later, Cowper's condition not having noticeably improved, Dr. Willis visited Weston to examine him. Willis, who spoke frankly of the "spectacle" of Mary Unwin, was convinced that Cowper should move to a house near his asylum in Lincolnshire, and he was perturbed when he found how unbudging both Mrs. Unwin and Cowper were on that score. All that Willis could do was to prescribe an additional drug, "a strengthener."[62]

Hayley visited Cowper twice after the Eartham visit of 1792, once in 1793 and again in 1794, the last time he saw Cowper. Hayley was deeply concerned in 1793 about the hostility toward himself on the part of both Cowper and Mrs. Unwin, and he wisely told Lady Hesketh that she called Mrs. Unwin "the Enchantress but the Magic lies not so much in any Qualities past or present of the Lady as in the very tender Heart & ardent Fancy of the Enchanted."[63] During this visit, Hayley claimed, Mrs. Unwin "prejudic'd our dear Friend in Darkness against me by an insidious Misrepresentation of an Expression that I believe I never used."[64]

In January 1794, the prospect of a visit from Johnny did not please Cowper: "I cannot see him, is there no way to stop him?"[65] The visit of William Crotch, an itinerant Quaker preacher, in the spring of 1795, did have a soothing effect. Crotch, who had not met Cowper, found himself in Weston and decided to call on the famous poet. Sam Roberts attempted to bar the way. "Go and tell thy master that a poor creature like himself wishes to see him." Cowper having assented to the visit, Crotch walked into the room where Cowper was, took him by the hand, and sat down by him. They sat hand in hand for an hour without speaking a word. Crotch then addressed Cowper and left.[66]

5   As Cowper's melancholy intensified, he withdrew more and more into his own secret world. He did not care for the company of Johnny or Hayley or even Lady Hesketh, who, by July 1795, decided to leave Weston. Her own health had worsened, and she could no longer participate in such a desolate existence. She had discussed the possibility earlier of Cowper going to Norfolk with John John-

son, and, in March 1794, she considered this the best solution to
the problem.

> he loves Norfolk on his dear Mother's account . . . and he has
> often told me how ardently he wished to see Norfolk once more
> before he dies—Now although it would delight me beyond con-
> ception to have the dear old soul come and live with me in
> Norfolk street, yet the bustle of London and the gaiety of that
> part where I reside are such insuperable objections that he
> cannot think of them a moment—The same objections hold
> good with all his other friends on the Father's side, they are all
> *about Town,* and obliged to be so because of their employ-
> ments under government—but these objections, my Johnny, do
> not exist among his Norfolk friends—there he might live undis-
> turbed, and enjoy the delights of society, *from which he has
> long been detained by the old enchantress,* and there we might
> visit him with tenfold pleasure, *and receive once more a long
> lost friend—'twould be like a resurrection from the dead* . . .[67]

This plan was formulated with the understanding that the removal
to Norfolk would only take place once Mary Unwin was dead, and
Johnny made inquires at that time as to where he and Cowper
could live. When Johnny arrived at Weston in July 1795, however,
Lady Hesketh, keenly aware of her failure to assist Cowper and
particularly bothered by Hannah's conduct, urged that both Cowper and Mrs. Unwin be taken at once to Norfolk. She assured
Johnny that the moment the move was settled she would "turn
her head to that subject—with all her might."[68] She also threatened
to place Cowper at Dr. Willis's (in effect, to have him incarcerated
in a private madhouse as he had been at Nathaniel Cotton's—but
with an extremely harsh taskmaster who would not hesitate to have
him confined to a strait-waistcoat), and in defiance of the reservations expressed to Johnny by his aunts, Mrs. Bodham and Mrs.
Balls, she insisted to John Johnson that there was nothing more
"worthy of his *Christian Profession* than in the Task of trying to
administer Comfort to the Afflicted."[69] Lady Hesketh prevailed on
Johnny (who claimed both he and Lady Hesketh could plainly see
in Cowper's "manner, though he says nothing, that he *wishes* to go
into Norfolk")[70] and won this particular battle. She left Weston,
however, with a sense of having suffered a bitter defeat in her war
with Mary Unwin, who still resolutely and defiantly held sway over
her cousin's affections.

15
Norfolk (1795–1800)

1   JOHN JOHNSON's view of the move to Norfolk was of unalloyed delight: "if any thing, *short of a miracle,* can restore the spirits of the most amiable of men. . . . it must be the step we are going to take."[1] Johnny thought the prospect of Cowper living with his Norfolk relations "charming," although he rather strangely asked his sister, Kate, on July 10, not to tell the Bodhams anything of the plan as he wanted to surprise them, *"without subjecting them to the fear of disappointment."*[2] Since Cowper did not wish to go to Dereham,[3] which he feared would be a market town much like Olney, Johnny had to ask his aunts for assistance in finding a suitable place to take him and Mrs. Unwin. Finally, Mrs. Balls learned that the Rectory of North Tuddenham, the village next to Mattishall, was vacant, and she arranged for Johnny and his party to stay there upon arrival in Norfolk.

During his last week at Weston, Cowper wrote two sets of lines on a panel of the window shutter of his bedroom. In the first, a couplet, he bid adieu to environs, however much they had been the setting of great distress, which had given him a measure of contentment:

> Farewell, dear scenes, for ever closed to me,
> Oh, for what sorrows must I now exchange ye![4]

In the other lines ("Me miserable! how could I escape / Infinite wrath and infinite despair!"),[5] he reiterated sentiments expressed constantly to Teedon since 1791.

At Olney and Weston, Cowper had never managed to escape completely the dominion of the awesome depressions which had overtaken him early in life, but in his rural retreat he had composed verse and prose of considerable merit. Now he saw himself as Milton's Satan forever excluded from the Eden that was Weston.[6] Three days before his departure, he wrote:

> To morrow to the intolerable torments prepared for me. See now, O God, if this be a doom, if this a condition such as a creature of thine could have deserved to be exposed to. I know that thou thyself wast not without thy fears that I should incur it. But thou would'st set me on the slippery brink of this horrible pit in a state of infatuation little short of idiotism, and would'st in effect say to me—Die this moment or fall into it, and if you fall into it, be it your portion for ever. Such was not the mercy I expected from Thee, nor that horror and overwhelming misery should be the only means of deliverance left me in a moment so important! Farewell to the remembrance of Thee for ever. I must now suffer thy wrath, but forget that I ever heard thy name. Oh horrible! and still more horrible, that I write these last lines with a hand that is not permitted to tremble!

He also claimed: "I perish as I do, that is, as none ever did, for non-performance of a task, which I know by after-experience to have been *naturally* impossible." His "unforgiveable sin," he now concluded, was his failure to follow God's command to kill himself.[7]

2   The journey began at one o'clock in the afternoon on Tuesday, July 28. There were two post chaises, with Mrs. Unwin, Hannah, and Ann Roberts in one, and Cowper, Johnny, and Sam Roberts in the other. Cowper did not display any reluctance to leave, after he was assured that Mrs. Unwin had been comfortably settled in her carriage. However, he fully expected that "the Tormentors would drag him out of [the carriage] at Olney, and tear him in pieces."[8] As the coach approached Olney, Johnny drew up the blind on Cowper's side, and the departure from Olney, as well as from Weston where Lady Hesketh had bid them adieu, passed without incident. In an attempt to draw Cowper's attention away from morbid thoughts, Johnny engaged in incessant conversation with Sam. Cowper joined in only when Johnny remarked on the roughness of the road between Turney and Bedford. Cowper "observed that he remembered it almost impassable—indeed so bad that a horse, in travelling it, used to be taken up to his belly in silt and dirt."[9] He continually remarked to himself, "I am in a pleasant delightful dream."[10] Johnny assured him that the dream was reality, that his

delight would continue. He rejoined, "what would I not give that it might do so!"[11] After Bedford, the road was of good quality, "the air balsalmic & the quantity of corn luxuriant—Mr C. made many remarks upon it 'en passant,' particularly on some beginning to be cut down."[12]

Fresh horses, which Johnny had ordered, were waiting for the travelers at the outskirts of Bedford, and the coaches went on to Eaton, "a very pretty Village on the great North Road, on the Buckinghamshire side of St Neots."[13] The party arrived at five o'clock at the Cock Inn in that village and stayed there for the night. After Mrs. Unwin had been settled, Cowper and Johnny walked into the churchyard immediately adjoining the inn. The walk was by moonlight and as they walked through the churchyard, Johnny felt that Cowper spoke and acted as he had when he had first met him in 1790: "alas, alas—during all the years that he lived after this, I never heard him talk so much at ease, again. It was chiefly about Thomson the Poet, that we talked."[14]

The party left Eaton at one o'clock the next day and made for Madingley Tollgate, where the horses were to be changed that day. Johnny had deliberately decided against a stop in Cambridge, and so the coaches passed through the University without stopping, arriving at Barton Mills beyond Newmarket at six o'clock. "It was a place still more retired than Eaton—and I expected in our walk after dinner, a similar pleasure to the one above mentioned.—But there was no such happiness in store for me. So I was obliged to be content with seeing my poor dear charge pass the evening . . . very composedly."[15] On the final day of the journey, chaises from East Dereham met the party at Brandon on the outskirts of Watton in Norfolk. Only here did Johnny learn that his sister and Margaret Perowne were waiting for them at North Tuddenham. At this relatively secluded spot with only a church, garden, and barn in addition to the parsonage, the journey ended at six o'clock. During their stay of almost three weeks, Johnson managed to persuade Cowper "out into the fields and meadows about this pleasant Parsonage and in our walks he would now and then notice a wild-flower or plant which was peculiar to our County."[16]

3   After arriving at North Tuddenham, Johnny devoted a considerable amount of energy to finding a place where he could next take his two invalids. At last, he was able to make arrangements

with a German apothecary, Dr. Kaliere, from whom he rented a house overlooking the sea at Mundesley, a quiet village on the Norfolk coast, a few miles south of Cromer. On August 18, the day before leaving the parsonage, Johnny persuaded Cowper to walk the four miles to Mattishall to visit Anne Bodham. At Mrs. Bodham's home, Johnny pointed out the Abbott portrait of 1792, and Cowper "clasping his hands, wished, with a heart-breaking sigh, that it was with him, as in those happy days—comparatively happy at least."[17]

Johnny had expected that he and his companion would find at the seaside "health & spirits."[18] Although Cowper took many "pleasant walks both above cliff & below and also in the fields about Mundesley, [Johnny] could perceive but small if any benefit either to his body and mind."[19] On August 31, Cowper, Johnny, and Samuel walked to Happisburgh, by the edge of the sea. Johnny recalled that Cowper ate an enormous meal of beans and bacon ("very old"), and apple pie ("the worst I ever saw"): "He ate, however, with a most complete relish of them all.—I never knew him enjoy a dinner any thing like it after that, to the day of his death."[20] To Cowper, however, Mundesley, with its rugged cliffs and deep ravine, was a place of horror, and his description of the coast of Norfolk is remarkably similar to his reaction to the hills of Sussex in 1792:

> The cliff is here of a height that it is terrible to look down from; and yesterday evening, by moonlight, I passed sometimes within a foot of the edge of it, from which to have fallen would probably have been to be dashed in pieces. But though to have been dashed in pieces would perhaps have been best for me, I shrunk from the precipice, and am waiting to be dashed in pieces by other means.[21]

Two miles from Mundesley on the coast was a solitary pillar of rock. Cowper visited this monument which the "crumbling cliff has left at the high water-mark" and he found in it an emblem of himself. "Torn from my natural connexions, I stand alone and expect the storm that shall displace me."[22] He was not unaware of the tragic irony that he had spent some of the happiest days of his childhood on the coast of Norfolk, but by this time he lived "a mere Animal life, which to a man of a mind naturally active, is, of itself, a misery nearly unsupportable."[23] At Mundesley, Cowper's "therapy," as it was to become throughout his stay in Norfolk, was walking, although, as he said, he "paid for"[24] these excur-

sions with swollen and inflamed eyelids. Toward the end of his
stay, Cowper wrote to Lady Hesketh about his vacillating heart
which could not find comfort anywhere.

> I shall never see Weston more. I have been tossed like a ball
> into a far country, from which there is no rebound for me.
> There indeed I lived a life of infinite despair, and such is my
> life in Norfolk. Such indeed it would be in any given spot upon
> the face of the globe; but to have passed the little time that
> remained to me there, was the desire of my heart. My heart's
> desire however has been always frustrated in every thing that
> it ever settled on, and by means that have made my disappoint-
> ments inevitable. When I left Weston I despaired of reaching
> Norfolk, and now that I have reached Norfolk, I am equally
> hopeless of ever reaching Weston more. What a lot is mine![25]

While Cowper spoke to Lady Hesketh, John Buchanan, and William Hayley, of "Perfect Despair,"[26] the ever sanguine Johnny reassured Kate: "I am happy to say that I have still better news for
you. [Cowper] is now almost wholly recovered—and is literally as
well, pretty nearly, as he was when I first knew him."[27] It is a
mark of the extraordinary discrepancy between the sensibilities of
these two men (and Cowper's ever-growing paranoia) that the
"well beloved kinsman" became at this time, and remained for the
rest of Cowper's life, "Mr. Johnson" and never again "Johnny."

Johnny divided his time between Mundesley and Mattishall,
where he stayed when performing his clerical duties at Yaxham and
Welborne each Sunday. Cowper and Mrs. Unwin were left behind
in the care of the Robertses and Hannah. Johnny had to search for
yet another residence, and he found one at Dunham Lodge, eight
miles from Dereham. On September 15, Cowper, Johnny, and Sam
Roberts drove by way of Cromer and Holt to view the prospective
residence. Cowper felt the house "was upon too grand a scale by
much for him. He had visited in such houses often, but had never
lived in such. On the whole however he did not say he *could* not
live at Dunham Lodge if necessary."[28] That night, the three men
stayed at Johnny's house at Dereham. Cowper was enchanted with
the study there, and he turned to Johnny and said, "I thank you
for this."[29] Johnny felt the expression of thanks was gratitude for
being allowed to pass the night in a restful place, "instead of *with
the Tormentors.*"[30]

Three weeks later, Johnny, Mrs. Unwin, and Cowper began their
journey to the "rambling, dreary Lodge upon the Hill at Dun-

ham."[31] (At Lady Hesketh's suggestion, Sam Roberts and his wife were left behind, to return to Weston. Hannah Wilson had been apprenticed in Norwich.) The party of three stayed at Johnny's house at Dereham for two weeks and then settled in at Dunham Lodge on October 22. A couple by the name of Johnson were engaged as servants, and Margaret Perowne was engaged to supervise the household. Peggy sent a cheerful note to Catharine Johnson on the morning after her arrival: "O that you could but have seen me and Mr Cowper sheeting the old Ladys bed Last Night. How nicely he spread the sheets for I was obleiged to unpack the linning . . ."[32]

Dunham is one of the highest points in Norfolk, and the Lodge a lofty, rambling house. The prospect from the bedroom windows was uninterrupted for more than thirty miles in each direction, and there was no protection from the wind. Soon after Johnson and his party arrived, there was a horrific storm. Johnny told Samuel Rose, "We expected nothing but being blown away into the wood."[33] However, the party "soon became tolerably settled, & fortunately found an exceedingly mild winter. Our days and evenings were chiefly spent in reading Novels."[34] Cowper became devoted to these sessions, although at Weston he could not stand cheerful novels and once ran out of the room when Lady Hesketh began a reading. At Dunham, these events became the center of his narrow existence: "so anxious is he for our evening Lecture that before the twilight is over he begins to fidget about the room, and when he thinks I don't observe him, he *slies* to the windows and lets down one of the Curtains—This is a signal for me to ring for candles—after which I go and help him to let down the other curtains, and before we have finished, the candles appear, and our maidens enter with their work-bags."[35] *Cecilia, Clarissa, Camilla,* and *Mordaunt* were among the books read to him. Although Cowper seemed to derive enjoyment from these occasions, he told Lady Hesketh that he lost "every sentence through the inevitable wanderings of [his] mind."[36]

As the winter progressed, Cowper was not physically well, and Johnny summoned his cousin, Dr. Donne from Norwich, to attend him. He prescribed opiates, which seemed to help. By March 1796, he had improved: "I think his *body* is mended—Oh that I could say his poor *mind* was mended too—but it was wounded by an immaterial *rod,* and must be healed by an immaterial *salve*—which nobody but GOD can make!"[37]

In the spring, Johnny, concerned about Mrs. Unwin's health, summoned the Powleys to Dunham Lodge. Johnny did not understand the hostility (obviously due to Mrs. Unwin's devotion to Cowper) which had developed between mother and daughter, and he referred to Mrs. Unwin's "un-natural anti-pathy to seeing her daughter . . . without any *conceivable cause*."[38] Cowper did not converse with the Powleys and answered their inquiries regarding his health with a *"mournful groan."*[39] During her visit, Susanna read a chapter from the Bible to her mother every morning, and Johnny continued the practice until her death. Cowper began to attend these sessions, apparently "without ever taking any notice."[40] Almost a week before the Powleys arrived, Johnson recorded in his diary a remarkable occurrence while he and Cowper were sitting by a table near the fire: ". . . on a sudden a most tremendous crash was heard just by us—like the noise of a hammer struck with great violence upon the table which stood between us.—I started very much, and asked him what it could possibly be—'Oh', said he, 'I know what it means'—but I could get no more from him—nor did he appear in the least degree, surprised."[41] Johnny was obviously as susceptible as Cowper to the awesome meanings which could be attached to such happenings. By May, Cowper was well enough to ride out with Johnny in a chaise, and by the end of June he began "peeping" into Wakefield's edition of Pope's Homer. "About this time he began to alter here and there a passage . . . And by the 6th of August, he was seriously embarked in a revision of his translation—producing, one day with another, about 60 new lines."[42]

Cowper's return to his Homeric labors briefly renewed him. He was constantly saying that "never, in his *born days,* 'till now, did he see what his Translation ought to be, and how, and *how only,* Homer can be properly translated."[43] Johnny passed this good news on to Hayley, whom he asked to visit *"before we leave Dunham Lodge,* to which he [Cowper] has begg'd that we may not return when we come from the sea, because he greatly prefers my house at Dereham. . . ."[44] Hayley did not take up the invitation, and the only visitor from the Weston days was Samuel Rose.

In September, Cowper, Mrs. Unwin, and Johnny left for Mundesley. Johnny's diary entry for the whole of September and October is cryptic: "Many walkes by the sea as before, when the weather was fine—but no particularly good effect from them."[45] Johnny continually tried to reassure Cowper that the dreadful calamities he feared would never happen, but, he unhappily lamented, "I might as well talk to the sea."[46] On October 29, 1796, the dispirited party went from Mundesley to East Dereham, where they were soon established at Johnny's "little abode."[47] Within ten days of their arrival at Dereham, Cowper required medical attention yet again from Dr.

Donne, and any hope of settling in comfortably at Dereham was dashed by the death of Beau on November 17 and of Mary Unwin exactly one month later.

Mrs. Unwin's health had deteriorated rapidly after the return to Dereham, and on December 16, the day before she died, Cowper asked one of the servants if there was "Life above-stairs."[48] Mary Unwin died at one in the afternoon on the seventeenth, and Cowper was with her a half-hour before this. As Johnny recalled, "Death was evidently in her countenance and he could not but see it was. He bore the sight, however, better than . . . expected, and went down . . . into the study to [the] customary employment of the Novel."[49]

> Before night, when she was laid forth, he went with me to look at her. It was nearly dusk, which I thought was better than day light for a sight so tremendous to this dear Soul. He bore it, however better than I expected. After looking at her a few seconds, with one hand holding back the head-curtain, he bore himself away in an agony and clasping his hands together, he lifted them up with great violence, and exclaimed, looking up towards the ceiling of the room—"*Oh God—was it for this?*"[50]

Johnny persuaded Cowper to return to the study, and, after that, Cowper never once named her to him, and he did not make any inquiries about the burial. Johnny claimed that Cowper never seemed "to think of her more,"[51] but, years before, Cowper had ceased to speak of Theadora, whose memory had obviously been vivid to him. As with his mother, he lacked the ability to accept or deal with the separation of death. So that Cowper would not be aware when the service was taking place, Mary Unwin was buried by candlelight at half past seven in the evening of December 23.

4   When she wrote to Johnny in January 1797, Lady Hesketh assumed that Mary Unwin's death had been a great relief to Johnny from "dead *weight*,"[52] but she was also puzzled that it did not seem to make any change for the better in her cousin's condition: "—since the death of his old Companion has produc'd no material Change in him I know not what can? this however may be *said* that the State she had been in so long, *has so much estrang'd him from her,* and made her so totally useless in all Respects, that he certainly cou'd not feel her Loss, as he wou'd have done, had she been taken from him some years ago—."[53] But Cowper certainly did feel the

loss. Although he had been extremely depressed up to the time of Mary Unwin's death and had retreated into himself from the beginning of 1794, his condition from late 1796 until his death deteriorated considerably. In the last four years of his life, he was convinced that he heard voices when awake—the voices from 1791 to 1795 had spoken to him only in dreams.

Cowper's voices and dreams from November 15, 1797, to April 23, 1799, were recorded by John Johnson in his "Pro et Contra" diary, and he also kept a journal from 1795 to 1800, "relating wholly" to Cowper. John Johnson was obviously trying to find a pattern to his cousin's unhappiness, and he hoped that by asking him to recount his visions Cowper might obtain some relief simply by sharing them with another person. Cowper himself classified his dreams: "dreams of contempt and horror—some of shame—and some were dreams of ignominy and torture."[54] In addition to acting as Cowper's confessor, Johnny intervened: "To day [March 29, 1707] I procured a workman to cut a groove in the wall behind our poor friend's bed, for the insertion of a tin tube, through which I hoped to be able to convey to him some comfortable sounds, to counteract those deplorable ones perpetually injected into his Mind's ear, by the unseen enemies of his Peace."[55] Such an intrusion did not really prove beneficial. On December 2, 1797, Johnny whispered through the tube: "Here's a happy New Year coming for Mr. Cowper, in this very house.—It will find you busy with your *Ho*-mer. Here's a happy New Year coming for Mr. Cow-per."[56] Cowper related the message to Johnny later that day and remarked that it was spoken rapidly to tell him "the time is come, by which I suppose he means the time of his torments."[57] Cowper was in such a depressed state that Johnny's meddlesome curiosity probably did not contribute to a furtherance of the melancholia, but it did not do any appreciable good since, by this time, Cowper would convert any message, however sanguine, into one of condemnation. John Johnson was desperate; he had to believe that ultimately he could assist Cowper to recover. It was an impossible task to reassure a person who for many years had wished never to have existed and who had once dreamed of happiness "but awoke never to find it again."[58]

In his visions, Cowper relived the traumatic events which had given rise to his unhappiness. He became convinced that John Johnson and Margaret Perowne despised him and would abandon him: "In his afternoon nap on the sopha, he dreamt that he saw Miss Perowne leaning upon Samuel's arm, to leave the house for ever."[59] He imagined that there was not elsewhere in the "universe so cruel a Being as you have in the form of Mr Johnson."[60] He was continually convinced that he would be turned out of doors. The voice would tell him, "You shall be left,"[61] or, more elaborately, it would tell him that Johnny would steal downstairs in the dark and leave him alone. He dreamed that Johnny took him to a strange house in London and then abandoned him there. Cowper's fear of exclusion was obviously heightened by the loss of his second mother, Mary Unwin, and in the delusions of old age, he experienced anew the loss of Ann Cowper.

The dominant pattern of images recorded by John Johnson is of food. Cowper remained the famished, guilt-ridden child. What he drank was of "the rankest poison,"[62] and he was warned that the more he imbibed the more miserable he would be. He saw his stomach full of monsters, and he imagined that what he ate formed a monster within him. He dreamed that he was attacked in the act of eating: "I saw a man darting a fork into my face last night, and I shall have it fulfilled to night or to-morrow morning, I know I shall."[63] When he had a bowel obstruction, he was told that "the substance formed there would harden to such a degree that no pill would touch it."[64] Infantile fantasies took over Cowper's sensibility, and he was drawn into a mire of self-loathing and terror. "Poor Mr. Cowper says *He* is Prometheus—and so it will be done to him!"[65]

Cowper existed in a world where he "was taken up in his bed by strange women,"[66] "saw a tree torn up by the roots, & knew that it meant himself,"[67] was "disjointed by the Rack,"[68] and "was to be let down to the bottom of the sea with ropes and drawn up again."[69] Like Teedon, John Johnson attempted to convert these prognostications of doom into what might be plausibly considered good omens. Hayley's ever sanguine mind worked in a different way. In a stroke of singular insight and imagination, he wrote to Cowper on June 24, 1797 in response to a short missive the poet had recently sent him describing his state of "Perfect Despair":

My keen sensations in perusing these heart-piercing Lines have been a painful prelude to the following ecstatic Vision—I beheld the Throne of God, whose splendour, tho' in excess, did not strike me blind; but left me powers to discern, on the steps of it, two kneeling angelic Forms. A kind seraph seem'd to whisper to me, that these heavenly petitioners were your lovely Mother, and my own . . . I sprang eagerly forward to enquire your Destiny of your Mother. . . . "Moderate the anxiety of

thy Zeal [said she] lest it distract thy declining Faculties! . . .
[I tell you that my son's] restoration shall be gradual; and that
his Peace with Heaven shall be preceded by the following
extraordinary circumstances of signal Honour on earth—He
shall receive Letters from Members of Parliament, from Judges,
and from Bishops, to thank Him for the service, He has render'd to the Christian world by his devotional poetry."[70]

Although it was obviously too late to do any good, Hayley's "Vision" of Cowper's mother speaking of the gratitude which others
owed to her son, to whom she was obviously devoted, hit at the
very source of Cowper's distress.

Hayley enlisted William Wilberforce and the Evangelical Bishop
of London, Beilby Porteus, to compose the first supposedly unsolicited letters. Wilberforce made his letter appear spontaneous by
sending a newly published pamphlet as a "small Testimony of the
high and sincere respect"[71] in which he held Cowper. Rather than
calming him, the letter distressed him. Porteous' letter was decidedly not helpful. He wrote "That *Love* [of God] you must possess surely in as full extent as any human Being ever did." Cowper
rejoined, *"Not an atom of it!"*[72] The concluding sentence of Porteus' letter was particularly unfortunate: "You must be enjoying in
the tranquility of private Life, the content, the composure, the
comfort . . . of having so essentially promoted the Glory of God
and the happiness of Mankind, & still more from the *certain expectation* . . . that your patient continuance in well-doing shall,
through the merits of your Redeemer, be rewarded with Glory,
honour, Peace and Eternal Life in the world to come."[73] A letter
from the Bishop of Llandaff arrived while Johnny was reading from
his *Apology for Christianity* to Cowper. The Bishop's assertion in
this letter that Cowper must be free from melancholy and super-
stitious apprehensions was especially galling. Cowper soon realized
that the "Vision" and the subsequent missives were part of a ploy,
for when Johnny later pretended to search for Hayley's letter of
June 24, which was then at Lady Hesketh's, Cowper told him not to
bother. Johnny protested by saying that "there is a kind of accomplishment of what is predicted."[74] "Well, be it so," said Cowper, "I
know there is, and I knew there would be, and I knew what it
meant."[75]

Hayley and Johnny may have been bumbling in their attempts to
"cure" Cowper, but they were benevolent men trying to relieve the

sufferings of their friend. After Mary Unwin's death, however, Cowper turned to solace to only one person, Margaret Perowne, whose gentle nursing became his only comfort. When she met Cowper in 1795, Peggy was forty-four years old (Mary Unwin was forty-one when he met her in 1765), the daughter of John Peroan, of Huguenot descent. Peggy, a friend of Catharine Johnson, was an impoverished gentlewoman who was paid to look after John Johnson's household. Johnny, who frequently referred to her as "Margarettina" or the "Old Maid,"[76] thought she was excessively dour. Like Mrs. Unwin years earlier, she took up her post sleeping in a corner of Cowper's bedroom. The poet continually dreamt that his new mother had abandoned him, and in one of his last letters (July 26, 1798) he told Lady Hesketh of his reaction to Miss Perowne's absence from Dereham: "I wrote a few days since to M. Pn., to tell her that as she had left me suddenly, and alarm'd me much by doing so, she would equally relieve me would she as sudden return."[77]

5   There were some encouraging signs in 1797. Cowper went riding with Johnny, and he began to gain weight. He grew plump in the face and legs, so much so that he could not deny Johnny's assertion that he "was master of a double chin & a ruddy cheek."[78] He drank a great deal of port, and after dinner Johnny would remain in his bedroom reading or writing. "On these occasions we used to contrive the looking-glass in such a manner between us that as he lay in bed he might see my image in it through an opening of the curtains at the feet—so that in the case of his waking he might not suppose himself forsaken, & left alone in the house . . ."[79] Cowper worked on the Homer intermittently from mid-June and then stopped in mid-August, perhaps because the "Vision" experiment had upset him.

Johnny suggested at that time in order "to draw him out of himself"[80] that he write his name in each of his four hundred books at the rate of 10 a day. "To this he readily agreed—though for an odd reason, dear Soul—viz. because he thought that he *must* live till they were all finished."[81] As his task progressed, Cowper, as Johnny had hoped, began to dip into some of the books. He finished this assignment on September 25 and took up the Homer revisions once again.

Johnny and Cowper visited Mundesley eight times in the summer of 1798. They visited the lighthouse at Happisburgh on June

7, and Cowper enjoyed looking through a telescope at the ships. Three weeks later, Cowper, Johnny, and Catharine rowed eight miles out to sea.

> When we were at the greatest distance from the shore we passed directly along side a Wine ship from Oporto—the Bacchus of Lynn. The Master offered to bring us to, holding a rope for that purpose ready to throw out to us,—but not supposing that Mr. C. would consent to go on board I took no notice of it to him. We had not however, left the ship three minutes before he observed that he had missed the only chance he should ever have of tasting *real* Port wine, and that he should have consented very readily to go on board had it been proposed to him.[82]

When the Dowager Lady Spencer visited him at Dereham on July 14, Cowper did not take much notice of her and merely answered her inquiries by a yes or no. According to him, Lady Spencer had only been interested in the furniture: "express'd herself much pleased with them, and spoke, before she went, of visiting them again hereafter."[83] (Georgiana Spencer, Thea's close friend, still wrote to her, and Cowper may well have realized that Lady Spencer would be sending a report on him to Thea.) Sir John Throckmorton met with a similar response when he called in December. When the chaise which carried him, Johnny, and Peggy overturned on the way back from their last trip to Mundesley in late October, Cowper "appeared not at all frightened but sat very quietly in the Chaise till it was lifted up again."[84]

Cowper completed his revisions to the *Iliad* in June or July, began the *Odyssey* on July 24, and finished work on it on March 8, 1799. Johnny tried to devise another project. He suggested that he complete "The Four Ages," revise his own poems, paraphrase some of the poetical portions of the Bible, modernize the poetry of their ancestor, John Donne, or translate Virgil's *Pastorals*. Cowper was not responsive to any of these suggestions.

Earlier in 1799, when Joseph Johnson published the ninth edition of Cowper's two volumes of verse, Cowper allowed Johnny to read to him all his poems—except *John Gilpin*, which he was now ashamed to have written. During this time, Johnson also read to him Gibbon's *Decline and Fall*, Boswell's *Johnson*, Bradshaw's *Josephus*, and Shakespeare. Cowper's last burst of creativity, perhaps inspired by these works, is found in the Norfolk Manuscript, which contains translations of some Latin poems by Vincent

Bourne and from the Greek Anthology. It also includes two original poems of arresting power and intensity: *Montes Glaciales* (*On
the Ice Islands*) and *The Castaway*, which Cowper subsequently
translated into Latin. Before he went to bed on March 11, the poet
told Johnny that "he had thought of six lines of Latin Verse, and
that if he could do any thing it must be to go on with that."[85] By
March 19, the "six lines" had grown to the fifty-three-line *Montes
Glaciales* and its sixty-four-line English rendition.

The inspiration for this poem was a newspaper piece on icebergs,
which Johnny read to Cowper. Among other writers in the eighteenth century, Erasmus Darwin had been especially interested in
such phenomena, and in *The Economy of Vegetation* (1791) he in-
structs his Nymph to direct the "ice-built isles" into the southern
waters; "veil'd in mist, the melting treasures steer, / And cool with
arctic snows the tropic year."[86] Influenced by Darwin, Cowper had
remarked to Hayley in June 1792: "50 times have I wish'd this very
day that Dr. Darwin's scheme of giving rudders and sails to the
Ice-islands that spoil all our summers, were actually put into practice. So should we have gentle airs instead of churlish blasts, and
those everlasting sources of bad weather being once navigated into
the Southern Hemisphere, my Mary would recover as fast again."[87]
Cowper's poem of 1799 is ultimately concerned, however, with the
inability of the ice islands moving south to cool the southern hemisphere and thus rendering a milder climate to the north. The poet
concludes with a warning to those islands:

> Seek your home; no longer rashly dare
> The darts of Phœbus, and a softer air;
> Lest ye regret, too late, your native coast,
> In no congenial gulf for ever lost![88]

This poem is about the impossibility of transformation, and its admonition to the ice islands to go back to their place of origin is a
grim reminder that they must accept their predestined lot or perish.
There is obviously an autobiographical bias in this poem, concerned as it is with the permanency of never-melting ice. However,
in his last poem, *The Castaway*, Cowper directly evoked his an-
guished heart.

On September 11, 1798, Cowper told Johnson that he dreamed
that he "saw a man who had suffered the most ignominious punishment—and envied him because his was over, and mine would never
be so."[89] This is, of course, the theme of *The Castaway*, and Cowper had earlier evoked in Olney Hymn no. 36 St. Paul's words in

1 Corinthians 9:27: "lest that by any means, when I have preached to others, I myself should be a castaway." "Fear" of being a castaway in Hymn 36 had given way to certainty by March 1799, and in his finest lyric poem he chose to write of abandonment by evoking the most potent image—the sea—in his verse. As a young man, Cowper had read in George Anson's *Voyage Round the World* (1748) of a seaman who, during a fierce storm, had fallen overboard:

> . . . and notwithstanding the prodigious agitation of the waves, we perceived that he swam very strong, and it was with the utmost concern that we found ourselves incapable of assisting him; and we were the more grieved at his unhappy fate, since we lost sight of him struggling with the waves, that he might continue sensible for a considerable time longer, of the horror attending his irretrievable situation.[90]

Cowper skillfully evokes the awesome torment of the "destin'd wretch" at the outset of his poem; then, the "I" briefly compares himself to the bereft seaman. The narrator then carefully describes the torment of the man who knows that he must soon die:

> Nor, cruel as it seem'd, could he
>   Their haste himself condemn,
> Aware that flight, in such a sea,
>   Alone could rescue them;
> Yet bitter felt it still to die
> Deserted, and his friends so nigh.[91]

At the end of the poem, the narrator introduces himself again and reminds his reader that "misery still delights to trace / Its 'semblance in another's case."[92] This narrator, having depicted the incredible anguish of the sailor and having offered what seems an obvious commonplace, adds a concluding comparison between the "wretch" and himself:

> No voice divine the storm allay'd,
>   No light propitious shone;
> When, snatch'd from all effectual aid,
>   We perish'd, each alone:
> But I beneath a rougher sea,
> And whelm'd in deeper gulphs than he.[93]

The stillness with which the poem concludes does not bring acceptance or understanding of God's mysterious ways—rather, it closes with the passive acquiescence of death and despair. *The Cast-*

away is the most chilling picture Cowper painted of his continual sense of abandonment.

Cowper's last extant letter (April 11, 1799, to Newton) was written three weeks after he had completed *The Castaway*. Here again, he evoked his sense of everlasting exclusion by using imagery reminiscent of his final poem. He had hoped, he told Newton, to spend eternity in paradise, but "I was little aware of what I had to expect, and that a storm was at hand which in one terrible moment would darken, and in another still more terrible, blot out that prospect for ever."[94]

6   In *Lavengro* (1851), George Borrow, who was born at Dereham in 1803, summoned up a picture, probably dependent upon the recollection of townspeople, of Cowper's final years: "the death-like face is no longer occasionally seen timidly and mournfully looking for a moment through the window-pane . . . the hind in thy neighbourhood no longer at evening-fall views, and starts as he views, the dark lathy figure moving beneath the hazels . . . and no longer at early dawn does the sexton of the old church reverently doff his hat as, supported by some kind friend, the death-stricken creature totters along the church path."[95] John Johnson's depictions of Cowper in 1799 augment Borrow's cameo. It was a melancholy time, but not, however, "of the blackest hue . . . but still very sad, and almost hopeless—He does not at all gain ground, but still incapable of interest from any thing without, gives his whole soul to the lacerating exercise of his poor dear miserable Self."[96] Samuel Parr, who had been Head Master of the Norwich Grammar School until 1785, called on the morning of September 5, "not in the hope of being able to see Mr C. but merely that he might say he had been under the same roof with so distinguished a character."[97] Earlier that summer, Cowper had ridden out with Johnny twice, once to visit Mrs. Bodham at Mattishall.

Upon the death of the Rector of Yaxham and Welborne in October 1799, Mrs. Bodham was able at last to present the livings, as had been previously arranged, to Johnny, whose income was thus augmented by several hundred pounds. It was now possible to think of a larger residence and Johnny decided on one three doors down which was "chearful—snug—and handsome,"[98] and which also had the advantages of a garden, and pleasant, retired walks. Cowper liked the dwelling when he visited it on October 28, and he "allowed that there was no comparison as to convenience & accommo-

dation between that and the house we now live in."[99] He even
talked of taking up gardening again. When the move took place on
the evening of December 11, Cowper "settled himself to sleep on
the sofa by the study fire immediately, and from the first moment of
our taking possession, appeared to like the House."[100]

Cowper soldiered on with further translations, including render-
ings of some of Gay's *Fables* into Latin. In January 1800, Johnny
began to read the corrected copy of the *Iliad* to him, but on January 30, Cowper's health had become "very poorly indeed."[101]
Johnny records that he suffered from a "prolapsus,"[102] but an apothecary the following day diagnosed dropsy (his legs were very swollen).[103] Two days later, he was seen by Dr. Lubbock from Norwich
who prescribed a "draft," which Cowper refused to take. He was
well enough on February 3 to ride out with Johnny. Except for a
few "Diuretic Drops" which, wrote Johnny, "we sly into his Coffee,"[104] he took nothing. Lady Hesketh recommended "Dantzick
Spruce,"[105] and Johnny asked Samuel Rose to send some. When
twenty drops of this cure were placed in a glass of wine for him,
Cowper declared he "neither could nor would drink such horridly
nauseous stuff."[106] Johnny was especially distraught at having received five gallons of the potion, and wished to annoint Rose with
it "from head to foot."[107] Hayley made a variety of suggestions:
electricity (as before), roasted broom seeds, tamarinds. Lady Hesketh
augmented her original suggestions with oysters, white wine with
lemon juice, Hock, Rhenish, and Rota Tent Wine, but Cowper
soon returned to his daily bottle of port in which he sopped toasted
bread.

In torment, Johnny told Hayley that he hoped for a few days
more to preserve "this amiable sufferer's cloudy existence—Death's
arrow, already on the nerve, will soon be on the wing."[108] On April
8, Johnny told Kate that Cowper's body was "covered with plaisters
where the bones would otherwise soon be through the skin."[109]
Hayley, whose own son Thomas Alphonso was dying, could not
journey to Dereham, but in his *Life of Cowper* he provided, presumably with information from Johnny and Margaret Perowne, an
account of the final week:

On Sunday the twentieth, he seemed a little revived.
On Monday he appeared dying, but recovered so much as to
eat a slight dinner.
Tuesday and Wednesday he grew apparently weaker every hour.
On Thursday he sat up as usual in the evening.

Friday the twenty-fifth, at five in the morning, a deadly change appeared in his features.
He spoke no more.[110]

Cowper died quietly at 4:55 on the afternoon of April 25. According to Dr. Woods, who saw him during his final illness, he "died of a worn-out constitution—not dropsy—with slight oedematous swelling of the legs, arising from extreme debility."[111] Cowper spoke his last words during Thursday night when refusing a cordial Margaret Perowne offered him: "What can it signify?"[112]

Cowper, the recluse, who was the most famous poet of his generation, was buried on Saturday, May 3, in the Chapel of St. Edmund in the North Transept of Dereham Church. Lady Hesketh, whose health had deteriorated considerably in the past five years, was too ill to attend the funeral, and no other member of the Cowper family was present. Despite the incredible depressions which had overwhelmed him so early in life and his inability to come to grips with the torments of exclusion and deprivation, all of Cowper's friends felt that their lives had been enriched and blessed by this kindly man.

7   Two years after Cowper's death, William Blake engraved six illustrations for Hayley's life of the poet. Blake designed only one of the plates, where the Peasant's Nest and three hares are placed at the bottom of the page. It was appropriate that Blake chose a rural sanctuary and tame animals to celebrate the poet of retreat and retirement. For the upper part of his design, Blake depicted lines 210–14 from book 1 of *The Task*:

> Peace to the artist, whose ingenious thought
> Devis'd the weather-house, that useful toy!
> Fearless of humid air and gathering rains,
> Forth steps the man—an emblem of myself!
> More delicate, his tim'rous mate retires.[113]

The "tim'rous mate" may be fearful, but she dwells in sun-drenched brightness. Blake may have perceived her radiant joyfulness as one aspect—a significant one—of a poetical sensibility he very much admired. The "fearless" figure is garbed in deepest black, his face is little in evidence, and he strides purposefully on his self-appointed round. In his rendition of the man who chooses to go into the darkness, Blake is showing the deeply negative side of Cowper's nature, but he also captures his determination to come to terms with hostile elements, be they the weather or deepest melancholia.

As his emblematical representation of Cowper reveals, Blake intuitively understood Cowper's troubled existence. William Cowper simply never discovered the meaning of his life, and this makes his last question to Margaret Perowne undeniably poignant. He ultimately fell victim to hostile inner demons, and he did not know or understand how they had come into being. He asserted that a vengeful God claimed him as victim. Despite his lack of comprehension of the forces which molded his life and which led him to become the "castaway," Cowper attempted in his poems and letters to write about the conflicts which shaped his destiny, and through his translation of Homer he tried to rejoin the world he had abandoned as a young man. Cowper did not win the battle against what he perceived as invading forces. Although he did not understand the great sadness that was for so long his life, he made real—though intermittent—attempts to vanquish the enemy. He did not succeed at this task, but his courage and determination were, at times, heroic.

Acknowledgments

LIKE so many others who have worked on William Cowper, I am deeply grateful to Miss Mary Barham Johnson, the great grand-daughter of the Reverend John Johnson, Cowper's Johnny, for her invaluable assistance in the preparation of this book. Miss Johnson permitted me to read her unpublished biography of Johnny, and she has allowed me to quote freely from manuscript material still in copyright. Other descendants of Cowper's relations and close friends have been of great help: the Misses C. and A. Cowper Johnson, Christian, Lady Hesketh, and Miss Catherine M. Bull. I should like to record my thanks to all the owners of manuscript material, who have kindly allowed me to quote from manuscripts in their possession. Much of my work on this book was done at the British Library and at Mills Memorial Library, McMaster University. I am grateful to the officers and staff of both for assistance.

My work in preparing this life of Cowper has been greatly eased by the multitude of papers and documents collected by two great Cowper scholars: the late N. C. Hannay and the late Kenneth Povey. I have also profited from the advice and wisdom of two other devoted Cowperians: Norma, Lady Dalrymple-Champneys (formerly Norma Russell) and Professor John D. Baird. Although I have avoided writing criticism of Cowper's work in this book, I am mindful of and have learned much from the many splendid books and articles which have been written on Cowper's poetry during the past twenty-five years, beginning with Morris Golden's *In Search of Stability* (1960).

My greatest indebtedness in the pursuit of things Cowperian is to my friend and coeditor, Dr. Charles Ryskamp. I first came to know Cowper when a student in his graduate seminar at Princeton. It has been a pleasure since then to work with him in preparing the Clarendon Press edition of Cowper's letters, and I hope this biography is worthy of the high standards Charles Ryskamp has brought to and insisted upon in the study of William Cowper.

The pursuit was made possible by generous fellowships from the Nuffield Foundation and the John Simon Guggenheim Memorial Foundation and a research grant from the Social Sciences and Humanities Research Council of Canada. I am grateful to those institutions and to McMaster University, which allowed me a sabbatical leave when such a privilege was not my due; in particular, I should like to thank Professor Richard E. Morton, Dean Alwyn Berland, and Vice-President Leslie King for their encouragement and practical support.

During the actual preparation of this book, I have incurred other obligations. Two former students of mine, Professors David Parkinson and Richard Arnold, did research of extraordinary finesse, the fruits of which have enriched my understanding of Cowper. I have also benefitted from the work on Cowper done by my colleague at McMaster, Professor Andrew Brink. Professor G. E. Bentley, Jr., Professor Donald C. Goellnicht, and Dr. Antony Luengo read the entire manuscript and made many useful suggestions. My old friend, Dr. John Covolo, enhanced this book by tactfully showing me in countless ways how grace and clarity of expression could be better achieved. My wife, Christine Dalton, resolutely believed in the merits of this biography, and the depth of my obligation to her is, simply, incalculable.

Abbreviations and Short Titles
Used in the Notes

Cowper's Letters

The primary printed source for Cowper's biography is his letters, as edited for the Clarendon Press (1979–84; vol. 1, 1979; vol. 2, 1981; vol. 3, 1982; vol. 4, 1984) by James King and Charles Ryskamp. Vol. 1 contains *Adelphi* and Cowper's letters from 1750 to 1781; vol. 2, letters from 1782 to 1786; vol. 3, letters from 1787 to 1791; vol. 4, letters from 1792 to 1799 and *Spiritual Diary*. (Cue titles: *Letters 1, Letters 2, Letters 3*, and *Letters 4*).

Cowper's Poems

Citations from Cowper's poetry from 1749 to 1782 are derived from: *The Poems of William Cowper*, vol. 1, ed. John D. Baird and Charles Ryskamp (Oxford: Clarendon Press, 1980). (Cue title: *Poems*).

Citations from Cowper's poetry after 1782 are derived from: *Cowper, Poetical Works*, 4th ed. (with corrections and additions by Norma Russell), ed. H. S. Milford (London: Oxford University Press, 1967). (Cue title: *Milford*).

Persons

C	William Cowper	JJ	John Johnson
WB	William Bull	JJO	Joseph Johnson
AC	Ashley Cowper	JM	Judith Madan
MC	Maria Cowper	PM	Penelope Maitland
TC	Theadora Cowper	JN	John Newton
SG	Samuel Greatheed	CR	Clotworthy Rowley
WH	William Hayley	SR	Samuel Rose
HH	Harriot Hesketh	ST	Samuel Teedon
JH	Joseph Hill	MU	Mary Unwin
CJ	Catharine Johnson		

Manuscripts

Annotations. This undated manuscript, "Remarks on Cowper's translation of Homer's *Iliad*," consists of eighty-four leaves, and contains detailed criticisms in

Fuseli's hand, mainly of individual lines, of books 1–17, 19, and 21–22 of Cowper's translation. There are occasional notes in Cowper's hand. Manuscript C210 in the James Marshall and Marie-Louise Osborn Collection, Yale University Library.

JJ Diary. The holograph memorandum book (twenty-two pages) of the Reverend John Johnson, relating almost wholly to William Cowper and Mary Unwin during their stay with him in Norfolk. Entries run from July 28, 1795, to February 3, 1800. Swarthmore College Library.

Memoranda. "Memoranda Respecting the Poet Cowper." A series of twelve observations (on four pages) on Cowper's life in Samuel Greatheed's hand. The information supplied was for Hayley's benefit. John Rylands Memorial Library, University of Manchester.

Pro et Contra. A diary (fifty-one leaves) kept by the Reverend John Johnson of the "dreams, voices, & notices of the poet Cowper." It records information from November 15, 1797, until April 23, 1799. Cambridge University Library.

Recollections. "Recollections of Cowper, A Poem." This narrative poem (approximately 1,500 lines), divided into two portions ("The Walk" and "The Lodge"), was composed by the Reverend John Johnson about 1831 to 1832. In the poem and the extended annotation to it which he prepared, Johnny recalled Cowper's life at Weston and many details concerning the poet's habits, attitudes, and conversation. Miss Mary Barham Johnson, Norwich.

Teedon. The holograph of the Reverend John Johnson's poem about Samuel Teedon is in the collection of Miss Mary Barham Johnson, Norwich.

Locations of Manuscript Material

Althorp	The Earl Spencer, Althorp House, Northamptonshire
Barham Johnson	Miss Mary Barham Johnson, Norwich
Barrett	Mr. Roger W. Barrett, Chicago
Bodleian	Bodleian Library, Oxford
British Library	The British Library, London
Bull	Formerly Miss C. M. Bull, Newport Pagnell
Fitzwilliam	Fitzwilliam Museum, Cambridge
Lambeth Palace	Lambeth Palace Library, London
Liverpool	Liverpool Civil Library, Liverpool
LRO	Lancashire Record Office, Preston
McMaster	Mills Memorial Library, McMaster University
Morgan	The Pierpont Morgan Library, New York City
Olney	The Cowper and Newton Museum, Olney
Pforzheimer	The Carl H. Pforzheimer Library, New York City
Princeton	Princeton University Library, Princeton
Rochester	The University of Rochester Library
Yale	Yale University Library, New Haven

Books and Periodicals

AR	*The Analytical Review*
Bishop	Morchard Bishop [O. Stonor], *Blake's Hayley* (1951)
CR	*The Critical Review*
GM	*Gentleman's Magazine*
Hayley	William Hayley, *The Life and Posthumous Writings of William Cowper* (3 vols., Chichester and London, 1803–4)
Homer	*The Iliad and Odyssey of Homer*, trans. William Cowper (2 vols., 1791)
Latin and Italian Poems	*Latin and Italian Poems of Milton, Translated into English Verse* (1808)
MR	*The Monthly Review*
N&Q	*Notes and Queries*
RES	*The Review of English Studies*
Russell	Norma Russell, *A Bibliography of William Cowper to 1837* (Oxford, 1963)
Ryskamp	Charles Ryskamp, *William Cowper of the Inner Temple, Esq.* (Cambridge, 1959)
Teedon Diary	*The Diary of Samuel Teedon*, ed. Thomas Wright (1902)

Unless otherwise indicated in the appropriate notes, place of publication is London.

Other sources of documentary information used in the writing of this book are Kenneth Povey, "Cowper and Lady Austen," *RES* 10 (1934), and "The Banishment of Lady Austen," *RES* 15 (1939); James King, "Cowper's *Adelphi* Restored . . . ," *RES* 30 (1979), and "An Unlikely Alliance: Fuseli as Revisor of Cowper's Homer," *Neophilologus* 67 (1983).

Notes

1 BERKHAMSTED AND WESTMINSTER

1 *Rural Rides,* vol. 1 (Everyman's Library ed., 1957), 86.
2 *Howards End* (Abinger ed.: Edward Arnold, 1973), 195.
3 HH to WH, January 28, 1802, MS Princeton.
4 *Adelphi (Letters* 1 : 18).
5 To JH, October 15, 1767, *Letters* 1 : 83.
6 Ibid.
7 T. H. King, "Cowper's Mother and an Early Lover," *N&Q* 98 (1924), 167.
8 *Milford,* 395.
9 To HH, February 26, 1790, *Letters* 3 : 348.
10 HH to JJ, April 28, 1800, MS Barham Johnson.
11 *Milford,* 395.
12 Ibid.
13 Ibid., 394.
14 To JH, November 6, 1784, *Letters* 2 : 294.
15 To Rose Bodham, February 27, 1790, *Letters* 3 : 349–50.
16 Vol. 1, ed. Holbrook Jackson (1932), 343. Burton also claims that "loss and death of friends may challenge a first place" in causing melancholia (357–58). He notes that from birth "the first ill accident that can befall [a child] is a bad nurse" (330). Burton is particularly sensitive to the influences parents wield over their children: "Parents, and such as have the tuition and oversight of children, offend many times in that they are too stern, always threatening, chiding, brawling, whipping, or striking; by means of which their poor children are so disheartened and cowed, that they never after have any courage, a merry hour in their lives, or take pleasure in anything" (333). The lives of melancholics, he also claims, are predetermined by the *"remembrance* of some disgrace, loss, injury, abuse, etc. [which] troubles them now being idle afresh, as if it were new done" (389). Modern psychoanalytical and psychological writers, in their concern with loss as a cause of depression, have elaborated on principles clearly documented by Burton. The most concise treatment of this topic can be found in Andrew Brink, "Depression and Loss, A Theme in Robert Burton's *Anatomy of Melancholy," Canadian Journal of Psychiatry* 24 (1979) : 767–72.

In the introduction to *The Romantic Mother* (Baltimore: Johns Hopkins

University Press, 1983), Barbara A. Schapiro, whose theoretical formulations are based on Kohut, Kernberg, Klein, among others, writes about theories which "focus on the earliest relationship with the mother as the core experience in one's psychic and emotional maturation" (ix): "The mother imago, the unconscious representation of the mother, is internalized in infancy and retained throughout adulthood. That unconscious representation is built upon the basis of the first real and fantasized relationship with the mother. Due to unavoidable shortcomings of maternal care, the relationship with the mother as our first love object is primarily characterized by ambivalence. . . . The child internalizes both the 'good,' loving mother and the 'bad' frustrating one. *If the relation with the mother imago is damaged by such disturbances as separation, death, or emotional rejection, the internal splitting becomes even more intense"* [emphasis mine].

"Splitting . . . is a major cause of ego weakness. Failure to resolve this primitive ambivalence, to integrate the internalized 'good' and 'bad' objects, prevents both the formation of a mature, cohesive self and the sense of a cohesive, concrete reality outside the self" (ix–x).

In *The Stranger Within* (Pittsburgh: The University of Pittsburgh Press, 1980), Stephen D. Cox, using eighteenth-century psychological theory, argues persuasively that Cowper's writings "show that sympathy and sensibility—which should aid the self in gaining new impressions and communicating more freely with the rest of the world—may actually reinforce the self's isolation" (126). However, Cowper's isolation derives from a sense of loss, and his sympathy and sensibility, although assisting him to know the feelings of himself and others, brought him acutely back to his own sense of emptiness and worthlessness. See also Andrew Brink, *Loss and Symbolic Repair* (Hamilton, Ont.: Cromlech Press, 1977).

17 Ibid., 358.
18 *The Stricken Deer* (1929), 18.
19 To Margaret King, August 4, 1791, *Letters* 3 : 551. Cowper's mental affliction has been variously diagnosed as toxicity of uremia (Jean Boutin, *Etude Medico-Psychologique sur William Cowper* [Lyon, 1913]); as manic-depression (J. H. Lloyd, "The Case of William Cowper, the English Poet," *Archives of Neurology and Psychiatry* 24 [1930]); and as apparent asexuality (H. K. Gregory in his unpublished doctoral dissertation presented at Harvard in 1951: "The Prisoner and His Crimes: A Psychological Approach to the Life and Writings of William Cowper"). See also William B. Ober, *Boswell's Clap and Other Essays* (Carbondale: Southern Illinois University Press, 1979), 153–75.
20 *The Standard Edition of the Complete Psychological Works*, vol. 14, ed. James Strachey (1962), 243–44.
21 Ibid., 246.
22 Evna Furman, *A Child's Parent Dies: Studies in Childhood Bereavement* (New Haven: Yale University Press, 1974), 12.
23 John Bowlby, *Separation* (1973), 369–70.
24 *Spiritual Diary* (*Letters* 4 : 469).
25 To MK, January 26, 1792, *Letters* 4 : 7.
26 To SR, October 19, 1787, *Letters* 3 : 42.
27 JJ to WH, October 13, 1801, MS Bodleian.

28 To Mrs. Bodham, November 21, 1790, *Letters* 3 : 430.
29 To John Buchanan, September 5, 1795, *Letters* 4 : 452–53.
30 To HH, June 23, 1791, *Letters* 3 : 530.
31 JJ to WH, October 13, 1801, MS Bodleian.
32 *Ryskamp*, 56.
33 To WU, September 26, 1781, *Letters:* 523.
34 *Milford*, 396.
35 Ibid.
36 *Adelphi (Letters* 1 : 5).
37 Ibid.
38 Ibid.
39 Ibid., 6.
40 Ibid.
41 To John Duncombe, June 16, 1757, *Letters* 1 : 79.
42 To John Duncombe, January 11, 1759, *Letters* 1 : 85.
43 To MK, December 6, 1788, *Letters* 3 : 237.
44 *Joseph Andrews*, ed. Martin C. Battestin (Middletown, Conn.: Wesleyan University Press, 1967), 230.
45 To Frances Hill, April 21, 1786, *Letters* 2 : 525.
46 SG to WH, August 26, 1800, MS Fitzwilliam.
47 To WU, September 7, 1780, *Letters* 1 : 389.
48 Ibid.
49 To JN, February 18, 1781, *Letters* 1 : 446.
50 *Memoirs* (1806), 52–54.
51 *Adelphi (Letters* 1 : 7).
52 To WU, May 23, 1781, *Letters* 1 : 482.
53 Ibid.
54 *Adelphi (Letters* 1 : 7).
55 *Milford*, 416.
56 Sir Louis Namier and John Brooke, *The House of Commons, 1754–90* (1964), vol. 3 : 327.
57 *Poems*, 290.
58 *Hayley* 1 : 13.
59 *Poems*, 62.
60 To Walter Bagot, November 28, 1785, *Letters* 2 : 404.
61 JJ to WH, June 8, 1805, MS Fitzwilliam.
62 Sophy Bagot, *Links with the Past* (1901), 193–94.
63 To HH, November 30, 1785, *Letters* 2 : 408.
64 To Walter Bagot, March 12, 1749/50, *Letters* 1 : 65.
65 To HH, November 30, 1785, *Letters* 2 : 408.
66 Ibid.
67 To John Duncombe, December 31, 1757, *Letters* 1 : 80.
68 To Mrs. King, May 30, 1789, *Letters* 3 : 288; to HH, post July 31, 1762, *Letters* 1 : 89.
69 HH to JJ, January 7, 1802, MS Morgan.
70 *Adelphi (Letters* 1 : 7–8).
71 *Letters of Spencer Cowper, Dean of Durham*, ed. Edward Hughes, *Publications of the Surtees Society* 165 (1956) : 129–33.
72 To SR, October 19, 1787, *Letters* 3 : 43.
73 To MK, March 3, 1788, *Letters* 3 : 120–21.

74 HH to WH, July 1, 1801, MS British Library.
75 S. E. Brydges, *Autobiographical Memoir* (Paris, 1826), 7.
76 To Thomas Carwardine, June 11, 1792, *Letters* 4 : 110.
77 To JN, July 19, 1784, *Letters* 2 : 265.
78 To Chase Price, February 21, 1754, *Letters* 1 : 72.
79 To Chase Price, about 1754, *Letters* 1 : 74.

2 THEADORA

1 To HH, April 17, 1786, *Letters* 2 : 523.
2 *Milford*, 636.
3 Gray to Thomas Palgrave, July 24, 1759, *Correspondence,* vol. 2, ed. Paget Toynbee and Leonard Whibley (Oxford: Clarendon Press, 1935), 631.
4 To HH, April 17, 1786, *Letters* 2 : 523.
5 To Mrs. Newton, about August 6, 1781, *Letters* 1 : 505.
6 To HH, December 23–24, 1785, *Letters* 2 : 428.
7 HH to WH, October 25, 1801, MS British Library.
8 Ibid.
9 HH to JN, October 23, 1800, MS Bull.
10 *Poems*, 32.
11 JM to MC, July 18–21, 1754, MS Bodleian.
12 HH to WH, February 21, 1802, MS British Library.
13 *Poems*, 73.
14 HH to WH, July 13, 1801, MS British Library.
15 H. F. Cary, "Biographical Notice of William Cowper," in *The Poetical Works of William Cowper* (1839), vii–viii.
16 *Poems*, 29.
17 Ibid., 31.
18 Ibid., 16–17.
19 Ibid., 33.
20 SG claimed C's father did not have any objections to the marriage. Memoranda.
21 HH to WH, September 13, 1801, MS British Library.
22 HH to PM, June 4, 1804, MS Bodleian.
23 HH to WH, August 30, 1801, MS British Library.
24 Georgiana Spencer to TC, June 6, 1756, MS Althorp.
25 Georgiana Spencer to TC, May 11, 1754, MS Althorp.
26 JM to MC, December 14, 1762, MS Bodleian.
27 JM to MC, January 4, 1763, MS Bodleian.
28 JM to MC, January 15, 1763, MS Bodleian.
29 Georgiana Spencer to TC, November 10, [1763], MS Althorp.
30 Memoranda.
31 TC to WH, May 10, 1807, WH's *Vindication*, MS Fitzwilliam.
32 To JH, August 5, 1769, *Letters* 1 : 207.
33 JM to MC, about August 18, 1769, MS Bodleian.
34 PM to HH, May 26, 1804, quoted in Southey to Gorham, December 23, 1835, MS Olney.
35 HH to PM, June 4, 1804, MS Bodleian.
36 Ibid.

37 E. C. Worsley to Mrs. Richard Gifford, February 12, 1806, MS Berg Collection, New York Public Library.
38 HH to C, October 10, 1786, MS Barrett.
39 HH to WH, June 23, 1806, MS British Library.
40 *Adelphi (Letters* 1 : 8).
41 Ibid., 9.
42 To Chase Price, February 21, 1754, *Letters* 1 : 72.
43 To Clotworthy Rowley, August 1758, *Letters* 1 : 81–82.
44 Alfred Leedes Hunt, *Evangelical By-Paths* (1927), 89.
45 To John Duncombe, December 31, 1757, *Letters* 1 : 80.
46 To John Duncombe, January 11, 1759, *Letters* 1 : 85.
47 *Poems*, 26–27.

3 LONDON

 1 To JN, March 5, 1781, *Letters* 1 : 456.
 2 To HH, January 30, 1788, *Letters* 3 : 92.
 3 WH to Eliza Hayley, August 25, 1792, MS Fitzwilliam.
 4 Ibid.
 5 SG to WH, August 26, 1800, MS Fitzwilliam.
 6 Recollections.
 7 JJ to JN, May 25, 1778, MS Bull.
 8 *The Monthly Magazine* 9, pt. 1 (1800) : 409.
 9 To WU, October 5, 1781, *Letters* 1 : 527.
10 To JN, September 24, 1785, *Letters* 2 : 377.
11 *Milford*, 220.
12 To George Montague, October 16, 1769, *Horace Walpole Correspondence*, vol. 10, ed. W. S. Lewis and others (1941), 298.
13 *Life of Johnson*, vol. 2, ed. G. B. Hill, rev. L. F. Powell (Oxford: Oxford University Press, 1934), 75.
14 To George Montague, February 7, 1761, *Horace Walpole Correspondence*, vol. 9, ed. W. S. Lewis and others (1941), 337.
15 SG to WH, August 26, 1800, MS Fitzwilliam.
16 Ibid.
17 Ibid.
18 JN to Hannah More, April 11, 1787, MS Morgan.
19 To JH, April 20, [1777]. *Letters* 1 : 268.
20 Ibid.
21 George Colman to C, January 22, 1785, *Poems of William Cowper*, ed. J. C. Bailey (1905), lv–lvi.
22 Boswell, *London Journal, 1762–3*, ed. F. S. Pottle (New York, 1950), 266.
23 Private Papers of James Boswell, MS Yale.
24 W. Kendrick, ed., *The Poetical Works of Robert Lloyd* (1774), vol. 1 : xxv.
25 W. W. Rouse Ball, *Cambridge Papers* (1919), 223.
26 To HH, September 4, 1765, *Letters* 1 : 113.
27 As cited in *Ryskamp*, 179.
28 See Charles Ryskamp, "New Poems by William Cowper," *The Book Collector* 22 (1973) : 443–78.
29 *Private Correspondence of David Garrick* (1832), vol. 2 : 338.

30 To wu, [March? 1780?], *Letters* 1 : 319.
31 Ibid., 320.
32 To Henry Mackenzie, December 10, 1787, *Letters* 3 : 66.
33 *Connoisseur* 120 (May 13, 1756) and 111 (March 11, 1756).
34 To John Duncombe, June 12, 1759, *Letters* 1 : 86.
35 JH to WH, February 19, 1802, MS Barham Johnson.
36 *Milford,* 361.
37 HH to WH, February 11, 1801, MS British Library.
38 To JH, November 1769, *Letters* 1 : 210.
39 *Milford,* 361.
40 See Sir William Holdsworth, *A History of English Law,* vol. 12 (London: Methuen, 1938), 16.
41 Ibid., 77.
42 *The Spectator,* no. 2 (March 2, 1711), vol. 1, ed. Donald F. Bond (Oxford: Clarendon Press, 1965), 9.
43 *Dunciad,* book 4, l. 568.
44 *Adelphi (Letters* 1 : 8).
45 See *Ryskamp,* 65.
46 To SR, June 20, 1789, *Letters* 3 : 298.
47 *Ryskamp,* 72.
48 To SR, July 23, 1789, *Letters* 3 : 305.
49 See *Ryskamp,* 68 n. 2.
50 To John Duncombe, November 21, 1758, *Letters* 1 : 83.
51 To the Nonsense Club, *Letters* 1 : 89.
52 As printed in *Ryskamp,* 206.
53 Ibid., 209.
54 Ibid., 208.
55 *Connoisseur* 138 (September 16, 1756).
56 Ibid., 134.
57 Ibid., 115.
58 To wu, October 31, 1779, *Letters* 1 : 307.
59 Ibid.
60 To wu, January 17, 1782, *Letters* 2 : 9.
61 JJ's notation (November 14, 1788) on the second flyleaf of C's copy of a 1715 translation of the *Iliad.* Collection of the late Sir Geoffrey Keynes.
62 To JJO, about January 15, 1781, *Letters* 1 : 433.
63 Ashley Cowper, *The Office of the Clerk of the Parliaments* (1763), 2–3.
64 *Adelphi (Letters* 1 : 14–15).
65 Ibid., 15.
66 Ibid., 16.
67 Ibid.
68 Ibid.
69 Ibid., 17, 18, 21.
70 Ibid., 24.
71 Ibid., 28.
72 To JN, October 20, 1787, *Letters* 3 : 44.
73 Robert Burton, *The Anatomy of Melancholy,* vol. 1, ed. Holbrook Jackson (1932), 386.
74 Freud, *The Standard Edition of the Complete Psychological Works,* vol. 14, ed. James Strachey (1962), 243–44.

75 *Adelphi (Letters* 1, 22, 23).
76 Horton Davies, *Worship and Theology in England, from Watts and Wesley to Maurice, 1690–1850* (Princeton: Princeton University Press, 1961), 12.
77 *Adelphi (Letters* 1 : 26).
78 As cited by T. C. Duncan Eaves and Ben D. Kimpel in *Samuel Richardson, A Biography* (Oxford: Clarendon Press, 1971), 553.
79 *Adelphi (Letters* 1 : 7).
80 A. C. Hobart Seymour, *The Life and Times of Selina, Countess of Huntingdon,* vol. 1 (1844), 165.
81 As cited by Falconer Madan, *The Madan Family* (1933), 109.
82 Ibid., 107.
83 To MC, March 11, 1766, *Letters* 1 : 134, and *Adelphi (Letters* 1 : 30–31).
84 Ibid., 32.
85 Book 4, l. 110. See *Adelphi (Letters* 1 : 28).
86 *Adelphi (Letters* 1 : 26).
87 Ibid., 28.
88 Ibid., 29.
89 Ibid.
90 Ibid.
91 Boswell Journal: MS Yale. I am indebted for this reference to my friend, Dr. Irma S. Lustig.

4 THE LIFE OF RETREAT

1   *Adelphi (Letters* 1 : 13).
2   See *Ryskamp,* 160.
3   *GM* 77, pt. 1 (1807) : 500.
4   *Adelphi (Letters* 1 : 33–40).
5   To HH, January 14–16, 1787, *Letters* 3 : 14–15.
6   *Adelphi (Letters* 1 : 38).
7   Ibid., 10.
8   Ibid., 43.
9   *Milford,* 166.
10 To HH, January 2, 1786, *Letters* 2 : 443.
11 *The Norfolk Poetical Miscellany,* vol. 2 (1744), 268–70.
12 HH to WH, October 25, 1801, MS British Library.
13 *Milford,* 166–67.
14 *Adelphi (Letters* 1 : 40).
15 Ibid., 42.
16 See C to JN, October 16, 1785, *Letters* 2 : 385.
17 *Spiritual Diary (Letters* 4 : 468).
18 To WH, April 6, 1792, *Letters* 4 : 51.
19 Patricia Meyer Spacks, *Imagining a Self* (Cambridge: Harvard University Press, 1976), 17. In the course of her essay on Cowper, one of the finest pieces of writing devoted to him, Professor Spacks says: "The history of the heart, as Cowper relates it, records a struggle to love: to love God, others, the self" (50). I agree. Although Cowper struggled to love, he was often incapacitated in this regard, and in this book I have tried to suggest the etiology of this inability.
20 *Rural Rides,* vol. 1 (Everyman's Library ed., 1957), 77.

21 To HH, September 14, 1765, *Letters* 1 : 115; to JH, October 25, 1765, *Letters* 1 : 121–22; *Adelphi* (*Letters* 1 : 46).
22 *Adelphi* (*Letters* 1 : 45).
23 Ibid., 46.
24 To Margaret King, March 12, 1790, *Letters* 3 : 359.
25 To JH, October 25, 1765, *Letters* 1 : 122.
26 Memoranda.
27 SH to WH, October 4, 1800, MS Fitzwilliam.
28 Elizabeth Pennington to Samuel Richardson. No date given. Letter was offered for sale by Winifred Myers, catalogue 351 (April 1948), 263. See T. C. Duncan Eaves and Ben D. Kimpel, *Samuel Richardson, A Biography* (Oxford: Clarendon Press, 1971), 453–54.
29 Cited by Myers.
30 SG to WH, October 4, 1800, MS Fitzwilliam.
31 Ibid.
32 HH to JN, May 29, 1795, MS Bull.
33 To HH, January 2, 1786, *Letters* 2 : 442–43.
34 SG to WH, October 4, 1800, MS Fitzwilliam.
35 To MC, October 20, 1766, *Letters* 1 : 152–53.
36 SG to WH, October 4, 1800, MS Fitzwilliam.
37 To JM, August 10, 1767, *Letters* 1 : 176.
38 Southey to Craddock, January 5, 1836, MS Fitzwilliam.
39 SG to WH, October 4, 1800, MS Fitzwilliam.
40 To JM, December 10, 1767, *Letters* 1 : 187.
41 To JH, October 25, 1765, *Letters* 1 : 122.
42 To JM, July 10, 1767, *Letters* 1 : 169.
43 Ibid., 170.
44 Ibid.
45 Ibid.
46 To JM, August 10, 1767, *Letters* 1 : 175.
47 To JM, March 1, 1768, *Letters* 1 : 191.
48 As cited by Josiah Bull in *John Newton* (The Religious Tract Society: London, n.d.), 27.
49 JN to WB, March 5, 1794, MS Bull.
50 *An Authentic Narrative* . . . (1764), 130.
51 Ibid., 41.
52 *An Authentic Narrative*, 159.
53 Horton Davies, *Worship and Theology in England from Watts and Wesley to Maurice, 1690–1850* (Princeton: Princeton University Press, 1961), 191. I am using the term "Anglican Evangelicalism" as defined by Davies. According to Davies, "Evangelical Methodism begins with Wesley's Aldersgate street experience in 1738, and Evangelical Anglicanism with either the conversion of William Grimshaw in 1742 or the appointment of William Romaine as Lecturer at St. Dunstan's in the West, London, in 1748" (210 n).
54 Ibid., 210.
55 As cited in G. R. Balleine, *A History of the Evangelical Party* (1908), 3.
56 Ibid., 18–19.
57 Journal entry for May 24, 1738, cited in *Balleine*, 19.
58 As cited in *Balleine*, 35.

59 Davies, *Worship and Theology*, 216.
60 *Letters* 1 : 566.
61 JN's diary for 1773, MS Bull.
62 *Cardiphonia* (2 vols., 1781), vol. 1 : 67.
63 Ibid., 76.
64 Ibid., 43.
65 Ibid., vol. 2 : 103.
66 Ibid., 200.
67 *MR* 65 (1781) : 203.
68 Josiah Bull, "The Early Years of the Poet Cowper at Olney," pt. 1, *Sunday at Home*, pt. 146 (1866), 349.
69 *The Holy and the Daemonic from Sir Thomas Browne to William Blake* (Princeton: Princeton University Press, 1982), 346.
70 To Mary Newton, March 4, 1780, *Letters* 1 : 321.
71 MS Princeton.
72 To JN, September 30, 1786, *Letters* 2 : 591.
73 To JN, April 11, 1799, *Letters* 4 : 466.
74 JN to MU, April 10, 1779, MS Lambeth Palace. In my discussion of John Newton, I have attempted to define his relationship to Cowper in terms of the known, not assumed, facts. I think there is ample evidence to prove that Cowper became uneasy with Newton's conception of literature and art and that he then renounced him as a mentor. I think there is little, or no, evidence to demonstrate that Newton's personality or religious beliefs unduly exacerbated Cowper's melancholia—just as I do not think that Evangelicalism is responsible for intensifying Cowper's depressive state.

Donald Davie in the 1976 Clark Lectures (*A Gathered Church* [London: Routledge & Kegan Paul, 1978] admits to many of the deficiencies which have been laid at the door of English Dissent, but he also provides a valuable analysis of a movement whose great strengths are sometimes neglected. It should also be noted that, although Cowper became a defender of Evangelicalism in *Poems* and *The Task*, those poems are not informed with a knowledge of the niceties of the theological doctrines of that movement.

5 OLNEY

1 See C to Mrs. Madan, March 1, 1768, *Letters* 1 : 191.
2 *Letters* 1 : 175 and n. 7.
3 *Poems*, 455.
4 To WU, June 8, 1783, *Letters* 2 : 139.
5 To WB, [August 3, 1784], *Letters* 2 : 269.
6 To JN, August 16, 1781, *Letters* 1 : 507.
7 Ibid.
8 Entry for February 2, 1779, MS Bull.
9 *Poems*, 393.
10 To JN, May 22, 1784, *Letters* 2 : 251.
11 To JN, December 24, 1784, *Letters* 2 : 314.
12 To JN, February 19, 1785, *Letters* 2 : 327–28.
13 To JN, November 17, 1783, *Letters* 2 : 180–81.
14 To JN, August 21, 1780, *Letters* 1 : 382.
15 To JN, March 29, 1784, *Letters* 2 : 229–30.

16   MU to Mrs. Balls, October 25, 1791, MS Barham Johnson.
17   MC to PM, March 25, 1786, MS British Library.
18   JN to C, February 17, 1781, MS Princeton.
19   As cited in JJ to CJ, July 31, 1810, MS Barham Johnson.
20   *Adelphi (Letters* 1 : 50).
21   Ibid.
22   Ibid., 51.
23   William Cole, as cited in *Ryskamp,* 10.
24   MS note by Richard Gough in his copy (Bodleian) of R. Masters, *The History of Corpus Christi College* (Cambridge, 1753).
25   *Adelphi (Letters* 1 : 51).
26   Ibid.
27   Ibid., 52.
28   Ibid.
29   Ibid.
30   Ibid., 53.
31   Ibid., 56.
32   Ibid., 58–59.
33   Ibid., 59.
34   Ibid., 60.
35   Ibid.
36   To WU, March 31, 1770, *Letters* 1 : 229.
37   *Adelphi (Letters* 1 : 53–54).
38   To JM, July 18, 1767, *Letters* 1 : 174–75.
39   WH, cited by WB in comments on JN's diary, MS Bull.
40   WB, commentary on JN's diary for 1771, MS Bull.
41   Entry for June 26, 1779, MS Bull.
42   *Connoisseur* 120 (May 13, 1756).
43   Quoted in Charles S. Phillips, *Hymnody Past and Present* (New York: Macmillan, 1937), 171.
44   Preface to *Olney Hymns* (1779), xiv.
45   Madeleine Forell Marshall and Janet Todd, *English Congregational Hymns in the Eighteenth Century* (Lexington: University Press of Kentucky, 1982), 92. In this excellent study, the authors justifiably point out that the tendency to read Cowper's hymns in an autobiographical manner must be tempered by the realization that many of the most seemingly personal portions of his hymns have strong similarities to the writings of other hymnographers. Although I think it is possible to read Cowper's hymns as a disguised spiritual autobiography, I agree that the conventionality of some of Cowper's hymns must be kept in mind. R. D. Stock in his comprehensive study, *The Holy and the Daemonic from Sir Thomas Browne to William Blake* (Princeton: Princeton University Press, 1982) makes a similar point (334–35).
46   *The New Oxford Book of Christian Verse* (Oxford: Oxford University Press, 1981), xxv.
47   *Poems,* 148.
48   Ibid., 158.
49   Ibid., 180.
50   See C to Mrs. Bodham, February 27, 1790, and n. 1, *Letters* 3 : 350.
51   Line 2 of the first *Divine Meditation.*

52 *The George Eliot Letters*, vol. 1, ed. Gordon S. Haight (New Haven: Yale University Press, 1954), 100.
53 *Poems*, 191.
54 Ibid., 177–78.
55 Ibid., 176.
56 To JH, November 5, 1772, *Letters* 1 : 258.
57 HH to WH, August 30, 1801, MS British Library.
58 JN to JJ, March 5, 1796, MS Barham Johnson.
59 Ibid.
60 Newton's fragmentary life of Cowper, MS McMaster.
61 Ibid.
62 WH to HH, September 27, 1801, MS British Library.
63 HH to WH, June 23, 1801, MS British Library.
64 *Spiritual Diary (Letters* 4 : 467).
65 To JN, October 16, 1785, *Letters* 2 : 385.
66 JN to JJ, August 23, 1779, MS Barham Johnson.
67 To HH, January 16, 1786, *Letters* 2 : 455.
68 MU to MN, October 7, 1773, *Letters* 1 : 260.
69 JN to Thomas Bowman, June 21, 1774, MS Osborn Collection, Yale.
70 To HH, February 9, 1786, *Letters* 2 : 475.
71 JN to JJ, November 28, 1795, MS Barham Johnson.
72 *Poems*, 209–10.
73 JN's diary, entries for August 14, 1775, and December 1775, MS Bull.
74 As quoted by Bernard Martin in *John Newton, A Biography* (London: Heinemann, 1950), 255.
75 WB to JN, August 4, 1780, MS Bull.
76 To WU, June 8, 1783, *Letters* 2 : 140.
77 *Poems*, 253, 360.
78 To WB, June 3, 1783, *Letters* 2 : 138.
79 To JN, May 10, 1780, *Letters* 1 : 342.
80 *GM* 54, pt. 1 (1784) : 413.
81 Ibid., 412.
82 Ibid., 414.
83 To JH, May 13, 1776, *Letters* 1 : 261.
84 To JH, June 6, 1778, *Letters* 1 : 282.
85 *Milford*, 177.
86 Ibid., 178.
87 Ibid., 178–79.
88 MS Bruce Papers, Bodleian.
89 To JN, December 16, 1786, *Letters* 2 : 618.

6 POEMS

1 *Hayley* 1 : 106.
2 To WU, May 1, 1779, *Letters* 1 : 291.
3 To JH, October 2, 1779, *Letters* 1 : 305.
4 To WU, June 8, 1780, *Letters* 1 : 350; to WU, June 18, 1780, *Letters* 1 : 353.
5 To JN, July 31, 1780, *Letters* 1 : 372.
6 To JN, February 6, 1780, *Letters* 1 : 313.
7 To WU, post November 9, 1780, *Letters* 1 : 404.

8   To JN, November 27, 1780, *Letters* 1 : 413.
9   To JN, December 2, 1780, *Letters* 1 : 418.
10 *Poems*, 234.
11 *CR* 51 (1781) : 74.
12 JN to C, February 17, 1781, MS Princeton.
13 To WU, August 6, 1780, *Letters* 1 : 375.
14 To WU, December 2, 1780, *Letters* 1 : 415.
15 To JN, December 21, 1780, *Letters* 1 : 424.
16 To JN, July 31, 1780, *Letters* 1 : 372.
17 To JN, December 21, 1780, *Letters* 1 : 425.
18 Ibid.
19 Ibid.
20 To JN, February 4, 1781, *Letters* 1 : 438.
21 To JN, February 18, 1781, *Letters* 1 : 444.
22 To JN, March 5, 1781, *Letters* 1 : 456.
23 Ibid., 455.
24 To JN, March 18, 1781, *Letters* 1 : 458–59.
25 Ibid., 459.
26 Ibid.
27 Henry James, *The Treacherous Years: 1895–1901* (New York: Avon Books, 1969), 16.
28 To JN, April 8, 1781, *Letters* 1 : 462.
29 To JN, April 23, 1781, *Letters* 1 : 465.
30 To JN, April 25, 1781, *Letters* 1 : 467.
31 To JH, May 9, 1781, *Letters* 1 : 470.
32 To WU, May 23, 1781, *Letters* 1 : 483.
33 To JN, July 12, 1781, *Letters* 1 : 497.
34 To JN, July 22, 1781, *Letters* 1 : 499.
35 To Mrs. Newton, about August 6, 1781, *Letters* 1 : 506.
36 To JN, August 25, 1781, *Letters* 1 : 512.
37 To JN, October 4, 1781, *Letters* 1 : 526.
38 As cited by Gerald P. Tyson, *Joseph Johnson, A Liberal Publisher* (Iowa City: University of Iowa Press, 1979), 1.
39 To WU, May 1, 1781, *Letters* 1 : 469.
40 To WU, May 23, 1781, *Letters* 1 : 480.
41 To JN, January 13, 1782, *Letters* 2 : 6.
42 To JN, May 21, 1781, *Letters* 1 : 478.
43 *Russell*, 40.
44 To JN, July 7, 1781, *Letters* 1 : 495.
45 To JJO, February 17, 1782, *Letters* 2 : 22.
46 To JN, October 4, 1781, *Letters* 1 : 526.
47 To JN, October 22, 1781, *Letters* 1 : 534–35.
48 *Poems*, 568.
49 JJO to C, February 18, 1782, MS Morgan.
50 To the Newtons, March 14, 1782, *Letters* 2 : 36.
51 Ibid., 37.
52 *Poems*, 569–70.
53 John D. Baird, "Cowper's Concept of Truth," *Studies in Eighteenth-Century Culture*, vol. 7, ed. Roseann Runte (Madison: University of Wisconsin Press, 1978), 372.

54   *Poems,* 258.
55   c to JJO, about January 15, 1781, *Letters* 1 : 433.
56   *Poems,* 254-55.
57   Ibid., 254.
58   Ibid., 261, 260.
59   Ibid.
60   Ibid., 279.
61   Ibid., 270.
62   Ibid., 262.
63   Ibid., 280.
64   Ibid., 346-47.
65   Ibid., 280.
66   Ibid., 321.
67   To WU, June 24, 1781, *Letters* 1 : 490.
68   *Poems,* 297.
69   Ibid., 316.
70   Ibid., 304.
71   Ibid., 300.
72   Ibid., 316.
73   To Mrs. Newton, about August 6, 1781, *Letters* 1 : 506.
74   To JN, October 22, 1781, *Letters* 1 : 534.
75   *Poems,* 360.
76   Ibid., 354.
77   Ibid., 383.
78   Ibid., 392.
79   Ibid., 396.
80   Ibid., 398.
81   To WU, June 18, 1780, *Letters* 1 : 353.
82   *MR* 67 (1782) : 262-63.
83   *GM* 52, pt. 1 (1782) : 130.
84   *The London Magazine* 51 (1782), 245.
85   *CR* 53 (1782) : 290.
86   To JN, [February 2, 1782], *Letters* 2 : 15.
87   To WU, May 27, 1782, *Letters* 2 : 49.
88   To WU, June 12, 1782, *Letters* 2 : 54.
89   To JN, November 7, 1781, *Letters* 1 : 538.
90   *Poems,* 256.
91   To HH, October 12, 1785, *Letters* 2 : 382-83.
92   To Mrs. Bodham, February 27, 1790, *Letters* 3 : 349.
93   Ibid., 350.
94   To Thomas Park, March 10, 1792, *Letters* 4 : 26.
95   To MC, October 19, 1781, *Letters* 1 : 531.

7   LADY AUSTEN AND WILLIAM UNWIN; COWPER'S LETTERS

1   SG to WH, September 18, 1800, MS Fitzwilliam.
2   SG to WH, September 9, 1800, MS Fitzwilliam.
3   To JH, July 7, 1781, *Letters* 1 : 494-95.
4   To WU, July 29, 1781, *Letters* 1 : 503.
5   To WU, August 25, 1781, *Letters* 1 : 515.

6 To JN, July 12, 1781, *Letters* 1 : 497.
7 To Lady Austen, December 17, 1781, *Letters* 1 : 560.
8 To WU, February 9, 1782, *Letters* 2 : 18–19.
9 Ibid., 19.
10 Ibid.
11 To WU, March 7, 1782, *Letters* 2 : 32–33.
12 To WU, February 24, 1782, *Letters* 2 : 24.
13 To WU, March 7, 1782, *Letters* 2 : 32.
14 Ibid., 33.
15 To WU, July 3, 1782, *Letters* 2 : 62.
16 To WU, August 27, 1782, *Letters* 2 : 73.
17 Ibid., 74.
18 To WU, about October 1782, *Letters* 2 : 81.
19 Ibid.
20 *Milford*, 352.
21 To WU, January 19, 1783, *Letters* 2 : 98.
22 To JN, February 24, 1783, *Letters* 2 : 110.
23 To JN, February 1784, *Letters* 2 : 210.
24 To HH, January 10, 1786, *Letters* 2 : 447.
25 SG to WH, September 9, 1800, MS Fitzwilliam.
26 To WU, July 12, 1784, *Letters* 2 : 262.
27 *Hayley* 2 (1806), 135–37.
28 Memoranda.
29 *Adelphi* (*Letters* 1 : 45).
30 Wilberforce to his wife, April 16, 1786, MS Fitzwilliam.
31 WU to JM, June 23, [1780], MS Rochester.
32 Ibid.
33 Ibid.
34 To WU, December 2, 1779, *Letters* 1 : 310.
35 *Poems*, 225.
36 To WU, February 6, 1781, *Letters* 1 : 440.
37 Ibid.
38 To WU, April 6, 1780, *Letters* 1 : 329.
39 To WU, about February 7, 1779, *Letters* 1 : 290.
40 HH to WH, November 9, 1800, MS British Library.
41 To John Duncombe, January 11, 1759, *Letters* 1 : 84.
42 To JM, January 15, 1768, *Letters* 1 : 189–90.
43 To JN, April 5, 1783, *Letters* 2 : 121.
44 To WU, February 27, 1780, *Letters* 1 : 316–17.
45 Ibid., 317.
46 To WU, June 8, 1780, *Letters* 1 : 348.
47 To WU, February 27, 1780, *Letters* 1 : 317.
48 To WU, June 8, 1780, *Letters* 1 : 348.
49 To HH, March 20, 1786, *Letters* 2 : 498.
50 To WU, August 6, 1780, *Letters* 1 : 374.
51 To JN, August 16, 1781, *Letters* 1 : 508.
52 To WU, December 22–24, 1781, *Letters* 1 : 567.
53 *The Complete Essays of Montaigne*, vol. 3, trans. Donald M. Frame (Stanford: Stanford University Press, 1965), 13.834 b.
54 Ibid.

8 THE TASK

1 Preface to *Posthumous Poems* (1815).
2 To WU, August 3, 1782, *Letters* 2 : 70.
3 To WU, about September 1782, *Letters* 2 : 77.
4 To WB, about August 3, 1783, *Letters* 2 : 153.
5 To WU, September 7, 1783, *Letters* 2 : 157–58.
6 *Milford*, 684.
7 Ibid.
8 Ibid., 501.
9 Ibid., 348.
10 Ibid.
11 Ibid., 351.
12 To WU, November 24, 1781, *Letters* 1 : 542.
13 Ibid., 542–43.
14 To JN, June 21, 1784, *Letters* 2 : 255.
15 To WU, February 9, 1782, *Letters* 2 : 16.
16 Ibid., 17.
17 To WB, about May 28, 1782, *Letters* 2 : 52.
18 To JN, April 20, 1783, *Letters* 2 : 127.
19 To JN, July 27, 1783, *Letters* 2 : 151.
20 To JH, February 4, 1784, *Letters* 2 : 210.
21 To WU, April 5, 1784, *Letters* 2 : 231.
22 To WU, July 12, 1784, *Letters* 2 : 263–64.
23 To WU, January 17, 1782, *Letters* 2 : 9.
24 *Prefaces, Biographical and Critical* . . . (10 vols., 1779–81), vol. 6 : 44.
25 To WU, January 17, 1782, *Letters* 2 : 10.
26 *The Literary Works of Matthew Prior*, vol. 1, ed. H. Bunker Wright and Monroe K. Spears (Oxford: Clarendon Press, 1959), 360.
27 To WU, about September 1782. *Letters* 2 : 76–77. Although it has been suggested by some commentators that Cowper adapted associationism to literary purposes (see T. E. Blom, "Eighteenth-Century Reflexive Process Poetry," *Eighteenth-Century Studies* 10 [1976] : 52–72; and Martin Priestman, *Cowper's Task, Structure and Influence* [Cambridge: Cambridge University Press, 1983], 22), Cowper's likely indebtedness to Hartley by way of Beattie has not been considered. In addition to Blom and Priestman, I have found three treatments of the structure of *The Task* particularly helpful in writing this chapter: Richard Feingold, *Nature and Society, Later Eighteenth-Century Uses of Pastoral and Georgic* (New Brunswick, N.J.: Rutgers University Press, 1978); Morris Golden, *In Search of Stability: The Poetry of William Cowper* (New York, 1960); and Patricia Meyer Spacks *The Poetry of Vision* (Cambridge: Harvard University Press, 1967).
28 To WU, April 5, 1784, *Letters* 2 : 231.
29 Ibid.
30 James Beattie, *The Minstrel . . . With Some Other Poems* (2 vols., 1779), vol. 1 : vii.
31 Ibid., 60.
32 Ibid., 67.
33 Ibid., 54.
34 Ibid., 75.

35 *Milford*, 183.
36 James Beattie, *Original Poems and Translations* (1760), 26.
37 *Poems*, 375–76.
38 David Hartley, *Observations on Man* (2 vols., 1749), vol. 1 : 383.
39 *Dissertations, Moral and Critical*, vol. 1 (Dublin, 1783), 95–96.
40 Ibid., 102–3.
41 Ibid., vol. 2 : 385–86.
42 Ibid., vol. 2 : 402.
43 Ibid., vol. 2: 388.
44 To JN, April 26, 1784, *Letters* 2 : 237. There have been various attempts to trace the influence of other eighteenth-century writers upon Cowper, but none of these arguments is convincing. For example, Cowper certainly read Thomson's *The Seasons*. However, there is almost no evidence to indicate Cowper's familiarity with this poem, except for his comment to William Unwin of January 17, 1782 (*Letters* 2 : 11) when citing practitioners of blank verse to whom Samuel Johnson might have turned to see the beauties of that form: "I should think too, that Thomson's Seasons might afford him some useful lessons." In the face of such evidence, Lodwick Hartley, *William Cowper, The Continuing Revaluation* (Chapel Hill: University of North Carolina Press, 1960) comes to the only realistic conclusion: "Thomson had used blank verse in the same sort of poetry and, like Cowper, his great model was John Milton. But Cowper imitated neither" (63); "Thomson, a convert to Deism, glorified Nature as an embodiment of the divine idea. Not so Cowper. In *The Task* he insists, as he had in 'Retirement,' that, though Nature bears 'the stamp and signature of God,' it is not God" (67).
      The earliest readers of *The Task* were reminded of Edward Young's *Night Thoughts* (see n. 93 below), and Nathaniel Cotton, Cowper's physician at St. Albans, had been a close friend of Young's. Cowper had certainly read Young's poem, but, again, the three references in Cowper's correspondence (*Letters* 2 : 68 and n., 552; 3 : 69 and n.) to *Night Thoughts* do not point to any real influence upon him. As in the case of Thomson, the influence is so diffuse as to be unrecognizable.
      A much more likely, earlier influence upon Cowper in *The Task* is Andrew Marvell, who constantly employed the conceit that the mind becomes most active, ironically, in retreat.
45 To WU, October 31, 1779, *Letters* 1 : 307–8.
46 Book 3, lines 19–26.
47 Book 7, lines 24–29.
48 Dustin Griffin treats Cowper's relationship to Milton comprehensively in "Cowper, Milton, and the Recovery of Paradise," *Essays in Criticism* 31, no. 1 (January 1981): 15–26.
49 To WU, April 5, 1784, *Letters* 2 : 231.
50 *Milford*, 129.
51 To HH, January 16, 1786, *Letters* 2 : 456.
52 To WB, February 22, 1784, *Letters* 2 : 217.
53 To WB, [August 3], 1784, *Letters* 2 : 269.
54 To WU, September 11, 1784, *Letters* 2 : 275.
55 To WU, October 10, 1784, *Letters* 2 : 284.
56 Ibid., 285.
57 Ibid.

58 To WU, October 20, 1784, *Letters* 2 : 285.
59 To JN, October 30, 1784, *Letters* 2 : 291.
60 See C to WU, November 1, 1784, *Letters* 2 : 292.
61 To JN, July 31, 1780, *Letters* 1 : 372.
62 To JN, November 27, 1784, *Letters* 2 : 300.
63 To WU, October 10, 1784, *Letters* 2 : 285.
64 To JN, November 27, 1784, *Letters* 2 : 301.
65 To WU, October 10, 1784, *Letters* 2 : 284.
66 To JN, November 27, 1784, *Letters* 2 : 300.
67 Ibid., 301.
68 To JN, December 11, 1784, *Letters* 2 : 309.
69 To JN, December 24, 1784, *Letters* 2 : 313.
70 Ibid.
71 To JN, June 25, 1785, *Letters* 2 : 358.
72 To WU, August 27, 1785, *Letters* 2 : 370.
73 To JN, August 6, 1785, *Letters* 2 : 367.
74 Ibid.
75 To WU, October 20, 1784, *Letters* 2 : 286.
76 To WU, November 20, 1784, *Letters* 2 : 299–300.
77 To WU, October 20, 1784, *Letters* 2 : 286.
78 Ibid.
79 To WU, November 1, 1784, *Letters* 2 : 293.
80 To WU, May 8, [1785], *Letters* 2 : 348.
81 *Milford*, 202.
82 Ibid., 203.
83 David Boyd in "Satire and Pastoral in *The Task*," *Papers on Language and Literature* 10 (1974), argues that Cowper was confused as to whether he was writing pastoral or satire. Although Boyd states his position in a way that is somewhat dismissive of Cowper, I do think there are two voices in the poem: one is essentially lyrical and confessional (pastoral) and the other castigates society and remains distrustful of art (satire).
84 *Milford*, 135.
85 Ibid., 172.
86 Ibid., 187.
87 Ibid., 188.
88 Ibid., 182.
89 Ibid., 241.
90 To WU, November 28, 1785, *Letters* 2 : 405.
91 *CR* 60 (1785), 251.
92 Ibid., 253.
93 *The London Magazine*, enlarged ser. 4 (1785) : 262.
94 *The London Chronicle*, no. 4521 (November 8–10, 1785) : 449.
95 *The European Magazine* 8 (1785) : 449.
96 Ibid.
97 *GM* 55, pt. 2 (1785) : 985.
98 *The New Review* 9 (1786) : 31.
99 *MR*, 1st ser. 74 (1786) : 416–17.
100 Ibid., 418.
101 See Lodwick Hartley, *William Cowper, The Continuing Revaluation* (Chapel Hill: University of North Carolina Press, 1960), 3–15.

102 See Abbie Findlay Potts, *Wordsworth's "Prelude": A Study of Its Literary Form* (Ithaca: Cornell University Press, 1953), 350–57. In his recent book *Cowper's Task, Structure and Influence* (Cambridge: Cambridge University Press, 1983), Martin Priestman devotes chapter 9 (162–98) to an extensive comparison of *The Task* to *The Prelude*.

103 For a more extended discussion of the two types of "employment" of Milton, see Wallace Jackson, *The Probable and the Marvelous: Blake, Wordsworth, and the Eighteenth-Century Critical Tradition* (Athens: University of Georgia Press, 1978), 93.

104 *Preface to Lyrical Ballads (1800)*, in *The Prose Works of William Wordsworth*, vol. 1, ed. W. J. B. Owen and Jane Worthington Smyser (Oxford: Clarendon Press, 1974), 118.

105 Ibid., vol. 3, 28. P. M. S. Dawson in "Cowper and the Russian Ice Palace," *The Review of English Studies*, n.s. 31 (1980), 440–43, suggests persuasively that the description of Kubla Khan's pleasure dome was influenced by Cowper's portrayal of Catherine the Great's ice palace; although Coleridge's schoolboy reminiscences in *Frost at Midnight* are autobiographical, their formulation in that poem may be derived from Cowper. In a similar way, Shelley's "herd-abandoned deer struck by the hunter's dart" (*Adonais*, l. 297) may be indebted to the "stricken deer" passage in book 3 of *The Task*, although both Cowper and Shelley are drawing upon a common source: the myth of Acteon.

106 To JN, January 13, 1787, *Letters* 3 : 10.

9   LADY HESKETH

1   Note in HH's hand at the top of the holograph of C to JJ, November 10, 1767.

2   To JM, July 18, 1767, *Letters* 1 : 174.

3   HH to C, October 10, 1785, MS Barrett.

4   HH to SG, May 31, 1800, MS Princeton.

5   HH to C, October 10, 1785, MS Barrett.

6   Ibid.

7   To HH, October 12, 1785, *Letters* 2 : 381.

8   Ibid.

9   Ibid., 382.

10 Abstract of Sir Thomas's will at LRO (DDF 413.2).

11 HH to William Farington, November 18, 1779, MS LRO.

12 HH to William Farington, April 18, 1780, MS LRO.

13 HH to C, October 10, 1785, MS Barrett.

14 HH to JJ, April 16, 1788, MS Barham Johnson.

15 *Northanger Abbey*, 3d ed., vol. 5, ed. R. W. Chapman (Oxford: Oxford University Press, 1933), 25.

16 HH to JJ, December 18, 1797, MS Barham Johnson.

17 *Persuasion*, vol. 5 : 150.

18 *Diaries and Letters of Madame D'Arblay*, vol. 1, ed. Austin Dobson (1904), 445.

19 Ibid., vol. 5 : 108.

20 *Thraliana*, vol. 1, ed. Katherine C. Balderston (Oxford: Clarendon Press, 1951), 444.

21 Ibid., vol. 1 : 478.
22 HH to WH, January 28, 1802, MS Princeton.
23 HH to SG, August 16, 1794, MS Princeton.
24 HH to WH, April 18, 1804, MS Olney.
25 Ibid.
26 HH to WH, October 24, 1805, MS Olney.
27 HH to JJ, September 16, 1799, MS Barham Johnson.
28 HH to WH, October 30, 1804, MS Olney.
29 HH to WH, November 24, 1804, MS Olney.
30 HH to WH, January 28, 1802, MS Princeton.
31 HH to William Farington, February 4, 1779, MS LRO.
32 *Thraliana,* vol. 1 : 411.
33 HH to William Farington, April 4, 1775, MS LRO.
34 HH to WH, April 18, 1804, MS Olney.
35 HH to WH, May 15, 1806, MS Olney.
36 HH to WH, July 12, 1806, MS Olney.
37 HH to WH, March 21, 1804, MS Olney.
38 Ibid.
39 To HH, November 9, 1785, *Letters* 2 : 393.
40 Ibid., 394.
41 To HH, May 1, 1788, *Letters* 3 : 154.
42 To HH, February 1, 1788, *Letters* 3 : 93.
43 See C to HH, October 12, 1785, *Letters* 2 : 382–83.
44 To HH, December 7–8, 1785, *Letters* 2 : 417.
45 To HH, January 23, 1786, *Letters* 2 : 461.
46 To HH, January 31, 1786, *Letters* 2 : 469.
47 To HH, January 10, 1786, *Letters* 2 : 446.
48 To HH, February 9, 1786, *Letters* 2 : 474.
49 To HH, May 15, 1786, *Letters* 2 : 540–41.
50 To HH, February 9, 1786, *Letters* 2 : 475.
51 To HH, April 10, 1786, *Letters* 2 : 517.
52 To HH, June 4–5, 1786, *Letters* 2 : 560.
53 To HH, June 12, 1786, *Letters* 2 : 564.
54 To HH, February 27, 1786, *Letters* 2 : 487.
55 To WU, July 3, 1786, *Letters* 2 : 572.
56 Ibid.
57 HH to TC, as cited by Thomas Wright, *The Life of William Cowper* (1892), 428.
58 To HH, February 27, 1786, *Letters* 2 : 490.
59 *Wright,* 420–21.
60 Ibid., 435.
61 To JN, September 30, 1786, *Letters* 2 : 591–93.
62 To HH, May 8, 1786, *Letters* 2 : 539.
63 *Wright,* 434.
64 To HH, November 26, 1786, *Letters* 2 : 599.
65 To WU, July 3, 1786, *Letters* 2 : 572.

10 WESTON

1 To WU, August 14, 1784, *Letters* 2 : 270.
2 To HH, May 1, 1786, *Letters* 2 : 531.

3 To JN, May 10, 1784, *Letters* 2 : 246.
4 To WU, September 11, 1784, *Letters* 2 : 277.
5 To HH, May 28–29, 1786, *Letters* 2 : 556.
6 *Milford,* 180 and 136–37, respectively.
7 *Hayley* 2 : 170.
8 Turvey-Abbey Scrapbook, MS Olney.
9 To HH, December 4, 1786, *Letters* 2 : 606.
10 HH to WH, July 5, 1787, MS Bull.
11 *The Universal Review* 26 (June 15, 1890).
12 To SR, August 27, 1787, *Letters* 3 : 17.
13 Hayley is the source of this observation. See G. E. Bentley, Jr., *Blake Records* (Oxford: Clarendon Press, 1969), 144–45 and n. 2.
14 HH to WH, January 16, 1805, MS British Library.
15 To MK, February 12, 1788, *Letters* 3 : 98.
16 To HH, February 15, 1789, *Letters* 3 : 259.
17 To WU, February 5, 1782, *Letters* 2 : 5.
18 *AR* 6 (1790) : 194.
19 Ibid., 5 (1789) : 482.
20 Ibid., appendix to 6 (1790) : 542.
21 Ibid., 5 (1789) : 357. The book's author was William Lawrence Brown.
22 Ibid., 5 (1789) : 206.
23 Ibid., 5 (1789) : 47–48.
24 Ibid. (1789) : 48.
25 Ibid., 4 (1789) : 30.
26 *Milford,* 379.
27 Ibid., 385.
28 To HH, November 27, 1787, *Letters* 3 : 57.
29 *Milford,* 365.
30 Ibid., 371.
31 Recollections.
32 Ibid.
33 Ibid.
34 Ibid.
35 Ibid.
36 To JJ, March 23, 1790, *Letters* 3 : 365.
37 To HH, January 23, 1790, *Letters* 3 : 334.
38 To HH, January 26, 1790, *Letters* 3 : 337.
39 To JJ, June 7, 1790, *Letters* 3 : 385.
40 Ibid.
41 To Rose Bodham, February 27, 1790, *Letters* 3 : 349.

11 HOMER: THE HEROIC TASK

1 See chapters 6 and 8 *passim.*
2 See, especially, *Letters* 3 : 4–597.
3 C to JN, December 10, 1785, *Letters* 2 : 420.
4 To John Duncombe, December 31, 1757, *Letters* 1 : 80.
5 *Prefaces, Biographical and Critical . . .* vol. 2 (1779), 222.
6 *Adelphi* (*Letters* 1 : 60).
7 To WU, September 3, 1780, *Letters* 1 : 387.

8   To JN, February 18, 1781, *Letters* 1 : 446.
9   To JN, December 3, 1785, *Letters* 2 : 411.
10 To JN, June 24, 1791, *Letters* 3 : 533.
11 Ibid.
12 To CR, February 21, 1788, *Letters* 3 : 110. A further irony in the relationship between the two poets is that Pope from the outset acknowledged that Homer must be attuned to modern taste, whereas Cowper, who felt that his own generation required a more historically accurate translation, was ultimately forced by his advisers, including Fuseli, to accommodate himself to a contemporary audience, whose taste, they argued, Cowper did not fully comprehend. Pope's desire to acknowledge the taste of his own generation is treated in H. A. Mason, *To Homer through Pope: An Introduction to Homer's Iliad and Pope's Translation* (London: Chatto & Windus, 1972). See also Steven Shankman, *Pope's Iliad: Homer in the Age of Passion* (Princeton: Princeton University Press, 1983).
13 SG to WH, September 9, 1800, MS Fitzwilliam.
14 *GM* 55 (1785) : 610.
15 *Prefaces*, vol. 7, 309.
16 *GM* 55 (1785) : 611.
17 Ibid., 613.
18 Ibid., 611.
19 Ibid., 613.
20 To HH, December 23–24, 1785, *Letters* 2 : 430.
21 To JH, December 24, 1785, *Letters* 2 : 431.
22 *Prefaces*, vol. 2, 220.
23 To HH, January 2, 1786, *Letters* 2 : 442.
24 To WU, July [28–29], [1785], *Letters* 2 : 365.
25 To HH, November 9, 1785, *Letters* 2 : 395.
26 To WU, November 28, 1785, *Letters* 2 : 405.
27 To HH, November 30, 1785, *Letters* 2 : 409.
28 To HH, December 7–8, 1785, *Letters* 2 : 417.
29 To WU, December 24, 1785, *Letters* 2 : 432.
30 To Walter Bagot, December 27, 1785, *Letters* 2 : 434.
31 To WU, December 31, 1785, *Letters* 2 : 437.
32 To Colman, December 27, 1785, *Letters* 2 : 436.
33 To HH, January 31, 1786, *Letters* 2 : 471.
34 To Walter Bagot, December 27, 1785, *Letters* 2 : 434.
35 To WU, December 31, 1785, *Letters* 2 : 438.
36 To HH, January 10, 1786, *Letters* 2 : 448.
37 To Walter Bagot, January 15, 1786, *Letters* 2 : 453.
38 To HH, January 16, 1786, *Letters* 2 : 454.
39 Ibid.
40 L. C. Knowles, *Life of Fuseli*, vol. 1 (1831), 67–68.
41 To JJO, January 25, 1786, *Letters* 2 : 468.
42 To HH, January 31, 1786, *Letters* 2 : 470.
43 Ibid.
44 To HH, January 23, 1786, *Letters* 2 : 464.
45 To HH, February 9, 1786, *Letters* 2 : 474.
46 To HH, February 11, 1786, *Letters* 2 : 478.
47 To HH, February 27, 1786, *Letters* 2 : 488.

48   Ibid., 489.
49   Ibid.
50   To JJO, February 1, 1786, *Letters* 2 : 472.
51   To JN, December 11, 1784, *Letters* 2 : 308.
52   To WU, October 31, 1779, *Letters* 1 : 307.
53   To HH, December 15–17, 1785, *Letters* 2 : 423.
54   Ibid.
55   To JJO, February 1, 1786, *Letters* 2 : 472–73.
56   "Z. Z." [Henry Fuseli], *AR* 15 (1793) : 2.
57   To HH, March 5, 1786, *Letters* 2 : 493.
58   Ibid., 494.
59   Ibid.
60   To WU, March 13, 1786, *Letters* 2 : 497.
61   To HH, April 3, 1786, *Letters* 2 : 511.
62   To HH, April 24, 1786, *Letters* 2 : 530.
63   *The New Review* 9 (March 1786), 164–68.
64   Pforzheimer *Proposals*, 4. Colman's annotated copy.
65   To HH, May 8, 1786, *Letters* 2 : 538.
66   Ibid., 537.
67   *Public Advertiser* (May 18, 1786), 2.
68   To HH, March 22, 1790, *Letters* 3 : 362.
69   To HH, May 15, 1786, *Letters* 2 : 543.
70   Ibid.
71   To HH, December 15–17, 1785, *Letters* 2 : 422.
72   To JH, June 9, 1786, *Letters* 2 : 562.
73   To Walter Bagot, July 4, 1786, *Letters* 2 : 575.
74   To Walter Bagot, August 31, 1786, *Letters* 2 : 587.
75   To Walter Bagot, July 4, 1786, *Letters* 2 : 575.
76   Annotations, 2r.
77   Ibid., 4v.
78   Ibid., 3r.
79   Ibid., 3v.
80   Ibid., 12r.
81   *Homer* 1, 54.
82   Annotations, 11v.
83   Ibid., 14r.
84   Ibid., 12v.
85   Ibid., 19v.
86   Ibid., 12v.
87   Ibid., 15r.
88   Ibid.
89   *Homer* 1 : 62.
90   Ibid., xvi.
91   *Public Advertiser* (May 1, 1786), 2.
92   To JJO, September 2, 1786, *Letters* 2 : 588.
93   Ibid.
94   To JH, October 10, 1786, *Letters* 2 : 593–94.
95   To HH, March 22, 1792, *Letters* 3 : 362.
96   To HH, December 11, 1786, *Letters* 2 : 616.
97   To HH, January 8–9, 1787, *Letters* 3 : 7.

98   Ibid.
99   To sr, August 27, 1787, *Letters* 3 : 17.
100 To wu, March 13, 1786, *Letters* 2 : 498.
101 To hh, about December 1785, *Letters* 2 : 440.
102 To hh, October 27, 1787, *Letters* 3 : 46.
103 To hh, November 17, 1787, *Letters* 3 : 55.
104 To Robert Smith, December 7, 1787, *Letters* 3 : 64.
105 Ibid.
106 To Walter Bagot, January 5, 1788, *Letters* 3 : 81.
107 To hh, [January 18], 1788, *Letters* 3 : 86.
108 To sr, February 14, 1788, *Letters* 3 : 101.
109 To mk, March 3, 1788, *Letters* 3 : 121.
110 To Walter Bagot, April 24, 1788, *Letters* 3 : 151.
111 To jh, May 24, 1788, *Letters* 3 : 164.
112 To cr, August 31, 1788, *Letters* 3 : 207.
113 To wb, October 30, 1788, *Letters* 3 : 228.
114 To jjo, December 6, 1788, *Letters* 3 : 239.
115 To jn, August 16, 1789, *Letters* 3 : 311.
116 To sr, January 3, 1790, *Letters* 3 : 325.
117 Ibid., 325–26.
118 To mk, January 4, 1790, *Letters* 3 : 327.
119 Fuseli to William Roscoe, November 25, 1789, ms Liverpool.
120 To jjo, September 7, 1790, *Letters* 3 : 410.
121 To cr, February 1, 1790, *Letters* 3 : 340.
122 To Mrs. Throckmorton, March 21, 1790, *Letters* 3 : 360.
123 To jj, July 31, 1790, *Letters* 3 : 402.
124 To jh, September 4, 1790, *Letters* 3 : 409.

12   HOMER: FINAL PREPARATIONS

1   *Homer* 1 : xi.
2   Ibid., ix.
3   James Boswell, *Life of Johnson*, vol. 3, ed. G. B. Hill, rev. L. F. Powell (Oxford: Oxford University Press, 1934), 333.
4   *Homer* 1 : xi.
5   Ibid., ix.
6   *CR* 4, ser. 2 (March 1792) : 245.
7   *On Translating Homer*, ed. W. H. D. Rouse (1905), 42.
8   *Homer* 1 : viii.
9   To cr, September 16, 1790, *Letters* 3 : 417.
10   To sr, November 30, 1790, *Letters* 3 : 437.
11   To jjo, December 17, 1790, *Letters* 3 : 443.
12   To mk, December 31, 1790, *Letters* 3 : 449.
13   To sr, February 5, 1791, *Letters* 3 : 462–63.
14   To Hurdis, March 6, 1791, *Letters* 3 : 475.
15   To sr, April 7, 1791, *Letters* 3 : 497.
16   To sr, April 29, 1791, *Letters* 3 : 504.
17   To jjo, May 23, 1791, *Letters* 3 : 515.
18   Ibid.
19   To jj, May 23, 1791, *Letters* 3 : 514.

20   To CR, February 21, 1788, *Letters* 3 : 111.
21   To HH, April 7, 1788, *Letters* 3 : 141.
22   Ibid.
23   To HH, June 27, 1788, *Letters* 3 : 188.
24   To CR, September 16, 1790, *Letters* 3 : 417.
25   To JH, September 17, 1790, *Letters* 3 : 418.
26   To CR, February 1, 1791, *Letters* 3 : 459.
27   To JJ, December 18, 1790, *Letters* 3 : 445.
28   To MK, March 2, 1791, *Letters* 3 : 473.
29   To JJ, February 27, 1791, *Letters* 3 : 471.
30   To Rose Bodham, April 8, 1791, *Letters* 3 : 498–99.
31   To JJO, June 15, 1791, *Letters* 3 : 527.
32   To JH, September 4, 1790, *Letters* 3 : 409.
33   To SR, April 29, 1791, *Letters* 3 : 504.
34   Ibid., 504–5.
35   To JJO, July 3, 1791, *Letters* 3 : 537.
36   To SR, July 6, 1791, *Letters* 3 : 538.
37   To HH, July 11, 1791, *Letters* 3 : 542.
38   To JH, July 12, 1791, *Letters* 3 : 545.
39   Cowper probably suspected that Johnson had made a great profit—one
     estimate goes as high as £10,000 (see Lodwick Hartley, *William Cowper, The
     Continuing Revaluation* [Chapel Hill: University of North Carolina Press,
     1960], 7)—from *The Task* without making him a partaker. On the other
     hand, Johnson probably saw himself as someone who continually took risks,
     only a few of which repaid him.
40   To Thurlow, about August 15, 1791, *Letters* 3 : 560.
41   To Thurlow, about August 22, 1791, *Letters* 3 : 563.
42   To HH, August 30, 1791, *Letters* 3 : 568.
43   *GM* 61, pt. 2 (1791) : 856.
44   To Hurdis, December 10, 1791, *Letters* 3 : 597.
45   *MR* 8, n.s. (1792) : 433–34.
46   *CR* 4, ser. 2 (1792) : 247.
47   Ibid., appendix (1792), 569.
48   *AR* 15 (1793) : 1–2.
49   Ibid., 3.

13   MILTON AND WILLIAM THE SECOND

1   To Walter Bagot, September 6, 1791, *Letters* 3 : 570.
2   To SR, September 14, 1791, *Letters* 3 : 572.
3   Ibid.
4   Ibid.
5   To SR, October 30, 1791, *Letters* 3 : 582.
6   To JN, November 16, 1791, *Letters* 3 : 588.
7   To Walter Bagot, December 5, 1791, *Letters* 3 : 594.
8   To Hurdis, December 10, 1791, *Letters* 3 : 597.
9   To JJO, July 8, 1792, *Letters* 4 : 144.
10   To WH, December 26, 1792, *Letters* 4 : 265.
11   As cited by J. Copley, "Cowper on Johnson's *Life of Milton*," *N&Q*, n.s. 24
     (1977) : 314. Cowper's contempt for Johnson the man is revealed in two

letters he wrote after reading extracts from *Prayers and Meditations* in 1785, which were published the year after Johnson died. See *Letters* 2 : 371–74.

12 Ibid.
13 Ibid.
14 Ibid.
15 Ibid.
16 Ibid.
17 Ibid.
18 *Latin and Italian Poems*, 213–14.
19 Ibid., 190.
20 Ibid.
21 Ibid., 235–36.
22 To WH, February 24, 1793, *Letters* 4 : 297.
23 Book 4, line 75.
24 *Memoirs of the Life and Writings of William Hayley*, ed. John Johnson (2 vols., 1823), vol. 2 : 425–27.
25 To WH, March 17, 1792, *Letters* 4 : 28.
26 Ibid., 29.
27 To Lady Throckmorton, March 19, 1792, *Letters* 4 : 32–33.
28 To Mason, June 25, 1782, *Horace Walpole Correspondence*, vol. 25, ed. W. S. Lewis and others (1955), 255–57.
29 Robertson to Gibbon, November 6, 1781, as cited in *Bishop*, 81.
30 To HH, May 5, 1792, *Letters* 4 : 72.
31 To Frances Hill, April 21, 1786, *Letters* 2 : 525.
32 To HH, November 17, 1785, *Letters* 2 : 397–98.
33 To WH, March 24, 1792, *Letters* 4 : 36.
34 WH to C, April 11, 1792, MS British Library.
35 To WH, May 1, 1792, *Letters* 4 : 70.
36 Ibid.
37 WH to C, April 11, 1792, MS British Library.
38 To HH, April 5, 1792. *Letters* 4 : 48.
39 WH to C, May 6, 1792, MS British Library.
40 Ibid.
41 To JJ, May 20, 1792, *Letters* 4 : 78.
42 WH to Romney. As cited in *Bishop*, 150.
43 MS British Library, as cited in *Bishop*, 151.
44 Ibid.
45 Ibid.
46 To HH, May 24, 1792, *Letters* 4 : 79.
47 To HH, May 26, 1792, *Letters* 4 : 82.
48 Ibid.
49 Ibid.
50 To WH, June 14, 1792, *Letters* 4 : 117.
51 To HH, June 21, 1792, *Letters* 4 : 125.
52 To WH, April 15, 1792, *Letters* 4 : 56.
53 Hayley's Memoirs (MS), vol. 6, 39, Yale University Library.
54 To HH, June 6, 1792, *Letters* 4 : 98.
55 To WH, June 19–20, 1792, *Letters* 4 : 123.
56 To HH, July 21, 1792, *Letters* 4 : 152.
57 To WH, July 22, 1792, *Letters* 4 : 153.

58   To HH, June 11, 1792, *Letters* 4 : 112.
59   To WH, July 29, 1792, *Letters* 4 : 160.
60   To JN, July 30, 1792, *Letters* 4 : 161–62.
61   Ibid.
62   To HH, August 11, 1792, *Letters* 4 : 168.
63   To ST, August 5, 1792, *Letters* 4 : 163.
64   As cited in *Bishop*, 26.
65   To SG, August 6, 1792, *Letters* 4 : 164–65.
66   *Bishop*, 26.
67   Ibid.
68   Ibid.
69   *The Emigrants . . .* (1793), v.
70   To HH, August 26, 1792, *Letters* 4 : 180.
71   To HH, September 9, 1792, *Letters* 4 : 190.
72   JJ to CJ, September 3, 1792, MS Barham Johnson.
73   Ibid.
74   Ibid.
75   Ibid.
76   Ibid.
77   Ibid.
78   HH to JJ, November 15, 1792, MS Barham Johnson.
79   WH to Eliza Hayley, September 23, 1792, MS Fitzwilliam.
80   JJ to Rose Bodham, September 23, 1792, MS Barham Johnson.
81   Edward Williams to Jonathan Rees, March 28, 1821, MS Olney.
82   To WH, September [20], 1792, *Letters* 4 : 196.

14   TROUBLE AT WESTON

1   JJ to Mrs. Balls, July 12, 1795, MS Barham Johnson.
2   Teedon.
3   To JH, June 29, 1785, *Letters* 2 : 360.
4   To HH, October 5, 1787, *Letters* 3 : 40.
5   HH to WH, April 7, 1803, MS British Library.
6   Teedon.
7   Ibid.
8   To ST, November 16–17, [1792], *Letters* 4 : 237.
9   *Teedon Diary*, 43, entry for November 4, 1792.
10   Ibid., 44, entry for December 1, 1792.
11   To WH, about September 8, 1793, *Letters* 4 : 392.
12   To ST, July 2–3, 1793, *Letters* 4 : 362–63.
13   To ST, October 25, 1793, *Letters* 4 : 417.
14   Ibid.
15   To ST, November 16–17, [1792], *Letters* 4 : 237.
16   ST to C, February 4, 1793, MS Princeton.
17   To ST, December 4, 1792, *Letters* 4 : 250.
18   To ST, January 25, 1793, *Letters* 4 : 279.
19   To ST, December 14, 1792, *Letters* 4 : 258.
20   To SR, November 9, 1792, *Letters* 4 : 232–33.
21   To HH, about October 25, 1795, *Letters* 4 : 222.
22   To ST, December 21, 1792, *Letters* 4 : 264.

23 To WH, December 8, 1793, *Letters* 4 : 439.
24 To WH, June 29, 1793, *Letters* 4 : 360.
25 To WH, July 7, 1793, *Letters* 4 : 364.
26 JJ Diary, March 11, 1799.
27 To SR, June 18, 1793, *Letters* 4 : 355.
28 To Phillips, June 23, 1793, *Letters* 4 : 356–57.
29 To JJ, September 6, 1793, *Letters* 4 : 390–91.
30 To Thomas Lawrence, October 18, 1793, *Letters* 4 : 415.
31 Memorials.
32 Ibid.
33 Ibid.
34 MS British Library.
35 To WH, January 20, 1793, *Letters* 4 : 277.
36 To HH, August 29, 1793, *Letters* 4 : 388.
37 To HH, May 22, 1786, *Letters* 2 : 550.
38 HH to JJ, July 10, 1794, MS Barham Johnson.
39 Ibid.
40 HH to JJ, July 10, 1794, MS Barham Johnson.
41 JJ to CJ, March 16, 1794, MS Barham Johnson.
42 Ibid.
43 HH to JJ, July 10, 1794, MS Barham Johnson.
44 HH to JJ, January 19, 1794, MS Barham Johnson.
45 HH to JJ, August 31, 1794, MS Barham Johnson.
46 Ibid.
47 HH to SG, May 23, 1794, MS Princeton.
48 HH to JJ, August 31, 1794, MS Barham Johnson.
49 To JN, December 24, 1784, *Letters* 2 : 315.
50 To HH, February 16, 1788, *Letters* 3 : 104.
51 To WH, July 15, 1792, *Letters* 4 : 148.
52 HH to JJ, September 27, 1793, MS Barham Johnson.
53 Ibid.
54 HH to JJ, July 19, 1800, MS Barham Johnson.
55 JJ to Margaret Perowne, July 24, 1795, MS Barham Johnson.
56 To HH, May 24, 1792, *Letters* 4 : 79.
57 WH to William Long, May 17, 1792, MS Fitzwilliam.
58 HH to JJ, July 17, 1794, MS Barham Johnson.
59 JJ to CJ, June 19, 1795, MS Barham Johnson.
60 Ibid.
61 HH to SG, May 17, 1794, MS Princeton. Cotton had died in 1788. Willis was often punitive in his treatment of patients. See John Brooke, *King George III* (1972), 331–36.
62 HH to SG, June 22, 1794, MS Princeton.
63 WH to HH, undated but 1793, MS British Library.
64 Ibid.
65 HH to JJ, January 24, 1795, MS Barham Johnson.
66 James Hurnard, *A Memoir Chiefly Autobiographical* . . . (1883), 51–52.
67 JJ to CJ, March 16, 1794, MS Barham Johnson. JJ is quoting a letter from HH to himself.
68 JJ to CJ, July 10, 1795, MS Barham Johnson.
69 HH to CJ, March 18, 1795, MS Princeton.
70 JJ to CJ, July 10, 1795, MS Barham Johnson.

15 NORFOLK

1 JJ to CJ, July 10, 1795, MS Barham Johnson.
2 Ibid.
3 JJ to Mrs. Balls, July 12, 1795, MS Barham Johnson.
4 *Milford*, 428.
5 Ibid.
6 *Paradise Lost*, book 4, lines 73–74.
7 *Spiritual Diary* (*Letters* 4 : 467–70).
8 JJ Diary, July 28, 1795.
9 SG to WH, August 1, 1795, MS Fitzwilliam.
10 Ibid.
11 Ibid.
12 Ibid.
13 JJ Diary, July 28, 1795.
14 Ibid.
15 Ibid.
16 Ibid.
17 JJ Diary, August 18, 1795.
18 Ibid., August 19, 1795.
19 Ibid.
20 Ibid., September 15, 1795.
21 To HH, August 27, 1795, *Letters* 4 : 450.
22 Ibid.
23 To Buchanan, September 5, 1795, *Letters* 4 : 452.
24 To HH, [September 5, 1795], *Letters* 4 : 454.
25 To HH, September 26, 1795, *Letters* 4 : 456.
26 To WH, about June 19, 1797, *Letters* 4 : 460.
27 JJ to CJ, September 6, 1795, MS Barham Johnson.
28 JJ Diary, September 15, 1795.
29 Ibid.
30 Ibid.
31 Ibid.
32 JJ and Margaret Perowne to CJ, October 23, 1795, MS Barham Johnson.
33 JJ to SR, October 24, 1795, MS Barham Johnson.
34 JJ Diary, October 22, 1795.
35 JJ to WH, April 25, 1796, MS Bodleian.
36 To HH, January 22, 1796, *Letters* 4 : 457.
37 JJ to WH, March 17, 1796, MS Bodleian.
38 JJ to WH, April 25, 1796, MS Bodleian.
39 Ibid.
40 JJ Diary, May 15, 1796.
41 Ibid., April 13, 1796.
42 Ibid., June 29, 1796.
43 JJ to WH, July 27–29, 1796, MS Bodleian.
44 Ibid.
45 JJ Diary, September 9, 1796.
46 JJ to WH, September 21, 1796, MS Bodleian.
47 JJ Diary, October 29, 1796.
48 Ibid., December 17, 1796.
49 Ibid.

50 Ibid.
51 Ibid.
52 HH to JJ, January 18, 1797, MS Barham Johnson.
53 Ibid.
54 Pro et Contra, January 7, 1798.
55 JJ Diary, March 29, 1797.
56 Pro et Contra, December 2, 1797.
57 Ibid.
58 Ibid.
59 Ibid., November 21, 1797.
60 Ibid., December 1, 1797.
61 Ibid., March 16, 1798.
62 Ibid., March 31, 1798.
63 Ibid., November 29, 1797.
64 Ibid., April 21, 1798.
65 JJ to WH, August 22, 1796, MS Bodleian.
66 Pro et Contra, November 17, 1797.
67 Ibid., November 19, 1797.
68 Ibid., November 25, 1797.
69 Ibid., February 25, 1798.
70 WH to C, June 24, 1797, as cited in *Bishop*, 218.
71 JJ to WH, September 30, 1797, MS Bodleian.
72 Ibid.
73 Ibid.
74 JJ to WH, November 22, 1797, MS Bodleian.
75 Ibid.
76 JJ to WH, April 25, 1798, MS Bodleian.
77 To HH, July 26, 1798, *Letters* 4 : 461–62.
78 JJ Diary, March 27, 1797.
79 Ibid.
80 JJ Diary, August 16, 1797.
81 Ibid.
82 JJ Diary, June 28, 1798.
83 To HH, July 26, 1798, *Letters* 4 : 461.
84 JJ Diary, October 27, 1798.
85 Ibid., March 11, 1799.
86 Lines 543–44.
87 To WH, June 19–20, 1792, *Letters* 4 : 122–23.
88 *Milford*, 431.
89 Pro et Contra, September 11, 1798.
90 Pp. 79–80.
91 *Milford*, 432.
92 Ibid.
93 Ibid.
94 To JN, April 11, 1798, *Letters* 4 : 466.
95 Everyman's Library ed. (1965), 20.
96 JJ to WH, October 23, 1799, MS Bodleian.
97 JJ Diary, September 5, 1799.
98 JJ to WH, October 23, 1799, MS Bodleian.
99 JJ Diary, October 28, 1799.

100   Ibid., December 11, 1799.
101   Ibid., January 30, 1800.
102   Ibid.
103   Ibid., January 31, 1800.
104   JJ to CJ, February 10, 1800, MS Bodleian.
105   JJ to SR, February 10, 1800, MS Bodleian.
106   JJ to CJ, February 19, 1800, MS Barham Johnson.
107   Ibid.
108   JJ to WH, February 26, 1800, MS Bodleian.
109   JJ to CJ, April 8, 1800, MS Barham Johnson.
110   *Hayley* 2, 219.
111   D. Woods to JJ, March 3, 1823, as cited by JJ in *Memoirs of . . . Hayley*, vol. 2 (1823), 106.
112   *Hayley* 2 : 220.
113   *Milford*, 133–34. Blake's response to Cowper is treated at length in Morton D. Paley, "Cowper as Blake's Spectre," *Eighteenth-Century Studies* 1 (1968) : 236–52.

Index

Brown, Lancelot "Capability" : 176
Brown, William Lawrence, *An Essay on Sensibility* : 181
Browne, Sir Thomas : 90
Buchanan, John, minister at Weston : 177, 253, 270
Buckland House, Berkshire : 175
Bull, William, dissenting clergyman of Newport Pagnell : 146, 205, 213; saw religious tasks Newton gave c as productive, 83; c and he share many traits, 89-91; suggests c translate Mme Guyon, 134-35
Bunyan, John : *Pilgrim's Progress* is one of the first books owned by c, 9
Burlington, Richard, 3rd Earl of : 108
Burney, Fanny : 161; *Camilla* and *Cecilia*, 271
Burton, Robert, *The Anatomy of Melancholy* : writes on loss as a significant cause of depression, 5
Busby, Richard, headmaster of Westminster in the Restoration : 12
Buston, Richard, c's medical attendant : 264
Butcher, Master, resident of Olney : 74
Butler, Samuel : 43, 110; *Hudibras*, 195
Bye, Deodatus, printer : 221
Byron, George Gordon, Lord : 141

Calvin, John : 9
Cambridge : 56, 77-81, 224, 268
Cambridge, University of : 128, 130, 187; generosity to the Homer subscription, 224-25
Caraccioli, Louis Antoine, Marquis de : 136-37
the Careys, one of the noble families from whom c descended on mother's side : 3
Cartwright, Edmund, reviewer : 115-16
Catfield, Norfolk village : 31; c as a child visits there, 9
Catherine the Great : 151
Catholicism : 172, 174-76, 177
Catullus : 23
Cawthorne, William, Mary Unwin's father : 61, 260
Cecil, Lord David : speculates on sense of defeatism in c's character, 6

Champion, Joseph, translator : 181
Chancery Lane : 37
Chapman, Mr., lawyer : c apprenticed to him, 18-19, 21, 38, 40
Charles I, King of England : 137
Charles Edward Louis Philip Casmir, the Pretender, also known as Bonnie Prince Charlie : 120
Charles Street, London : 160
Charlotte, Queen : 163
Chaucer : Clerk of the Works at Berkhamsted, 1
Cheltenham : 161
Chesterfield, 4th Earl of, Philip Dormer : 98, 108
Chetwynd, Martha, Lady Hesketh's mother-in-law : 164
Cheyne, George, physician : claims melancholia is the English malady, 8
Chicheley : 16
Chichester : 179
Christ Church, Oxford : 33, 49
Churchey, Walter, lawyer and would-be poet : 215, 224
Churchill, Charles : 12, 33, 35; c's great admiration for him, 43
Clapham Sect : 90
Clarendon, 1st Earl of, Edward Hyde : 137
Clench, Bruni, Ann Donne Cowper's maternal grandfather : 3
Clench, Catherine (Hippesley), Ann Donne Cowper's maternal grandmother: lives near St. Martin's in the Fields, 3
Clifton : 121, 124, 127, 161, 164
Cobbett, William : writes on Hertforshire, 1; comments on Huntingdon, 58
Cock Inn, Eaton : 268
Cockerell, Mary : Hayley's mistress, incorrectly identified by John Johnson as Thomas Hayley's mother, 247
Coleman, Dick, orphan befriended by c and later his servant : 58, 75, 260
Coleridge, Samuel : 156
"Collegium Insanorum," Dr. Cotton's asylum : 50, 52-57
Collins, William : 110, 155, 156

probably caused both breaks with
Lady Austen, 126; ill health, 234,
241; paralytic stroke, 241, 243;
makes good recovery, 242, 245;
health worsens, 249, 253; hostile to
Teedon, 251; she becomes focus of
Lady Hesketh's resentment, 257–
63; her health deteriorates further, 271; death, 273–74
Unwin, Morley, clergyman husband of
Mary : 60–61, 62, 128; jealous of
c's hold over his wife, 63–64; dies
accidentally, 64; wanted c and
Mary to live together in the event
of his death, 86
Unwin, William Cawthorne, clergyman : 57, 65, 103, 118, 132, 134,
149, 167, 169, 172, 174, 179, 180,
188, 190, 195, 213, 235; meets c, 60;
lyrics sent to him, 95; is misled by
c concerning *Anti-Thelyphthora*,
96–98; is finally told that c is publishing a volume of verse, 100, 127;
tells c that his verse is too uncompromising, 112; acts as c's intermediary with Lady Austen, 123,
126–27; becomes c's agent in dealings with Joseph Johnson, 128,
146–47; deeply attached to c from
the outset of their friendship, 128;
has important connections at Cambridge, 128; holds advanced views
on abolition of slavery and penal,
political, and social reform, 128;
disliked by parishioners at Stock,
128–29; dutiful friend to c, 130;
c's renewal as a letter writer is
first evident in 1779–81 letters to
him, 131, 133; hostile to Madame
Guyon's theology, 135; *Tirocinium*
is dedicated to him, 149–50; death,
172, 178, 212; Hurdis reminds c
of him, 246
Uxbridge, Henry Baley, *afterward*
Paget, Earl of : 213

Vane, Frederick, schoolmate of c's at
Westminster : 213

Vauxhall : 32
Vicarage, Olney : 72, 89, 124–25, 168–69,
170
Vincent, William, Under Master at
Westminster : 14
Virgil : 203
Voltaire, *Henriade* : 78

Wagstaff, Mr., tanner at Olney : 76
Wakefield's edition of Pope's Homer :
272
Waller, Edmund : 23
Walpole, Horace : 32, 239
Warrington Pew incident : 74
Warton, Joseph : 34, 155, 156
Warton, Thomas : 155, 156
Watts, Isaac : 83–84
Wesley, Charles : 83–84
Wesley, John : 49, 66–67, 82, 83, 90
Westminster Abbey : 12, 47
Westminster School, c's public school :
2, 34, 35, 49, 191, 197; the great
Whig school, 12; classics the basis
of an education there, 13, 189
Weston Hall, Throckmorton resi-
dence : 174, 175, 184; description,
176
Weston Lodge, c's residence : 172, 174–
75, 184, 185–86, 241, 249, 257;
description, 176–77
Weston Underwood : 94, 171, 177, 178,
185, 188, 212, 240, 248, 262, 265, 267,
270; description, 174–75, 185–86
Weymouth : 31, 163, 184
Whitefield, George : 66, 67–68
Wilberforce, William : 128–29, 213, 276
Wilkes, John : 33
William Pindar, one of c's nicknames :
33
William the Conqueror : 1
Williams, Edward, poet : 248
Willis, Francis, clergyman : attends c,
263–64, 265
Wilson, Hannah, Patty's daughter,
Mrs. Unwin's niece : becomes the
focus of Harriot Hesketh's anger,
260–62, 265, 267, 270; apprenticed
at Norwich, 271
Wilson, Patty, Mrs. Unwin's half-sister,
wife of Dick Coleman : 260

Library of Congress Cataloging-in-Publication Data
King, James.
William Cowper : a biography.
Includes index.
　　1. Cowper, William, 1731–1800—Biography.　2. Poets,
English—18th century—Biography.　I. Title.
PR3383.K5　1986　　821'.6 [B]　　85-25352
ISBN 0-8223-0513-5